INSIDE INDIA TODAY

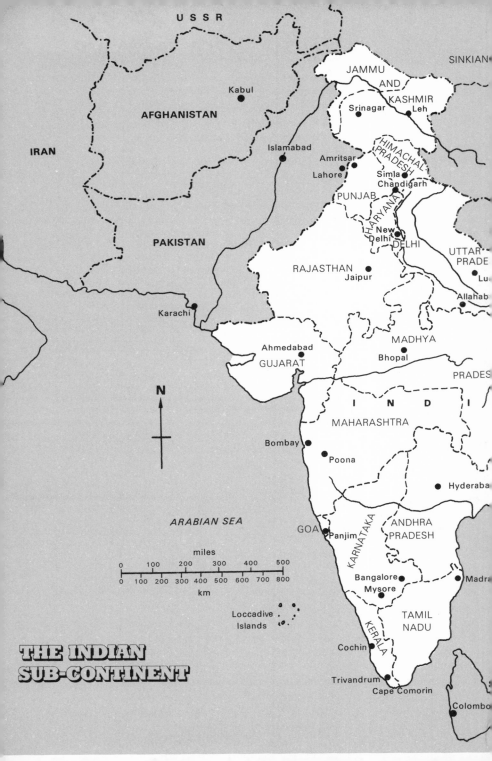

THE INDIAN
SUB-CONTINENT

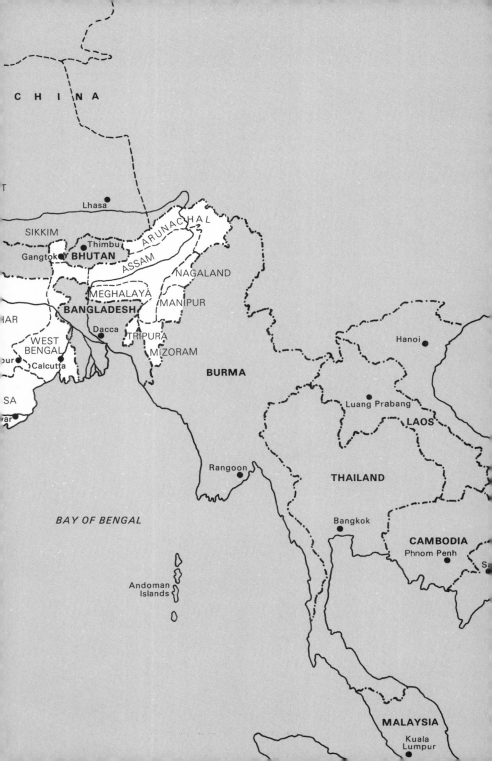

The Untouchables of India
Black British, White British
A Triangular View (A novel)
To Anchor a Cloud (A play)
Apply, Apply, No Reply **and** A Clean Break (Two plays)

DILIP HIRO

INSIDE INDIA TODAY

REVISED 1979

MONTHLY REVIEW PRESS
NEW YORK AND LONDON

To Jeanne S.

Library of Congress Cataloging in Publication Data
Hiro, Dilip.
    Inside India Today.
    Bibliography: p. 321
    Includes index.
    1. India—Politics and government—1947-   I. Title.
JQ215 1977.H57   320.9'54'05   77-76161
ISBN 0-85345-424-8 CL
ISBN 0-85345-481-7 PB

Monthly Review Press
62 West 14th Street, New York, N.Y. 10011
47 Red Lion Street, London WC1R 4PF

10 9 8 7 6 5 4 3 2 1

Manufactured in the United States of America

CONTENTS

PREFACE

My initial research on India, conducted some six years ago, made me realize the absence of a single, comprehensive book, which informs the general reader, Indian or non-Indian, as to how this most complex political entity in the world functions at both the popular and institutional levels. It also made me realize that such a book was needed, and that the best approach to the project would be to combine library research with extensive field work.

And, over the next few years, this is what I did.

I collected material for the book by interviewing people throughout the country, and perusing several newspapers and periodicals, and dozens of specialist books, which often deal with no more than an aspect or two of the Indian polity. I spent the best part of nineteen months – from October 1970 to April 1972 -- travelling around the sub-continent, conducting informal and formal interviews. I covered almost all the constituent States of the Republic; and in each State I visited the capital and at least two villages.

As someone familiar with half a dozen Indian languages – which are spoken in the northern, central and western parts of the country – I conversed with my interviewees, in these regions, directly. Elsewhere, I had an interpreter with me. In every village I visited, I talked to members of different social strata: landless labourers, poor peasants, middle peasants, rich farmers, landlords, and artisans. Similarly, in the cities, I interviewed menial workers, industrial proletariat, petty traders, white collar employees, professionals and government bureaucrats. I conducted these interviews, without a set questionnaire, talking informally, changing and directing conversation as I went along. My intention was to secure first-hand information about the socio-economic status of my subject, as seen by him, and his social and political views in fairly simple, direct terms.

I followed a similar technique while interviewing journalists, academics, political leaders, party workers, trade unionists, and industrialists. But my questions, in their case, were designed primarily to seek their views on, and analysis of, the social order and political events. These interviews, thus, became not only a source of information to me, but also analysis.

Further information and analysis came from various Indian news-papers and periodicals, published almost always in English. (This may seem unrepresentative, but is not, because the small minority that reads, writes and speaks English dominates the political, economic, and intellectual life of the country.) Until the imposition of emergency and censorship, in June 1975, the press in India was, theoretically speaking, free. In practice, however, most of the popular publications, which command a disproportionately large section of the total newspaper circulation, were either guarded in their criticism of the ruling party – the centrist Indian National Congress – or attacked it almost invariably from a rightist position. This was so for political and commercial reasons, which are explained, at some length, in Chapter 18 (pp. 243–4). The task of the free press was therefore performed mainly by the official organs of various political parties, and a few small, independent journals of opinion. Among the latter category, the *Economic and Political Weekly* deserves a special mention. A liberal, radical, small-circulation periodical, published in Bombay, it remains (within the current restrictions on the press) well-informed and per-ceptive, in both its editorials and the dispatches of its correspondents.

Finally, the books on India: there is by now a sizeable library of specialist books on the country, written by journalists (often Indian) or academics (both Indian and Western); and I went through most of it. Whatever the subject of the book, or the nationality of the author, none of them seemed antagonistic towards, or highly critical of, the present socio-political system; and none recommended anything more revo-lutionary than a few reforms *within* the existing political-administrative framework. This is worth noting.

So much for my published sources and their general bias.

I have divided my book into five parts. Part I is a report on life in contemporary India. It is composed of information culled from inter-views conducted by me, from various other surveys and studies, and from news items. The purpose here is to portray the country in human terms, to enable the reader to form a general idea of the people who, individually and collectively, constitute Indian society. Since most of them live in villages, the report begins with rural India, then moves on to the major cities – which are the repositories of power, political and economic – and ends with a wide-ranging description of the corruption rampant in society today.

Part II outlines, in some detail, the constitutional framework within which the above situation exists, and the mechanism of contesting and winning elections. As the Congress has been the only party that has ruled the country at the national level, since the British left in 1947, the rest of this section is devoted to its history, performance in office, achievements and failures in agriculture and industry, and its attempt to dominate the trade union field which, on the eve of independence, was under the influence of the Communists.

Part III begins with a history of the Communist movement, then traces the split in the movement, and describes the emergence of three Communist parties, their inter-relationship with one another, and their attitude towards the established order. It ends with a chapter on the State of West Bengal, where the dramatic success of the leftist movement during the period 1967–72 was followed by a shift in the other direction.

Part IV examines the composition and strength of the rightist forces in the country, both political and institutional – that is, the military and para-military forces, police, and intelligence; and shows how the Congress government at the Centre makes frequent use of these institutions either to weaken the leftist movements or to maintain the country's unity.

The final section describes both the strains within the Indian Union and what causes them: alienation of religious, linguistic, and racial minorities from the majority community. It also describes the internal cohesive forces at work – the national administrative services, the government-controlled broadcasting agency, and the pro-establishment press – and the external support provided by the foreign blocs led by *both* Russia and America. It then explains how, when the strains became unbearable, the Congress regime in Delhi declared a national emergency in June 1975, jailed political opponents on a large scale and imposed press censorship; and why. The section ends with an outline of the most likely scenario for the country in the coming decades.

A word about the terms, personal names, and abbreviations used. The Congress means the Indian National Congress, now being led by the Prime Minister, Indira Gandhi, who is always described by that name. (Gandhi refers to M. K. Gandhi, a Congress Party leader popularly known as Mahatma Gandhi, who died in 1948; and Nehru to Jawaharlal Nehru, the first Prime Minister of India, and father of Indira Gandhi.) The Syndicate-Congress means the right-wing faction of the Congress which established itself as a separate entity in late 1969, but whose leaders claim it to be the continuation of the original party.

The term Socialist means a member of any of the three Socialist parties that have been in existence at one time or another, since the early 1950s; the Socialist Party, the Praja (i.e. People's) Socialist Party, and the Samyukta (i.e. United) Socialist Party.

The term Communist applies to the Communist Party of India as it existed until the split in 1964. The two resulting parties are referred to as the CPI, which is pro-Moscow in its international policies, and the CPI(M) – i.e. Communist Party of India (Marxist), a party which follows an independent line in the international arena, and whose members are commonly known as the Marxists, or Marxist-Communists. The third Communist party, which came into existence in 1969 and took a pro-Peking stand, called itself the Communist Party of India (Marxist-Leninist). Its members were popularly described as Naxalites. By the mid-1970s, however, the term Naxalite had come to apply to all militant Communists – whether members of the CPI(M-L) or not – who do not participate in the country's parliamentary processes.

It is common in India to describe sums in lakhs (one lakh = 100,000) and crores (one crore = 100 lakhs = 10 million). The approximate exchange rate for the Indian rupee is taken to be 5 British pence or 14 American cents.

INTRODUCTION

It was towards the end of May 1975 that I finished the penultimate draft of this book. A month later came the declaration of emergency in India, followed by a series of restrictive regulations. Incorporation of these events into the final text of my book presented no problem, however, as I had ended the previous draft with a scenario predicting a move towards authoritarianism of some kind.

The events in India since June 1975 fit only too well the general thesis I had formulated a few years earlier by studying, in depth, the Congress Party's history, style of operation, and, above all, its basic dilemma: how to continue to pose as the party of the poor to win the popular vote while pursuing policies that primarily benefit the upper-middle and upper classes, who control the party organisation at all levels. The device of emergency enabled the Congress to resolve the dilemma temporarily. The critics were silenced; the press censored. The people were bombarded with pro-Congress and pro-Indira Gandhi propaganda of the crudest type.

However, once the opposition was paralysed, normal democratic restraints removed, and electoral considerations brushed aside, the true socio-economic bias of the ruling party became increasingly obvious. Its policies and actions (but *not* slogans) became openly anti-labour, pro-capital; anti-peasant, pro-landlord. The civil servants, police, and intelligence became more corrupt and oppressive than before. The campaigns for mass sterilisation and 'beautifying' the cities (by demolishing, almost overnight, entire colonies of the underprivileged), were launched, and won, by treating the poor, both in country and town, as sub-human. Little wonder then that when these very people were offered a chance to exercise their right to vote on the merits, or otherwise, of emergency, they came out decidedly against both it and the party that imposed it.

I revisited India at the time of the March 1977 election. Despite its claims to have reduced corruption in Indian life by the provisions of emergency, the Congress Party employed the same corrupt methods in its election campaign as it had done on previous occasions—even more so. But these methods proved inadequate to swing enough voters to its side to enable it to continue its rule.

Despite various handicaps, the Janata (People's) Party, formed *after* the announcement of the general election on 18 January 1977, ended up victorious. In a sense the Janata Party is new; in a sense not. Certainly, the elements that coalesced (and later merged) to create the new party have been there for a long time, and are described and analysed at some length in Chapters 6 and 15.

Although the imposition of emergency released the executive from the normal democratic checks and balances, the structure or the working mechanism of such important institutions as the civil service, police, military, and the broadcasting services, through which the executive operates, did not change. In that sense the description and analysis of life in India and the Indian institutions in the book remain as valid today as they did in the pre-emergency period.

LIFE IN INDIA:
A REPORT

VILLAGE INDIA

Most of the urban intellectuals, administrators, and businessmen
have . . . hardly any idea of the conditions prevailing in the
villages, only a few miles from the metropolitan centres. . . . To
be frank, for a good part of my life also I did not have any idea
of the extent of this [rural] poverty.

Arvind Mafatlal, an Indian industrialist[1]

What meets the eye [in rural India] are utter poverty, misery,
inequality, exploitation, backwardness, stagnation, frustration, and
loss of hope.
Jaya Prakash Narayan, a popular Sarvodaya (i.e. Universal Welfare
movement) leader[2]

My wish in life is just to get enough to eat, nothing more.

Gopal Naicker, a landless labourer[3]

The rich have the power of wealth.
K. Subramaniam, an educated, unemployed rural youth[4]

India, the world's second largest country, is by far the most complex,
the most variegated. This variety pertains not only to physical
geography – snow-capped mountains, tropical forests, deserts, flat
countryside – but also to language, religion, art and architecture, social
customs, race, and, most importantly, different stages of economic
development – from prehistoric shift cultivation to modern atomic
power plants. 'At one jolly go,' writes Ashok Mitra, an Indian
economist, 'one can traverse [in India] the entire spectrum of pastoral
life, feudalism, mercantilist behaviour, unbridled capitalism, and
blotches of socialist earnestness.'[5]
What is most striking, visually, about the Indian people is the
racial variety. Leaving aside the Mongoloids, who are marginal both in
terms of their numbers and habitation – in the mountainous areas in the
north and north-east – there are three main races: Australoid, Dravidian,
and Aryan, and various mixtures of them. The 42 million, predominantly Australoid, aborigines are spread out, albeit unevenly,

3

throughout the country, and speak dozens of different dialects. The 150 million Dravidians, constituting a quarter of the total population, are to be found mainly in the four southern states – Andhra Pradesh, Karnataka, Kerala, and Tamil Nadu – each with a distinct language of its own. The Aryans, and part-Aryans, are the most numerous in the rest of the country where seven major languages and scores of dialects are spoken.

Underlying these racial and other differences, however, are three major unifying factors: Hinduism, which claims the religious loyalty of 83 per cent of the Indians; the caste system, which is peculiar to Hindus, and has a religious sanction; and a long history of domination by aliens. The British were the last in a line of foreign conquerers, having been preceded by the Mughals and Afghans (Muslim tribes originating from Central Asia), and Aryan tribes from the southern Russian steppes and Iran. They were also the most successful in bringing all of the sub-continent under their authority and setting up an effective political-administrative machinery. However, since the major reason for them to secure, and then to retain, India was economic – first trade and then, with rapid industrialization in Britain, ample supplies of raw materials for their factories, and guaranteed colonial markets for their manufactured goods – they discouraged industrialization of India. Consequently, today, India is a predominantly agrarian country, with four-fifths of its over 600 million people living in villages, where most of them depend on land for their livelihood.

Agriculture in India is unevenly developed. There are some areas, admittedly small, where shift cultivation, which pre-dates settled cultivation and the use of plough, is the norm. Then there are areas, again relatively small, where tractors, chemical fertilizers, high-yield varieties of seed, and wage labour are commonplace – that is, agriculture is highly developed and capitalized. Elsewhere the mode of production is feudal or semi-feudal – that is, the peasant, possessing all the requisite tools of production, either serves the landlord as a serf or pays him, or his agent, an excessive rent for the use of his land.

As a result of land reform legislation in various States of the country since the early 1950s the class of traditional (absentee) landlords, known in India as zamindars or *jagirdars*,[6] has been replaced or superceded by a class of rich peasants, who engage themselves directly in farm management, and a much larger class of middle peasants. The latter produce enough to feed their families and to exchange the surplus for the non-food necessities of life. In order to achieve the maximum production, they have to hire the services of poor peasants and the landless in the village who, more often than not, are either lower caste Hindus or outcastes (officially referred to as Scheduled Castes), or aborigines. The reasons for this socio-economic relationship are to be found in history.

When the Aryan tribes began to colonize India around 1500 BC, they excluded their non-Aryan subjects, called Sudras, from their social and religious life, and assigned them nothing higher than menial work on land or in the service of their masters. Later, the three social orders, Brahmin, Kshatriya, and Vaisaya, then existing among the Aryans, and the Sudras, were incorporated into the *chaturvarna* – i.e. the four castes – system. Brahmins continued their traditional tasks of being priests, teachers, and advisors to kings; Kshatriyas, as warriors and rulers; Vaisayas, as traders and farmers; with Sudras acting as farm servants, agricultural labourers, and artisans. Then there were those who were excluded from the caste system altogether – the *panchjanahas*, the fifth people – the outcastes, the Untouchables. They were assigned the tasks of sweeping the streets, scavenging, and disposing of dead animals and condemned to live outside the village, a practice which still persists.

During the Muslim rule, which lasted from the early thirteenth century to the mid-nineteenth century, many among the lower Hindu castes and the outcastes embraced Islam as a means of social emancipation, in which they were not particularly successful, since Muslims came to be regarded, by the upper caste Hindus, as just another out-caste group whose place lay, literally, outside the village boundary. This continues. Almost all of the thirty-one villages visited in the course of this study – conducted during the period of 1970–2, to form a general socio-economic profile of rural India – had separate hamlets for the Untouchables, Muslims, and aborigines.

As expected, different parts of the country reflected different moods. Whereas the general feeling in the north-western region, with about a tenth of the country's population, was of hope, the dominant feeling in the eastern region, having a third of the national population, was of despair and despondency. Elsewhere the picture was mixed. Similarly, in any given village, different sections of the community, viewed their socio-economic condition differently. All in all, however, the aggregate picture, as conveyed by reports on the four villages of Kajha (in Bihar), Nihal (in the Punjab), Dusi (in Tamil Nadu), and Sahajapur (in West Bengal), reflects the state of rural Indian society fairly well.[7]

Kajha lies about two hundred miles east of Patna, the capital of Bihar, the second largest State in the country. It is a sprawling village of over 1,200 people, with two hamlets, one populated by twenty-five Muslim families, and the other by some fifty Hindu outcaste families. The village proper comprises fifteen upper caste (i.e. Brahmin and Kshatriya) households, sixty middle caste (i.e. Vaisaya) households, and eighty-two lower caste (i.e. Sudra) households. Only the upper caste families and a section of the middle caste households own land; the rest, the vast majority, are landless. Some of the landowners have as much as 200 to 500 acres each. Two of them own a tractor, worth at least R2 20,000 (£1,000) – a sum that equals sixty times the average annual income of an Indian.

One of the tractor-owners is Kishan Chand Chaudhry, a dark man of 40, with a clean-shaven face and head, and a slightly angular body. He owns the largest building in the village, a brick and mortar structure, with a veranda bordered by round, whitewashed columns, and a spacious courtyard that is strewn with steel pipes, meant to be installed into an irrigation tube well, an indication of the interest he takes in the development of his land. He also likes to supervise the work of those he hires, especially the farm servants, and is in the habit of beating them if he finds them neglecting their job.

Having just thrashed a farm servant, produced before him in the courtyard, for negligence in his duty the previous day, Chaudhry sat down on a cot in the veranda. 'The labourers are not work-minded these days,' he said. How much did he pay them? 'Two to three rupees [10 to 15p] a day,' he replied. 'Or, Rs 1.50 [7½p] plus breakfast and lunch.' How many labourers did he engage? 'Depends on the harvest,' he replied cryptically, aware that a precise figure would reveal the size of his landholdings which, apparently, were above the ceiling – 20 to 60 acres per person in a joint Hindu family, depending on the quality of land – fixed by law. He knew about the land ceiling Act, and that it had not been enforced. Why was this so? 'If the government takes over the surplus land after allowing for each individual in a joint Hindu family, it won't be able to give land to more than a quarter of the landless,' he said. 'If that happens, the remaining three-quarters of the landless would turn against the ruling party [i.e. the Indian National Congress]. That's why the party is not serious about this.' (By this logic, almost all the landless in the State should be voting against the Congress since very few have received any land; but this is not so.)

While the Congress government has, for a variety of reasons, failed to help the landless,[8] it has, in the name of raising food production, done much to help such large landowners as Chaudhry. For instance, a co-operative society was set up in the village with government aid, in 1966, with Chaudhry as its president, to advance short-term loans to cultivators for the purchase of chemical fertilizers and high-yielding varieties of seed. But since loans are to be given *only* to those who own land, 81 per cent of the local families find themselves ineligible to borrow. On the other hand, some of the better-off landowners borrow from the co-operative society at the annual interest rate of 6 to 8 per cent, and then lend it to others at an annual rate of 36 to 72 per cent! Chaudhry is aware of this abuse, but is not the least bit concerned. '*Jis ke paas jitna hai, utana use milta hai* [to him that has much, much is given],' he said, quoting a Hindi proverb.

His major concern, of course, has been to increase the yield of his own land by the use of machinery and modern techniques. A few years ago he applied to the government-managed land mortgage bank for a loan to buy a tractor. The loan was granted. But because he refused to bribe any of the bureaucrats involved he had to wait for a whole year for his cheque to come through. Finally, he went to Patna to collect the cheque only to be told that some 'technical difficulties' had arisen. Thinking that it was cheaper to give a bribe than incur large hotel and other expenses in Patna, he paid a substantial sum to a bank official. The realization that being the president of a local co-operative society did not make him immune from the illicit demands of civil servants was a bitter blow to his ego.

Who was to blame? 'The politicians,' he replied. 'It's because they are corrupt that the lower ranks in the government become corrupt.' Politics, he went on to say, had become a form of business. 'To get started in politics, a man needs Rs 10,000 to 20,000 [£500 to £1,000]. Now, if this man gets elected to some position he must get his money back first, then make more and try for a higher position in politics.' A 'higher position' meant a seat in the Lok Sabha, the popularly elected lower house of central Parliament, in Delhi, the elections to which had been held earlier that month (March 1971). Chaudhry had actively supported the conservative Syndicate-Congress candidate but he had lost to his opponent from the Indira Gandhi-led Congress party. For all practical purposes, however, the two candidates were interchangeable. 'Before the elections, the Indira [Gandhi]-led Congress tried to get him back to its fold by offering him Rs 100,000 [£5,000], but he refused,' said Chaudhry. 'The politics of this country has gone all wrong. India's future is dark.'

A similar note of despair and cynicism was struck by Aganlal Musahar, a young landless labourer with wavy black hair. 'These elections do us no good,' he said. 'Our condition has not changed, and there is no hope.' The poverty of Musahar was apparent. He could not even afford a mud hut: the walls of his thatched-roof hut were made of bamboo and palm leaf. He had no shirt on, only a lungi. Didn't the introduction of a metalled road, an irrigation canal, and electricity in the village, that had occurred over the past decade, mean that progress was being made, and that there was hope? 'The road is useful to those who have cars, jeeps, and buses,' said Musahar. 'The canal is for those who own land. As for us, the landless, we see the water flowing, and feel happy.' He grinned sardonically. 'Electricity? It is for those in brick houses, not those in bamboo huts. We have hardly enough to eat.'

Although he had had to leave school at 14, because his father could not afford to pay for his books and clothes, he had not stopped learning, in an informal way, and was generally well-informed. For instance, he

knew about the law on land ceiling, and that it had not been applied
in the village. If so, why didn't the landless go to court to have the law
implemented? 'Courts,' he said. 'How can we win against the rich
landlords? They have one lakh [100,000] rupees [£5,000], and we have
only five [25p].' Gori Lal, a middle-aged peasant, looking perplexed
and unwell, nodded in agreement. 'People with money always get their
way,' he said. 'It's always the poor who get into trouble, get beaten up
by the police and put in jail.'

Lal is marginally better off than Musahar: he owns one-eighth of
an acre of unirrigated land. It is a single-crop land, with an average
yield of 450 lb. of wheat. This is insufficient for seed, and for feeding
himself, his wife and child, for a year. So he works for a rich landowner,
as an agricultural labourer, for three months in a year. Then there are
casual labouring jobs, and these keep him busy for another three
months. But wages are low: Re 1 [5p] a day plus a simple lunch of
chapatis (i.e. pancakes) and a vegetable. During the harvesting period,
he gets Re 1 [5p] a day plus breakfast and lunch, or one-sixteenth of
what he harvests. (These wages are far below what Chaudhry, a local
landlord, claimed to be paying to his labourers.)[9] His wife works
whenever she can find it, which is not often. They try to save; but it
is an uphill task. The best they can do is survive; no more. The last
time Lal could afford a 20 naye paise (1p) worth bus ride to Purnea, a
town 15 miles away, was eight months ago!

What was his wish in life? 'To cultivate a few acres of land as a
sharecropper,' said Lal. It was a modest wish since, according to the
government statistics, 40 per cent of rural households in the district
(of Purnea) are sharecroppers. To safeguard the interests of such a
substantial section of society, the State administration, as befits a
popularly elected institution, stipulated by a law passed in the 1950s
that a sharecropper should give no more than a third of the produce
(as rent) to the landowner. But the law was worthless – so said Lal,
Musahar, and two elderly sharecroppers who were interviewed.

In practice, a sharecropper gives one-half to two-thirds of the
output to the landlord as rent. 'In addition,' said a local sharecropper,
'we give free labour to the landlord by working on his land for nothing.
If we refuse, the landlord throws us out of his [leased] land.' It is
fairly simple for the landlord to do so because – explained the two
elderly sharecroppers – all these leases are oral, and the sharecropper,
almost always indebted to the landlord, is hardly in a position to
challenge him. They had leased 2 acres of land each, and were both
indebted to the landlord, a fate they shared with two-thirds of the
landless in the district. It was customary for them to borrow grain
from the landlord for seed, and return twice as much at the time of
harvest, and thus pay the landlord an interest rate of 100 per cent in
five months. (This practice is quite widespread in the country.) What

was the reason for the existence of such a situation, with a few people, like Chaudhry, being rich, and many being poor? 'It's God's will,' said Musahar. 'No, it's due to the government's policies,' said Lal. 'Also, the rich had their fathers owning a lot of money and property,' said one of the sharecroppers. 'And when you have more to start with, you make more.'

How did their present living condition compare with that prevailing ten or fifteen years ago? It had grown worse as far as food was concerned, they said, but clothing had improved a bit.[10] Interestingly enough, a four-month study of Khandola, a village in Uttar Pradesh, the largest State in the country, carried out in the mid-1960s by Gilbert Etienne, an official of the Food and Agriculture Organization of the United Nations Organization, led to the following conclusion:

> Despite some nuances . . . the common trait of agricultural workers and artisans is the precariousness of their standard of living. . . . How many times have I been given the same, sad, rather bitter answer 'kuchh nahin (nothing)' when I have questioned them on the progress made during the last ten or fifteen years. Twenty out of 22 agricultural labourers, together with 18 of the artisans and tradesmen questioned, gave this reply.[11]

Whereas Bihar and Uttar Pradesh, accounting for a quarter of the national population, are almost at the bottom of the table of the per capita income, the Punjab and Haryana, two of the smallest States, are at the top. In recent years both these States have registered a much higher rate of economic growth than the rest of the country. This has been mainly due to the 'green revolution' – a term used to signify an extraordinary increase in the output from agricultural land – that has been taking place in this region since 1965, when the introduction of a high-yielding variety (HYV) of seed for wheat was accompanied by an increase in irrigation facilities, chemical fertilizers and pesticides, credit, and farm machinery, especially tractors. The number of tractors, for instance, went up from 7,800 in 1961 to over 25,000 in 1969.[12] The village of Nihal, situated 75 miles south-west of Chandigarh, the joint capital of the Punjab and Haryana, reflected this change thus: in 1961 it had no tractors at all; in 1971 it had 7.

Nihal is a conglomerate of unplanned squares and circles, and streets with open drains running by the side of houses which are equally haphazardly constructed. Some of the houses are made of unbaked bricks and mud; others of pale red bricks and cement; and the rest are thatched huts. A flagpole, standing somewhere in the middle of the village, is flying a yellow triangular flag, an indication that Sikhs – followers of Guru Nanak, a Hindu by birth, who, in the early sixteenth century, preached a monotheistic creed and opposed hereditary priesthood and the caste system – form an important part of the community.

Indeed, 80 of the 150 households in the village are Sikh; and almost all of them are landowners. The rest are Hindus, mainly lower caste and outcaste, who are, with a few exceptions, landless. In other words, a little over half of the families in the community possess all of the 1,700 acres of land belonging to the village, with the top ten families owning two-fifths of the total. It is families such as these who have been the principal beneficiaries of the green revolution.

Sardara Singh, an old Sikh cultivator with a flowing white beard, summed up the economic situation in the village thus: 'In the old days even those who had much land did not have enough resources or knowledge to make money out of it. Now, with electricity at the farm [that came in 1965] and miracle seed [that came in 1966], the situation has changed. These fellows have raised the yield of wheat from 12 to 13 maunds [maund equals 82 pounds] to 22 to 23 maunds. They are really well off now – constructing buildings, buying more tractors and motorcycles, and drinking it up. That is, those with 15 acres or above. Those with 15 acres just survive. It takes them ten years or more to construct one brick building. And those with less land or none at all are in a tight situation.' Since nearly three-quarters of the landholdings in the State, as well as in this village, are below $7\frac{1}{2}$ acres, the fruits of the green revolution have gone mainly to a small minority. Typical of this minority is Gurdayal Singh, a local Sikh of 36, who owns 17 acres of land. By switching to modern methods of production in the mid-1960s, he increased his profits from land rapidly – and saved, to the extent that in 1971 he managed to buy a second-hand tractor and harrow, worth Rs 16,000 (£800), by using his savings and borrowing small sums from his relatives.

The increased output from land, and the awareness of this, have led the landlords to raise their rent from the customary 50 per cent to 60–75 per cent of the produce. If a sharecropper refuses, or is unable to pay the higher rent, he finds himself ejected from the land, and swelling the ranks of agricultural workers. (Not surprisingly, the State witnessed an increase of over 100 per cent in the proportion of agricultural workers during the decade of 1961–71 – from 9.7 per cent of the rural workforce to 20·4.) However, a rising demand for labour due to intensive cultivation, multiple cropping, higher yields, and an increased activity in the non-agricultural sector has meant that rural labourers are finding more work than ever before, a situation which is not to the liking of the landlords.

'In the old days labourers used to work hard because they had hunger in their stomach,' said Sardara Singh of Nihal. 'But now they have less hunger in their stomach; and so we have to watch their work. Also, they have alternative jobs available to them. And they prefer to work on roads and buildings, and as coolies in towns – away from the fields.' He then referred to the families of *bazigars* (literally, public entertainers), a group outside the pale of the traditional Hindu or Sikh society, who live in a hamlet of their own, and whose men were then earning substantial wages (of Rs 2.50 to 7 (12½p to 35p) per day, depending on the output) as labourers in the grain warehouses of the nearby town of Patran.

But this was seasonal work, available only for a few weeks during the harvesting periods. At other times, the only reliable source of income for these twenty-three *bazigar* families is the sale of milk of their buffaloes, which fetches them no more than Rs 3 (15p) a day, part of which is spent on feeding the animal. Their material poverty is apparent from the fact that they make their sons work as soon as they are 8 or 9. The boy takes out the cattle of the rich and middle farmers for grazing, a job for which he receives Rs 25 (£1.25p) and a maund (82 lb.) of wheat a month. The other alternative – sending the child to school – costs money: Rs 10 (50p) per month per child, according to Dulari, a young, articulate *bazigar* woman. No wonder, then, that despite the existence of a primary school in the village, only six of the forty-six *bazigar* children of school-going age attended school, three of them being the children of Dulari.

How did they, the *bazigars*, compare their present living conditions with those prevailing some years ago? In recent years, they said, they had experienced an improvement in their life style. They, an itinerant people by tradition, had settled down, and had been finding more work on more days of the year than ever before. A similar feeling had earlier been expressed, by Gurdayal Singh, about the village community. 'In the past, people used to eat *chapatis* without any vegetable; now they do so with vegetables,' he had said. 'Clothing is better too. Now nobody is naked, and very few are to be seen in tattered clothes.' This is generally true of those wheat-growing areas in the country which have irrigation facilities since the 'miracle' seed can give the expected high yield only if there is ample water supply at the right time. (By 1970–1, only a third of the wheat-growing area was being cultivated with 'miracle' seed.)

It is rice, however, that is the staple diet of Indians; two and a half times as much land is used to grow rice as wheat. Progress here has been modest. By 1970–1, only one-seventh of the rice-growing area had been brought under 'miracle' seed; and the overall increase in production had been marginal. A recent study of the rice-growing district of West Godavary in Andhra Pradesh, by Francine R. Frankel, consultant to the United States Aid Mission in India, showed that the introduction of new technology had increased rice production by only 17 per cent. This was due to the existence of unfavourable 'agro-climatic conditions' and a very high proportion of small land-holdings (of 2–3 acres), which are unsuitable for an efficient use of the new technology.[13]

The example of Dusi, a village 50 miles south-west of Madras, the capital of Tamil Nadu, is typical of the rice-growing areas. More than four-fifths of the landholdings here are below 5 acres. Of the 610 families in the village and its two hamlets (one for the Untouchables and the other for Muslims), only six families own land above 10 acres. All of them are Brahmin, the highest caste.

S. Vedantam is one of them. He is a fat, jolly man of 29, with a white sandalwood paste mark on his forehead, who lives in a white-washed, brick house with a stone-paved platform in front of the entrance, in Brahmin Lane, the main street of the village. Although his family consists of five members (himself, his wife and child, a widowed sister, and father), a fairly typical situation, he constantly refers to it as 'the joint family', an indication that he wishes to mask the real size of the agricultural land owned and managed by him. 'The joint family,' he said, 'owns 40 acres of land.' (This was probably an understatement.) Of these, 25 acres were rented out to tenants or sharecroppers, and the rest were under 'self-cultivation', a curious statement to make since, as an orthodox Brahmin, Vedantam does not touch a plough.

He made no mention of the policies of the State government which had enabled him, along with thousands of large and medium-sized landlords in the State, to double the rice output from his 'self-cultivated' land, but instead railed against the State administration for placing a ceiling on land. 'The principle of ceiling is to equalize everybody,' he said. 'It's a ruse to get the poor people's vote. It'll never work. Suppose the government really enforces this law – which it has not – and gives some land to the landless, and even some capital. What will the poor fellow do with this land or capital? Nothing; because he doesn't know. It's like giving a coconut to a monkey: he can't eat it. We know these [poor] people. It's us, here, who can look after them, not those fellows in Madras. We are like one big family with our farm workers. We give them loans without interest. We trust them, and they trust us. That is why there is no need to make written agreements with our sharecroppers. Word of mouth is enough.'

The sharecroppers, however, viewed the situation differently. Vardan Vanniyar, a wiry, gaunt-faced Naicker, the largest caste in the village, for instance, would have liked to have a written agreement. 'Then I would not be threatened with eviction by the landlord every-time he felt I have not produced enough,' he said. 'These threats worry me. The land is in short supply in the village, and there are always people anxious to become sharecroppers even if the rent is high.' He cultivates $1\frac{1}{2}$ acres of land that belongs to an absentee Brahmin landlord. It is one-crop land, and the average yield is fifteen sacks of paddy (i.e. unmilled rice). Eight sacks go as rent to the landlord; and another one and a half sacks as seed and wages to labourers he must engage for harvesting. So, in the end, he is left with five and a half sacks, or a little over a third of the produce.

Those sharecroppers who get their seed and fertilizer from the landlord, as do all the Untouchable sharecroppers, living in the Harijan[14] colony, have to pay 70 per cent of the produce as rent to the landlord. 'Getting only 30 per cent of the produce does not make it worthwhile for us to work on land,' said M. Pazani, a 27-year-old Harijan sharecropper. 'But if we protest we get kicked out. Yes, I know of the tenancy law [which specifies a maximum of 40 per cent of produce as land rent], but it does not apply here. The landlords are influential, and we poor have no unity. Actually, we went on strike once, five or six years ago; but we could not hold out for long. Still, the landlords agreed to raise our share from 25 per cent to 30–35 per cent.'

One of the reasons for a lack of unity among the poor is the social chasm that exists between the outcastes and the caste Hindus. Despite the existence of the Untouchability (Offences) Act, passed by the national Parliament in 1955, which outlaws the enforcement of disabilities 'on the ground of untouchability' in regard to entrance and worship at temples, access to shops and restaurants, use of water resources, etc., the Untouchables in Dusi continued to be barred from the barber and tea shops as well as temples and wells – until 1967. In that year, someone claiming to be the State government's Harijan Welfare Officer arrived in the village, and led a party of Untouchables to a tea shop, and threatened to lodge a complaint with the local police if they were not served. They were, and have continued to be. But nothing more. They are still barred not only from the village wells and temples but also from the local sub-post office, which is in Brahmin Lane, a street that is out of bounds to them.

Why did they, the Untouchables, not make a determined bid to break the social bar completely? 'If we tried,' said Pazani, 'all the higher caste Hindus would join together and beat us.' Wouldn't the police intervene? 'No,' said A. M. Krishnan, the government-appointed headman of the Harijan hamlet. 'The policemen themselves are caste Hindus. There is only one Harijan among them, and he does not help us at all. Besides, there are other ways of punishing us. For example, the village karnam [i.e. land revenue officer] could refuse to put his signature on our papers. And we need that for any and every transaction we want to make.'

In general, the Untouchables are most shunned by Brahmins, the highest and purest of the four castes. The traditional antagonism is accentuated by the fact that, in this region, Brahmins are, more often than not, landlords while the Untouchables are sharecroppers or agricultural workers. The alienation between the two groups is best illustrated by their attitude towards the Communists. 'If the Communists come to our colony I'll join them,' said Pazani, reflecting a general sentiment of his community. 'If the Communists gain power then there will be no difference between the rich and the poor.'

'The Communists antagonize relations between landlords and peasants, and are a menace,' said Vedantam, a Brahmin landlord. 'They should be banned.' He then referred to a 'violent' agitation of the agricultural workers for higher wages, led by the Communist Party of India (Marxist), that had occurred a few years earlier in the district of Thanjavur, 150 miles to the south, and which had brought about a change in the situation, summarized by a Thanjavur landlord thus: 'Things used to be very peaceful here some years ago. The labourers were hardworking and respectful. But now . . . the fellow who used to stand in the backyard of my house to talk to me comes straight to the veranda wearing slippers and all. At 5.30 p.m. sharp he says, "Our leader is speaking today at a public meeting. I have to go." His leader holds a meeting right next door to me and parades the streets with the red flag. These fellows have become lazy and arrogant, thanks to the Communists. They have no fear in them any more.'[15] Similar sentiments were expressed frequently, during the period of 1970–2, by the landlord class in West Bengal, following the formation of leftist coalition ministries, first in 1967 and then in 1969, with the CPI(M) as the major partner.

Over the past decade or so, West Bengal has been getting poorer in relative and absolute terms. Both its rank in the table of per capita income and the actual per capita income have been coming down. Between 1968 and 1969, for instance, the annual per capita income declined from Rs 330 (£18.33) to Rs 326 (£18.11);[16] and the trend has continued since then. The general economic downturn is to be seen in most of the rural areas, such as Sahajapur, where three-fourths of the State's 48 million people live.

Sahajapur, situated a little over a hundred miles north-east of Calcutta, has 290 households and nearly 1,500 inhabitants. Of these, 30 households are upper caste Hindus, 140 are lower castes; and the remaining are Santal (a tribal group), who live in a hamlet of their own. As is the case elsewhere in the country, the upper caste Hindus own most of the agricultural land. But, since land distribution is once again uneven, only ten of these families are really well off. The richest of them is the Mandal family.

Neelkant Mandal, a slim, nut-brown man of 25, looks after the land of the joint family, which includes three generations and twenty members. How large was the land? He parried the question; but, in the course of a long conversation that followed, it emerged that his grandfather had bequeathed 350 acres to his five sons, all of them still alive. That is, each of the surviving sons had an 'effective' ownership of 70 acres – or almost three times the size (then) allowed by the State's land ceiling law.

He knew of the law on land ceiling, Neelkant said. 'But we keep the excess land in the name of our children, to provide for their future.

It is bad to go against the law, but we are only looking after our interests.' If educated people like him did not abide by the law, how did he expect the illiterate to do so? 'Yes,' he said, 'it is understandable why the illiterate do not follow the law. But then the last [CPI(M)-dominated] United Front government tried to take the land away even from those who had less than 25 acres. The attitude of the poor has changed – for the worse. They no longer respect those with land. This began to happen soon after the first United Front government came to power [in 1967]. The poor think that the rich are getting richer. I think the poor want the money without working for it.'

Deepapada Mandal, his 72-year-old uncle, wearing a white shirt and *dhoti*, and polished shoes, agreed. 'In the olden days, things were orderly,' he said. 'No more. Nowadays people do a lot of stealing and get away with it. For example, fish is being stolen from my tank, but nothing can be done about it.' (Later, many villagers were to state categorically that the tank in question was common property of the village.) He threw a loving glance at the water tank from his chair in the veranda of his guest room. 'The British were so much better,' he continued. 'Things went wrong with Nehru coming to power. Communists are worse. They want all to be equal which is not possible. They are bad because they go for violence. If the CPI(M) comes to power again, it will take away all my property and all my money. Then I won't be able to help the poor people. Only the other day, a CPI(M) party worker (in the village) came to me for help, for his father's funeral. I gave him Rs 10 (50p). Why doesn't the CPI(M) give him some money?'

'Because the CPI(M) has no money: it is a poor man's party' came a reply from one of the persons in the group of men and boys that had, by then, collected around Mandal's veranda. The speaker was a short, thin man in his mid-thirties. His name was Netai Chundur Majhi; and he knew both the local CPI(M) and the Mandals. He owed the Mandals Rs 300 (£15) for his dwelling, a thatched mud structure, he said (later – away from the Mandals), but was unable to pay. When he was threatened by the Mandals with court action, he consulted his friends; and they advised him to join the CPI(M), 'the poor man's party'. He did. That is, he was often seen in the company of a CPI(M) activist in the village, a teacher. This deterred the Mandals from going to court; but to penalize him they refused him work on their land which, until then, had been a steady source of income for him.

His dwelling is in that part of the village where lower caste Hindus, mostly landless peasants like him, live. The houses are derelict; and the residents, weak and undernourished, look older than their years. 'On an average, we work one day in four – say, one week a month – on the land of big landowners here,' said Majhi. 'The daily wages are Re 1 [5p] and 3½ lb. of rice. Now, to feed my family twice a day I need half a rupee [2½p] and 4½ lb. of rice. So, you can see that I must find other work. I gather fruit and sell it, thatch roofs sometimes, carry loads. But even then, it is not everyday that we have two meals. We can survive on one meal a day, and often that is all we have. Today, for example, I have eaten nothing yet, for there is not a grain at home.'

It is not only the landless but also most of the poor farmers and some of the middle peasants who have been suffering a decline in their living standards due to the continued maldistribution of land and a rapidly rising population. The case of the Kundu family is illustrative. Kalipada Kundu, a 68-year-old weaver-cultivator, with a holy thread round his bare chest, is the father of four daughters (all married) and three sons (two married). Forty years ago he inherited 14 acres of land; now he is down to 2. Every time he married his daughter he sold some land to meet the expenses of dowry and the customary feeding and entertaining of scores of near and distant relatives. Once he had pneumonia; and in order to pay the doctor's and pharmaceutist's bills (amounting to £16) he had to sell an acre of land. Then there was a severe drought once; and the only way he could survive was by selling land. Other times he did so to clear his debts and save himself the heavy interest charges. In short, in order to get over his immediate financial crisis, he disposed of part of his land-capital, which reduced his income-producing base and thus hastened the process of his impoverishment.[17]

What saved him from penury was weaving, a craft he had learnt from a neighbour in his youth. Over the years, this has become an increasingly important source of income to the joint family, especially when two of his sons too have learnt the craft, one from him and the other at a nearby technical college. The family has two looms, cheap home-made contraptions; and between the three of them they weave 60 cotton towels a week, working 12 hours a day, and earn Rs 27 (£1·35) a week. The third son cultivates the family's 2 acres, and has 5 more acres on lease as a sharecropper. 'It is thus that we, the sixteen of us in the joint family, manage to eat twice a day, all year round,' said Kalipada. 'Mind you, we *never* really have a full meal. But still, we are better off than many in the village.'

But he had other frustrations, or rather his youngest son, Narhari, had. 'Narhari was a good student and got a government scholarship to go to a technical college,' he said. 'He secured a diploma in weaving – three years ago. He sent out many applications for a job; but not even once did he get an interview. In the end he gave up. He began weaving at home.' He pointed to the room at the back which had the hand-looms and where Narhari was then weaving. 'What is the use of all that education and expense?' he asked. 'Now Narhari is doing exactly what my other son is doing, working on a handloom at home; and that one never even went to high school. We are all going downhill here.' The man sitting next to him on the veranda nodded agreement.

He was Bhola Nath Lohar, an old, sunburnt, low caste Hindu, all bones and wrinkled skin, with a salt and pepper goatee, who worked as a sharecropper on 4 acres of land. Although he supplied all of the inputs and labour for the land, he received only a third of the produce. 'As a result,' he said, 'it is only during the harvesting season and a few months after that that we eat two meals a day. Then we cut back to one meal a day. There are days, just before harvesting begins, when we have to go without food. With more mouths to feed than ever before, and with prices of things – salt, rice, mustard oil, *dhotis* – rising, our condition is growing worse.'

The rapid rise in prices has hit particularly hard those who do not work on land, and do not therefore receive payment in kind, an arrangement that partly cushions the effects of inflation. Haripada Karmakar, a blacksmith, is a case in point. A small, emaciated-looking man, he makes his living by making and repairing agricultural tools – spades, scythes, rippers, and axes – and cooking implements such as ladles and colanders. 'Nowadays I can hardly manage to support my wife, three children, and mother,' he said. 'It costs Rs 6 [30p] a day to maintain them. The prices are rising so fast that every day it becomes more difficult to survive. I had a bicycle which I had inherited from my father. Last month my financial condition was so bad that I had to sell it to buy some rice. I had this bicycle for twenty-two years. It was old, but it was useful. I would use it to bring galvanized iron and scrap iron from Bolpur [the nearby town]. Now I have to bring these by bus or bullock-cart; and that costs money. But what else could I have done? I needed the money so badly last month.'

A similar sense of despair and frustration, arising out of growing impoverishment of the masses, is to be noticed in Calcutta, the State capital. The tensions and pressures of city life, coupled with an appalling degree of overcrowding and filth, make existence for most Calcuttans far less bearable than is the case in the countryside, where open spaces and lush growth, especially during the monsoon, tend to soften somewhat the rigour of material poverty.

2

URBAN INDIA

Three-fourths of the population in our metropolitan areas have no private latrine, or bathroom, or water tap, or sewerage facilities.
Sindhu Phadke, an Indian economist[1]

3·39 per cent of urban households own 45·31 per cent of the country's total urban wealth.
A Report by the Reserve Bank of India[2]

About 80 per cent of the primary school children are prone to disease due to gross undernourishment, according to a sample survey conducted on 20,000 school children in Madras.
News item in *The Times of India*[3]

Calcutta is certainly the world's most overcrowded metropolis;[4] and a visitor gets a taste of it right at the point of arrival, the city's two main railway stations. The pattern continues outside; for the streets are choked with people dressed in a wide variety of clothes, rickshaws, pulled by thin, ill-clad men, taxis, cars, trams, and buses weighed down with passengers packed solidly inside, and clinging desperately to the steel bars welded to the doors and windows of the vehicles. Even the pavements are crowded, since a pavement is more than a footpath: it is also a bedroom, a drawing room, a shop, a dining room, a business premise, a bathroom, and a playground. And no part of the city is spared.

Right in the centre of the metropolis, in the shadow of the offices of the country's leading industrial houses, can be found a barber cutting hair on the pavement, a man sleeping, a scribe filling in a money-order form, half-clad children playing, a hawker selling fruit, while only a few feet away a man may be urinating against the wall, a half-naked man having a bath, and a cow leisurely chewing up orange peels and coconut husks. In spite of the vast *maidan* (open space) that flanks the central area of Chowringhee, the air is mixed with smells of urine, rotting garbage, and cowdung. And the garbage heaps outside the New Market, the city's most prestigious shopping centre, attracts not only stray dogs, pigs, and chickens of the neighbourhood, but also some of its destitutes. The public services in the area are as bad as elsewhere. The streets are pot-holed, hydrants leaky, and drains clogged; and every wall is a virtual urinal. This is symptomatic of a bigger and wider problem.

The situation has deteriorated to this point as a result of the continued lag in housing, sanitation, water supply, and public transport with respect to a rapidly rising population – up from 2·11 million in 1941 for the city and district (officially called the Calcutta Metropolitan District) to 7 million in 1971. Most of the increase has been due to the inflow of the landless and poor peasants from the countryside of West Bengal and the neighbouring States, and Hindu refugees from the then East Pakistan (now Bangladesh).

The people of the Calcutta Metropolitan District are the most ill-housed in the country. Only 8 per cent live in a self-contained flat or house; whereas 20 per cent have nowhere to live except in shops or other business premises such as factories, offices, docks, or construction sites, and another 28 per cent live in structures made of bamboo, mud, or unbaked bricks, with insufficient or non-existent sanitary and hygienic facilities. The rest live in pucka (i.e. made of baked bricks and mortar) or semi-pucka structures with shared facilities.[5]

Among those who are compelled to live on their business premises is the 60-year-old Keshab Banik, a shopkeeper in the Gariahat area, whose income from the shop is so meagre (Rs 10 (50p) a day) that he cannot afford the daily 64 naye paise (4p) bus journey from Rajur, a town 30 miles south of Calcutta, where his family lives.[6] Another such Calcuttan is Subodh Nayak, a 19-year-old house servant, who sleeps in the veranda of the flat of his employer – a middle-class family in south Calcutta. Of the Rs 20 (£1) received as monthly wages, he manages to send Rs 15 (75p) to his family – consisting of five brothers and sisters, and parents – in Payerchali, a village 150 miles west of Calcutta.[7] (Half of the families in this village were then substantially dependent on remittances from Calcutta for their survival, whereas a decade ago this was true of only a quarter of the families, an indication of the growing pauperization of the countryside.)

Soon after he left school at fourteen, Nayak found that his labour was not needed for the 2-acre farmland that his father owned, and was glad to leave when, two years later, his uncle, already working in Calcutta, got him a job as an office boy. But this did not last long; and he was soon back in the village, idling away his time. Then his elder brother found work in Calcutta, as a doorman with an electrical firm, at Rs 90 (£4·50) a month, and called him to the city. Together, they opened a tea stall in the compound of a newspaper office. Just as business was picking up, the newspaper management decided to build a garage where their tea stall stood; and so they had to go. It was then that Nayak was helped by a friend to become a house servant, a job with long hours and poor pay, but with the fringe benefit of free accommodation. His example illustrates the rising pressure on land in the countryside and the utter insecurity of life in the city.

It is significant that of the three members of the Nayak family working in Calcutta, only one – the uncle – was living away from his employer, in a *bustee*, a term used for a settlement of one or more barrack-like structures. There are 3,000 *bustees*, dotted around the metropolis; and many among the city's working and lower-middle classes can afford nothing better.[8] A typical room in a *bustee* measures 12 feet by 5, often lacks ventilation and electricity, and is occupied by as many as five people. The paths within a *bustee* are almost always unpaved, unlit, and littered with uncollected garbage. The water supply and sanitary facilities are, to say the least, grossly inadequate. The *bustee* in Deodar Street, south Calcutta, for example, is equipped with only two water taps and one latrine; and its 150 inhabitants have to make do with these.[9] A line for the use of the only latrine starts so early in the morning that by the time Ramchandra Mahato, one of the residents, joins it at five o'clock there are enough people ahead of him to keep him waiting for an hour.

Mahato, a thin, dark man of 35, shares his room with his 65-year-old father and 16-year-old brother. He and his father have a vegetable-cum-firewood business which they set up, each morning and evening, on a pavement, just outside the *bustee*. In the morning, while his father attends to the sales, he chops up the old furniture he buys from junk shops and prepares bundles of firewood. Then he goes off, pushing his cart, on some coolie errands. Later, he and his father have lunch together, and a short nap, which is followed by a few games of cards with neighbours. By then it is time to set up the sales counter for vegetables and firewood. Business continues until about half past eight; then they have dinner, a wash up, and a few more games of cards. They retire to bed at about half past eleven.

They follow this routine seven days a week, every week of the year. Yet all they earn is a sum of Rs 125 to 150 (£6·25 to 7·50) a month. Of this, Rs 35 (£1.75) go for rent, and Rs 90 (£4·50, at the rate of one rupee, 5p, per person per day) for the upkeep of the three of them. So, in the end, they have Rs 5 to 25 (25p to £1·25) left over, each month, to send to their family in rural Bihar. Declining sales, caused by a steady deterioration in the living standards of their clients ('Those who used to buy one kilogramme of potatoes are now buying only three-quarters of a kilogramme,' said Mahato), are making their remittances home smaller and irregular. Yet there is no question of a return to the village, for all it offers him, or his father, is half an acre of ancestral farmland.

Their neighbour, Lakshman Singh, a 40-year-old man with greying hair, who runs a tea stall in the *bustee*, was also feeling the effect of the declining living standards of his clients, and finding his petty business increasingly uneconomical. Ideally, he said, he would like to be a factory worker, with an assured income at the end of a month, along with such fringe benefits as a provident fund for old age. But, with overall employment in industry on the decline, since the mid-1960s,[10] there was no chance of that happening. In any case, the factory workers themselves were experiencing a fall in their living standards, as was manifested, for example, by their mounting indebtedness. During a brief span of two years, a worker in the jute industry (one of the leading industries in the State) increased his borrowing from his provident fund by more than a third.[11]

A similar trend is to be noticed among the lower-middle class of the city. 'A grim prospect of semi-starvation, destitution, mounting debts and sordid living without any sign of redemption stares at every lower middle class family,' reports the News Team of the *Statesman* of Calcutta. 'Almost all are caught in the cobweb of debts. Fresh loans are invariably taken to pay off old debts, and the process continues indefinitely. . . . Food is just enough to keep the body going. Fish is rarity. So is milk. Malnutrition is rampant. Recreation is non-existent.'[12]

Balaram Roy and Jatin Majmudar are cases in point. Roy, a low-grade employee of the State government, travels to his office perching on the footboard of a tram car so as to evade payment of fare which he can ill afford. He avoids all social meetings which might entail expenses. 'The other day I did not attend the marriage of my nephew who was brought up in our household,' he said. 'Everyone was given to understand that I was ill. But I know why I was forced to stay back. [It was lack of money.]' The principal meal of his family is rice or flour mixed with a meagre quantity of sweet molasses or lentils. Even then he cannot always provide for all of his family. Sometimes he and his wife have to forgo meals to see that their children do not go hungry. Majmudar, a lower-division clerk, keeps two glasses of water underneath his table in the office. 'Besides quenching thirst, water has another purpose,' he said. 'It does away with headache born out of weakness.' His weakness stems from malnutrition which is a result of his insufficient earnings – Rs 230 (£11·50) a month. 'Sometimes I cannot buy enough coal to light the oven in my house twice a day,' he said.[13]

For Dhiren Chaterjee, a small, intelligent-looking bachelor of 28, lack of money means, and will continue to mean, having to remain unmarried. A son of a lawyer, he had to cut short his university education when his father had a stroke. Lack of a university degree meant that a white collar job was out of the question for him since, even among those with a degree, no more than a half can ever hope to find one. He therefore tried for a job on a factory floor, and got it. He became a machine operator in an ordnance factory, and then an engineering firm with a workforce of nearly 2,000 and an active trade union. He earns

Rs 250 (£12·50) a month. House rent, his daily bus fare, lunch at work, and cigarettes cost him Rs 100 (£5) a month; and the rest is barely enough to maintain the four adult members of the family in a style that befits a middle-middle-class Bengali household. And so, to balance his budget, he has to borrow periodically from the company's co-operative society.

However, Chaterjee sees his predicament in a larger context, as a symptom of the growing economic degeneration of the existing social order, and seeks a social, not an individual, solution which, he believes, lies in bringing about a genuinely socialist revolution in the country. He has come to hold this view as a result of his contact with the Communist movement, which began during his college years. Now he is an active member of his union, which is led, in the main, by the CPI(M). When the first CPI(M)-dominated coalition government came to power, in 1967, he and other union activists observed many strikes and *gheraos* – i.e. encirclement of individual managers by workers as a tactic for winning concessions – that occurred in the nearby factories. This collective experience of theirs proved useful when they called on the workers in their own factory to strike. The strike lasted fifty-four days, and won the workers better wages and working conditions.

Indeed, during that period, the late 1960s, the 200,000 engineering workers in Calcutta, and elsewhere, managed to secure a 20 per cent increase in their wages. This was long overdue since wages of industrial workers in the State were a third less than those in the rest of the country.[14] 'We pay the workers here [in Calcutta] one-half to two-thirds of what we pay them in and around Delhi,' said Ranjan Roy-Chowdhry, the works manager of a medium-sized rubber factory. 'We keep them as temporary hands because making them permanent entitles them to fringe benefits and gives them security. We do this by breaking their service, because the law says that a worker with 210 days of continuous service is entitled to becoming permanent. Anybody who even vaguely attempts to start a union is dismissed immediately.'[15] It was the awareness of such facts that made S. S. Dhavan, a liberal, Cambridge-educated lawyer, then serving as the governor of West Bengal, state: 'The proletariat of Calcutta is the worst exploited in the world.'[16]

The brief rule of the leftist coalition ministry, during the period of 1967–70, which gave the State's working classes some sense of confidence, was decried by most of the city's industrialists and businessmen. 'Thanks to the presence of the CPI(M) in the United Front government, our employees became *excessively* militant,' said B. K. Dutt, chairman of a large bank. 'These CPI(M) fellows have no sense of proportion.'[17] S. Gupta, chairman of a large industrial house, described at length the 'acute discomfort' caused to the manager of one of his firms, in early 1969, when he had been led out of his air-conditioned office by a group of workers and union representatives, and made to stand in the sun while they negotiated their wages and working conditions with him. 'With the extremists and Communists as ministers in the United Front government, our workers lost all sense of discipline,' he concluded.[18]

Most of the businessmen and company directors, earning Rs 5,000 to Rs 50,000 (£250 to £2,500) a month, show their 'sense of discipline' by habitually falsifying their income tax returns, and contriving to transfer their personal expenses of accommodation, transport, domestic help, and the general running of a household on to the company account. They maintain their 'sense of proportion' by including in their weekly shopping list expensive French champagne, available at Rs 300 (£15) a bottle.

The life style of this class is summed up by AM, a Calcutta journalist, thus:

Clubs and parties, golf and horse races have been the staple of their existence. For them, it has been a separate, esoteric world: they would slink to office, nursing yesternight's hangover, at around ten-thirty; by eleven, coffee will be served by dainty secretaries; one or two perfunctory meetings concerning office chores, or one or two letters for dictation; come twelve-thirty, the chauffeur-driven cars will be summoned, and the sahibs will migrate to the clubs, aperitifs will be followed by yet other aperitifs, indolent gossip about other people's jobs and wives, a languorous luncheon, a slovenly, contented reappearance in office around three or three-fifteen; but by four-thirty, the sahibs will call it a day, some will head toward a few hurried rounds of golf, others to the luxurious bungalows or apartments for a brief rest and recreation before the gruelling round of boisterous cocktails and parties commences in the evening.[19]

However, for a time, during 1970–1, when members of the Communist Party of India (Marxist-Leninist), popularly known as Naxalites, carried out individual 'annihilation' of 'class enemies', the élite considered it prudent to curtail its social activities. In fact, many among them, especially those of non-Bengali origin, sent their families off to other cities, chiefly Bombay, which was regarded as politically safe and economically sound.

Mainly because of its proximity to Western and Middle Eastern markets, Bombay has come to enjoy a pre-eminent position in India's commercial and industrial life. During the late 1950s and early 1960s, when the country had some success in expanding its industrial base, Bombay witnessed a substantial economic growth. Since then the city's rate of economic growth has declined considerably, but not its attraction to the rural poor. Indeed, the decennial growth in its population went up from 40 per cent during the 1950s to 43·8 per cent in the

1960s.[20] And yet there has been no visible deterioration in such municipal services as road sweeping, garbage collection, and an efficient public transport system.

The housing situation in Bombay, however, is no better than that in Calcutta; nor are the water supply and sanitary facilities any better. Nearly three-quarters of the 6 million Bombayites live in one-room tenements and lack private bathroom, water tap or latrine.[21] Of these, more than two-fifths are to be found living in the city's make-shift slums, where they lack adequate protection from the monsoon, which lasts three months in a year and brings an average rainfall of 70 inches.

'Walking through the slush and filth of the slums along Rafi Ahmad Kidwai Road in Sewree and Wadala [in north Bombay], one sees huts crushed by rain or blown by the winds,' reports a correspondent of the *Times of India*.

> With bamboos, tin sheets, tarpaulin bags, and other waste
> materials, the inmates keep trying to reconstruct the huts. . . .
> Through the narrow, dark streets run rivulets of grey water. . . .
> The area becomes like a vast Turkish bath when the sun shines and
> the water begins to evaporate rapidly. From the heaps of garbage
> emanates a pervasive, repulsive odour. Flies swarm around excreta
> of human beings and dogs. Rats as big as kittens scale the dirty
> walls, and sickly hens roam the streets in search of food. . . .
> Some of the bamboo and tarpaulin structures are so low that
> one cannot enter without bending double. Aluminium utensils,
> stinking rags, and sickly children are crammed inside. Water
> drips into the huts all the time, and women are busy the entire
> day scooping it out.[22]

What is worse is that both the number and size of the slums keep increasing. It is estimated that in the vast slum complex of Dharavi, north Bombay – with a population of 300,000! – a make-shift hut goes up every hour of the day and night.[23] This happens because of the continuing influx of rural migrants, the natural increase in the population of the existing slums, and a continual displacement of those living in cheap housing which has deteriorated to the extent of becoming unsafe. The Shivajinagar slum in Sion, north Bombay, is a case in point.[24]

When, in 1959, a few rows of unsafe barrack-type tenements, near the municipal hospital in Sion, were razed to the ground, many of those displaced occupied the open space just across the road, and built huts. By 1964 there were sixty huts; and, by 1971, three times as many, accommodating 900 people from all parts of the country. Nearly a third of them are Maharashtrians, i.e. the people of the State; another third are from the northern States of Uttar Pradesh and Bihar; and the remaining from the southern States of Andhra Pradesh and Tamil Nadu. They make their living as hawkers, coolies, night watchmen, domestic servants, mill and dock workers, hospital sweepers and attendants, and bootleggers.

The huts are arranged in rows with a narrow path, barely 4 feet wide, separating them. They lack drainage and sanitary facilities, with the result that a black slush covers the paths even when it is *not* raining, and children can be seen defecating in open daylight on pavements around the slum. Each hut is 10 feet by 8, with a door that is hardly 5 feet high. The inside, without any ventilation or electricity, is often cramped with a two-tier bed. The small area under the narrow awning outside serves as kitchen. The air is full of smells of putrefying garbage and human excreta, aromatic spices – and illicit liquor.

The smell of illicit liquor emanates from a 'cold drink' shop, which is owned by S. Rumulu, a plump, black, spectacled man of 32. Born in Hyderabad, Andhra Pradesh, Rumulu grew up to be a *bidi* (i.e. cheap hand-rolled cigarette of unprocessed tobacco) worker. He and his wife, who assisted him in making *bidis*, between them managed to earn Rs 9 (45p) by working a twelve-hour day. They found this inadequate; and so, attracted by stories of fortunes that could be made in Bombay, they set out for the Big City in 1963. On arrival, they camped on the pavement outside a railway terminus. He worked as a coolie while his wife cooked. One day he met a fellow Andhraite who had his own *bidi* works. He agreed to roll *bidis* for his new-found friend; and the latter brought the Rumulus to the present slum. Here, they constructed a hut of their own at the cost of Rs 60 (£3). They worked hard, and saved. Rumulu opened a small 'cold drink' shop, a front for selling illicit liquor, a thriving business.[25] He prospered. On top of that, in 1969, he won a lottery of Rs 10,000 (£500), a windfall, which gave a further boost to his business, and made him an important part of a ring of bootleggers, who maintained an excellent relationship with the police by paying them regular bribes.

There are many in the slum who admire and respect Rumulu for his material success and, knowing his cordial relations with the police, were only too willing to elect him the secretary of the local Hutment Owners' Association, that was formed by the residents, a few years ago, to resist any attempt that might be made to evict them from the illegally occupied land. Among his admirers is Satya Shankar, a shy, boyish-looking man of 25, a landless peasant from Andhra Pradesh, who has to work from 4 a.m. to 10 p.m. to be able to make a living.

His first job of the day is to deliver fifty to sixty bottles of milk to various households. This necessitates his getting up at four in the morning to secure a place in the front of a long line that forms at the (government-run) distribution kiosk, where milk is sold. He uses a bicycle and a 10-year-old helper to do this job, which fetches him and his help Rs 2 (10p). Then he washes cars for two hours, and earns a rupee (5p). He has a quick breakfast, and is off to do household chores for a family for two hours, for which he is paid 50 naye paise (2½p) – a rate that amounts to a third of what an unskilled factory worker gets. He returns to his hut, washes milk bottles, and is off again to do the afternoon round of milk delivery, a job that earns him 50 naye paise (2½p). Only after that, around five in the afternoon, does he find time to cook and eat, and have a short nap. At seven in the evening, he begins his second round of household chores which continues until 10 p.m., and brings him 75 naye paise (3¾p). Then he has dinner, and goes to bed around 11 p.m. That is, sixteen hours' labour earns him Rs 4½ (22½p) – or Rs 135 (£6·75) a month. This seems pitiably low; and yet this is about what the two Mahatos – father and son – in Calcutta earn.[26] In a way, this is a measure of the difference in the economic condition of the two cities.

Indeed, some of the poor in Bombay still manage to move up the socio-economic ladder a step or two. The case of the Garude family, living in a one and a half room pucka tenement in north Bombay, is illustrative. Until his retirement a year ago, Kondiram Garude, a bespectacled man of 60 with a stoop, worked as a labourer at the government's railway workshop, a job he held for thirty-eight years. He managed to bring up his eight children, four sons and four daughters, by supplementing his income by making shoes (something he, a leather-worker by caste, had learnt at an early age) in his spare time. The expense of educating them was borne by the State government which provides scholarships to members of the Scheduled Castes (such as leather-workers, street-sweepers, scavengers, etc.) up to university level, and reserves a certain percentage of jobs in the civil service for them. It was thus that his eldest son was able to secure a BA and a white collar job. (Later, he married and moved to an outer, cleaner suburb of Bombay.) Now, one of his three grown-up daughters is at a university college; another is studying midwifery; and the third is a seamstress in a clothing factory. What changes had he, Garude, seen in his block of tenements over the past generation? 'Electricity has come, and a water tap inside each tenement,' he replied. 'As for the residents, some have moved up [economically] and left the tenement block; others have gone down.'[27]

In a general sense, therefore, the condition of the poor has remained basically what it was a generation ago. The rich, on the other hand, have been growing richer. This is indicated by the rising demand in the city for such smuggled luxury goods (by Indian standards) as foreign transistor radios, tape recorders, cameras, watches, liquor, cosmetics, nylon saris, etc.; and luxury housing. In the summer of 1971, for instance, a small flat measuring 30 feet by 20 in a fashionable part of the city was selling for Rs 100,000 (£5,000) or renting for Rs 900 (£45) a month, the average gross monthly salary of a junior business executive; and the demand outstripped supply.[28] Many of the rich make exorbitant profits by getting involved, directly or indirectly, in financing such operations as smuggling, bootlegging, foreign currency exchange racket, and buying and selling luxury housing and office accommodation. A similar situation, albeit on a smaller scale, exists in Madras, the country's third largest port-city, where luxury goods are smuggled in from Singapore and Hong Kong. The purchasers are to be found among the city's commercial and industrial élite, much enlarged by the growth in the city's industry and commerce that occurred, mainly, in the late 1950s and early 1960s.[29]

As there was no corresponding rise in the supply of cheap accommodation in Madras for the increased labour force, drawn mainly from the countryside, the already bad housing situation became worse. During the 1960s, the number of slums nearly doubled, as did the percentage of the city's population living in them (from 22 to 43 per cent).[30] Among the new slums that mushroomed during that period was Annanagar, established near the garbage-dumping ground at the southernmost tip of the city, in 1966, by some of the residents of the already existing slum in Rayapuram some miles away.[31]

Initially, the colonizers were afraid of being evicted by the local authorities; but when the Dravida Munnetra Kazhagam (i.e. Dravida Progressive Federation), a regional party they supported, won control of the Town Hall in 1967, they felt secure. They then planned the colony properly – laid wide parallel streets, allotted a sizeable plot to each family, and built a temple *and* an office for the Annanagar Hutment Dwellers Association. They dug a well, but it yielded brackish water; and so the local authority had to supply them with drinking water, which it did by sending a water tanker, each morning and evening. By early 1971 they had acquired properly-built public latrines. But there was little they could do about the swarms of flies and stench that came from the nearby dumping-ground where trucks, piled high with the city's rubbish, rolled in all day, and where a few of the colony's old women and children could be seen competing with pigs and dogs to find something worth eating or keeping.

A few other old women of the colony find solace in sitting under a tree, in front of a small heap of red chillies and a few cucumbers with the intention of selling them, a scene that makes Jairaman Milli-Chetty, with four handlooms installed in his house, appear as a man of immense enterprise. He is a large, bare-chested man of 62, who had earlier left his weaving trade to become a factory hand. He lost his job when he tried actively to establish a pro-Communist union in the factory. It was then, at 45, that he became what he calls 'an independent weaver'. Now he and his three assistants produce lungis worth Rs 100 (£5) a week. After he has paid the labour and material costs, he is left with Rs 20 (£1) a week. This is just about enough for the rice, vegetables, lentils and fish, and firewood and paraffin that he needs for the upkeep of himself, his wife, and their child. 'The only consolation in this business is that you are your own boss,' he said. 'There is very little profit in it nowadays. That is why I advised my two sons to do something else. One is a night watchman and the other is a house-painter. [This is in contrast to the situation of the Kundus in rural West Bengal, where the economy of the village offered the two sons no alternative to weaving.[32]] It is the fast rising prices that are hurting us badly.'

Vijay Lakshmi Mani, the 33-year-old wife of a man who has an embossing business at home, summarized the impact of inflation on their life thus: 'Sixteen years ago, when I married, my husband earned Rs 60 [£3] a month. We had rent to pay; but we saved enough to buy these embossing machines. Now we earn Rs 150 [£7·50] a month; and even though there is no rent to pay, we just scrape through. Ten years ago, rice cost 80 naye paise [4p] a measure; now it costs Rs 2 [10p]. Milk used to be Rs 1·25 [6p] a measure; now it is Rs 3 [15p].' She envied her neighbour, T. Subramani, who is a coolie with the Food Corporation of India at the docks, and whose wages are tied to the cost-of-living index.

Subramani, a lean, handsome man of 29, secured this job in 1965, when the FCI was formed by the Indian government to handle the import and distribution of foodgrains from abroad. Before that he worked for a private firm which did the loading and unloading of ships. It was contract work and paid well while it lasted, but there was no job security. 'With the FCI now the money is not so good, but there is security,' he said. An average of seven days' work in a month, along with unemployment benefits, brings him a total of Rs 106 (£5·30) a month after deductions for provident fund and life insurance. Working as a coolie somewhere else on his off days and sale of milk from his buffalo augment his monthly income by another Rs 50 to 80 (£2·50 to £4). He finds this more than enough to maintain himself, his wife, and two small sons, and has managed to purchase a bicycle out of his savings. 'Things are getting better,' he said. 'For example, I can borrow money from the FCI co-operative society at a reasonable rate of interest. And I am insured for Rs 2,000 [£100].' He finds the idea of life insurance attractive. 'Anything bad could happen to me, but that would not affect the future of my sons,' he added. 'They would be able to pursue their education with my insurance money.' He would like them to pass the high school finals, at the least, and secure a white collar job, preferably in the government.

Subramani was thus voicing an attitude which is widely prevalent among the country's poor. Time and again (in the course of their interviews), poor parents, in both rural and urban India, said that the best thing that could happen to their sons would be for them to become civil servants. They have a high regard for a white collar job because they feel that only someone who has had 'education' – something they traditionally associate with Brahmins, the highest caste – can get one, and also because the caste system places those working with their hands low on the social scale. Most of them are seemingly unaware of the mounting economic difficulties that white collar employees are now facing.

The economic plight of lower-grade employees of the State government was summed up by C. Dev-Nathan, the president of the Tamil Nadu Non-Gazetted Officers (so called because their appointments and transfers are *not* notified in the Government Gazette) Union, thus: 'Almost all NGOs are indebted to private moneylenders. They find themselves taking loans at the interest rate of 6 to 12 per cent a month. Say you want a loan of Rs 100 [£5]. First, you have to give a bond of Rs 200 [£10]. Then you have to pay the interest for the first month right away. That is, you get in hand Rs 88 to 94 [£4·40 to 4·70], depending on the interest rate. And, if you fail to keep up the payments, the moneylender will take you to court for twice the sum you actually borrowed.'[33] A similar situation prevails elsewhere. A survey of clerks in Bombay in 1971 revealed that 80 per cent of them borrowed Rs 45 to 75 (£2·25 to 3·75) – i.e. one-sixth to one-fourth of their starting monthly salary – a month from private moneylenders.[34]

The survey also showed that 95 per cent of them live in one-room tenements, and that only 35 per cent can afford a table fan which, given the hot and humid climate of Bombay for six months in a year, is almost a necessity. V. K. Malhotra, a clerk with the Central government since 1960, is a case in point. He and his family of eight – aged parents, a widowed sister, wife, and four children – manage to live in a one-room flat in central Bombay, an accommodation that costs them Rs 50 (£2·50) a month. After he has paid for his children's education and transport cost, and covered his own pocket expenses, he is left with Rs 253 (£12·65). And to feed nine mouths for a month out of that sum is something of an 'ordeal', as he puts it.

The condition of those working in retail trade and private industry is even worse. They have neither the job security nor the fringe benefits that go with a job in the civil service; and their salaries are often low. Haribhai Baga, a clerk with a small chemical firm, for example, earns no more than Rs 225 (£11·25) a month; and, despite his twenty-eight years' service, Kalyanji Parikh, an accountant-salesman with a hardware merchant, receives a monthly salary of Rs 280 (£14). 'The large majority [of clerks and low-grade officials] live from hand to mouth, and battle relentlessly with the trials of day-to-day life,' concludes K. K. G. Nambiar, the researcher.[35]

The condition of clerks in Delhi – where they are employed by the thousand, by the Central government – is equally bad. Here, their major problem is finding reasonably priced accommodation. In principle, the Central government is expected to house its employees in its own property, and charge them 10 per cent of the salary as rent;

in practice, however, the waiting list is so long that even those who had joined the service in 1950 had not secured government accommodation twenty years later. Most of the civil servants, therefore, accept 15 per cent of their salary as housing allowance and do their best to find accommodation they can afford, an increasingly difficult task. In one year alone (1971), rents went up by as much as 50 per cent; and a typical one-room tenement in south Delhi was renting for Rs 150 to 250 (£7·50 to 12·50) a month, which was more than the basic starting salary of a government clerk.[36]

During the same year, 1971, the sale of imported liquor in Delhi went up threefold, an indicator of the growing prosperity of the rich – top government officials, politicians, businessmen, industrialists, and 'contact men' of large industrial houses. Some other facts, too, point in the same direction. Whereas the city's population rose by less than 100 per cent during the period 1958–70, the number of 'fast moving vehicles', mainly private cars, went up 600 per cent.[37] Each year witnesses the opening of still more luxury hotels, and those already established offer more luxurious services. In early 1972, for instance, the prestigious Ashoka Hotel inaugurated a new supper club with an all French cuisine, offering – as a local correspondent of the *Hindustan Times* informed his readers in a long, laudatory write-up – 'the most expensive *hors d'oeuvre*' of '*Foi Grass Truffe de Strasbourg* priced at Rs 120 [£6] for two persons followed by *Caviar de la Gaspienne* for Rs 70 [£3·50]'.[38]

A few weeks earlier, the city's English-language dailies had vied with one another in describing, at some length, the 'Big Fun' that awaited the local élite at the New Year's Eve ball at the luxury hotels. Demand for tickets – at prices that would feed an average Indian family of five for a fortnight – had been greater than ever before. 'Most of them [luxury hotels] had already sold out the available seats by the evening [of 30 December],' reported a correspondent of the *Indian Express*:

> For the New Year's celebration, Oberoi-Intercontinental . . . is charging Rs 140 [£7] per head. The hotel is having celebrations at three different places on its premises. With a total capacity of 1,000 people, plans are nevertheless fast filling up. . . . The Ashoka Hotel in its Cosmic Hall with 750 people is already two-thirds full. . . . Claridges is offering two tariffs. . . . The Maharani Restaurant with 'three floor shows and a very special menu' will charge Rs 95 [£4·75]. Only about ten seats are left unsold. The Banquet Hall with only 'two floor shows and delicious buffet supper' will cost Rs 75 [£3·75]. . . . The Imperial Hotel, though pricing its tickets at Rs 100 [£5] per head, will be having a cabaret and Indian dancing.[39]

This is just one example of the extravagance of the city's rich. The lavishness shown at weddings is another. The members of the élite compete with one another in being ostentatious at weddings by inviting hundreds of guests, plying them with food and drinks, and giving expensive presents to the couple. It is not uncommon for a Class I civil servant to invite a thousand guests to the wedding of his son or daughter, and spend as much as Rs 50,000 (£2,500) on entertaining them and meeting other expenses.[40]

How can someone with a monthly salary of Rs 1,000 to 2,000 (£50 to 100) afford this? By being corrupt, receiving bribes and kickbacks from businessmen-industrialists in exchange for administrative and other favours. The top civil servants have little to fear because their political masters, the Central government ministers, are, more often than not, equally corrupt. Thus it is in Delhi, the nation's capital, that the corrupt politician and civil servant join hands with the businessman to enrich themselves at the cost of millions of the country's consumers.

Corruption was not unknown in the past. But – as Romesh Thapar, the Delhi correspondent of the *Economic and Political Weekly*, points out – 'Seldom have we known corruption on the scale at which it flourishes today. Yes, it flourishes, because it is patronized – and very often by the most powerful in the land, within the government and outside. And there is no ceiling on it.'[41] Its dramatic growth in recent times has been fuelled mainly by 'black money' – a term loosely applied to incomes and profits earned either through illicit operations or retained by evading taxes – which, by virtue of free circulation, has created a large 'black money' economy, which, in turn, is already deeply enmeshed with the 'white money' economy.

3

A CORRUPT SOCIETY

Tax evasion and black money have now reached a stage which can only be described as a menace to the economy.

Interim Report of the Direct Taxes Enquiry Committee in 1972[1]

In each State there is an anti-corruption department, and there has never been a better misnomer.

Denis Joseph, an Indian journalist[2]

According to a Health Ministry survey, every third eatable in India is adulterated. . . . Tea waste, processed gram waste, coffee husk, cashew-nut end-crop, and coal tar dyes have been found to be the main adulterants in tea.

Chandrakant Tamhane, an Indian journalist[3]

Black money was first created in India during the Second World War when thousands of commercial and industrial firms made enormous profits on which they managed to avoid paying taxes. They did so by maintaining two sets of books – one for the auditor and the tax man, and the other for private use and record – a practice which continues. Since then, both the size and velocity of black money have increased enormously as businessmen and industrialists have contrived to evade income tax as well as excise duties and sales tax. According to conservative, official estimates, during the period of 1947–72, the amount that escaped the income tax net increased ninety-one times – from Rs 48 crores (one crore = 10 million; £24 million) to 4,380 crores (£2,190 million).[4] By then, 1972, the size of black money was put at Rs 10,000 crores (£5,000 million), which was *more* than the official money supply during that year![5] What is worse is that black money has been multiplying much faster than white. While the average return on white money was only 8 to 10 per cent a year, conceded the Central Minister of State for Finance, in 1974, the annual rate of return on black money was often above 200 per cent.[6] The country has reached a point where the malpractices that create black money and enlarge it have become an integral part of its everyday economy.

Often a manufacturer buys part of the raw material he needs, in cash, and processes it without recording it at any stage. He bribes the government's excise staff, stationed at the factory, and gets his goods out to a wholesaler, who sells them to a retailer. The latter buys part of the goods in the normal way and the rest in cash, without any written records. He has no problem selling the 'black' part of his stock, because customers are often only too willing to forgo the receipt, since that saves them the sales tax they are expected to pay. It is thus that suppliers, manufacturers, wholesalers, and retailers build up stocks of black money. They can either use this money to finance more illicit operations, or change it into white money, which is a reasonably simple operation.

Say a retailer wishes to convert a 'black' sum of Rs 50,000 (£2,500) into white. All he has to do is look for a house worth Rs 100,000 (£5,000), where the vendor is willing to sign a sale deed for Rs 50,000 (£2,500), take that sum by cheque, and accept the remainder in (black) cash. This is quite easy, because the arrangement works in favour of the vendor too: it reduces his margin of profit and, therefore, his tax. What about the black money left into the hands of the vendor? He can use it for another property transaction or, better still, buy smuggled gold. Gold is an ideal investment: it is a safe bet against inflation and its possession can be masked easily in ornaments which Indians, especially women, are in the habit of wearing.

Gold smuggling brings the foreign exchange racketeer into the picture, because each year no less than 250 *tons* of gold – or about one-fifth of the world production – are smuggled into India, mainly through Bombay, from Dubai in the Persian Gulf, because the gold merchants in Dubai sell it only for American dollars or British pounds.[7] These operators are part of the vast network which is involved in smuggling out such Indian goods as antiques, precious stones, and marijuana for sale abroad, and acting as instant banks and exchange bureaux for the Indian expatriates who wish to remit monies home and for the foreigners visiting India. They attract business from foreign tourists by offering them higher than the official rates of exchange, and by having their agents approach them in the street. The extent of this practice can be judged by the fact that each day some $100,000 are exchanged unofficially in and around Connaught Circus, New Delhi's fashionable centre, and anything up to 1,500 people are involved in the racket.[8]

Many of the foreign tourists do business with them not only because they get more for their money but also because it saves them the ordeal of having to fill in half a dozen forms, produce such personal documents as passport and visas, and stand in line for an hour or more at a bank, merely to change their money at the official rate. And yet the procedure at the banks – commercial establishments interested in

attracting as many customers as possible – are by no means as bureaucratic and cumbersome as those prevalent at government offices, which
exist for purely administrative purposes.

'The procedures and practices in the working of government offices
are cumbersome and dilatory,' states the Report of the Committee on
Prevention of Corruption, appointed by the Central government in
1962.

> There is a general impression that it is difficult to get things
> done without corruption. Scope for corruption is greater and the
> incentive to corrupt stronger at those points of organization
> where substantive decisions are taken in matters like assessment
> and collection of taxes, determination of eligibility for obtaining
> licences, ensuring fair utilization of licensed goods obtained there-
> under, giving of contracts, approval of works, and acceptance of
> supplies.[9]

In the case of income tax, often dishonesty of the assessee is matched
only by the cunning of the assessor. While many doctors, lawyers,
accountants, and shopkeepers either do not issue receipts for the
sums received from their clients/customers, or give receipts for sums
lower than the actual, the tax men find their ways of harassing them
with a view to extract bribes, a pursuit in which they are helped by
frequent changes in the law. (In one year alone, 1970, the provisions
of the Income Tax Act in force underwent 250 insertions, 230 sub-
stitutions, and a hundred omissions!)[10]

Consider a shopkeeper selling cloth, or patent drugs and cosmetics,
who makes it a point not to issue (handwritten) receipts for all the
sales he makes,[11] and thus manages to produce a lower sales figure
than the actual. The income tax inspector rejects this, and proceeds to
form his own estimate. For this, he visits the shop one day to check
the books, making sure to do so during the early part of the month
when sales – often to customers who, being on a monthly salary, do
most of their shopping during the first days of the month – are much
higher than during rest of the month. The inspector thus arrives at a
higher sales figure than the actual, and puts the shopkeeper on the
defensive. He then volunteers to 'rescue' the trader for a certain 'fee'.
The trader finds that the bribe amounts to about a third or a quarter
of the extra tax he would have to pay if the inspector stuck to his own
figures. So, he ends up bribing the inspector; and both of them enrich
themselves at the cost of the public exchequer.

But the public treasury suffers far bigger losses in the case of large
business houses, where illicit bargaining occurs between top civil
servants and their political cohorts, the government ministers, and the
industrialist. 'Say you have income tax cases pending,' said S. Gupta,
chairman of a large business house in Calcutta. 'One day, somebody

comes along, and refers to your cases, and says that the minister [concerned] will let you go if you pay so much. You pay, and things get done.'[12] But it is not always the case that an industrialist waits for the other side to make a move. In fact, almost all large and medium-sized business houses employ full-time 'liaison' men, who – in the words of the Committee on Prevention of Corruption – 'make a careful study of the character, tastes and weaknesses of the [government] officials with whom they have to deal, and these weaknesses are then exploited.'[13]

The other major illicit activity of the large business houses pertains to obtaining import licences for raw materials and basic chemicals, a policy instituted by the Central government in the early 1950s in order to distribute the raw materials in short supply in the country on an equitable basis and have them put to the best possible use. Most of the big industrial houses either secure import licences in the name of firms and individuals that exist only on paper,[14] or obtain licences for amounts much larger than they actually use – dishonest exercises in which they are helped by chartered accountants, who issue 'duly certified' documents, and corrupt government officials and ministers. They then sell the excess raw materials at large premiums, varying from 50 per cent to 300 per cent, to other, comparatively small manufacturers (the type described earlier on p. 33) who, as a rule, feel so intimidated by the complex procedures and red tape involved in obtaining import licences that they do not apply at all and, instead, rely on supply from the 'black market'.

While this kind of corruption, which is in essence tied up with the country's recent progress in industrialization, has added a new and menacing dimension to the national economy, the traditional corruption in such government departments as land revenue, customs and excise, police, and public works has become more widespread. 'We were told by a large number of witnesses that in all contracts of construction, purchase, sales and other regular business on behalf of the government, a regular percentage is paid by the party to the transactions, and [that] this is shared in agreed proportions among the various officials concerned,' states the Committee on Prevention of Corruption. 'We were told that in the construction work for the Public Works Department, 7 to 11 per cent was usually paid in this manner [as bribes] and [that] this was shared by persons of the rank of the Executive Engineer and below down to the *mistry* [i.e. mechanic].'[15] In that sense, Abdul Hafiz, a contractor to the Public Works Department of the Bihar government, is fairly typical of his class. He customarily pays 10 per cent of the value of the contract to the government officials: 3 per cent to the overseer; 2 per cent each to the assistant engineer, the executive engineer, and the accountant; and 1 per cent to the cashier.[16] In return for the bribes received, the officials overlook the shoddy workmanship and sub-standard materials used by the contractor.

When the government undertakes public works itself, as it does in drought-stricken areas to create employment for the people, the officials line their pockets by inflating the number of labourers engaged and by paying them less than the specified rate. The records of the Rajasthan government, for instance, showed that the famine relief work of 1969 provided labouring jobs to 85,000 people at Rs 1.50 (7½p) a day each. But, in point of fact, only 50,000 people were employed and paid Re 1 (5p) per day each. This meant that the difference between the official and actual expenditures – amounting to 61 per cent of the total – was appropriated by the government bureaucrats![17] A year later, the same thing happened in the drought-stricken district of Banaskantha, in Gujarat. An estimated 35 to 40 per cent of the government expenditure of Rs 2 crores (£1 million) on famine relief was siphoned off by the officials.[18]

The police department is another government agency which is corrupt – *and* inefficient. It seldom loses a chance of extracting monies from citizens, either at random or in a well-organized fashion. For instance, it is customary for the police in most Indian cities and towns to levy a police 'cess' on shopkeepers and vendors, and collect it regularly. 'Every Sunday in one locality in Old Delhi a team of policemen go round with a bag and a notebook to make their collections from the vendors,' reports Chand Joshi of the *Hindustan Times*.

> On Saturdays the collection is made from the shopkeepers. After distribution and payments, an average corrupt Station House Officer in one of the more profitable police stations makes a net profit of Rs 15,000 [£750] a month and not-so-profitable ones Rs 5,000 (£250). . . . [The average salary of a Station House Officer is Rs600 (£30) a month]. The average SHO's residence has a radiogram, fully carpeted rooms, refrigerators . . . and all the modern amenities which would do a business executive proud.[19]

The police do not offer any extra service in return for the levy; and yet any shopkeeper or vendor who refuses to pay it invites harassment by the police.

The local police are of course only too willing to strike a 'deal' with any special interest group that wishes it. In Jamshedpur, Bihar, for instance, the police have allowed the owners of the city's 500 taxis not to use the meter for a levy of Rs 10 (50p) per taxi per week.[20] Similarly, the police authorities in the Greater Delhi area offer private transport companies insurance against prosecution on such matters as vehicle safety, overloading, speeding, etc., for a flat fee of Rs 500 (£25) per month per truck *not* involved in the (illegal) inter-State smuggling, and Rs 1,000 (£50) for the ones engaged in smuggling.[21]

Often the police refuse to act in cases where they should, until and unless they are bribed. The tenant–landlord relationship in the cities is a good example. A tenant must pay the police before they move to protect him from the illegal harassment by his landlord. In Delhi, the police charge a 'standard' bribe for this: two months' rent. On the other hand, the police are quite prepared to become dilatory if the person bribing them wants them to. 'Even murder can be condoned [by the police] for Rs 5,000 to 10,000 [£250 to 500] if it is an unsensational one,' states Chand Joshi. 'For a sensational murder no price is too high.'[22] The police help the party by doctoring the case. This is done – as a recent report of the Uttar Pradesh Police Commission points out – by delaying the recording of the crime report until the Station House Officer visits the scene of crime and formulates his line of action to 'square up' matters with 'what should be written in the [police] diary'.[23]

Corruption has by now spread even to courts, especially the lower courts. It is not uncommon for someone who has been found guilty and fined to be given a court receipt for a sum lower than what he had paid earlier as fine (announced verbally by the magistrate), with the difference being distributed later among the magistrate, his stenographer, the reader of the court, the custodian of the court files, and the court clerk. The general situation in the courts is summed up by Ranjan Marwah, an Indian journalist, thus: 'The files have to be produced, so you pay. Your case is fixed for a convenient date, so you pay. Your case is delayed, so you pay.'[24]

A similar situation exists in many government departments where – in the words of Dharam Vira, the governor of Karnataka – 'Nothing happens without money changing hands.'[25] Often those dealing with a government bureaucrat find that the only way to get results within a reasonable period of time is by bribing him, offering him what is euphemistically called 'speed money'. But even the term 'speed' is to be interpreted in the context of the time-scale of an Indian civil servant which, in turn, is defined by labyrinthine procedures. 'When an official letter addressed to me is delivered by the post office, it goes to the "inward" clerk first, then to his supervisor, and finally the joint secretary of my department; and only then does it come down to me,' said V. Mohan, a cultural officer in the public works department of the Kerala government. 'I put a note on the letter that a reply may be given on the following lines; and the whole chain starts again. It takes *three weeks* for the reply to be sent out, provided nobody in this chain is on leave.'[26]

The experience of Francis Hope, a British journalist, with the postal department in India is typical.

I had got this validation [of my credit card for sending overseas cables by the Indian Post and Telegraph department] in New

Delhi, and therefore left it quite near my deadlines to file [my despatch] from Calcutta [he wrote]. The telegraph office was unimpressed. 'You have piece paper?' 'Credit card? Yes.' 'We cannot accept a credit card without validation.' 'I have the validation too.' Pause for the study of the second piece paper. . . . 'This is a Delhi validation. You need a Calcutta validation. You must go to the post office finance department. Unfortunately they are closed.' This was nine in the morning. A full rehearsal of the day's events would be tedious.

One journey up unswept stairs ('unfortunately the lift no longer functions') is much like another; one office furnished only with files closely resembles the next. . . . You enter, to see a harassed man half hidden behind a barricade of buff files. He ignores you. Closing one file, he selects another, almost certainly at random. He flicks through it until he finds something. He frowns very angrily at whatever is there, as if hoping it will simply flee in terror. He then still more angrily makes a mark in the margin with a pen, which does not work. The only thing which does write is the plastic tube from a broken biro, with which some cross observation is noted. Then he closes the file, sighs, rubs his eyes behind his glasses, and asks: 'What can I do for you?' The answer usually turns out to be nothing. I went through such rituals with eight people: some once, some twice, one three times. The administrative machine, like the lift, simply does not function – or at least, does not function simply.[27]

Hope managed to get his job done in one day, a remarkable achievement, mainly because he was a journalist and a European.

The delays suffered by those who live and work there, and have to deal with the government, are unbelievable. 'Grants from the [State] government's education department [in Calcutta] often come *after* the academic year is over,' said Ashim Sengupta, the headmaster of a government-supported secondary school in Paruldanga, a village in West Bengal. 'If you write to the department in Calcutta, no reply follows. Teachers remain unpaid for three to four months in a row, and suffer much hardship. They end up borrowing monies at exorbitant rates of interest.'[28] This happens because of the labyrinthine procedures followed by the finance department which controls the purse strings. Thanks to the prevalence of bureaucratic sloth and red tape, budgeted amounts for social services and developmental projects seldom get spent fully.

Even such commercial activities of the government as airlines, railways, and telephones are not free from red tape and corruption. The result is not only inconvenience and hardship to the public but also huge losses to the national exchequer. Whereas no aeroplane of the

government-owned Indian Airlines ever flies with full load, many of
the prospective passengers are denied a ticket, because of the cumbersome, bureaucratic procedures regarding ticket reservation. Similarly,
while the telephone system remains under-utilized, thousands of
applicants for a new connection are kept waiting for months, even years.
The Public Accounts Committee report of 1971 pointed out that at
least 162,000 additional telephone connections could have been given
and a sum of Rs 45.2 crores (£22·6 million) earned.[29]

Meanwhile, many telephone subscribers find that they have to pay
for out-of-town calls they never made. This happens because unscrupulous telephone exchange employees make private deals with
some subscribers and, by tampering with lines, transfer their out-of-
town calls to others.[30] Those using postal services soon discover that
the only way to ensure delivery of letters with postage stamps of
medium or high denominations is by sending them by registered mail
or under postal certificate, because otherwise postal employees remove
the stamps and throw away the letters.

Nor is the railway goods service free from pilfering which occurs
because, more often than not, the members of the Railway Protection
Force, employed to 'protect' goods in transit, co-operate with the
pilferers. At one point, when copper was in short supply, and the
government, beset with foreign exchange problems, could not afford
an increase in its import from abroad, the professional pilferers extended
their activity to stealing overhead electric (copper) cables used on part
of the railway system. Commenting on the 155 cases of theft of overhead cable, in the first quarter of 1971, a correspondent of the
Hindustan Times wrote: 'Though the electrical portion of the railways
uses high voltage for traction, the thieves, who operate in gangs, are
adept in short-circuiting the system by throwing wet ropes across the
overhead wires and cutting lengths which can be removed easily.'[31]

The technical expertise shown in the above case is just one aspect
of the complex operation which involves the criminal underworld,
railway employees, the police, businessmen, and the Congress politicians,
without whose active co-operation to 'protect' the gangsters from the
police, this racket, or any other, could not be sustained. The general
milieu in which all this happens can only be described as morally
decadent. 'Everybody, just about everybody, is vaguely aware that the
state of morality in the country has reached its nadir,' observes the
Economic and Political Weekly. 'What is however more shocking is that
. . . there is no expression of shock or indignation on anybody's part.'[32]

Corruption is no longer considered morally stigmatizing. Those who
give bribes and those who receive them do so without any moral
qualms. And if anybody gets caught – which is rare indeed – the social
and political élite are only too ready to forgive him, for they themselves
are tarred with the same brush, and know it. The following incident,

narrated to Richard P. Taub, an American academic, by a senior civil servant in Delhi, sums up the situation aptly:

> Shortly after we moved into it [our newly-built house], we heard in the house next door, loud weeping and wailing and beating of breasts. My wife went next door to see what the trouble was. . . . It turned out that that was the house of an executive engineer of a large project, and he had been proceeded against for corruption. He was being sent to jail, and that's what all the weeping was about. [However] about a year and a half later, we noticed a big party going on there with a band and music, and *half the élite of Delhi.* We thought it was for a wedding. It turned out to be a celebration of his release from prison. The moral standards have clearly gone down.[33]

A similar situation exists in politics which is dominated by the Congress. 'The Congress Party machine which she [Indira Gandhi] controls wallows in the tar barrel [of corruption], and many of her ministers, both Central and State, are deeply immersed,' states Peter Gill, the Delhi correspondent of the *Daily Telegraph.*[34] This being so, the number of ministers (of whom there are nearly 400 in Delhi and various State capitals), not to mention ex-ministers, who are corrupt, can well be imagined. And yet, no more than ten ministers or ex-ministers have been investigated by a quasi-judicial commission of inquiry over the past twenty-five years; and none of those found guilty has ever been sent to prison. In fact, often those found guilty have had no difficulty in reclaiming their past position of power – after a brief, very brief, period of oblivion.

The case of four former Congress ministers in Bihar, including R. L. S. Yadav, is typical. They were investigated by *two* commissions of inquiry (at the cost of Rs 2,500,000(£125,000) to the taxpayer) and found guilty. Their houses were searched twice, in September 1970 and April 1971, by the Central Bureau of Investigation with a view, ostensibly, to starting court proceedings against them. But in the end nothing came of it. Indeed, soon after the last of the house searches, Yadav found himself emerging as a protégé of Indira Gandhi and securing, with her active support, the leadership of the Congress group in the State Assembly, and becoming Bihar's Chief Minister! 'We take it for granted that, amongst those who have succeeded in reaching the top, there will be a certain number against whom there will be *prima facie* evidence of moral turpitude,' states the *Economic and Political Weekly.*

> We also accept . . . that some of them may be temporarily under the shadow and asked to vacate their official positions; but . . . we [also] accept as another part of the same reality that these

gentlemen . . . would, soon, recapture the ruling party's
organization in their respective States [and] inch their way up. . . .
In no time, the Prime Minister [Indira Gandhi] would be closeted
with them for hours on end to discuss affairs of the polity.[35]

The irony is that all this goes on while the Congress leaders vie
with one another in condemning corruption – with S. S. Ray, the
Congress Chief Minister of West Bengal, outbidding them all by
suggesting that corrupt Chief Ministers should be hanged![36] and
while the special Prevention of Corruption Act, passed by the Congress
ministry in Delhi in 1947, remains in force; and the Central Vigilance
Commission, established in 1956 – following a recommendation by an
officially appointed committee to investigate corruption in the civil
service and the railways – continues to function; and every State
government has its own anti-corruption department.

But perhaps this is not ironic, because condemning corruption is
a ritualistic exercise which the Congress leaders perform out of sheer
habit and political expediency; and the actual impact of the Central
Vigilance Commission and various anti-corruption departments is
almost negligible. During 1969–70, for instance, the Central Vigilance
Commission initiated investigations against no more than 880 civil
servants of the Central government, and caused the dismissal of only
twenty-two of them.[37] And this in an establishment with 3,000,000
employees, at least a quarter of whom indulge in some form of bribe-
taking many times a year! The effectiveness of the anti-corruption
department is reduced considerably by the fact that it is part of the
police machinery of a State government which is almost invariably
corrupt. Furthermore, this department is under constant pressure
from government ministers who like to determine themselves which
cases should be pursued and which ones dropped. In the end, these
departments manage a passable performance by catching some of those
who receive petty bribes while ignoring those who are involved in
more serious misdemeanours.

It may well be that attention ought to be paid to the effects of
corruption rather than the phenomenon itself, and that it be considered
in pragmatic, not moralistic, terms. Quite simply, does corruption help
or hinder economic growth? There are some who regard corruption as
a necessary lubricant for an economic system such as India's, and
something which, on balance, has a tonic effect on the economy. Then
there are others who, like Gunnar Myrdal, the internationally known
Swedish economist, feel that 'the prevalence of corruption provides
strong inhibitions and obstacles to [economic] development'.[38] This
applies to both agricultural and industrial sectors.

What is involved here [in agriculture] is corruption that is coupled
with incompetence, and, by being a steady and slow drain, is a

real deterrent to economic progress [states Gilbert Etienne]. The contractor who makes irrigation channel with poor cement, the State tube well operator who refuses to dispense water unless he receives *bakshish* [i.e. gratuity], the co-operative supervisor who, because of his corrupt practices, turns peasants against the rural credit system, the official who drags out the necessary formalities when dealing with a request for electricity connection – these men hold back development.[39]

In the industrial sector, the single most important corrupting factor is the sale of import licences at grossly inflated premiums which, in the final analysis, are paid by the consumer. This causes a transfer of an enormous sum – estimated at Rs 750 crores (£375 million) in 1970, or about half of all the black money generated in that year[40] – from millions of consumers to a small minority. By thus enriching the already rich at the cost of the poor, this form of corruption impedes progress towards rapid and sustained industrialization, and is thus detrimental to economic growth. So, from both moral *and* economic standpoints, corruption is harmful to the interests of the country.

In short, the state of the Indian polity today is hardly enviable. The economy is faltering; the gap between the rich élite and poor masses is widening; and society is fast losing its moral and ethical bearings, and becoming increasingly corrupt. The onus for the present state of affairs lies on the shoulders of the Congress, a centrist party, which has been ruling the country since independence, in 1947, within a political-administrative framework defined by a Constitution which was conceived and passed by a Constituent Assembly dominated by it.

PART II

POLITICS AND ECONOMICS OF CENTRISM

4
PRESENT POLITICAL-ADMINISTRATIVE STRUCTURE

> In many respects . . . the 1950 [Indian] Constitution was the
> 1935 Constitution [framed by imperial Britain] writ large, and the
> men who had acquired the experience of operating the 'slave'
> Constitution were by no means tyros when they undertook the
> task of operating the 'free' one.
>
> A. H. Hanson and Janet Douglas, British political scientists[1]

The 385-member-strong Constituent Assembly, called to session in Delhi by the colonial government in 1946, reflected the political situation then prevailing; 292 members were chosen by the legislative assemblies of the eleven provinces (ruled directly by the British), elected on a restricted franchise of about one-fifth of the adult population; and 93 were appointed by the rulers of the 'native' states that existed under the overall hegemony of the British Indian Viceroy. Partitioning of colonial India into two independent dominions of India and Pakistan by the British government, in August 1947, reduced the size of the Indian Constituent Assembly to 298, with 208 members owing allegiance to the Congress. It functioned as both the Constitution-making body and Parliament until January 1950, when it formally adopted the new Constitution. With this, India became an independent republic, but *within* the British Commonwealth.

This arrangement, secured with the co-operation of the British Parliament, was just one example of how the former rulers continued to colour the thoughts and attitudes of India's nationalist leaders. The 1950 Constitution itself had drawn heavily not only on Britain's North American Act of 1867 (for Canada) and the Commonwealth of Australia Act of 1900, but also from the Government of India Act of 1935, which the Congress leaders had once denounced as the 'slave' Constitution.

On the other hand, the Congress movement had grown on a two-pronged programme of opposition to alien rule – epitomized in the oppressive powers vested in the hands of the agent of the British Sovereign, the Viceroy, and the provincial governors – and support for the idea of arming the citizens of an independent India with certain basic human rights. As such, the Congress leaders felt duty bound to incorporate their promises of the past into the new Constitution.

The 1950 Constitution, therefore, begins with a list of such fundamental rights as 'right to freedom of speech and expression, assembly, association, occupation, and acquiring, holding or disposing of property', and 'the right to freedom of religion'. This is followed by a set of directive principles which, though 'not enforceable by any court', are 'fundamental in the governance of the country', and are meant to guide the state in making laws, primarily, 'to promote the welfare of the people by securing and protecting as effectively as it may a social order in which justice, social, economic and political, shall inform the institutions of the national life'.

The state is directed, in particular, to follow a policy which ensures: '(a) that the citizens . . . have the right to an adequate means of livelihood; (b) that the ownership and control of the material resources of the community are so distributed as best to subserve the common good; (c) that the operation of the economic system does not result in the concentration of wealth and means of production to the common women . . . ; (e) that citizens are not forced by economic necessity to enter avocations unsuited to their age or strength.' Furthermore, the state is expected to 'make effective provision for securing the right to work, to education and to public assistance in cases of unemployment, old age, sickness and disablement, and in other cases of undeserved want', and for 'securing just and human conditions of work and maternity relief'. (None of these directives, it must be noted, is as yet within a shade of realization.)

These provisions, and the establishment of the Supreme Court with powers to interpret the Constitution, and the election of the President of the Republic are about the only major points of difference that the Indian republican Constitution has with the colonial Government of India Act, passed by the British Parliament in 1935.

The Constitution specifies a parliamentary form of government for the Republic of India, which is described as a 'Union of States'. The executive powers of the Union, including the supreme command of its armed forces, is vested in the President, and is exercised by him through officers subordinate to him. He is elected, for a five-year term, by an electoral college, consisting of elected members of both houses of the Union Parliament and the legislative assemblies of the States, with each member's vote weighted to reflect the size of his constituency. He is assisted by a Vice-President who is elected, for five years, by an electoral college composed of only the members of the two houses of the Union Parliament, with each member's vote weighted to reflect the size of his constituency. The Vice-President is the *ex officio* chairman of the Rajya Sabha (i.e. the Council of States), the upper house of

Parliament, and replaces the President when the latter is absent or incapable of fulfilling his office.

The President has the authority to recall the two houses of Parliament and address messages to them. He formally promulgates the legislation passed by Parliament, and has the power to issue ordinances when Parliament is in recess. He may proclaim a state of emergency for the Union. In that case, or when he feels that the normal constitutional set-up of a State has ceased to function, he may suspend the State's constitution and place it under direct federal control. This action of the President needs to be approved by the Union Parliament. However, the state of emergency cannot be extended beyond three years, even if Parliamentary approval is available.

Although formal executive authority rests with the President, actual power is exercised by a Council of Ministers headed by the Prime Minister, who, by virtue of commanding or being likely to command a majority in the Lok Sabha (i.e. the House of the People), the lower house of the Union Parliament, is called to office by the President. All but two of the 524 members of the Lok Sabha are elected by direct universal suffrage for a period of five years. All but twelve of the 250 members of the Rajya Sabha are elected by the members of the legislative assemblies of the constituent States for a period of six years, with those remaining being the nominees of the President. (The Lok Sabha can be dissolved by the President before its tenure is up; whereas the Rajya Sabha cannot, since, like the American Senate, it is a perpetual institution, where a third of the members retire every other year.) Issues are decided by a simple majority vote in both houses, provided there is a quorum of one-tenth of the members; and a bill must pass both houses before it is sent to the President for signature and promulgation.

The constitutional set-up in the States (which are listed in the Constitution) is almost similar to the one prevalent at the Centre. The formal executive power lies with the governor who is a nominee of the President. He administers the State with the 'aid and advice' of a council of ministers, headed by the chief minister, who has or is likely to have support of the majority in the State legislative assembly. The council of ministers is collectively responsible to the assembly, but all its decisions must be conveyed to the governor.

The legislative assembly, elected on the basis of a universal franchise, has a normal tenure of five years, but can be dissolved earlier by the governor. Some States also have a legislative council, a body whose members are nominated partly by the governor, and partly by such sections of society as university graduates, teachers, local municipal councillors, etc. It is a perpetual institution, with a proportion of its members resigning every other year. Legislation passed by these bodies cannot become law until and unless the governor ratifies it. (All legislation is open to challenge in the State High Courts or the Supreme Court, on constitutional or other grounds.)

The governor also has the right to recall legislative bodies, address messages to them, and issue ordinances when they are in recess. If and when the governor feels that the administration of the State cannot be carried on under normal constitutional provisions, he informs the Union President accordingly, and thus invites Central take-over of the State government.

The Constitution spells out the areas where the Union and State governments have the exclusive right to legislate, and where the two share this power (the 'concurrent list'). The 'Union list' includes defence, armament and ammunition, atomic energy, foreign affairs, citizenship, immigration, the Reserve Bank of India, currency and coinage, Central finances, company legislation, banking and insurance, taxes on income (except from agriculture), customs duties, company taxes, etc. The 'concurrent list' includes civil rights, penal code and legal procedures, trade and industry, economic and social planning, trade unions and labour, and price control. In case of duplication, the Central laws over-ride those of a State. Thus, a State's exclusive legislative powers are limited, in the main, to such subjects as law and order, local government, education, public health, agrarian relations, forestry, and property law and taxes.

There is, likewise, a division of taxation powers between the Centre and the States. The Union government has the authority to collect customs and excise duties; and to tax income, capital and property, public and private companies, and railway fares and freights. The States have the right to levy taxes on agricultural income, consumption of electricity, sale of goods, vehicles, animals and boats, professions, land revenue, succession and estate duties on agricultural land, and impose excise duties on buildings, land, and mineral rights. The Central government hands over some taxes (such as those on property and railway fares) to the States and shares some others (such as income tax and customs duties) with them. The Centre also has the authority to give grants-in-aid to 'such States as Parliament may determine to be in need of assistance'. Over the years, the inequitable distribution of powers of taxation have led the States to rely far more on the grants from the Centre than had been visualized in 1950.

This is the situation in normal circumstances. In times of emergency – which the Union President is entitled to declare if he believes that 'the security of India or of any part of the territory thereof is threatened whether by external aggression or internal disturbance' – a State government can be reduced to a non-entity, since Parliament then is authorized to 'confer on the President the power of the Legislature of the State to make laws'.

In short, in both financial and legislative spheres, the Constitution is heavily biased in favour of the Centre and against the States. Its working over the past twenty-five years has borne out the criticism of Dr Sampurananand, the Congress chief minister of Uttar Pradesh, in 1950, that the Constitution-makers had sought to reduce the State governments to the position of 'agents of the Centre'.[2] In fact, the Constitution does not guarantee the territorial integrity or even the existence of a State. The Union Parliament can, by a simple majority vote, set up new States or alter the areas, boundaries, and names of the existing States. And it has done so in the past: once to reorganize almost all the States on a linguistic basis; and then to carve out Nagaland, Meghalaya, and Mizoram, in successive stages, from the old State of Assam, and Haryana from the previous State of the Punjab. Conversely, Parliament has the authority to amalgamate all the States and thus set up a unitary form of government.

It is within this broad constitutional framework that day-to-day administration is conducted by bureaucrats, and where most of the contact between the predominantly rural citizenry and the government occurs. Here too there has been the least possible change from the pre-independence times. The main burden of administration continues to fall on the members of the élitist Indian Administrative Service,[3] which, except for the slight change in the name, is the old Indian Civil Service of the colonial days, and which was given a permanent status by an Article in the Constitution. The principles of recruitment and training for the Indian Administrative Service are almost identical to those employed by the alien rulers to govern India.

The only major break with the colonial past that occurred was in the field of self-government of rural areas. A nationalistic pride in the existence of a panchayat (i.e. council) in each village in bygone days had led the Congress leaders to commit themselves to the revival of the institution. They therefore inserted an Article in the Constitution which directed the State to 'take steps to organize village panchayats and endow them with such powers and authority as may be necessary to enable them to function as units of self-government'. However, specific legislative action, defining the composition, powers, and tenure of a panchayat, was slow to follow, since local self-government is a State subject, and most of the State governments were reluctant to share power with village bodies. During the period of 1950–5, the number of village panchayats in the country rose only by 34,600 to 117,600. Of these – said the Report of the Enquiry Commission, appointed by the Central government, in 1957 – only a third provided lighting and sweeping facilities to the community, and none made 'more than negligible' contribution towards economic development.

The only way to strengthen the panchayat system, it seemed, was by integrating it with development and welfare activities in the rural areas. A recommendation to that effect by the Enquiry Commission was warmly endorsed by the Central government – particularly when its earlier efforts to establish the Bharat Sevak Sangh (i.e. Indian Volunteer Association) to galvanize popular support for the economic uplift of the countryside, as visualized by the Five Year Plans, had ended in a fiasco – and passed on to the State governments, which acted on it in due course.

What then emerged was a three-tiered system whereby the old district boards, first established by the British as partially representative organizations with limited powers, were replaced by zilla parishads (i.e. district councils) with responsibility for co-ordinating development plans to be channelled through panchayat samitis (i.e. council committees), consisting of a number of popularly elected panchayats encompassing one or more villages – all interlinked through indirect elections. This system, popularly known as the panchayati raj, was first introduced in Rajasthan and Andhra Pradesh in 1959, and then extended to other States.

A typical panchayat represents about 1,000–3,000 voters in one or more villages, and consists of twelve to fifteen members, two-thirds of whom are elected (one from each ward), and the remaining co-opted from among women, Scheduled Castes and Tribes, etc., for a period of three years. The sarpanch (i.e. chief councillor) is elected directly. The following annual budget of the Chinaogirala panchayat (population 3,100) in Andhra Pradesh, for 1969–70, throws some light on the working of a panchayat: income, Rs 23,133 (£1,156); expenses, Rs 33,800 (£1,690), including Rs 20,000 (£1,000) on road repairs. Income is raised by taxing houses, grass grown on the banks of a canal, carts and bicycles, fishing, and shops and factories; and imposing surcharges on land registration fees and land revenue. The expenses consist of salaries of the staff, street lighting, and the maintenance of library, roads, school, and community welfare centre.[4]

Forty to fifty panchayats are banded together to form a panchayat samiti (covering a population of 30,000 to 100,000). Its membership consists of the sarpanches of constituent panchayats and ten co-opted members representing women, Scheduled Castes and Tribes, and other minorities. Its functions include community development, agriculture, primary education, animal husbandry, health and rural sanitation, and cottage industries. It is entitled to levy taxes on land and a surcharge on stamp duties, etc. In practice, however, a major part of its income comes from the State government as grants for running schools and as allocations for community development programmes. Eight to twelve panchayat samitis, covering the geographical area of a district, are grouped together to form a zilla parishad. Its membership consists of the presidents of the panchayat samitis, the members of the State legislative assembly and Union Parliament, and the president of the district co-operative bank – with the district collector, the highest civil servant in the district, acting as an *ex officio* member. Its major function is to allocate development funds (averaging Rs 1.5 crores, (£750,000), a year), which originate with the State government, to its constituent panchayat samitis.

In order to remain faithful to their traditional view of a panchayat as an organ of 'consensus democracy' at the village level, the national leaders of the Congress decided, as a matter of policy, not to issue party tickets to their members contesting panchayati elections. This decision, however, was never taken seriously by the Congress functionaries at the State level who, rightly, saw in these elections a valuable opportunity to extend their party's influence in the countryside. The other parties thought likewise. Consequently, the panchayati raj system now exists in a larger political environment of electoral politics, where different parties compete against one another to win votes by stressing differences amongst them rather than their common objectives, a process that dates back, in India, to 1909.

5

ELECTORAL POLITICS

It is as hard for a poor man to enter an Indian legislature as for a rich man to enter the Kingdom of God.

Duncan B. Forrester, a British social scientist[1]

It has been a most regrettable development in recent years that money power has come to play such a dominant role in the elections to legislatures.

V. V. Giri, former President of India[2]

The government has banned political donations by the companies. But, political parties approached me for money last week. They expect you to find illegal ways of paying them.

A. Sivasalam, an Indian industrialist[3]

It may well be that by and large the voting act is devoid of political content. . . . Indeed, the decision to vote for one candidate rather than another may be governed entirely by non-political considerations, and the voter may often be unaware of the political choice he makes through the act of voting.

Gopal Krishna, an Indian academic[4]

The Morley–Minto reforms of 1909 marked a break with the past in so far as they introduced the principle of representation in the government at the provincial and central levels. The quota of the 'non-official' Indian members of the Imperial Legislative Council (first established in 1861 with only three 'non-official' Indian members) was raised to twenty-seven, forming nearly a half of its increased strength of sixty; and these members were to be elected by provincial councils with 'non-official' majorities, which, in turn, were to be elected by local municipalities and district boards, chambers of commerce, universities, land-holders, etc. But these councils, central and provincial, could do no more than make recommendations to the Viceroy or a provincial governor, who continued to monopolize executive power.

The Montagu–Chelmsford reforms that followed a decade later replaced the Imperial Legislative Council with the Central Legislative

Assembly, and instituted a system of 'dyarchy' in the provinces where ministers in charge of certain departments were responsible to provincial councils and others to the governor. An electoral system based on property and tax payments enfranchised about 3 per cent of the adult population for elections to the provincial councils, and about one-fifth of that number for elections to the Central Assembly. The 1935 Government of India Act improved on this. It made the provincial assemblies almost fully representative, and the council of ministers responsible to the legislature. It extended the right to vote to all those who owned property or paid taxes or were literate – that is, about eighteen per cent of the adult population. Since property, mainly agricultural land and residential housing, was mostly in the hands of the upper castes and a section of the middle castes – the two groups forming no more than 31·5 per cent of the total Hindu population in 1931[5] – and since literacy too was limited, in the main, to these castes, the latest reform by the British government still left the vast propertyless majority without any political say.

Introduction of universal suffrage, in the wake of the 1950 Constitution, did not revolutionize the situation, because the already established caste-classes concentrated within themselves not only political authority, but also social prestige and economic power; and the hitherto disenfranchised sections of society needed some time to realize fully the importance of a vote given to them from the top, and to overcome their historic sense of inferiority; and because, most importantly, the (feudal type) economic dependence of the lower caste-classes on the upper caste-classes remained unchanged. Furthermore, traditional leaders of the lower sections of society lacked both education and political awareness, and could not conceive of the possibility of ousting the upper caste leaders from the seats of power. The most they could, and did, do was to bargain with the leaders of competing upper castes, or factions within them – that is, offer them a block of votes in an election for money and/or social concessions.

No wonder, then, that the institution of the panchayati raj system in many of the States did not foster a new breed of leaders, dedicated to a radical socio-economic change (as had been hoped by some in the Congress hierarchy), but merely sanctified the older order, with upper caste leaders, or their henchmen in the lower castes, still in the saddle. A survey of the panchayat samitis in an Andhra Pradesh district, in the mid-1960s, for instance, showed that 'high caste, more land, more money, and more education' continued to be 'the requisites for political success'.[6]

A similar situation exists at the State level, since a typical State legislative assembly constituency, having 70,000 to 100,000 voters, encompasses two or three panchayat samiti blocks, and since most local (landowning) caste rivals or factions regard State elections as no more than an exercise in their traditional rivalry to be conducted, this time, in a comparatively larger arena, either under the wings of one or the other faction of the Congress, in which the party is often divided at the State level, or the banner of different political parties.

On their part, it is here, at the State level, that the political parties make their proper appearance. They do so by nominating a member as the party's official candidate. This can be a daunting affair if a party wishes to contest all or most of the over 3,600 State assembly seats which often come up for election simultaneously. However, no party has the resources or organization to do so, except the Congress. The candidate selection system of the Congress normally takes three to four months to complete, because some 25,000 applications (an average of six to seven applications per seat) have to be processed through a complex route, which reflects the organizational structure of the party.

The basic unit of the party is the block Congress committee which covers the same area as a panchayat samiti. Then come the district Congress committee and the pradesh (i.e. State) Congress committee. One-eighth of the members of various pradesh Congress committees in the country, along with the party's President and some co-opted members, comprise the 750-member-strong All India Congress Committee, which meets a few times a year to outline general policies for the party. Then there is the Plenary Session, which is held every other year, and which consists of nearly 5,000 delegates elected directly by ordinary members of the party. These delegates elect the party President who then forms his 'cabinet' – called the Working Committee or High Command – of twenty members, half of them being his appointees, and the other half being the elected representatives of the All India Congress Committee. The Working Committee then appoints a Parliamentary Board of eight members (including the President) for the purpose of regulating and co-ordinating parliamentary activities of the party in various legislatures in the country. The Parliamentary Board, along with seven elected representatives of the AICC, form the party's Central Election Commission which has the authority to conduct election campaigns and select candidates. It does so by sending out a circular five to six months before the elections to the pradesh or district Congress committees (depending on the level at which the candidates are to be vetted first), outlining the criteria to be used for selecting candidates.

The applicant is generally asked to: (a) outline his social, economic, cultural, and political outlook, that is, express his views on such subjects as untouchability, land reform, minority rights, labour welfare, etc.; (b) relate the 'national and public' service he has rendered, that is, his involvement in such programmes as the co-operative movement, village industries, Harijan welfare, community development projects; and (c) state his experience in the legislative field from the village panchayat upwards. A sitting member seeking renomination is asked to describe how well he maintained his contact with his constituents, how regular were his contributions to the party fund, and how consistent was he in obeying party whips during the Assembly sessions.

The other parties, which often have a similar organizational structure to the Congress, follow more or less the same procedures and policies in selecting candidates. However, these parties contest a limited number of seats, and competition for party tickets in their case is nowhere as keen as with the Congress. The Jan Sangh (i.e. People's Union), a right-wing party, fights State elections only in those constituencies where it has at least 600 primary members, and issues party tickets solely to those who have been active members of the party for at least three years. It is the same with the Communists: the candidate must be an active member and must have a substantial influence in the constituency.

However, in practice, political parties are guided more by pragmatic considerations than high-sounding 'official' policy statements. These are: Is the candidate a local man? If yes, how widespread is his personal and social network? How does his caste or religion (in the case of a non-Hindu) relate to the caste and religious composition of the constituency? How well can he manipulate traditional social loyalties in his favour? How experienced is he in public and electoral affairs? How effective is he in dealing with government officials? And, most importantly, how large are his financial resources?

A local man is preferred to an outsider because elections at the State level still remain, essentially, contests between individuals rather than between parties or policies. As such, an applicant with an extensive network of family and caste ties within the constituency has a greater chance of securing a party ticket than the one with a high ideological loyalty to the party but low social assets. And, despite the frequent condemnation of the 'evil' of 'casteism' by the political parties of various shades, almost all of them take special note of the caste origin of the applicants for the party ticket. The Congress, a consistent opponent of 'casteism' in its policy statements, is the worst offender. 'Congressmen constantly refer to caste as an essential component in recommending selection of candidates,' notes Ramashray Roy, an Indian academic. 'The frequency of reference to the caste composition of constituencies and to the desirability of giving representation to dominant castes and communal groups leave no doubt concerning the relevance of caste and communal considerations in the selection of candidates.'[7]

The significance attached to the caste origin of a prospective candidate is not surprising; because in the absence of a genuine political consciousness among rural voters (except in a few States), who form the bulk of the electorate, caste is a natural rallying ground for the electors;

and because caste loyalty is a common thread between the politics of a village and those of a rural constituency of a State Assembly. In the circumstances, if candidates of rival parties belong to different or competing castes, then caste becomes the most important element in the electoral contest. If, however, candidates of different parties belong to the same caste, then their social standing and, most significantly, the size of their financial resources often determine the election result.

As the party contributes only a minor share of the election campaign expenses, the candidate has to be rich himself, or be able to draw on the resources of rich relatives and friends, because fighting elections, at the State and federal levels, is expensive. This has to do with the size of the electorate in a constituency and the area to be covered, not to mention the practice of buying votes.[8] Even in West Bengal, the country's second most densely populated State, a typical rural State assembly constituency comprises about a hundred villages, scattered over 200 square miles. A serious candidate needs to visit each of these villages in the company of a few supporters, something which entails either buying a second-hand jeep (which costs a minimum of Rs 20,000 (£1,000)), or hiring one. An indication of the expenses involved was given by a candidate of the Communist Party of India (CPI) for a rural constituency in Andhra Pradesh, when he stated that in the 1967 elections he had spent Rs 18,000 (£900) and secured nearly 20,000 votes, whereas his Congress opponent had spent nearly Rs 100,000 (£5,000) and received 40,000 votes.[9] In the elections to the State assembly of Uttar Pradesh, in early 1974, no serious candidate was reported to have spent 'less than Rs 100,000 [£5,000]'.[10] Candidates contesting the comparatively small urban constituencies have to spend a lot of money on holding public meetings, distributing pamphlets and posters, conducting door-to-door canvassing, and providing free transport to voters on the polling day.

Yet there exists the Representation of the People Act 1951, which among other things stipulates a limit on election expenses in order, ostensibly, to minimize the influence of money in the country's political life, and enable those with modest means to become legislators. Exceeding the limit can lead to disqualification from contesting elections for up to six years. The present ceiling, which varies from State to State and ranges between Rs 5,000 (£250) and Rs 13,500 (£675), is modest; and this means simply that it is violated by a large number of contestants. The scale of violation can be gauged by the fact that 40 per cent of the legislators in Tamil Nadu (in 1967) *themselves* admitted spending more than twice the legal limit, and 6 per cent as much as ten times the limit![11]

What is more, the law states that a successful candidate must submit his election expenses under oath (and show them to be within the legal limit) before he is allowed to take his seat in the legislature. The

only way in which most of the legislators can get through this require-
ment successfully is by lying. 'He [a legislator] begins his political
career with a blatant lie, with a white lie, by signing papers that he has
kept his election expenses within the ceiling prescribed by the law,'
states M. L. Gautam, a member of the Rajya Sabha. 'But he has not,
in most cases, in 90 per cent of the cases. . . . He writes in his election
returns, "Paid Rs 25,000 [£1,250] to my party". And thereafter the
party may spend as much as one lakh [i.e. Rs 100,000 (£5,000)] of
rupees (and get away with it) because . . . what the party spends is not
covered by the law.'[12] Nor does the law cover the expenses incurred by a
non-political association or body of individuals, or personal friends or
supporters of a candidate. When, in October 1974, the Supreme Court
ruled that the expenses 'authorized', but not spent directly, by a
Congress Member of Parliament, should be included in calculating
his election expenses, the Congress government in Delhi nullified the
Supreme Court's ruling immediately by issuing an ordinance in the
name of the Union President, which read:

> Notwithstanding any judgment, order or decision of any court
> to the contrary, any expenditure incurred or authorized in
> connection with the election of a candidate by a political party
> or by any other association or body of persons (other than the
> candidate or his election agent) shall not be deemed to be, and shall
> not even be deemed to have been, expenditure in connection with
> the election incurred or authorized by the candidate or by his
> election agent.[13]

The figures quoted above pertained to the 1967 Parliamentary
elections, when average expenses by a serious candidate were estimated
to be Rs 200,000 (£10,000), which were considerably less than those
for the 1971 elections (averaging Rs 480,000 (£24,000)).[14] However,
these sums have to be viewed against the fact that a Parliamentary
constituency has 500,000 to 750,000 voters, and that, in rural areas, it
covers 600 to 1,000 villages scattered over 1,000 to 3,000 square miles.
The vastness of a Parliamentary constituency and the distance, both
physical and psychological, that exists between the average voter and the
national Parliament in Delhi, create a situation where a Parliamentary
candidate has to be 'sold' to voters more as an agent of a political
party than merely as a local celebrity. The identity of a political party,
however, is often established not by explaining its election manifesto
or its socio-political differences with other parties, but by popularizing
the electoral symbol allotted to it by the Chief Election Commissioner.
And in this, party candidates for State assembly constituencies – five
to seven of which are grouped together to form one Parliamentary
constituency – play an important part in those States where elections
to the two legislative bodies are held simultaneously. While canvassing

for themselves, under the party's electoral symbol, they urge the electors to cast their Parliamentary vote too for the same symbol, a service which secures them financial assistance from the party's Parliamentary candidate. In short, at the federal level, the need for both money and organization is so high that an individual candidate cannot manage on his own and has to depend, simultaneously, on the State assembly candidates (for organizational skills) and the treasury of the party headquarters (for money).

To meet this demand, a party must raise an enormous election fund if it is serious about winning a majority, on its own, in a Parliament that has 524 seats and a total electorate of 273 million. Such a task is clearly beyond the capacity of any party, except the Congress. But even this party has to stretch itself beyond such methods of fund-raising as launching membership drives[15] and encouraging its local members and sympathizers to present money purses to party dignitaries at election rallies, and approach rich landlords, businessmen, and industrialists, who, as a rule, are sympathetic to it.

The rapport between the Congress and business community dates back to the early 1900s when the rising Indian industrialist class supported the party in order to counter the influence that British capital, its well-established competitor, had with the colonial government. This continued throughout the pre-independence period when the party came to depend, for its financial survival, almost entirely on the periodic donations made by some of the leading Indian business houses.[16] After independence, these donations, some made in cash and others by cheque, became the main source for the party's central election fund. This happened in the first general election in 1951–2, and again in 1957.

Later that year, when the new Companies Act, meant to rationalize the working of companies, came into effect, the public limited firms found themselves barred from making donations to political parties. But this did not last long. An amendment to the Companies Act, passed in 1960, allowed these companies to donate 5 per cent of their total annual profit or Rs 25,000 (£1,250), whichever was higher, to political parties. A study of the financial statements of 144 major companies for 1961–2, which included the period covering the 1962 general elections, showed that they had contributed Rs 7,904,000 (£395,200) to the Congress, or nearly half of the party's total 'official' expenses in the State and Parliamentary elections; and Rs 2,076,000 (£103,800) to the right-wing Swatantra (i.e. Freedom) Party, or nearly three-fifths of the party's total 'official' election expenses.[17]

The involvement of big business houses in the 1967 elections was much greater and more open than in the past, with the companies now backing the opposition parties, mainly to the right of the Congress, to a larger extent than before. Piqued by this, and the loss of power in many of the major States in these elections, the Congress party in Parliament amended the law in 1969, and banned donations by companies to the political parties. The net effect of this change was to drive the practice underground and make it more business-like than in the past, and thus benefit the Congress which, being the ruling party, could offer an almost instant *quid pro quo* to businessmen making 'donations' in black money.

On the eve of the mid-term elections to Parliament, in March 1971, the Indira Gandhi-led Congress approached all the prominent members of the business community, and – to quote K. K. Shah, then a minister in the Central government – 'there was no big businessman or industrialist who refused money to the ruling Congress'. And the sums involved were higher than ever before.[18] 'These . . . [industrialist] owners of [major newspaper chains] are said to have given Mrs Gandhi roughly Rs 15 crores [£7.5 million] for election purposes,' stated Kuldip Nayar, an Indian journalist and author.[19]

In addition to making cash payments to a few top Congress leaders in Delhi, most of the big business houses instructed their sales agents in the country to help the local Congress candidate, in cash, and assured them that they would be reimbursed through proper 'adjustments' in their commission on sales. They also asked their constituent firms at the local, State and national levels to buy advertising space in hundreds of souvenirs and election news sheets to be published, or 'scheduled' to be published, by the district Congress committees, before the elections, while the Companies Act officials went out of their way specifically to inform the large industrial houses that advertising was an 'admissible' business expense. 'The Prime Minister's [Congress] party is flouting it [the 1969 amendment to the Companies Act banning donations to political parties] by promising to publish 400 souvenirs for her party just before the elections,' reported Frank Moraes, an Indian journalist. 'Each page in each souvenir costs Rs 2,000 [£100] . . . . [This means] one industrial house or business company can contribute Rs 800,000 [£40,000] to Mrs Gandhi's Congress by taking one page in each souvenir.'[20]

Why do business houses give large sums to the Congress? For ideological and pragmatic reasons. They know that notwithstanding the periodic resolutions passed by the party in favour of 'socialism' and the considerable praise lavished on the concept of 'democratic socialism' by some of the party leaders, the Congress government's actions and policies are meant to further their economic interests. 'The big business houses support the Congress with huge sums because they know that the party believes, *in practice*, in capitalistic development,' said Abhijit Sen, an industrialist in Calcutta. 'The Chamber of Commerce here would tell us before elections that Atulaya Ghosh [of the Congress] would approach each of us for money; and he did. And we paid.'[21] Pragmatic reasons are equally important. 'Industrialists give money to the Congress for elections as a business transaction, to get licences and all,' said Arvind Mafatlal, an industrialist in Bombay.[22] These licences are for importing raw materials or capital goods, or expanding already existing industrial units, or starting new units; and the 'price' for obtaining one rises as the polling day approaches. 'Much larger chunks of money [than those involved in presenting money "purses" to Congress leaders at public rallies] continue to clink in the Congress coffers to the rustle of industrial licences changing hands,' reported Rajinder Puri, an Indian journalist, on the eve of the March 1971 Parliamentary election. 'Rs 2 lakhs [£10,000] is the reported average fee for each licence cleared in a jiffy.'[23] Furthermore, according to a report in the *Financial Express*, import policies concerning foreign cotton and wool-tops were liberalized by the Congress administration in deals respectively with the Indian Cotton Mills Federation and the Woollen Manufacturers' Association for a total sum of about Rs one crore (£500,000).[24] In addition, monies were raised, as usual, from contractors who supply goods or services to such federal government agencies as the armed forces, the Central Public Works Department, etc.

A somewhat similar situation exists at the State level. Here various ministers are expected to tap their sources for 'contributions' to the Congress election fund. For instance, the transport minister approaches bus operators licensed to ply buses on certain routes; the public works minister, construction and supply contractors; the co-operatives minister, heads of co-operatives; the excise minister, licensees for the sale of alcoholic drinks; and the industries minister, local industrialists who depend on the State government for water and power supply, protection of property, and harmonious labour relations.

Since other parties have never enjoyed power at the Centre, and done so only briefly and intermittently in some of the States, they have not been able to emulate the example of the Congress in collecting election funds even if they wished to. However, due to its openly pro-capitalist stance, the close links between its top leadership and some of the large business houses, and the affluence of most of its candidates, the Swatantra Party is quite well off. The Jan Sangh, another right-wing party, manages to finance its election campaign by selecting rich peasants or former feudal lords as its candidates in rural constituencies, relying heavily on the dedication of its volunteers who work without any remuneration, and by collecting small sums from a large number of middle-class people, including small industrialists and businessmen, and shopkeepers. The two Communist parties, especially the CPI(M), also collect small amounts from a large body of members and sympathizers. In addition, they often make informal arrangements with the leaders of the trade unions sympathetic to them, and collect monies to build up an election fund to contest a limited number of seats. (They do so because the trade union law forbids trade unions from giving money to political parties from their general fund.)

While selection of candidates and collection of election funds are in progress, top policy makers of each party issue an election manifesto. For all practical purposes, this is a ritual which is taken seriously, if at all, only by some newspapers: they publish summaries of the manifestos and their own comments on them. But since a mere 2 per cent of newspaper sales are in villages, where 80 per cent of the electors live, the overall impact of this exercise is insignificant.

In any case, with the exception of the CPI(M), all other parties differ only slightly from the Congress. This can be seen by examining the manifestos issued on the eve of the 1971 Parliamentary elections, when the Congress faced a serious challenge from the 'Grand Alliance' of the Syndicate-Congress, Swatantra Party, Jan Sangh, and Samyukta (i.e. United) Socialists. While the Congress expressed its wish 'to ensure a better life to the people and to satisfy their aspirations for a just economic and social order,' the right-wing Jan Sangh declared its commitment to 'nationalism, democracy and the building up of an egalitarian society . . . in which there could be no place for economic exploitation or social disparity', and 'the building up of modern India on the basis of liberty, equality, and fraternity', and the conservative Syndicate-Congress proclaimed its 'main objective' to be 'the creation of a democratic, socialist, secular society in India' which 'alone will ensure social justice and equality of opportunity to all, and freedom of the individual'.[25] It was only the CPI(M) which stated specifically that 'unless economic and political power of the capitalist and landlord classes is attacked . . . the way to real freedom and democracy will not be open'.

'Poverty must go,' said the Congress manifesto. 'Disparity must diminish. Injustice must end.' The Jan Sangh document was no less rhetorical: it declared a 'national war on poverty' with the objective of winning a 'total victory'. Similarly, the Syndicate-Congress manifesto declared 'abolishing poverty' to be its '[main] objective'. 'Equality and social justice are the guiding values of socialist policies and pro- grammes,' said the Praja (i.e. People's) Socialist Party. But that did not deter it from making it 'explicitly clear' that 'the party is not opposed to private property as such'. So did the CPI 'wish to make it clear' that 'it does not stand for the abolition of the right to property'. Both the Congress and Jan Sangh documents said that they had no intention of abolishing the institution of private property. It was again left to the CPI(M) to be explicit, and recommend that 'necessary amendments to the fundamental rights as laid down in the Constitution' be made so as to 'make it possible for Parliament and the State legislatures to legislate against the private property of foreign and Indian monopolists, former princes and big landlords, and other top strata of society'.

Even on such specific subjects as land relations and private enterprise, the main parties ended up in general agreement. 'A positive programme of agrarian reform is necessary,' said the Congress document. 'The Jan Sangh upholds the principle of "land to the tiller",' read its manifesto. The CPI, which had coined the 'land to the tiller' slogan in the 1930s, was now content to merely recommend that 'land reform in favour of peasantry' be 'carried out'. Even the Swatantra Party strung along. 'Land reform should be speedily completed and implemented,' it said. 'Monopoly [in the industrial sector] has to be combated.' The CPI agreed, and went on to suggest that this be done by 'radical measures of nationalization'. Both the centrist Congress and 'leftist' Praja Socialist Party shared the view that private enterprise should be helped. 'The private sector will be stimulated to the maximum extent possible,' promised the Congress. 'Socialism does not mean killing individual initiative and spirit of enterprise,' said the Praja Socialist Party.

'The [election] promises carry little hope of definite action,' observed Thilo Bode, the Asian correspondent of the *Suddeutsche Zeitung*, a West German daily, for whom the 1971 election was the fourth Indian election to be covered. 'All parties want democracy, progress and stability, but no party is prepared to define these terms. They are just slogans, stunted in their growth and limited to personalities.'[26] M. Raymond Girard, a veteran French documentary film-maker, drew a similar conclusion. 'Apparently what is important to politicians in this country [India] is personalities,' he said. 'In my talks with Mrs Gandhi I couldn't get her once to say what her issues were. She just wouldn't answer that question. Neither does any other politician. They keep talking about their plans in vague terms, and the only thing they are specific about is personalities.'[27]

Excessive stress on personalities and deification of top leaders have long been important elements of the Congress style of politics. In pre-independence days, mass popularity of the Congress was carefully built around the triumvirate of M. K. Gandhi, J. Nehru, and V. B. Patel. The deaths of Gandhi (in 1948) and Patel (in 1950) left Nehru as the sole popular leader, *the* national statesman almost, above partisan politics – an image he allowed to be cultivated and perpetuated, and the one his party exploited to the hilt to win elections until his death in 1964. This tradition has continued with his daughter, Indira Gandhi, who became the Prime Minister in early 1966 (when, following the death of L. B. Shastri, the immediate successor to Nehru, the Congress members of Parliament elected her their leader), a position that enabled her to project herself as the *national* leader, during and after the 1967 elections, something no other leader, within or outside the Congress, could do then, or can now. The use of the popularity of any other leader for electoral purposes is limited, at best, to the region of his origin – such as K. Kamraj Nadar's to Tamil Nadu[28] and Morarji Desai's to Gujarat. This is done by having the leader's picture appear on all posters and handbills.

However, the single most important image for a political party to project is its election symbol, a device used to help the vast majority of voters to overcome their illiteracy. The symbols are allotted, by the Chief Election Commissioner, from a list considered to be 'neutral' (i.e. without any positive or negative associations in the popular mind); and each party strives to popularize it to the point where most electors feel that they are voting for the symbol rather than party. 'The main campaign technique of each and every candidate is to lay great emphasis on his election symbol rather than his political label,' state C. P. Bhambhri and S. P. Verma, Indian political scientists.[29] Until the split in the Congress, in 1969, its election symbol was a yoked pair of bullocks, the most useful of the domesticated animals in rural India since the ancient times. '[It] suggested all kinds of favourable connections,' notes Norman D. Palmer, an American academic. 'Many Indians could be persuaded that they should not vote against bullocks, which symbolized the source of their livelihood, and their main source of power and transportation.'[30] The 'cow and calf' symbol, allotted to the Congress, led by Indira Gandhi, on the eve of the 1971 elections, has a positive religious undertone – for the Hindu voters, who account for more than four-fifths of the electorate.

The most popular method of communicating the symbol to the voters is through posters, handbills, and signs on the walls. Often parties combine the election symbol with slogans, and pictures of their national or regional leaders. The two most widely used posters of the Congress in the 1971 elections, for example, were composed thus: one carried Indira Gandhi's picture and the party's election symbol, and the slogans – 'Onward To Democratic Socialism – On With Indira Gandhi', and 'Vote Congress/For Progress'; and the other had the pictures of M. K. Gandhi, J. Nehru, and Indira Gandhi, with an appropriate slogan printed next to each image – 'Slavery to Freedom' (M. K. Gandhi), 'Freedom + Democracy + Economic Growth' (J. Nehru), and 'Democracy + Secularism + Socialism' (Indira Gandhi). Similarly, the Dravida Munnetra Kazhagam, a popular regional party in Tamil Nadu, made an extensive use of the pictures of its personages – C. Annadurai (now dead), popularly known as 'Anna' (i.e. the Big Brother), and M. Karunanidhi, the State's chief minister. When a party lacks a charismatic State or national leader, or when it follows a deliberate policy of refraining from creating a personality cult (as is the case with the two Communist parties), it relies solely on combining its election symbol with catchy slogans. The Jan Sangh, for example, coined such slogans as 'For honest and efficient administration/Vote . . .', 'For unity and security of the country/Vote . . .', 'For freedom of agriculture and business/Vote . . .'.

Posters are displayed in both rural and urban areas, but handbills are often distributed only in urban centres, where literacy among voters is comparatively high. However, the main burden of propaganda (other than familiarization with electoral symbols) is carried by word of mouth. Party slogans and exhortations are shouted through loud-speakers attached to such vehicles as rickshaws, jeeps, taxis, and trucks. A more deliberate job is done by party speakers at public meetings. These vary in size from the informal neighbourhood get-togethers of twenty to fifty people to street meetings of a few hundred to elaborately stage-managed public rallies of tens of thousands which are often addressed by a prominent party leader. Attendance at these rallies is considered an indication of the popularity of a party, a form of 'un-scientific' opinion poll.

Since speeches are usually made in urban areas, the vast majority of voters, living in villages, are not exposed to them. Their votes are won, in the main, quietly, through the intercession of community or caste leaders. In general, the lower the social status – and, as a corollary, the educational and economic standing – of the caste, the higher the influence of caste leaders over their members; and vice versa. The candidates know this, and in courting different community and caste leaders employ different tactics. In dealing with the established leaders of higher castes they make use of their own caste origin, personal friendships, and factionalism existing at the village panchayat level, and make lavish promises about bringing government-financed development projects to the village (which, as stated earlier, in Chapter 1, pp. 6–7, 10 and 12, benefit mainly the upper caste-classes). In the case of the leaders of lower castes, especially outcastes, where the traditional leader has much influence over the members of his caste, most of the serious candidates resort to the tactic of buying votes. The practice is widespread and is prevalent in both rural and urban constituencies. A typical situation is summarized by E. A. Ramaswamy, an Indian academic, who studied the suburban constituency of Singanallur, in Tamil Nadu, in the 1971 Parliamentary elections, thus:

Fears were frequently expressed that a well-to-do rival might upset all calculations by purchasing votes on the night before the poll. . . . An almost universal belief was that Harijan scavengers in the employment of the municipality responded only to direct inducements. Feeding them on the night before the poll was believed to be the only way of bagging their votes. This was expensive since entire streets . . . had to be fed. . . . The feeding continued till the small hours of the morning. The Harijans were then herded to the polling booths and lined up for voting.[31]

All this goes on despite the fact that the Representation of the Peoples Act 1951 prohibits bribery, undue influence, appeal by a candidate or his agent on the grounds of religion, race, caste, community, or language, hiring or procuring vehicles for carrying voters, incurring expenditure in excess of the prescribed limit, and procuring the assistance of government employees for furthering the chance of election of a candidate.[32] The most frequent and blatant violator of the law is the Congress, the ruling party.

It uses the government machinery in various ways to help its candidates to win. In the 1971 Parliamentary elections, for instance, it made use of the Defence Department to secure jeeps (which are the single most important item needed for an election campaign, and which are always in short supply, necessitating a long wait for the buyers) for its candidates.

The ruling party plans to requisition 1,000 to 2,000 jeeps [said Madhu Limaye, a Socialist member of Parliament, in January 1971]. The minister-in-charge of Defence Production has allowed the [only] manufacturer to postpone immediate delivery of jeeps to Defence Department and instead supply these to hire-purchase companies. These companies will then 'hire' these out to the Congress. . . . After elections these jeeps will be taken back, reconditioned, and sold to the Defence Ministry.[33]

Also, as in the past, the Congress administration used the government-managed broadcasting service to its advantage by having it report at length, and favourably, the activities of the senior party leaders, particularly Indira Gandhi. In fact, since the early days of the internecine quarrel within the party, which developed in the summer of 1969 and matured into an open split some months later, the Congress government made an extensive use of radio to project Indira Gandhi as a daring and radical leader who had chosen to cross swords with the old, reactionary party bosses and expose their conservatism and affinity for the 'vested interests'.[34] (The existence of 12.77 million radios in use in 1971, which was more than twice the number in use at the time of the 1967 general election, made radio broadcasts – in a largely illiterate and sub-literate country – a most powerful instrument of propaganda.) Now, on the eve of elections in 1971, the Congress ministry went one step ahead. It encouraged such government institutions as marketing boards, co-operatives, land mortage banks, and the recently nationalized commercial banks to advertise their goods and services on radio (which had been allowed to accept commercial advertising on a limited scale only a year earlier), and thus help engender a feeling among the electorate that bank loans, 'miracle' seeds, chemical fertilizers, etc. were theirs for the asking.

The Congress governments in the States have not fallen behind the Centre in this matter. It is not uncommon for them to sanction new development projects, and even have some of them completed speedily, if need be, in order to win some seats. The example of a rural constituency in Rajasthan, in the 1967 election, is fairly typical. 'During the short campaign,' states Anand Chakravarati, an Indian researcher, 'the Congress candidate R. K. Vyas made sure that construction of a 3-mile road from Chomu to a village nearby was completed . . . a [medical] dispensary at village Khejroli was sanctioned and work begun . . . [and] an extension of electricity for agricultural purposes was given to a number of farmers.'[35]

The most blatant example of the Congress using government machinery and influence, at both the federal and State levels, to win votes, occurred in the 1974 State assembly elections in Uttar Pradesh. 'The machinery of state was unashamedly used to ensure the Congress Party's electoral survival,' reported Sarwar Lateef, an Indian journalist, in the *New Statesman.*

> Supplies of essential commodities like foodgrains, kerosene and cement – now in short supply throughout India – were diverted [from other States] on a priority basis to Uttar Pradesh. A number of decisions were announced which can only be described as pre-election bribes. Wages and salaries of government and other employees were raised. Sugarcane prices were increased for the benefit of 10 million cane-growers. Employment and land were offered to Harijan voters.[36]

But a far more effective and insidious method to ensure electoral victory that the Congress employs, is to deftly interweave party organization with government and quasi-government institutions. This is what the party has done in some States, particularly Maharashtra. And the details of this plan were spelled out by no less a person than a member of the Maharashtra's Congress ministry – Dr Rafiq Zakaria:

> Take the zilla parishad. Each one has a president, and four chairmen of specialized committees. Everyone of them is paid a salary of Rs 500 [£25], and given a bungalow and a car. A district is divided into four to six *taluqas* (i.e. sub-counties); and each *taluqa* has a president who gets paid by the government. [These presidents are involved in the execution of development plans, and a lot of money passes through their hands.] Then each district has a co-operative bank, which gives short-term loans for the purchase of seed, fertilizers, etc., with a chairman and a board of

directors who are paid salaries by the bank. There is also a land mortgage bank, which gives long-term loans for capital investment in tube wells, water pumps, engines, tractors, etc., in each district, with a paid chairman and a board of directors, not to mention the district marketing boards and the sugar co-operatives.[37] The cadres of the Congress are absorbed in these institutions. Here they can promote the interest of the party and get paid for it. Once you have got such a system working for you, it's difficult to get thrown out of office.[38]

The Congress indulges in such malpractices in a milieu where about half the voters are illiterate and another third are barely literate,[39] the voter turnover is low, varying between 45 per cent and 55 per cent; and the political awareness of the electors is so low that often no more than a quarter can name the State's chief minister or the party he belongs to.[40] A study of the voting behaviour in the 1967 general elections, considered the most exciting yet, showed that 71 per cent of the electorate were either 'apathetic' or 'peripherals' or 'spectators', that is, they had little or no knowledge of the election issues.[41] Most of those who consciously sided with or canvassed for a candidate did so for reasons which were essentially non-political.

Nonetheless, a study of one or more election results can throw some light on the profile of support for different parties and indicate a trend in voting. A national sample survey of voters spread over 47 Parliamentary constituencies, in the 1967 elections, by Rajni Kothari, an Indian political scientist, and his associates, revealed some interesting facts. They found that whereas 42·1 per cent of rural electors voted for the Congress, only 30·9 per cent of urban voters did so;[42] 43·1 per cent of the over-35s voted for the Congress while 31·4 per cent voted for the opposition, with the rest not voting at all;[43] and 40·3 per cent of the illiterate electorate voted for the Congress whereas only 30·5 per cent of them did so for the opposition, with the remaining not voting at all.[44] 'Younger age, higher education and urban exposure contributed to the alienation [of the voter] from the Congress party,' they concluded.[45]

In ethnic and caste terms, the Congress drew 'most heavily from middle caste groups (largely peasant castes), Scheduled Castes and Tribes, Muslims and voters from other religious minorities',[46] that is, 58 per cent of the total electorate. And since Muslims and Scheduled Castes, who form more than half of this segment of the electorate, are fairly evenly distributed throughout the country, the Congress is assured of a certain minimum percentage of votes in individual constituencies, which is not the case with any of its rivals. It is further helped by an electoral system which awards victory to the candidate with the highest number of votes, even if this falls short of the majority of total votes.

Actually, the Congress has never won a majority of the popular vote. Its vote in the first three Parliamentary elections (in 1952, 1957, and 1962) fluctuated between 44·7 per cent and 47·8 per cent, but its share of seats in Parliament did not fall below 75 per cent. In the fourth general election, in 1967, the party faced an electorate which was deeply dissatisfied with its performance. A national sample survey of voters showed that 84·4 per cent of them felt that the party had failed to hold prices down, 78·1 per cent said that the party had failed to root out corruption, 75·5 per cent stated that the party had failed to distribute food to the people, and 59·9 per cent said that it had failed to help the farmers.[47] And yet the party managed to secure 55 per cent of the seats in Parliament on a popular vote of 40·7 per cent. This happened because of the existence of a 'high degree of identification with Congress as the government party' among the voters,[48] who could not visualize a government in Delhi without the Congress party being in charge; and because of a general lack of political consideration by the electorate in deciding to vote for one party rather than another; and because of the absence of a viable opposition party or alliance, with an all-India image and organization.

Four years later, however, four opposition parties – Syndicate Congress, Jan Sangh, Swatantra, and Samyukta Socialists – having a total of 153 seats in Parliament (versus the Congress's 223), banded together to form a 'Grand Alliance', which offered itself as a viable alternative to the Congress. Although the Alliance secured 23·4 per cent of the popular vote, it won only 9·4 per cent of the seats in Parliament. In contrast, the Congress obtained 43·1 per cent of the vote and 67 per cent of the seats.

The 'Grand Alliance', it seemed, had been too hastily stitched together to succeed in projecting itself as a viable entity and a genuine alternative to the Congress. And, contrary to the expectations of the leaders of the Alliance parties, a particular weakness of a constituent party was transferred to the Alliance as a whole. For instance, the unpopularity of the Jan Sangh among Muslims and Scheduled Castes deprived even the non-Jan Sangh candidates of the votes of these substantial communities. Similarly, the image of the Swatantra Party, as a party of the capitalists and feudal lords rubbed off on all the Alliance candidates, particularly when the Congress propaganda managed to keep the (essentially inconsequential) issue of the abolition of privy purses of the former princes in the forefront.[49]

Lacking any coherent or positive programme to hold the Alliance together, its leaders personalized the election campaign to an unusual degree by making 'Remove Indira Gandhi' their *only* slogan, while Indira Gandhi constantly reiterated her commitment to the cleverly coined slogan of '*Garibi Hatao*' – 'Remove Poverty'. Given the general conservatism of the Alliance parties, excepting the Samyukta Socialists, the smallest constituent, she had little difficulty in portraying the Alliance as a tool of the rich, whom she attacked, repeatedly, in public. Launching her party's election campaign in the largest of the Indian States, Uttar Pradesh, she lashed out at 'capitalists, newspaper barons, rajas, and maharajas', who, she claimed, were all out to thwart her government's 'march towards socialism'.

But only a few days earlier, she had, according to Sumanta Banerjee, an Indian journalist, assured a group of prominent industrialists in Bombay that 'they need not have any fears of a new government after the elections', and Naval Tata, a leading industrialist, had in return assured her that 'industrialists were not against her'.[50] They could not have been, for they were the ones who had given her party huge sums of money to fight the elections. 'Indira Gandhi is having the best of both worlds, hobnobbing with big business when it suits her, and still passing off as a socialist,' said Tarkeshwari Sinha, a Syndicate-Congress leader.[51]

However, Indira Gandhi was doing no more than follow the long-established pattern of behaviour of the Congress leaders. 'When the Congressmen talk to a Chamber of Commerce they say one thing, and when they talk to labour they say something quite different,' observed M. V. Arunachalam, a leading industrialist of Madras.[52] Nor is the situation any different in rural areas. There, notes Myron Weiner, an American political scientist, leaders of the Congress 'speak different messages and make different promises to the landless labourers and to the peasant proprietors'.[53] This might seem opportunistic, but, in point of fact, the Congress was never conceived as a party of the poor *against* the rich. After all, it was established, in the mid-1880s, by those Indians who were already socially and economically well-off and wanted to upgrade their status further by petitioning the foreign ruler.

6

THE CONGRESS PARTY:
FACING BOTH WAYS

The hard core of the gradually democratizing Congress coalition was, in sum, non-aristocratic, middle-class and moderately reformist, generally not desiring complete liquidation of superior classes and generally not desiring radical effort to enhance the position of the lowest classes.

> Howard L. Erdman, an American political scientist[1]

'We spoke of socialism because that was what went down well with the masses,' Mrs Gandhi told me [in July 1969].

> Kuldip Nayar, an Indian journalist and author[2]

The Congress has many socialist slogans, but no socialist policy or action.

> Abhijit Sen, an Indian industrialist[3]

My [Congress] party has adopted a particular way to socialism in which both capitalists and non-capitalists can co-exist.

> Indira Gandhi, Prime Minister of India[4]

The establishment of the Indian National Congress in 1885 had the active encouragement of the British Viceroy, who saw in it a 'controlled' vehicle of protest for the Indians. And it was a retired English member of the covenanted services, A. O. Hume, who brought about the merger of the three existing provincial organizations – the Indian Association of Bengal in Calcutta, the Mahajan Sabha in Madras, and the Bombay Presidency Association in Bombay – to create a national body. The seventy self-elected delegates, who attended the inaugural session, were middle-class professionals – lawyers, teachers, and journalists; and the major 'social' problems they discussed were the possibility of holding examinations for the covenanted services simultaneously in England and India, raising the age limit for these examinations, and increasing the number and types of government jobs available to the Indians. The colonial administration responded to this by appointing a commission which, in due course, recommended, among other things, that the covenanted services be renamed the 'Indian Civil Service'.

THE CONGRESS PARTY   71

For the next generation, the Congress continued to concern itself almost exclusively with such 'social' problems as the improvement of the upper-class Indians in British administration; and its leadership remained in the hands of the members of the Western-educated upper-middle class, while its financial support came from landowners, princes, and the industrial house of the Tatas.[5] That is, it failed to widen either its supporting base or its objectives, and began to decline. But the partition of Bengal on administrative grounds by Lord Curzon in 1905, gave it a new lease of life. It enraged Bengali sentiment, and drove the protesting educated lower-middle class in Bengal and Bombay Presidencies – already suffering economic distress due to shortage of government jobs – into the arms of the Congress.

As a result, the Congress acquired a 'radical' wing which proved sufficiently influential to have the party demand, in 1908, a self-governing dominion status for India (under the British tutelage). But this did not mark an end to the conflict that had developed between the moderate and radical wings within the party. Indeed, with the country becoming involved in the First World War, this conflict sharpened. The death of G. K. Gokhale, a leader of the moderates, in 1915, tilted the scale in favour of the radicals, who were led by B. G. Tilak, a man who hinted at the 'efficacy of violence' and demanded Home Rule. His failing health, however, prevented him from mustering popular support for his demand.

It was at this time (1917) that M. K. Gandhi began to make his mark in Indian politics. Born of *bania* (i.e. trading caste) parents, in north Gujarat, he had studied law in England, and then settled in South Africa, where he led a civil disobedience movement by the Indian settlers against the official policy of racial discrimination. This was his initiation into politics, leading a non-violent militant action against an oppressive authority. Two years after his return to India in 1915, he organized *satyagraha* – passive resistance – against the colonial government by the peasants working on British indigo plantations in north Bihar. Later, in 1919, when the British responded to the Congress's demands for self-rule with repressive laws, Gandhi gave a call for *satyagraha* and mass civil disobedience against the government, and received popular support in Gujarat, Bihar, and Uttar Pradesh (then called United Provinces). This helped transform the Congress from being, essentially, a pressure body to being a mass party, and secured Gandhi the highest place in the party leadership.

Gandhi won popularity among different sections of society for different reasons. He appealed to Hindu masses because he was able to communicate modern political events and ideas in traditional religio-philosophic terms of Hinduism which they understood and appreciated.[6] He appealed to them also because he lived simply and was religious. But he was far from being orthodox, particularly in the crucial area of the caste system and the practice of untouchability. Here, he was a reformer, and attracted not only Untouchables to the Congress but also many Hindu social reformers. He became popular with the landowning and cultivating peasants (and the middle-class groups in small towns that were related to them) because he took up their grievances regarding land revenue and levies with the colonial government. He also managed to secure the co-operation of many businessmen and capitalists. His caste background – a *bania*, merchant – and place of birth, north Gujarat, made him readily acceptable to the business communities of Gujarat, and the adjoining Rajasthan, financially the two most powerful groups in the country. Furthermore, he believed in, and actively worked for, co-operation and harmony between workers and capitalists – whom he considered to be mere 'trustees' of capital on behalf of the community – and this suited the capitalists perfectly.[7]

Within the Congress itself, Gandhi came to play the crucial role of a mediator between the conservative and pragmatic Patel and the radical and impulsive Nehru, and harnessed their talents for the party's good. Although he supported Nehru in having the party raise its political demand to total and complete independence from the British (and not merely dominion status under the British sovereign) in 1929, and the concept of economic planning in Free India in 1931, Gandhi made no effort to loosen the hold that Patel and his conservative wing had over the party machine. Nehru, who considered himself above such mundane chores as supervising the running of a party machine, let things be, with the result that the conservatives often had their own man elected as the Congress President.

Only once, in 1938, did S. C. Bose, a charismatic radical, manage to bypass the conservative party bosses, appeal to the Congress delegates directly, and win the party Presidency. But the following year, when he tried to do the same again, he ran into open hostility from the con-servative troika of Patel, Rajendra Prasad, *and* Gandhi. Now was the time for Nehru to take sides, to prove his radical *bona fides*. Instead, he did nothing: he remained neutral. (Bose won; but in the face of continued hostility of the conservatives in the party hierarchy, felt too disgusted to go on, and resigned from the party altogether.) Later, Nehru published a pamphlet in which he, more or less, disowned the mildly Marxist ideology he had come to acquire in the late 1920s, and went on to state that there was no right and left in the Congress, only the modernists and Gandhians (i.e. traditionalists), both of whom were 'essential' to the Congress and the nation.[8] In other words, Nehru ceased to be a radical partisan, and, instead, became a mediator himself, an 'upholder of the middle course'.

His subsequent actions showed this. For instance, on being called to form an 'interim government' in Delhi, by the British Viceroy, in 1946, Nehru put Patel in charge of the crucial Home Ministry. This gave an opportunity to Patel to retain almost intact the British method of administration with its essentially colonial biases and philosophy, to treat the feudal rulers of the 'native' states with much care and sensitivity, and to use the maximum possible police and military force to crush the Communist movement in the Telangana region in the South. By the time he died, in December 1950, Patel had left an unmistakably conservative stamp on the government administration of an independent India, and placed an arch-conservative, P. D. Tandon, as the President of the Congress.

Meanwhile, following the country's independence, in August 1947, the Congress Party had given itself the task of establishing 'a co-operative Commonwealth based on equality of opportunity and of political, economic and social rights'. But no attempt had been made either to define the term 'co-operative Commonwealth' or to restructure the party to achieve it, or to resolve the deleterious tension that had developed between the organizational and parliamentary wings of the party ever since it assumed office at the Centre in 1946.

The election of Tandon as Congress President made the already bad situation worse, and indeed, following Patel's death, the friction between the two wings of the party, now led respectively by Tandon and Nehru, came to a head. Tandon thought it prudent to resign in order to save the party the disastrous possibility of facing the electorate in the first-ever general election based on universal suffrage, in 1951–2, without the charismatic, vote-catching Nehru being (seen to be) in full command. Nehru led his party to an impressive victory, winning 364 out of 489 Parliamentary seats, and 2,246 out of 3,283 State assembly seats. The Congress emerged strong in all the States, except Orissa, where a local conservative party led by former princes proved more popular, and the old States of Travancore-Cochin and Madras, where the Communists posed a serious threat to the Congress.

Nehru frustrated the Communist attempt to secure power in Madras, through coalition with non-Congress groups in the assembly, by calling on the services of C. Rajagopalachari, a wily and staunchly anti-Communist Congress leader in the State. At the same time he tried to show that his party and administration were 'progressive'. When he launched the First Five Year Plan, in late 1952, he described it as a unique combination of economic planning, a concept commonly associated with Marxist-socialist governments, with Western-style democracy. He maintained friendly relations with Soviet Russia, and followed up the signing of an agreement with the People's Republic of China on 'Trade and Intercourse between the Tibet Region of China and India', in April 1954, with an official visit there, some months later, when he praised the progress that China had made in a short span of five years. In January 1955, he had the Congress session at Avadi, near Madras, adopt a resolution that:

In order to realize the object of the Congress and the
Constitution and to further the objectives stated in the Preamble
and the Directive Principles of the State Policy of the
Constitution of India, planning should take place with a view
to the establishment of a socialistic pattern of society where the
principal means of production are under social ownership or
control, production is progressively speeded up, and there is
equitable distribution of national wealth.

What did a 'socialistic pattern of society' mean? The answer came
not from the Congress, but from the Planning Commission, a government body. 'The socialistic pattern of society is not to be regarded as
some fixed or rigid pattern,' stated the Planning Commission's Document on the Second Five Year Plan (1956–61). 'It is not rooted in any
doctrine or dogma. The accent of the socialist pattern is on . . . the
raising of living standards, the enlargement of opportunity for all, the
promotion of enterprise among the disadvantaged classes, and the
creation of a sense of partnership among all sections of the community.'[9] Certainly nobody, whether socialist or capitalist, could have
opposed such an all-embracing, altruistic concept.

As expected, the new slogan was much bandied about by the Congress
in the general elections of 1957 – to good effect. The party won 371 out
of 494 seats in Parliament, and 2,012 out of 3,102 seats in the State
assemblies, and assumed power at the Centre and in all the States,
except the newly-formed State of Kerala, where the Communists won a
narrow majority. One way to counter the Communist influence was by
making the Congress adopt more 'radical' policies, Nehru seemed to
think. He therefore had the Congress session in Nagpur, in early 1959,
adopt a resolution in favour of 'joint co-operative farming', ceilings on
agricultural land, and the allotment of surplus land to local panchayats
with a view to having them cultivated by co-operatives of landless
labourers. This caused some stir among conservative elements within
and outside the Congress, who denounced the impending 'collectiviza-
tion' of Indian agriculture, and went on to form the unambiguously
conservative Swatantra Party. They need not have bothered, since
nothing concrete came of the famous Nagpur Resolution. Indeed,
very little was heard of the 'co-operative farming' in the country or at
subsequent Congress sessions.

The Congress leaders at the State and federal levels, often themselves
large landholders and property owners, were too busy safeguarding
their own interests, or enriching themselves, by misusing political
power, to seriously initiate and implement programmes for the welfare
of the poor classes. And, by the early 1960s, this had begun to tarnish
the popular image of the party. 'The Congress image as an organization
of selfless, non-violent soldiers of freedom [from foreign rule] is being

quickly replaced by an image which depicts it as a band of self-seeking, unscrupulous and corrupt politicians in active alliance with the rapacious, selfish, anti-social and dishonest elements of society,' noted C. P. Bhambhri and S. P. Verma.[10] There was a steep decline in the membership of the party – from 10·08 million in 1958 to 2·02 million in 1963.

Nehru tried to stop the rot by making many of the Congress State chief ministers and Central cabinet ministers resign their posts and devote themselves fully to party work. He also had the Congress session in Bhubenshwar, in early 1964, commit itself to 'democratic socialism with planned economic development as the instrument for realizing it'.[11] But, once again, this was an empty ritual. To most Congressmen, this meant nothing more than replacing their worn-out catch-phrase of 'socialistic pattern of society' with a new slogan of 'democratic social-ism', to be used for winning the next general election. 'Some years ago,' said Rani Bir Chundur, a son of a prominent Congress leader in West Bengal, 'I was travelling with some Congress leaders, and I heard one leader say to another, "As long as we beat the drum of socialism we'll always be in power".'[12]

Anyway, Nehru died soon after; and L. B. Shastri, who succeeded him, seldom, if ever, uttered the word 'socialism' either in public or private. He even abandoned the idea of economic planning, which the Bhubenshwar Resolution of the party had described as 'the instrument for realizing democratic socialism'. He declared a 'plan holiday' in 1965. When Indira Gandhi followed Shastri as the Prime Minister, in early 1966, she continued the 'plan holiday', and declared herself to be a 'pragmatist'. She proved this by visiting America within the next few months and calling President Johnson, then in the process of escalating American involvement in Vietnam, a 'man of peace'; and, shortly after, devaluing the Indian rupee by a massive 58 per cent, under none-too-subtle American pressure.

However, as the time to fight the general election of 1967 approached, she and other party leaders reached out for clichés likely to appeal to the poverty-ridden masses. 'The Indian National Congress has placed before the country the goal of a democratic socialist society,' declared the party manifesto. 'It is of the highest importance that the provision of basic needs of every individual is ensured and a national minimum comprising the essential requirements in respect of food, clothing, housing, education, and health is established as speedily as possible. . . . It would be reasonable to expect that the objective will be substantially realized by the end of the Fifth Plan [in 1976].' But this time, neither radical rhetoric nor generous promises of a bright future to come proved adequate to cover the glaring failures of the Congress adminis-tration – food shortages, inflation, rising unemployment, higher taxes, and an economic recession. Consequently, the party's strength in

Parliament fell from 371 to 281, with 150 of the seats won by a margin of 500-odd votes in constituencies with an average electorate of 500,000; and the party lost control of the assemblies in nine major States, which, between them, account for two-thirds of the national population.

Shocked by the election results, and yet determined to regain the lost ground, the party's High Command went on to commit itself (in May 1967) to achieve the following ten-point programme by 1976: (1) 'social control' of the banks; (2) nationalization of general insurance; (3) progressive take-over of export-import trade by state agencies; (4) a national policy of public distribution of foodgrains; (5) organization of consumer co-operatives in urban and rural areas; (6) effective steps to curb monopolies and concentration of economic power; (7) steps to ensure provision of minimum needs of the entire community; (8) restrictions on individual holdings of urban land; (9) prompt implementation of land reforms; and (10) abolition of the princes' privileges 'other than privy purses'. (A flush of 'new radicalism' led the All India Congress Committee meeting, held the following month, to drop the qualification 'other than privy purses'.)

But there still remained the immediate problem of containing the rising popularity of the CPI(M) in the country, particularly in Kerala and the industrially and strategically important State of West Bengal, where the party dominated the non-Congress coalition governments. The conservatives in the Congress High Command suggested collaboration with rightist elements in the non-Congress coalitions in the States in order to isolate the Communists politically, and then an open use of government force to crush their movement. But Indira Gandhi chose not to act in the hope that these heterogeneous coalitions would fall apart. They did; and, within two years of the general election, a fresh poll had to be held in Bihar, Uttar Pradesh, Punjab, and West Bengal.

The Congress, however, fared worse than before in all the States, with the CPI(M) improving its position further in West Bengal at its cost, and emerging as the largest single group in the assembly. This sharpened the differences within the Congress High Command regarding the tactics to be employed to counter the march of the Communists. Should the party move right or left? 'I want to take the wind out of the sails of the Communists, and I can do that only by moving to the left of the centre,' said Indira Gandhi. 'Morarji Desai does not believe in that policy.'[13] The rabidly anti-Communist Morarji Desai – who, among other things, supported American action in Vietnam – had the backing of S. K. Patil, a favourite of the industrialists in Bombay, Atulya Ghosh, the archangel of Calcutta's business community, and the conservative S. Nijalangappa, the party's President. They wanted an alliance with the Jan Sangh and Swatantra Party, and an open shift to the right in economic policies.

At the party session in April 1969, in Faridabad, Nijalangappa referred to the inefficient management of the public sector of the economy, and suggested greater incentives to private enterprise. Indira Gandhi responded to this by proposing at the party's High Command meeting, held on the eve of the All India Congress Committee session in July in Bangalore that the public sector should be encouraged by either directing all the banks to reserve larger resources for 'public purpose' or nationalizing the top five or six banks. Furthermore, she recommended 'nationalization of import of raw materials; curbing of restricted trade practices; and diligent enforcement of the land reform laws already existing'. All this was part of her 'stray thoughts hurriedly dictated' that she presented to the High Command. And she won their *unanimous* agreement! Aware of the political disadvantage of being seen, publicly, to be less 'socialistic' than their colleagues, and knowing in their mind that very little, if anything, would come of it, the conservatives in the High Command supported Indira Gandhi's 'stray thoughts'. (At the same time, these leaders went around muttering, 'What's stopping Mrs Gandhi from actually implementing these radical policies? After all, she's the head of the government' – a valid criticism.)

This narrowed the conflict between the two groups to the single issue of choosing the party nominee for Union President, a position that had fallen vacant prematurely due to the sudden death of President Zakir Hussain in May. Here, the party's Parliamentary Board rejected Jagjivan Ram, a senior Central cabinet minister and a nominee of Indira Gandhi, and adopted Sanjiva Reddy, the Speaker of the Lok Sabha. This made Indira Gandhi realize that although the conservative party bosses had gone along with her on the issue of radicalizing economic policies, they had no intention of loosening their grip on the party machine. As she was determined to secure control of the party organization, she decided to undermine the authority of the party bosses by not accepting their decision regarding the party nominee for Union President, and instead working actively for V. V. Giri, who was Union Vice-President, then officiating as the President. She also decided to use her political authority to the full.

Within a week of the Bangalore session of the party, she nationalized the top fourteen banks by having the (Acting) Union President issue an ordinance, and forced Desai to resign the post of Finance Minister. Both these decisions of hers were played up by the government-controlled All India Radio; and many among the urban lower and middle classes were led to believe that they would benefit from the new and enlightened policies to be followed by the nationalized banks. 'Almost overnight,' noted Ranajit Roy, an Indian journalist, 'the political climate changed in her favour and she became the people's heroine, who, they believed, wanted to do good to the people and curb the proprietary classes.'[14] This was ironic, because it was the selfsame

Indira Gandhi who had rejected the idea of bank nationalization only three years earlier, when the subject had been raised seriously at the Central cabinet level,[15] despite the fact that every one of the party's election manifestos since 1951 had mentioned it and the party had first adopted the idea in 1931.

Anyway, the timing and manner of her actions undoubtedly boosted her popular standing, and made many of the fence-sitters among the Congress legislators in the country jump to her side. This enabled her to defeat the 'official' Congress candidate for Union President, although only by a small margin.[16] Now that she had control of both the parliamentary and organizational wings of the party, there was nothing to stop her from implementing all of her radical reforms she had outlined in her 'stray thoughts' in Bangalore. And yet, when pressed by popular demand for 'immediate nationalization of import trade', she argued that 'We have first to consolidate the first step [of bank nationalization] and its gains, and study the overall impact of it'.[17]

While she remained essentially flexible and 'pragmatic' in her economic policies, she took an uncompromising stand towards the old party bosses, who, now chastened by the defeat of their candidate for Union President, held out an olive branch. She spurned it, and initiated a move to oust Nijalangappa from his office in the party – a step that won her her own 'expulsion' from the organization. She demonstrated the weakness of her rivals by having 441 of the 750 members of the All India Congress Committee assemble in Delhi, in November 1969, and pass a no-confidence motion in Nijalangappa. A similar division in the two houses of Parliament showed that she had the support of 222 of the 283 erstwhile Congress members of the Lok Sabha, and 114 of the 154 Congress members in the Rajya Sabha. (The rest of the Congress members in Parliament formed a separate group which came to be known, in common parlance, as the Syndicate-Congress.) Clearly, Indira Gandhi was the victor.

What made her win as decisively as she did? Her position as the Prime Minister gave her an advantage over her opponents in the party, and she used it to the fullest possible extent. Also, she showed much greater stamina for infighting and flair for dramatic action than her rivals had suspected her to be capable of. Whereas she made use of those in the party organization who disliked the overlordship of the party bosses, the conservative leaders failed to co-ordinate their forces with those of the right-wing parties, and the subsequent defeat of Reddy, their nominee, undermined their position considerably. Outside the Congress ranks, members of Parliament belonging to religious and/or linguistic minorities, such as Sikhs, Tamils, etc., sided with Indira Gandhi rather than her obscurantist rivals. And all the radical and leftist members of Parliament, being antipathetic to the conservative Congress leaders, backed her. The CPI, enjoying a substantial support among the working and lower-middle classes in the Greater Delhi area, did so by organizing pro-Indira Gandhi demonstrations and processions, and keeping up a daily stream of 'visitors' to her residence in New Delhi, thus providing the local and national press and, most importantly, radio with news favourable to her image as *the* 'leader of the masses'.

Her conservative opponents in the party tried to use this support for her in the streets, by the CPI, as proof that she was herself a Communist, but failed. 'Some people say that I am a Communist, and that I want to lead the country to an ultra-left path,' she said to a meeting of Congress workers in February 1970. 'There are others who think that I am not sufficiently inclined to the left. Both are wrong. I am following the middle path.'[18]

At the same time she wished to guard against the possibility that 'following the middle path' did not end up as doing nothing, or very little, to institute the much-needed economic and social reform, as had happened in the past. Moreover, she had to be seen to be *doing something* in order to maintain the mass popularity she had gained during the intra-party dispute. A perusal of the ten-point programme, adopted by her party in May–June 1967, showed that there were only two points which could enable her to sustain her newly-found image of being radical and *against* the rich. One was a ceiling on urban property; and the other was abolition of the former princes' privileges. But 'urban property' came under 'land', a State subject, where action could only be taken by individual State governments; and so she could initiate action only in the field of the former rulers' privileges, which included an annual privy purse, exemptions from income tax, wealth tax, estate duty, and local taxes, immunity from prosecution, the right to fly their own flag, etc.

The princes had been granted these privileges, on the eve of India's independence, in return for surrendering their hereditary right to rule their 'native' states, by Patel, the then Home Minister; and this arrangement had later been guaranteed by two Articles (291 and 363) in the Constitution. Many of the former rulers had then taken to democratic politics – particularly in Madhya Pradesh, Rajasthan, Orissa, and Gujarat, the States which were composed, mainly or substantially, of the old 'native' territories – and contested elections either as independents or candidates of the Congress, which had welcomed them with open arms. But the founding of the Swatantra Party in 1959, and the steadily rising popularity of the Jan Sangh in north and central India, began to draw them away from the Congress.[19] This process culminated in 1967, when their substantial support to the right-wing parties, specially in the above-mentioned States, badly damaged the electoral performance of the Congress, and made them a target of attack by the radical minority within that party (then functioning as the Congress

Forum for Socialist Action)—a group which succeeded in having the All India Congress Committee session, in June 1967, amend the last of the ten-point programme from 'abolition of the princes' privileges other than privy purses' to 'abolition of the princes' privileges'.

But these privileges could only be abolished by amending the Constitution; and that needed the support of two-thirds of the members present in each of the two houses of Parliament. Indira Gandhi's government introduced the appropriate Constitutional amendment in the Lok Sabha, in September 1970, which passed it by 339 votes to 154, with the Syndicate-Congress and other right-wing parties opposing it, and then in the Rajya Sabha, where it failed to get the necessary support by one vote. Indira Gandhi then acted through the Union President, who issued an Order abolishing the princes' privileges. The princes took the matter to the Supreme Court which ruled, in December, that the Order was *ultra vires*. This provided Indira Gandhi with a concrete example, to show to the people, as to how her party's 'march to socialism' was being frustrated by right-wing elements, recently bolstered by the emergence of the Syndicate-Congress, led by the old party bosses. The temptation to use the princes' privy purses as a major weapon in an electoral battle with her opponents to the right was irresistible. At the same time, she wished to end the irksome dependence of her minority government, commanding only 222 votes out of a total of 520, on the 43 votes of the CPI and CPI(M). These considerations therefore led her to dissolve the Lok Sabha a year earlier than the end of its normal life, and seek a fresh mandate from the electorate.

By employing a combination of tactics – including collection of large sums of money from businessmen and industrialists, and a massive misuse of the government machinery for the benefit of her party – she managed to raise the strength of her party in Parliament to 351 and reduce that of the Syndicate-Congress from 61 to 16. This caused disarray and demoralization in the ranks of the Syndicate-Congress. Many of them sought admission to the Indira Gandhi-led Congress; and, despite all the invectives hurled at them, as members of the Syndicate-Congress, by the latter, only a few weeks earlier, they were welcomed back.

What further helped this mood of 'forgive and forget' was the outbreak of a popular rebellion in the then East Pakistan against the military hierarchy of West Pakistan soon after the Indian Parliamentary elections in March, an event that engaged the attention of the Central government in Delhi and engendered a feeling of unity in India against Pakistan, and which led, nine months later, to a war between the two countries, with India emerging as the victor, and the old East Pakistan establishing itself as the independent state of Bangladesh. This improved the popular standing of Indira Gandhi, and caused a further erosion in the ranks of the Syndicate-Congress. The result of the elections to the legislative assemblies in sixteen States, in March 1972, established this unambiguously: the Syndicate-Congress secured only 3·4 per cent of the 2,563 seats at stake, whereas Indira Gandhi's Congress won 70·4 per cent of the seats.

With her party firmly in power both at the Centre and in the States, including the strategically important West Bengal, Indira Gandhi could afford to return to the 'pragmatic' path which she had been treading before the intra-party dispute developed in mid-1969. And she did. 'Ever since the *"Garibi hatao"* [i.e. "Remove poverty"] slogan was coined on the eve of the parliamentary general election last year, Mrs Gandhi has been telling her colleagues in the government, the party officials and the rank and file . . . that she was no slave to doctrinaire politics and that she would work for the attainment of the socialist goal in her pragmatic way,' wrote a staff correspondent of the *Overseas Hindustan Times* in early June of 1972.

In fact, at a private meeting of the Congress members of Parliament in Delhi, in June 1972, she went so far as to snub the radicals – her faithful allies in her battle with conservative party bosses – merely because they had asked for a more faithful implementation of the party's promises as outlined in the election manifestos, particularly on the issue of ceiling on agricultural land and urban property, than had been conceded by the party's High Command and Congress governments in various State capitals. 'Do these people want another split in the party?' she was reported to have asked rhetorically. 'Opposition within the party . . . cannot exceed the limits of our aims and objectives.'[20]

Some weeks later, a group of right-of-centre Congress MPs were encouraged to constitute themselves as the Nehru Study Forum to act, primarily, as a counterpoint to the left-of-centre Congress Forum for Socialist Action. A conflict, in the form of heated public exchanges, between the two Forums seemed inevitable. And when this happened, Indira Gandhi seized on the opportunity, and asked (in April 1973) that *both* Forums be disbanded; and they were. With the dissolution of the Congress Forum for Socialist Action, first established in 1966, Indira Gandhi was relieved of any pressure that could be applied on her by the left wing of the party. 'She [Indira Gandhi] need no longer feel constrained to chirp about the virtues of socialism in season and out of season,' wrote a special correspondent of the *Economic and Political Weekly*, 'that matter could [now] be postponed till the next election.'[21]

So, by the spring of 1973, the Congress Party's composition was back to where it had stood four years before, when the first sign of a rift within the party hierarchy was discerned, with the marginal difference of the loss of some leaders, only two of whom – Morarji Desai and K. Kamraj Nadar – had any popular support in the State of their origin. Hence, for all practical purposes, the Congress Party at present led by Indira Gandhi is to be considered as the original party, which has had an unbroken spell of power at the Centre since 1947, and which is therefore to be held responsible for the achievements and failures of the Indian government since then.

THE CONGRESS GOVERNMENT: THE UNFULFILLED PLANS

There is a backlog of 84 million houses to be built in India. Every
year 2 million more are needed. The country builds only 300,000.
Philip Knightley, a British journalist[1]

Mrs Gandhi said that the progress in living standards could be
seen on the faces of the people, even in remote areas. But this
progress has hardly been impressive as indicated by the
government's own statistics.
A Special Correspondent of the *Amrita Bazar Patrika*[2]

Average annual growth [in India] in the 1950s was only 3·8 per
cent and in the 1960s 3·7 per cent. Meanwhile the population
has been growing over 2 per cent a year. Even the apparent small
increase [average 1·3 per cent] in income per head was largely
accounted for by foreign assistance.
Philip Bowring and Lawrence Lifschultz in the
Far Eastern Economic Review[3]

India's economic progress since independence has been negligible;
and this was conceded by none other than Mohan Dharia, junior
Minister of Planning in the Central government. 'Between 40 per cent
and a half of all Indian citizens are living in conditions of abject poverty,'
he told Parliament in August 1972. 'This number is as large [today] as
it was two decades ago.'[4] This was all the more ironic, because, almost
exactly twenty-five years ago, on the eve of independence, Prime
Minister Nehru had, in a radio broadcast to the nation, deplored the
fact that 'our people' lacked food and clothing and 'other necessaries',
and were caught in 'a spiral of inflation and rising prices', and had then
gone on to promise to 'plan wisely so that the burden on the masses may
grow less and their standards of living go up'.[5] The country was given a
taste of 'planning wisely' when the First Five Year Plan was inaugurated
in 1952.

This, and the subsequent two Plans, contained the following major
objectives: to have all children of school-going age in school by 1965;

to lower the annual birth rate from 4·2 per cent (in 1961) to 3·2 per cent (in 1974); to reduce unemployment in both rural and urban areas; to accelerate industrialization so as to lower the proportion of agricultural workers to total workers from 70 per cent (in 1950–1) to 60 (in 1975–6); to lessen disparities and imbalances between different regions of the country; to reduce concentration of economic power and inequalities in personal income and wealth; and to end dependence on foreign aid by 1965–6, mainly by becoming self-sufficient in foodgrains and having a developed capital goods industry. The overall economic aim of the Plans was to double the per capita income, preferably by 1970–1, but certainly by not later than 1977–8 – that is, to achieve an annual increase in income of $3\frac{1}{2}$ to 4 per cent for the next twenty to twenty-five years.

As yet *none* of these objectives has been attained. Even such a modest target as having all school-age children at school remains unachieved. There was some progress between 1950 and 1965, when the percentage of such children went up from 42·6 to 76·6; but since then there has been no increase. But the actual significance of this fact is much less than what the figures convey, because (a) two-fifths of these children drop out after the first year and can be termed 'literate' only in a technical sense of the word, and (b) all such statistics, based on information supplied by government-paid employees – in this case teachers and headmasters – are invariably inflated.

A typical situation in primary schools was described by Chris Mullin, a British volunteer who worked in rural areas near Madurai, in Tamil Nadu, thus:

> A primary school had been built in 1957, and two teachers came daily from Madurai. When I asked the president [of the local panchayat] how many children attended the school he told me, 'Eighty or ninety' . . . One day I paid an unannounced visit to the school and counted only thirty-eight pupils and one teacher. There are believed to be about a hundred children of primary school age in Kamatchi [village].[6]

No wonder then that, in the column headed 'Percentage of children in primary schools, 1968–69', *Statistical Outline of India, 1972–73* states the figure of 105 for Tamil Nadu: that is, more children were registered in primary schools of Tamil Nadu than actually existed![7]

Although the national literacy rate has gone up modestly – from 18 per cent in 1947 to 30 per cent in 1971 – the situation, in absolute terms, has grown *worse*. In 1951, there were 298 million illiterates in the country; twenty years later their number had grown to 386 million! This was because of the staggering increase in population which was allowed to happen due to the government's failure to institute an effective birth control programme in time.

All through the 1950s the Congress administration took no action in this field, and the annual birth rate soared to 4·2 per cent. In the Third Five Year Plan (1961–6), it managed to spend only one-sixth of the sum budgeted for population control programmes. A severe food shortage in the country, in 1966, highlighted the problem of fast-rising population, and forced the government to treat it with some urgency. It fixed the target of reducing the annual birth rate to 3·2 per cent by 1974, and undertook effective means to achieve it. By the end of 1971, it claimed to have brought the birth rate down to 3·7 per cent, and established enough family planning centres and sub-centres to serve half the national population. Major stress has been on sterilization; and it was claimed that, by the end of 1972, some 12·5 million men and women had been sterilized.[8] The next most popular method has been the use of the intra-uterine contraceptive device; and, by 1972, nearly 4·5 million women were claimed to have been fitted with the device. All told, these methods are supposed to have covered more than one-eighth of all couples in the reproductive age group (i.e. with the wife in the 15–44 age bracket) in the country.

However, once again, these figures, based on information given by government employees, must be treated sceptically. A recent survey conducted in a district, where many of the men had undergone a vasectomy operation, often under the inducement of cash payment (of Rs 80/£4) or a cheap transistor radio, revealed that 35 per cent of those sterilized had wives aged 45 or above, 20 per cent were widowers or separated, and another 6 per cent were unmarried.[9] In other words, 61 per cent of the men who had been sterilized did *not* belong to 'the couples in the reproductive age group'.

Meanwhile, the consequences of the past governmental neglect in this area, and the general failure of the Congress administration's economic policies are to be seen in the rapidly rising unemployment. Between 1956 and 1974 (the years which marked, respectively, the beginning of the Second and Fifth Five Year Plans), the backlog of unemployed went up from 5.3 million to over 15 million. The number of *registered* unemployed (only a fraction of the total) jumped from 335,000 in 1951 to 9,315,000 in 1975, a twenty-eight-fold increase in twenty-four years![10] (In contrast, the employment exchanges could hardly offer 614,000 jobs.) Nearly half of the registered unemployed had some educational qualification, including a university degree. Often those with higher education become so desperate that they end up applying for any and every job. When, for example, ten posts of peons, carrying a monthly salary of Rs 190 (£9·50), were advertised by Kerala University, Trivandrum, in September 1971, over 10,000 persons, including many university graduates, applied. 'Recently, the [Tamil Nadu] Electricity Board advertised for 600 clerical posts; and there were 25,000 applications,' reported a correspondent of the

Overseas Hindustan Times. 'There were 16,000 jobless engineers and diploma-holders registered with employment exchanges at the end of March this year [1972].'[11] They were part of the national pool of over 80,000 unemployed degree- and diploma-holding engineers. This was the situation in a country where the government had dedicated itself to rapid industrialization, through economic planning, more than a generation ago!

No wonder then that only negligible progress had been made in lessening the dependence of the population on agriculture as a means of livelihood. The 1950s witnessed no change in the pattern of employment, and the 1960s very little: the proportion of agricultural workers to total workforce declined by a mere 1 per cent, from 69·5 per cent to 68·6.[12] Of this, only 0·4 per cent were absorbed into industry.[13]

Another major aim of planning – reducing disparities and imbalances between different regions – remains unattained. If anything, regional disparities have grown wider. In general, the eastern and north-eastern States (i.e. Bihar, Orissa, West Bengal, Assam, and the small border States and sub-States), with about a third of the national population, have lagged behind the rest of the country, especially its north-western region. While the Haryana government, for instance, could claim in 1971 to have electrified all its villages, only 9 per cent of Bihar's villages had been electrified. Similarly, Punjab's administration could by then claim to have provided 70 per cent of the State's cultivated land with irrigation facilities, whereas West Bengal's government could say so for only 22 per cent of the land. (The national figure then was 23·3 per cent.) The average wheat production in the Punjab–Haryana area was at least twice as high as in Bihar. 'Those areas [of the country] . . . which, by chance or otherwise, have moved into a regime of high rates of growth, continue to maintain such high rates of growth, and those parts which have fallen behind continue to be afflicted by doggedly low rates of growth,' states AM, an Indian journalist. 'Even in these States [of low economic growth] the top 10 per cent of the population have, duly, made their pile and enjoyed a fantastic rise in real incomes and standard of living in the course of these twenty-five years (of independence).'[14]

What is worse is that further enrichment of the already rich has occurred at the cost of the poor. Between 1953 and 1961, for instance, the share of the top tenth of the population in the national income rose from 28 per cent to 37 per cent, whereas that of the bottom two-fifths declined from 20 per cent to 15 per cent;[15] and the trend has continued. 'Taking a conservative estimate of Rs 15 [75p] per capita per month [at 1960–1 prices] as the minimum level of living in the Indian rural area, a recent survey has shown . . . [that] the percentage of the population below the minimum level in rural India went up from 38 in 1960–1 to 53 in 1967–8, thus registering a rise of about 40 per cent in less than a decade,' notes Paresh Chattopadhyaya, an Indian academic. During the same period, the corresponding percentage in urban India rose from 32 to 41.[16]

The growing impoverishment of the Indian masses can be gauged by the simple statistics that per capita *availability* of foodgrains declined from 16·1 ounces (457 grams) per day, in 1954,[17] to 14·7 ounces (417 grams) in 1973, and that of cloth from 14·4 metres to 12·1.[18] These figures presume equal and uniform distribution of food and clothing, which is hardly the case. 'The top 5 per cent appear to be responsible for as much as 22 per cent of the national income which is slightly higher than [that] received by fully one-half of the population,' stated S. Patel, an Indian economist, in 1971.[19] This situation exists in an economy which has, over the period 1951–71, registered an average annual growth of mere 1.3 per cent, far below the target of 3·5 to 4 per cent visualized by the planners in 1951, and their successors.

Foreign aid is another area where the intention of the successive Plans has not been realized. When foreign aid was first sought and received, it was stated categorically, by the Congress administration, that it was to be a temporary measure, since the general aim was to reach the point of economic 'take-off' by the mid-1960s. Actual events have been to the contrary. Foreign aid financed 8 per cent of the total government investment in development, during the First Five Year Plan, 25.2 per cent during the Second, and 30·5 per cent of the Third![20] In 1951, at the beginning of the First Plan, external aid formed no more than one-third of 1 per cent of the total national income, whereas in 1967–8, it constituted 4 per cent, a twelve-fold increase. 'Even as we talk more and more about self-reliance [and reduction in foreign aid] . . . we are now pleading for aid in local currency to the [maximum] possible extent,' noted the *Economic and Political Weekly* in 1972. 'Increasingly, also, aid is not being related to development or growth; it is emerging as a means of keeping us where we are.'[21] The growing reluctance of foreign countries to lend money to India in their own currencies is understandable. After all, India had allowed its foreign debts to increase 217-fold in twenty-one years, from Rs 32 crores (£16 million) in 1950–1 to Rs 6,954 crores (£3,477 million) in 1971–2![22]

One of the factors causing this deterioration has been the huge import bill for food that the country keeps on paying because of its continued insufficiency in it. Import of food first began in 1948 when, following partition, India lost large areas with food surpluses to West Pakistan, and communal disturbances and the uprooting of millions of people caused a loss of production in India's own fertile north-western region. Since then, notwithstanding periodic assertions by the Congress ministers that self-sufficiency is around the corner, imports of food-grains have been consistently on the rise, as the following quinquennial figures in million tonnes, from 1951 to 1971, show: 12·1, 19·13, 25·35, and 31·44. (A sharp decline in food imports – to below the half a million tonne mark – in 1972 was followed by import of 3·62 million tonnes in 1973, and over 5·5 million in 1974.)[23] Imports during the period of 1966–71 would have been even higher, had not the 'green revolution' made some impact on production at home, which, despite a massive investment of Rs 3,336 crores (£1,668 million) in community development programmes, land reclamation, and irrigation projects during the first three Plans, had, by 1960–4, reached a plateau of 80–82 million tonnes a year.

The 'green revolution' was launched in 1965 when the extension of the recently instituted Intensive Agricultural Area Programme – consisting of providing chemical fertilizers, credit, price incentives, marketing facilities, and technical advice – from the original 15 districts to 114 coincided with the arrival, from abroad, of the 'high yielding varieties' of seeds for wheat and rice. The subsequent increase in the yield of these foodgrains encouraged more and more agriculturists to adopt the new techniques. The area under 'miracle' seeds went up from 4·67 million acres in 1966–7 to 34·6 million in 1970–1, and covered about a third of the total wheat-growing land and one-seventh of the rice-growing land. As a result of increase in both the acreage under wheat cultivation, and productivity of land due to the new techniques, the production of wheat doubled during these four years.

Most of this occurred in Punjab and Haryana, since these States have a large number of peasant proprietors, and since the State governments had invested heavily in building up an infrastructure of irrigation systems (and irrigation is the first prerequisite for the new techniques to be effective), roads, and electricity, and supported it with a reasonably efficient system of credit and distribution of new seeds, chemical fertilizers, farming equipment, etc. During the 1960s, in the Ludhiana district of Punjab, for instance, the land under irrigation increased from 45 per cent of the total to 70 per cent, the consumption of fertilizer from 18 lb. per acre to 242 lb., the wheat acreage under new seed from 1 per cent of the total to 90 per cent; and the average yield of wheat per acre from 1,385 lb. to 3,280 lb.[24]

However, Ludhiana, where four-fifths of the owner-cultivators operate plots of *more* than 10 acres, is far from typical, even in the prosperous Punjab. In the large wheat-growing States of Uttar Pradesh and Bihar, four-fifths of all cultivating households operate farms of *less* than 8 acres,[25] and thus lack the resources needed to have a reliable source of irrigation, often a deep tube well, which is the key to increased production.

In any case, nationally, rice cultivation, which occupies 92 million acres (versus wheat's 37 million acres), is the more important. The average landholding in the rice belt is much smaller than it is in the wheat zone, and consequently the proportion of landowners, who lack the resources needed to utilize the new technology, is much higher. (The average landholding in the rice-growing districts of West God-avary, Andhra Pradesh, for example, is 1·4 acres.)[26] Overall, states Francine R. Frankel, an American expert on Indian agriculture, farmers with 20 acres or more in the rice belt have made 'the greatest absolute and relative gains' by mechanizing farm operations and diversi-fying their cropping pattern, and those with 5 to 10 acres have ex-perienced 'some improvement in net income' while the vast majority – 'probably as many as 75 per cent to 80 per cent' – have suffered a 'relative decline in their economic position'.[27] In other words, new technology and fresh capital are being injected into that segment of agriculture which is owned mainly by the rich farmers – a process that suits both them and the Congress, which relies heavily on their support for its sustenance, but which must also, for electoral reasons, commit itself periodically to the idea and programme of land distribution and 'land reform'.

8

AGRARIAN RELATIONS: THE HALF-HEARTED REFORM

All our political problems and discussions are but a background to
the outstanding and overwhelming problem of India – the land
problem.

Jawaharlal Nehru in 1933[1]

The political power structure being what it is, there is no basis at
all for hoping that a radical measure on the lines of the Japanese
land reforms during American occupation after the Second World
War will be adopted in India.

M. S. Appu, Central Land Reforms Commissioner,
in 1971[2]

The imposition of ceiling on agricultural holdings in India is a
case of inchoate policy, imperfect legislation, and inefficient
implementation.

A report to the Central Land Reforms Committee
by the Union Ministry of Agriculture[3]

It is agriculture which contributes the single largest share of the national
wealth, and provides employment to most of the working people. And
it is in this field, more than any other, that the average citizen comes
into direct contact with the government. This has been so for many
centuries past; but the nature of this contact has undergone a considerable change. In the early days of the recorded Indian history,
contact between the cultivator and the king, who collected taxes, was
simple and direct. This continued until the twelfth century when
Muslim tribes from Central Asia began to colonize the sub-continent.
Initially, they often chose to impose tribute upon the conquered Hindu
king, thus reducing him to the status of a tributary chief, who acted as
an intermediary between the peasant and the supreme Muslim ruler.
Later, when they chose to govern most of the conquered areas directly,
they appointed revenue contractors and revenue farmers (called zamindars), and assigned large estates to their Court nobles and administrators
(called *jagirdars*), and thus created a whole new class of intermediaries,

whom they paid either a certain percentage of the land taxes collected or gave, outright, tax-free land to cultivate.

The complex relationship that evolved between the cultivators and the government over the centuries was not rationalized until the time of Emperor Akbar of the Moghul dynasty. During his reign, from 1556 to 1605, proper land records were compiled; and the farmers were invested with ownership rights of land and, simultaneously, made responsible for the payment of land tax to the government either directly or through the traditional village headman or the officially appointed zamindar, and the role of the intermediaries was correspondingly reduced. But the gains made by the peasants were lost considerably when, with the decline of the Moghul rule during the ˙mid-eighteenth century, the authority of the state weakened, and the cultivators came to rely more and more on the intermediaries. Their position worsened when the British East India Company, which succeeded the Moghuls and which was interested in collecting the largest amount of tax in the shortest period of time, started auctioning the zamindari rights of villages to the highest bidder every five years. This caused rack-renting of the cultivators by the zamindars and led to a severe famine condition and minor peasant rebellions in the 1770s.

Lord Cornwallis – the British administrator from 1786 to 1792, and again from 1797 to 1805 – stopped the practice of periodic auctioning and introduced a system of permanently settled estates with land revenue, fixed in perpetuity, to be paid by the zamindars. ˙He applied the new system to all of Bengal Presidency (which then included Bengal, Bihar, and Orissa), the northern part of Andhra, and most of present-day Uttar Pradesh. It was hoped that this would win the British administration loyalty of the zamindar class; and it did. But the other hope, that this would encourage the zamindars to give security of tenure to their cultivators, did not materialize. In fact, the zamindars, now assured of their property rights in perpetuity, exacted extra sums from their tenants and ejected them when others offered a higher rent. Also, permanent security encouraged many of them to migrate to towns and cities, and leave the mundane affairs of rent collection and administration to agents and sub-agents. In due course, a whole chain of intermediaries grew; and the gap between the rent collected from the cultivators and the revenue paid by the zamindars to the government widened enormously.

The British administration realized this as well as the disadvantage of being frozen out (due to the terms of the Permanent Settlement) of the increase in prices of both land and agricultural commodities that had occurred since the late 1790s. So, the Permanent Settlement system was discarded in favour of ryotwari – i.e. proprietary rights were given to the ryot,[4] the cultivator – in those areas that fell into British hands later – during the first half of the nineteenth century – namely, the central and southern parts of Madras Presidency, all of Bombay Presidency, Central Provinces, East Punjab, and Assam. In short, by the mid-nineteenth century, British India had two systems of land ownership: zamindari, a caricature of English landlordism; and ryotwari, a caricature of French peasant proprietorship. (In the 'native' states, ryotwari co-existed with *jagirdari*.)

At the turn of the twentieth century, the zamindari system covered well over half of the cultivated land in India; and this made the zamindars, forming only 2 per cent of the population, the most powerful element in society. In general, they were in sympathy with the Congress, since its aim then was to win concessions from the British government through appeals, and not confrontation. But as the party became progressively nationalist, and thus anti-imperialist, particularly after the Jallianwalla Bagh massacre in Amritsar, in 1919 (when hundreds of unarmed Indians were killed or injured), zamindars began to lose interest in it.

On its part, the Congress, even at its most radical, was benignly neutral towards zamindars. The peasant agitations against special imposts or high land revenue, led by Gandhi and Patel, in 1917 and after, were, by virtue of being in ryotwari areas (such as Gujarat) or on British-owned plantations (such as in north Bihar), directed either against the British government or capital. 'So long as peasant interests were adversely and directly affected by [the British] government, the Congress . . . defended peasant interests with vigour,' states Walter Hauser, an American historian. 'But where peasant interests were circumscribed by [the indigenous] landed interests, the Congress under Gandhi counselled mutual trust and understanding.'[5]

The economic programme that the Congress adopted in 1931 reflected this attitude. It recommended nothing more than lowering of rents, limiting the right of zamindars to evict their tenants, and extending the status of permanent tenants to a larger segment of them than had been the case hitherto. There was nothing novel or radical about this. Indeed, having realized that rack-renting by zamindars was, in the final analysis, detrimental to the economic and political fibre of the State, the British government itself had, starting in 1885, periodically passed legislation to safeguard the interests of the tenants, such as stipulating that zamindars and tenants exchange documents stating 'reasonable' rent to be paid in cash and/or kind, and authorizing a tenant to take his zamindar to court if the latter tried to exact an excessive rent from him. (What the government had *not* done was to set up an effective enforcement machinery.)

It was not until 1936 that, under pressure from its radical wing, the party's plenary session condemned the 'antiquated and repressive land tenure and revenue system' as a major cause of poverty among the peasants, and called for a 'thorough change of the land systems'. (There was as yet no clear-cut demand for abolition of zamindari.) But a year later, when the party won power in eight out of eleven provinces of British India, not all its ministries passed laws in line with the mild 1931 resolution, much less undertook a 'thorough change of land systems'. Even where legislation was passed to give, say, security to tenants, some provisions for eviction were allowed. These were enough to enable the zamindars to do, more or less, what they wished. In short, as late as the end of the 1930s, no direct conflict between the zamindars and the Congress had developed.

However, the situation changed abruptly when the Second World War broke out in 1939 and the colonial administration joined the Allies without consulting the Congress, or any other Indian leaders. In protest, the Congress ministries resigned *en bloc*; and later, in 1942, the party, led by Gandhi, launched a countrywide 'Quit India' movement against the British. The zamindars, who had all along been the main props of the colonial regime in the countryside, now lined up behind the government and the War effort, and against the nationalist movement.

The Congress retaliated in kind. 'The reform of the land system, which is so urgently needed in India, involves the removal of intermediaries between the peasant and the state,' said its manifesto for the election of 1945–6. 'The rights of such intermediaries should therefore be acquired on payment of suitable compensation.'[6] The Congress Economic Committee, presided over by Nehru, also made similar recommendations in 1948.

At that time, zamindars owned 55 to 60 per cent of all cultivable land in the country; and rack-renting was so severe that the ratio of the land revenue paid by them to the government to the rents received by them from the tenants, varied between 1:7 as in Bihar,[7] and 1:23 as in (pre-partition) Bengal,[8] and Uttar Pradesh.[9] A substantial part of Uttar Pradesh was then under the land system of *taluqdari*, a particularly oppressive variation of zamindari, which enabled the big zamindar to become a petty local chief, at once 'a tax collector, policeman, judge, and moneylender',[10] and control the political life of the area through his revenue agents, some of them being his tenants, and others directly dependent on him.

No wonder then that Uttar Pradesh was the first State to abolish zamindari. 'All estates situated in the Uttar Pradesh ... shall stand transferred to and to vest ... in the State free from all encumbrances,' declared the Uttar Pradesh Zamindari Abolition and Land Reform Act of 1950. Actual vesting occurred on 1 July 1952. That is, all the rights, titles, and interests of the intermediaries (between the cultivator and the government) were passed on to the government except in the case of groves and 'self-cultivated' land. As it happened, 94 per cent of all zamindars managed to show themselves to be owners of groves and/or 'self-cultivated' land,[11] and contrived to retain almost 7 million acres of the 33 million acres of land that they possessed before the law became operational.[12] Likewise, in Rajasthan, a State composed almost entirely of former princely states, following the enforcement of the Rajasthan Land Reform and the Resumption of Jagir Act (of 1952), in 1954, a little over 8,000 *jagirdars*, owning nearly 17,000 villages, managed to retain a third of the original 15 million acres of arable land they owned.[13] As for the land taken over by the government, the zamindars and *jagirdars* in various States were awarded compensation, in cash and government debentures or bonds, to the tune of Rs 600 crores (£300 million).[14]

Consider the case of zamindar X in Uttar Pradesh who had, say, 5,000 acres of land, divided up in 500 plots, with each plot leased to a tenant for cultivation. He lived in a city where, through his agents and sub-agents, he received rents from tenants, a small fraction of which sufficed to pay the land revenue. When, in 1937, the newly installed Congress ministry showed mildly pro-tenant bias, he ejected fifty of them and took over their 500 acres of land for 'self-cultivation', a perfectly legal step, since the new law did not deprive him of the right to 'resume' a certain portion of his land for self-cultivation. Later, in 1948, when the Zamindari Abolition Bill was first published, he evicted more tenants and managed, through his influence with the local land revenue officials, to show that, say, another 500 acres had all along been 'self-cultivated'. So, on 1 July 1952, he retained the actual possession of the 1,000 'self-cultivated' acres, and received compensation for 4,000 acres, and thus managed to sabotage considerably the original intent of the Act.

A similar situation has prevailed in the sphere of tenancy legislation, which the Congress ministries instituted to regulate land rent, and to confer on tenants security of tenure and, finally, ownership rights. For this, either already existing laws were amended or new ones passed. The Congress government in Uttar Pradesh, for instance, issued an ordinance in 1948 nullifying those provisions of the law (that it had itself passed in 1937) which allowed the landlords to evict their tenants. The law enacted in Karnataka, in 1952, stipulated that a tenancy once begun could not be terminated until the end of five years, and that those who had cultivated a particular plot of land for twelve consecutive years were to be treated as 'protected' tenants with security of tenure and a right to pass on the lease to their successors. The law concerning sharecroppers/tenants-at-will in West Bengal stated that no sharecropper could be evicted, and that the share paid to the landowner as rent was not to exceed 25 per cent of the produce. Similarly, the Adihar Protection and Regulation Act of 1948 in Assam fixed the landowner's rent at no more than 20 per cent of the produce. But to be able to enjoy these rights, a tenant must be 'registered' as such. And since registration is done by the land revenue official of the village, who is almost invariably friendly with local landlords and who does not have to give reasons for refusing a tenant's application for registration, most tenants are, for all practical purposes, barred from becoming 'registered'.

'The position regarding the record of tenancies . . . is not satisfactory anywhere in the country,' states the Planning Commission's Review of Land Reform in 1972, 'and no record exists in some areas.'[15] Among the areas lacking a record of tenancies is the Andhra region of Andhra Pradesh; and the bureaucratic machinery is so slow that – as a correspondent of *Link* pointed out – it would take five years to compile a record of rights, and meanwhile, 'most of the tenants may be evicted'.[16] This is by no means a false alarm. Between 1961 and 1971, the process of evictions, disguised as 'voluntary surrenders' by tenants, had reduced the number of landholding cultivators in the State by 1·56 million and raised the figure of landless labourers by 1·43 million.[17] As regards those who are still tenants, in the country, 82 per cent do *not* have fixity of tenure – so said a recent report by the Central government's Home Ministry![18]

Another aspect of land reform legislation has been the concept of maximum size of present landholdings and future acquisitions. The Uttar Pradesh Zamindari Abolition Act of 1950, for example, limited future purchases of land to a maximum of 30 acres. This policy of gradual reduction in disparities in landownership was considered by the Congress leaders to be a useful electoral tactic as well as an antidote to the radical Communist movement in the Telangana region in the south, which had successfully accomplished the task of redistribution of land in a short span of four years (1946–50) through militant action. Later, this was backed by the Planning Commission, appointed in 1951, on purely utilitarian grounds. Aware of the damage done to agriculture, due to the neglect of land and irrigation facilities by the zamindars and *jagirdars* of the past, the predominantly technocrat members of the Planning Commission recommended a wider ownership of land as a means of boosting production. These factors, and the increasing respectability of the slogan (if not the content) of the 'socialistic pattern of society', first raised by Nehru in early 1955, made an increasing number of State administrations consider imposing a ceiling on landholdings. The actual progress, however, was slow. The case of Rajasthan is illustrative.

The Congress government of Rajasthan appointed a committee, in November 1953, to study the idea of fixing a ceiling on landholdings. This committee took four years to submit a report! It was another two years before the legislative assembly passed the appropriate Bill and fixed a limit of 30 standard acres – a standard acre being an acre of land of excellent quality with perennial irrigation facilities and at least two crops a year. By the time the Act received the Union President's assent, it was March 1960. But nothing happened then, because the date and manner of the enforcement of the Act had to be decided by the State government later. And it was another three and a half *years* before the Congress ministry got around to framing draft rules and having them discussed by the legislative assembly. Then, just before the Act was to have become operational on 15 December 1963, some landlords challenged it in court. Another year went by before the Supreme Court finally dismissed the landlords' case. The State government then announced 1 April to be the date of enforcement only to postpone it, inexplicably, to 1 October. This was postponed again in order to – as the government statement put it – 'meet the demand of military personnel on the Indo-Pak border' (in the brief two-week-long war between India and Pakistan towards the end of September 1965). At this point, large landholders began to argue that if the Act were to be enforced in its original form, those (small) peasants who had bought land from them since 1963 would be dispossessed. So, the enforcement of the Act was once again postponed!

Following the 1967 election, when the Congress scraped back to power by a majority of one, the government announced that it would start taking over land above 90 standard acres, but did not do so. It was only when the landless and land-poor peasants in northern Rajasthan, led by the CPI(M), launched an agitation for land, that the government finally decided to act. It agreed to remove certain exemptions to the ceiling, granted in the original Act, but later it tied this amendment to another which legalized all the *malafide* transfers that had taken place until 31 December 1969.[19] This reduced the expected surplus land from 2·3 million acres to 1 million.

The Congress ministries in other States have been equally tardy in passing and executing a land ceiling law. In Andhra Pradesh, for example, the Congress government issued an ordinance, in September 1957, which required all landowners with 20 acres of land to notify the government (at leisure, since no time limit was specified); but the actual Bill on land ceiling was not published until the following July. Then two years were spent in resolving two fairly simple points: (a) should an individual be used as a unit for fixing a ceiling, or a family; and (b) should the area of a landholding, or income from it, be used as a yardstick for specifying a ceiling. After the Bill was drafted and passed by the State assembly, the Union President took seven months to sign it. Meanwhile, large landowners went about partitioning their property and 'transferring' it to their relatives and friends. As a result of these malpractices, and excessively high ceilings (from 27 to 324 acres, depending on the quality of land), only 519 acres, out of a total of over 28,000,000 acres of arable land, became available to the government as surplus land! In Bihar, the appropriate legislation openly allowed a landowner to transfer his land a year *after* the enforcement of the Act to 'his son, or daughter, or to such person or persons who would have inherited such land or would have been entitled to a share therein had the landlord died intestate'. No wonder then that the law yielded only 9,000 acres of surplus land out of a total arable land of 29,000,000 acres.[20] And in Assam the ceiling Act, passed in 1958, provided for the transfer of surplus land to anybody the landowner wished until April 1970.

The land ceiling law continues to be violated widely, as the reports on the villages in West Bengal, Bihar, and Tamil Nadu, in Chapter one, amply indicate.[21] 'It is possible for an individual in the delta area [of Andhra Pradesh] to control several hundred acres of land,' notes Myron Weiner.[22] And, a decade after the passing of the ceiling Act, in Bihar, which specifies a limit of 20 to 60 acres of land per member in a 'joint' family, there existed hundreds of landlords with 500 acres or more.

Some landlords even managed to improve their economic condition, as a result of these laws, by cheating the public exchequer. 'There are cases where landlords have realized lakhs of rupees as compensation from the government without losing an inch of land from the hundreds of acres they own,' reported a correspondent of the *Statesman*.

> A typical case, recently unearthed, relates to a zamindar, formerly a minister who, jointly with his brother, owned 1,000 acres before the [West Bengal Land Reform] Act came into effect in April 1955. Apparently he had come to know well in advance that the legislation would be introduced; the joint property was then transferred under the ryotwari arrangement to five sons of one of the brothers who, in turn, distributed part of their land among their wives and children as sub-ryots. Among the *benamdars* [i.e. *malafide* owners] were also servants of the family and others. Since such distribution of the land covered less than half of the total holding, 534 acres of land were declared to be fisheries (which were exempted from the application of ceiling) although the land was being used for farming. When the Act came into force, both the ryots and sub-ryots (who were mostly members of the joint family) started paying land revenue directly to the government. As the original owners of the land – the two brothers and the ryots [i.e. five sons of one brother] – lost the rent they used to get, they were entitled to compensation from the government. They received Rs 700,000 [£35,000] as compensation, while retaining within the family's possession whatever land they owned originally.[23]

Often the law on land ceiling was so shot with loopholes that a rich landlord did not have to be ingenious to maintain control of his original land. In Madhya Pradesh, for instance, the law not only exempted 'religious institutes, cow-breeding centres, schools and charitable institutes, sugar factories, and land given to commercial concerns' from the provisions of the Act, but also 'efficiently managed farms and mechanized farms'. The list of exemptions from the ceiling, in Punjab, included 'specialized farms engaged in "cattle breeding, dairying or wool raising", efficiently managed farms, and land belonging to registered societies'. Not surprisingly, the number of (often bogus) co-operative societies in the State shot up after the enactment of this law.

In Uttar Pradesh, the land ceiling Act came into effect (in 1960) about the same time as the Co-operative Farm Act did. This enabled the big landlords to redesignate their holdings as co-operative farms, appoint themselves as managers, and dispose of the profits any way they liked.[24] This was all the more ironic because the concept of 'joint co-operative farming' had been inspired by Nehru's vision of a 'socialistic pattern of society', and the recommendation contained in the famous Nagpur Resolution of the Congress session in 1959 that the surplus land yielded by the land ceiling law be entrusted to the panchayats 'for getting it cultivated by co-operatives of landless labourers'.

A similar situation exists in the area of co-operatives for credit and marketing, the establishment of which was encouraged by the State governments after the Nagpur Resolution of 1959. These co-operatives have rendered practically no help to small farmers – i.e. those cultivating less than 5 acres of land – who constitute two-thirds of all rural households, simply because they cannot offer, to quote the words of the National Commission on Agriculture, 'security in the shape of tangible assets'.[25] On the other hand, these co-operatives have proved extremely beneficial to the top 6·8 per cent of the rural families, who own as much as 46 per cent of the total land in the country, especially when, following the inauguration of the Intensive Agricultural Development Programme in 1965, the State governments used them as the main channel for providing finance for new techniques and farming equipment – a development which caused the number of small diesel engines, used for irrigation water pumps, to increase from 449,000 to 1,640,000 during the period of 1965–70, the number of tractors from 54,000 to over 100,000, and the consumption of chemical fertilizers from 697,000 tonnes to 1,059,000 tonnes. 'Rather interesting is an official assessment (not released to the public) which candidly admits that co-operation is an activity of, for and by the richer sections of the agriculturalists of the State [of Maharashtra],' writes Saral Patra, an Indian journalist.[26]

'Thus the overall assessment has to be that programmes of land reform adopted since Independence have failed to bring about the required changes in the agrarian structure,' states the Review of Land Reform by the Planning Commission in 1972.[27] What are the reasons for this failure? 'The lack of political will is mainly responsible for [this],' says the Planning Commission's Review.

In most parts of the country they [i.e. the potential beneficiaries of land reform] are passive, inarticulate, and unorganized. . . .
Furthermore . . . the general attitude of the administration has been

one of apathy in the matter of implementing measures of land reform. As a matter of fact, in India the bureaucracy is, by and large, a part of the powerful anti-land reform bloc. The lower echelons of the [land] revenue department [charged with the implementation of land reform laws] are often . . . under the sway of substantial owners who have a vested interest in evading the enacted laws.[28]

The 'lack of political will' means quite simply lack of will on the part of the Congress, its continued inability to effect land reform. This is not surprising because the party is dominated by landed interests, particularly at the State level, where laws on land relations are designed and implemented. 'The State Congress consists mainly of big and middle peasants, and the membership of the legislative party overwhelmingly represents the big "bagaitdars", i.e. the irrigationwallas,' notes the Maharashtra correspondent of the *Economic and Political Weekly*.[29] This is the case elsewhere as well. An exhaustive study of the Congress party in Kaira district, Gujarat, and Ramdrug sub-district, Karnataka, in the mid-1960s, led Myron Weiner to conclude that the party recruits its active members and leaders mainly from among 'the 5 per cent of the landowning population with more than 30 acres', and that 'the Congress party activists are representatives of the upper strata of agriculturists . . . not of the landless tenants and farm labourers'.[30]

It is apparent that the more numerous but 'passive, inarticulate, and unorganized' landless and land-poor peasants need to be forged into a militant peasant organization if the deeply entrenched power of the landlords, rich peasants, and bureaucracy is to be neutralized and a genuine land reform accomplished; and that the Congress is not the party to foster such an organization. As stated earlier, any peasant agitations that the party ever led during the pre-independence days were directed against British capital or government, *not* the Indian landed interests;[31] and these were at best sporadic exercises.

It was the Socialists and Communists, then functioning within the Congress, who took a sustained interest in the condition of the Indian peasantry, a condition that worsened considerably when the economic depression of 1929 caused a severe drop in the prices of such agricultural commodities as wheat, jute, cotton, etc. By the mid-1930s, enough local peasant organizations had grown up in the country to necessitate the formation, in 1936, of the All India Kisan (i.e. peasant) Congress, an event in which leading Socialists and Communists were assisted by a few radical Congressmen. The following year, the leftist leadership changed the organization's name to All India Kisan Sabha (i.e. Association), adopted a red flag as its standard, and criticized the Congress for its refusal to commit itself to a programme of zamindari abolition and the Congress ministries, then functioning in many provinces, for their ambivalent attitude towards agricultural tenants and poor peasants.

During the Second World War, and soon after, the All India Kisan Sabha, which had by then become Communist-dominated, conducted peasant agitations in many districts of Bengal, Bihar, Uttar Pradesh, Punjab, and Madras against eviction of tenants and excessively high land rents, and for the settlement of the landless on government land, illegally taken over by landlords. The most militant and successful peasant movement led by the Communists, however, occurred in the Telangana region of the old princely State of Hyderabad. It began in 1946, and by the time the Indian government took 'police action' against Hyderabad's ruler for refusing to join the Union of India voluntarily, in September 1948, it had succeeded in abolishing landlordism in one-sixth of the State's area, covering 4 million people, and distributed nearly 1 million acres to the landless and land-poor.

The takeover of the Hyderabad State administration by the Congress government in Delhi led, not to a consolidation of the gains made by the poor peasantry, but to an immediate onslaught on the Communist movement, followed a year later by an Order abolishing the *jagirdari* system in the State. And it was only in 1950, two years after Delhi's 'police action', that the government enacted the Hyderabad Tenancy and Agricultural Lands Act, which gave hereditary rights to those tenants who had been occupying land for six consecutive years. Even so, compared to Rajasthan, where *jagirdari* was not abolished until 1954, and Uttar Pradesh, where hereditary rights were not given to tenants until 1952, progress was quicker and more extensive in Hyderabad; and this happened because of a strong leftist-led peasant movement in the State. 'Indeed,' as N. K. Krishnan, a CPI leader, was to point out in 1972, 'it was the Telangana struggle which brought into sharp nation-wide focus the question of radical agrarian reform on the very morrow of Indian independence.'[32]

The 'radical agrarian reform' actually carried out boiled down to abolishing zamindari and *jagirdari* throughout the country and bringing nearly 20 million cultivators, in the country, into direct contact with the government. However, this and the Congress's commitment, in 1955, to the creation of 'socialistic pattern of society', were enough to disorientate the leftist peasant movement. The increasing conflict between the moderate and radical sections of the Communist Party, which began in the mid-1950s and continued until 1964, when the party split, further weakened the movement. This process continued until the mid-1960s, when the situation changed.

By then, the failure of land ceiling and tenancy laws had become apparent. The surplus land taken over by various State governments amounted to no more than 2 million acres – that is, a meagre 0·6 per cent of the total agricultural land – with only a third of it actually allotted to the landless.[33] The net effect of tenancy laws was to transform secure tenants into insecure, and long-term tenants into short-term. Introduction of new technology, from the mid-1960s onwards, further encouraged the landowners to take over land from their erstwhile tenants for 'self-cultivation', and thus cause a dramatic increase in the number of the landless. Between 1961 and 1971, the number of landless labourers in the country went up by 81 per cent, from 17·3 million to 31·3 million.[34] The 'green revolution' further widened the gap between the rural rich and poor. During the 1960s, the assets of small peasants in Maharashtra, for instance, declined by 10 per cent whereas those of rich farmers improved by 76 per cent.[35] 'The "green revolution" *occurring within the framework of an outmoded agrarian structure*, not only perpetuates the poverty of the rural masses but also enables the top few to gain at the expense of the many,' states P. C. Joshi, an Indian economist.[36]

In the circumstances, discontent among the rural poor started to rise; and the leftist parties, particularly the Communists, began to take a renewed interest in the land problem. The installation of non-Congress ministries in many States, in the wake of the 1967 general election, provided a congenial atmosphere for the launching of agitations by tenants for tenurial security, and by the landless workers for increased wages and allotment of surplus and other land. This was particularly so in West Bengal and Kerala, where the CPI(M) was the senior partner in the coalition government. Consequently, between early 1967 and mid-1969, West Bengal experienced 346 occupations of the (illegally retained) surplus land by the landless.[37] This State also became one of the few in the country, where members of the newly established Communist Party of India (Marxist-Leninist) – the Naxalites – undertook 'annihilation' of individual landlords and moneylenders, with a view to arousing political consciousness of the poor. In the summer of 1970, the CPI, in association with the two socialist parties, conducted a nation-wide 'land grab' movement in which nearly 150,000 landless and poor peasants participated.

The Congress government in Delhi reacted to the situation in the way it had, in 1948, to the militant Communist movement in Telangana: it followed a dual policy of repression and reform. It actively helped to curb the Naxalite movement by loaning its Central Reserve Police, and even the army, to the State governments of Andhra Pradesh, West Bengal, and Bihar. Simultaneously, it impressed upon the State administrations – both Congress and non-Congress – the need to expediate implementation of the old land reform laws and consider lowering the land ceilings further. It prepared, and widely publicized (in December 1969), a critical report entitled *Causes and Nature of Current Agrarian Tension* – an exercise which also fitted the radical image that

Indira Gandhi wished to project of herself and the party led by her, soon after the formal split in the Congress in November 1969.

A year later, Indira Gandhi was reported to have prodded a meeting of the chief ministers on the subject of land reform by reminding them that 'In recent times the growth and prosperity of nations like Mexico, Japan, and Iran had started off with land reform. . . . On the other hand, the Austro-Hungarian Empire and Tsarist Russia had failed to heed the need for land reform, and both regimes had perished.' But this was not enough to sway all those present. V. P. Naik, the then chief minister of Maharashtra, for example, argued that it was wrong to tackle the land problem 'on the basis of slogan shouting and political considerations'.[38] In the end, it was decided that 'all aspects' of the proposition regarding new land ceilings be examined by the newly formed Central Land Reforms Committee headed by the Union Minister of Agriculture.

This committee submitted its report, in August 1971, recommending that the ceiling for a family of five be fixed in the region of 10 to 18 acres of land that is perennially irrigated or is capable of growing two crops a year, and at 54 acres of land with no irrigation facilities. (The ceilings then existing varied between 12 to 15 acres per family, as in Kerala, to 27 to 324 acres per family member, as in Andhra Pradesh.) The party organization accepted this recommendation and incorporated it in its manifesto for the State assembly elections of early 1972.

It should have been fairly simple for the Congress, returned to power in almost all the States with a comfortable majority, to implement this promise quickly. But instead the party hierarchy initiated a long debate on the following points: what should be the size and composition of a family? should the new law include land irrigated by private resources? and how far back should the law be made applicable? The 'radicals' in the party wanted a family defined as five members including three children, no matter what their age. The 'moderates', led by the chief ministers, wanted a family to include only three *minor* children, and thus allow each major child to own property in his/her own right. The 'radicals' did not wish to make any distinction between land irrigated by private resources or government. The 'moderates', on the other hand, argued that land irrigated by private means should be exempted from the new ceilings so as not to discourage landowners from constructing their own irrigation facilities, particularly deep tube wells. (This would have meant exempting nearly 60 per cent of all irrigated land.) They also wanted the new legislation to be effective not from February 1970, as had been originally planned, but from January 1971.

It was not until July 1972 that the Congress High Command formally resolved the debate – in favour of the moderates. It laid down the following broad outline: the standard family should consist of husband, wife, and three minor children; the ceiling for the privately-irrigated land should be 25 per cent higher than that for the government-irrigated land; and the new law should be made retrospective from January 1971. Indira Gandhi fully supported these proposals. Arguing in favour of the 'moderates', led by the chief ministers – whom, only two years earlier, she had admonished for failing to implement land reform legislation – she said, 'Where is the organizational structure and the administrative set-up to implement a more radical policy?'[39] But who was responsible for failing to create an appropriate administrative machinery to carry out a radical land reform? None other than her own party – the Congress.

'Under the prevailing conventions of corruption,' wrote the *Patriot*, a newspaper sympathetic to the Congress, 'it will have to be assumed that quite a number of "families" will sprout where hitherto there had been only one, the age of children will take an upward leap (so as to make them major, and therefore eligible to possess land in their own name), and certainly much first quality land will become second or third quality, depending on how powerful the given rich peasant group is and how much the ministers concerned value its patronage.'[40] Not that the large landowners had been idle *before* the Congress High Command announced its decision. Over the previous few months they had gone about feverishly splitting their land, transferring it, and having such deeds backdated. In other words, the new legislation had been effectively emasculated long before it had even been drafted. No wonder then that, by the summer of 1975, less than 3·5 per cent of the 4,000,000 acres that had been 'expected' to become available as surplus in the country as a result of the revised ceiling laws had been declared surplus and taken possession of by the various State governments.[41] In short, the new land ceiling laws, enacted in the early 1970s, proved as ineffective as the ones passed a decade earlier.

What *could* have been achieved by a proper conception and implementation of land ceiling law can be gauged by the estimates made by Francine R. Frankel and K. N. Raj, an Indian economist. Frankel states that an average ceiling of 20 acres per rural household, applied in 1961, should have yielded 55 million acres of surplus land (versus the actual 2 million).[42] Raj states that, on the basis of the National Sample Survey of 1961–2 of 'operational' landholdings, 'all rural households can be provided with holdings of not less than 4 acres [each] in the relatively dry zone of "north-west", "central", and "west" India if a ceiling of twenty acres is enforced; and of at least 2 acres [each] in "north", "west", and "south" India if a ceiling of 10 acres is enforced'.[43]

And yet there are steps that the Congress could even take *now* to help bring about some measure of social justice in rural India. 'A lower ceiling has to be prescribed for *future acquisitions* of land so that gradually a homogeneous agricultural community may be expected to emerge, with families holding land between 5 and 15 acres,' recommends the *Economic and Political Weekly*.

Landlords who claim to be owner-cultivators will have to be statutorily required to live in the village for the major part of the year. Tenants holding non-resumable land will have to be declared owner-cultivators and given rights to transfer their land to institutional credit agencies for obtaining investment credit so that newly conferred land ownership is backed by provision of credit. Land records will have to be brought up-to-date and provision made for recognition of share-croppers' rights.[44]

This seems fair and rational; but it is unlikely to happen because the social background of the Congress activists and leaders militates against such a possibility. The agrarian situation can therefore be summed up as one where social injustice has continued to exist with only a marginal improvement in production. This, however, is not the case in industry, which has registered an impressive progress in many areas.

INDUSTRIAL POLICIES: 'SOCIALISTIC' CAPITALISM

In spite of much radical posturing and pledges of socialism, there is in fact no departure from the concept and practices of mixed economy as defined in the 1948 Industrial Policy Resolution.

Economic and Political Weekly editorial in 1972[1]

Some capitalists are quite good; and I hope others too will become good.

Indira Gandhi, speaking at a public rally, in 1971[2]

While G. D. Birla [of the Birla business house] was financing the Congress in mid-term elections in Bihar and Uttar Pradesh [in 1969], the Congress government in Delhi was instituting an inquiry into his firms. Birla knew that he'd be criticized in public while he'd get his things done on the quiet.

A. Sivasalam, an Indian industrialist[3]

The socialism contemplated in India . . . is a system under which private competitive enterprise has and will continue to have a vital role to play; it is a system which respects private property and provides for private property.

H. V. R. Iyengar, governor of the Reserve Bank of India[4]

In contrast to the growth in food production, which has barely been able to keep pace with rising population, the pace of industrial development has been outstanding. While population increased by 50 per cent during the period 1951–71, the industrial production index rose by 333 per cent – from 54·8 to 180·8.[5] The production of steel went up from 1·3 million tonnes in 1955 to 4·6 million tonnes in 1971; that of cement from 4·6 million tonnes to 14·9 million tonnes, soda ash from 79,000 tonnes to 483,000 tonnes, cotton textiles from 6,278 million metres to 7,356 million metres, and commercial vehicles from 9,500 to 40,800. The rise in industrial production looks as dramatic as it does partly because the initial base was small and partly because Congress Government has been sincere in its commitment to the policy of rapid industrialization –

a concept which has all along had the active support of the Indian businessman-capitalist class.

As far back as 1887, the Bengal National Chamber of Commerce, formed 'to aid and stimulate the development of commercial enterprise in Bengal . . . and generally . . . [aid] the interests of the commercial classes of Bengal', conferred honorary membership on the prominent leaders of the Congress.[6] The commercial classes in Calcutta – and Bombay and Madras, the two other ports developed by the British – then consisted of compradors (i.e. local agents of foreign commercial and industrial establishments), traders and bankers, who were mainly involved in the supply of cotton, jute, and tea to Britain, the demand for which had grown after the opening of the Suez Canal in 1869. Their close contact with British capitalists, who had begun setting up factories in and around Calcutta and the two other port-cities, enabled the compradors to grasp the intricacies of industry; and some among them thought of starting their own factories. But they were unable to do so because they were denied the necessary permission by the British government. This generated a lot of frustration among the Indian commercial classes; and they held the first All India Industrial Conference, in 1905, at the same time and place as the Congress Party's annual session, in order to press their demand for an official permission to enter the manufacturing field.

As a result, the colonial regime relented; but it was not until the outbreak of the First World War in 1914, when trading between India and Britain came to a virtual halt, that the Indian commercial class got its real chance to foster industry. The cotton textile industry was a major beneficiary of this; and the increased involvement of Indian capital and management led to the formation, in 1918, of the Indian-dominated Bombay Millowners' Association, which sympathized with the Congress, and which, along with the local textile traders' organization, backed the *swadeshi* (i.e. 'of one's own country') movement for the boycott of foreign goods and support of indigenous industry that M. K. Gandhi had initiated in 1921, with a symbolic bonfire of British-made cloth, in Bombay.

The rising Indian entrepreneurial class considered it necessary to articulate its needs through national organizations of its own. And the Indian Chamber of Commerce, established in Calcutta in 1926, and the Federation of Indian Chambers of Commerce and Industry, founded in Delhi in 1927 with a membership consisting of local Chambers of Commerce and traders' associations, came to play this role. These bodies demanded higher tariffs to protect infant indigenous industries, encouragement to new industries, more credit facilities, and lower taxes, but were rebuffed by the colonial regime. 'India is only a subordinate branch of the British administration', said D. B. Kaitan, the president of the Federation of Indian Chambers of Commerce and

Industry, in 1928. 'The interests of India are to us, who are connected with Indian business, the sole consideration; the interests of India are . . . to the [British] Government of India of subsidiary consideration, as the Secretary of State and, through him, the powerful British commercial interests have always a strong say.'[7] This attitude of the alien ruler helped maintain the traditional affinity between the business community and the Congress. What further reassured businessmen, many of them being from Gujarat and Rajasthan, was the fact that the party was coming under the growing influence of M. K. Gandhi, a man whom they found congenial, both socially (he was, after all, a Gujarati-speaking *bania*) and ideologically (since he believed in and worked for, harmony between capital and labour).[8]

Periodic flashes of radicalism, to which the Congress became susceptible during the 1930s, did not disturb this rapport, because, as Weiner explains, 'so long as the Congress was not in itself formulating [government] policy, hardheaded businessmen worried little about the vague socialistic biases of the [Congress] movement'. When finally, in 1937, the Congressmen won power at the provincial level, they desisted from following policies that they felt would 'divide the Congress, accentuate class struggle, and dry up financial resources of the party'.[9]

It was not until 1942 – when, in the middle of the Second World War, the Congress launched its 'Quit India' campaign against the British and the War effort – that a minor crack appeared in the alliance between business and the Congress. Although a substantial segment of this class continued to sympathize with the party, the War emergency laws precluded any possibility of a business establishment withholding its co-operation from the government. In any case, war-time conditions provided unprecedented opportunities to capitalists to expand business and industry, and amass wealth through excessive profiteering, black-marketing, and hoarding. Such anti-social activities of the business community, never liked even at the best of times, made it unpopular with the masses.

These factors, plus a Gandhian bias in favour of small-scale industry, and a populist sentiment that seemed to temporarily seize the Congress hierarchy on the eve of independence, led the All India Congress Committee session in 1947 to recommend that industries producing articles of food and clothing and other consumer goods should only be in the small sector, and that large-scale industry be brought under government control and a process of transfer from private to public ownership of existing large undertakings be initiated within five years.[10] The business community reacted to this by going on an 'investment strike', causing a decline in industrial production. Unnerved, the newly installed Congress government in Delhi gave repeated assurances to the industrialists that there were no plans whatsoever for nationalization or take-over of any *existing* establishments, and went on to incorporate these into an Industrial Policy Resolution and have it passed by Parliament in April 1948. 'For some time to come, the State could contribute more quickly to the increase of national wealth by expanding its present activities wherever it is already operating and by concentrating on new units of production in other fields, rather than on acquiring and running existing units,' said the resolution. 'Meanwhile, private enterprise, properly directed and regulated, has a valuable role to play.'

The resolution further stated that the manufacture of arms and ammunition, production and control of atomic energy, and the ownership and management of railways were to continue to be the monopoly of the Central government; and that in such basic industries as coal, iron and steel, aircraft manufacture, shipbuilding, manufacture of telephone, telegraph and wireless apparatus (excluding radio receiving sets), and mineral oils, the State was to be concerned only with starting new establishments, while existing undertakings were to be allowed all facilities for expansion for at least the next ten years; and that the rest of the industrial field was to be left open to private enterprise, with the Central government regulation and control limited to only eighteen industries, including heavy chemicals, cement, machine-tools, and fertilizers.

Interestingly enough, this resolution had many similarities with the Industrial Policy Statement, issued during 1944–5, by the Planning and Development Department of the British Viceroy's administration for adoption in the post-war period. The Policy Statement had classified industries in three categories: the first category, consisting of twenty major industries, was to have been under direct Central government control; the second, comprising industries of 'national importance' (namely, aircraft, automobiles and tractors, iron and steel, chemicals and dyes, machine tools, electro-chemicals, and non-ferrous metals), was to have come under State ownership in those cases where adequate private capital was not forthcoming; and the third, comprising the remaining industries, was to have been left to private capital, but under various degrees of State control.[11] In other words, the net result of the first 'socialist' impulse of the Congress administration was the adoption of an industrial policy that had been recommended by the departing colonial regime.

The outcome of the second 'socialist' impulse of the Congress – signalled by the coining of the slogan of 'socialistic pattern of society' – was no more revolutionary. 'All industries of basic and strategic importance, or in the nature of public utility services, should be in the public sector,' said the revised Industrial Policy Resolution passed by Parliament in April 1956. 'Other industries which are essential and require investment on a scale which only the state, in present circumstances, could provide have also to be in the public sector.' Accordingly, the public sector category (now called Group A) was expanded to include such capital-intensive industries as coal, iron and steel, aircraft manufacturing, shipbuilding, oil, and mining; and some of the industries, such as machine-tools, heavy chemicals, and fertilizers, which were previously in the (controlled) private sector, were brought into the mixed sector (now called Group B); and the residual industries were left as before, in the private sector (now called Group C).

When the industrialists protested against the expansion of the public sector, they were told by the Congress government spokesmen that the private sector had failed to provide capital for heavy industry during the First Plan, and that expansion of basic industry with public capital, contemplated during the Second Plan, would benefit the privately-owned consumer goods and light engineering industries. And this is precisely what happened. During the four-year period 1955–9, which covered the major part of the Second Plan, the net income of joint-stock companies rose by 41 per cent and their pre-tax profit by 37 per cent.[12] Thus the strain between the Congress and business proved temporary.

The general features of the Third Plan (1961–6), which, among other things, opened seven of the seventeen industries listed in Group B in 1956 to private enterprise, were such that Karamchand Thapar, the president of the Federation of Indian Chambers of Commerce and Industry, acknowledged publicly that allocation of resources between public and private sectors had been 'broadly similar' to what had been proposed earlier by the FICCI.[13] While Nehru told the annual session of the FICCI, in 1962, that 'private enterprise is a good thing', and that 'the suppression of private enterprise is bad',[14] G. D. Birla, India's leading industrialist, reassured a gathering of American businessmen in 1963 that 'the public sector [in India] is going to act as a generator of private enterprises'.[15] This was not surprising, because, as Michael Kidron, a British economist, points out, 'The private business community, whatever the rhetoric of the moment, has always been substantially represented within the Nehru government and the Congress Party.'[16]

During his eighteen years in office, the 'socialistic' Nehru never deviated from the policy of choosing a Finance Minister, a key post in his cabinet – and he chose six of them – who was first and foremost acceptable to the business community. As for the party organization, business interests have always been well-entrenched at different levels – local, State, and national. More than two-fifths of the party members in Kanpur, a textile centre in Uttar Pradesh, for instance, were found to be 'traders, shopkeepers, and businessmen'.[17] And a study of the party in Madurai, an industrial city of half a million in Tamil Nadu, led Myron Weiner to conclude that it is 'largely dominated by businessmen', with traders and shopkeepers taking keen interest in the local party organization, and the industrialists concentrating their major effort and contacts at the State level.[18]

It is a common practice among local businessmen to provide both money and manpower for the annual and biennial sessions of the State and national party. 'Under the guidance of T. S. Krishna [manager of T. V. Sundaram, an industrial house], $60,000 [£30,000] were raised to build the meeting hall [in Madurai] and generally to organize the entire programme [of the All India Congress Committee session],' noted Weiner. 'White collar workers from T. V. Sundaram offices were given responsibility for greeting visitors at the airport, maintaining a reception centre at the railway stations, providing food for delegates, maintaining snack canteens, and so on.'[19] And, as stated earlier, business-men provide the bulk of election funds for the party at the State and national levels.[20]

The split in the party, and the efforts of the faction led by Indira Gandhi to present itself as radical and socialistic, did not materially alter the relationship between business and the party. When business-men expressed disapproval of the speed with which fourteen leading commercial banks were nationalized in July 1969, Indira Gandhi appealed to them, in a public speech, not to consider bank nationaliza-tion as 'a step directed against them',[21] and went on to instruct such government-controlled financial institutions as the Life Insurance Cor-poration, the Industrial Development Bank of India, and the Industrial Finance Corporation to help tide businessmen over any difficulty they might experience as a result of bank nationalization. Not that these institutions had neglected the private sector in the past, when large commercial banks, owned by some of the top industrial houses, existed to the almost exclusive benefit of private commerce and industry. Indeed, most of the loans granted by the government institutions had gone to the seventy-three large business houses. This was to continue; and it did, so much so that, as of March 1972, twenty-two of these houses accounted for two-thirds of the loans given by the Life Insurance Corporation, and twenty-two of them for more than half of those granted by the Industrial Development Bank.[22]

So, like other 'radical' actions or resolutions of the party in the past, bank nationalization too was to leave undisturbed the trend towards a growing concentration of commercial and industrial capital that had first been noticed in the late 1950s. The degree of such concentration can be judged by the fact that, in 1951, the twenty richest family groups owned 29 per cent of all private capital,[23] whereas in 1968 the ten top family groups possessed 28 per cent of total private capital.[24] An official survey revealed that, in 1964, seventy-five top business houses, con-trolling less than 6 per cent of all non-banking firms in the country, owned 47 per cent of total company assets. By 1969, their share had gone up to 54 per cent of the total company assets, with the top twenty houses registering individual gains of 55 per cent to 196 per cent.[25]

Various steps taken by the Central government to counter the growing concentration of private capital have proved ineffective. This is as true of the law abolishing the practice of the (company) managing agency as of the introduction of the system of licensing for the expansion of existing plants or manufacture of new products, and the enactment of a law against monopolies and restrictive trade practices, and the establishment of the Monopolies and Restrictive Trade Practices Commission.

A close relationship, financial and family, between the industrial class and compradors, had led to the emergence of the managing agency system. This arrangement enabled the original comprador, and his family and close relatives, to maintain control over a large number of diverse trading, financial and manufacturing firms, while, at the same time, being paid handsome 'fees' for 'managing' these companies. A dramatic expansion in the country's industry and commerce, particularly during the late 1950s and early 1960s, brought the nepotistic and monopolistic ills of the practice to the fore, and necessitated action by the Central government. It passed a law to abolish the system – in stages. By April 1970, the system was supposed to have been totally non-existent, and yet K. N. Narang, a young Indian industrialist, wrote in November 1971, 'Even today the managing agents control, within the same [business] house, up to one hundred companies with businesses which are completely unrelated'.[26] A report on management patterns in the corporate sector, over the past quarter-century, by the Central government's Company Affairs Department, published in July 1972, stated that 'managing agency families have by and large succeeded in retaining their control over the companies they formerly controlled'. In this, the Birlas were singled out to be the most ingenious: they had adjusted their management pattern in such a way that they continued to wield all 'effective power' in running a company by placing one or two family members on the board of directors to guide such salaried executives as president or vice-president of the company.[27] The Birlas also appear as the main guilty party as far as misuse of industrial licences is concerned.

Industrial licensing was introduced about the same time as the First Plan was launched, in 1952, with the objectives of (a) promoting essential industries and discouraging inessential ones, and (b) helping to bring about a wider ownership of industry. An inquiry by R. K. Hazari, an Indian economist, in 1966, revealed that the twenty-eight largest industrial houses were more successful than others in receiving licences for substantial expansion of existing units or manufacturing a new product. 'Some [business] houses follow the practice of putting in a number of applications for each product,' he wrote. 'Multiple applications for the same product and for a wide, very wide indeed, variety of products are meant to foreclose licensable capacity. This appears to be particularly true of Birla applications. . . . Birla enterprises . . . tend to pre-empt licensable capacity in many industries.'[28]

The governmental practice of processing each application individually, on a first-come-first-served basis, and not considering similar applications in batches and awarding a licence to the best possible applicant, favours those who manage to get an inkling of the government's intentions before the others; and these are almost invariably the larger business houses, since they are the ones who have considerable political influence and maintain special 'contact men' in Delhi. No wonder, then, that a report by the Industrial Licensing Policy Enquiry Committee, published in 1969, stated that the small sector had been brushed aside even in industries where large units of production did not enjoy economies of scale, and that the main beneficiaries of industrial licensing had not merely been the big industrial houses but the very biggest, with the Birlas, once again, being the front-runner.[29] The Committee's recommendation that a Monopolies Commission be appointed to keep a watchful eye on the large business houses was accepted by the government, and such a body was established, in August 1970, under the Monopolies and Restrictive Practices Act, which had been passed a year before.

On the other hand, this happened a decade after Nehru had told the annual session of the Federation of Indian Chambers of Commerce and Industry, in 1960, that 'Not to encourage monopoly is a common matter, common thing not confined to socialistic thought. Every modern capitalistic thought is opposed to monopoly',[30] and five *years* after the Monopolies Enquiry Commission had published a disturbing report on the growing concentration of private capital.

The powers of the Monopolies Commission are, however, severely limited. It can act *only* on the cases referred to it by the government, and it does not have the final say. This seems to have had an inhibiting effect on it: of the 149 cases of application for an industrial licence referred to it during the first twenty-one months of its existence, it recommended rejection only in five instances.[31] Furthermore, it has been brought into the picture only in the sphere of industrial licences and has not been directed, or encouraged, by the government to investigate either instances of growing concentration in industry or subtle methods of control employed by a small number of families to direct numerous firms. This could prove a fruitful area of investigation because, as A. N. Oza, an Indian economist, points out, almost every one of the twenty largest business groups controls at least one or two giant companies which, in their respective industries, are in a 'dominant or oligopolistic position'.[32]

But this is unlikely to happen, particularly when, following its return to power in March 1971, the Congress administration chose to quietly downgrade the 'radical' posture adopted by it before the elections, and, in the name of rising production *per se*, gradually liberalized its policy towards big business. 'The elimination of concentration of economic power has to be balanced with the growth in the economy,' said K. V. Raghunatha Reddy, junior Minister for Company Affairs, in May 1972.[33] The balance has shifted more and more in favour of large industrial houses. 'Yojana Bhauan [literally, Planning Mansion, the secretariat of the Planning Commission] has made it known that the initiative of the Ministry of Industry and Civil Supplies . . . – supposedly to unshackle the productive forces in the private sector, including the big business houses – will receive full support from the planners,' reported BM, an Indian journalist, in February 1975. 'What is [however] never made explicit – and is, in fact, denied – is that a market-oriented industrial policy is thus being pursued or that the government is effectively loosening its regulations and controls over industry.'[34]

The Congress leadership behaves the way it does because it knows that an open declaration of change in favour of business would be an electoral liability, since the urban-dwelling capitalist often arouses jealousy, even hostility, among the predominantly poor electors, and unlike the rich peasant or landlord in the countryside, he lacks any traditional influence over a substantial section of voters. On the other hand, the business community has the power to withdraw co-operation from the government, through subtle and not-so-subtle means, and cause reduction in production and investment, and thus have the government alter its policies to favour business.

The Congress's predominant concern for production *per se*, however, pre-dates the recent political developments. As early as 1946, soon after the party won power in various provinces, its ministries actively considered boosting production by banning strikes and stipulating compulsory arbitration to resolve industrial disputes. But their plans were frustrated by the non-co-operation of the Communist-dominated All India Trade Union Congress, which was the only central trade union organization in existence then, and which had been established at the initiative of some radical Congressmen shortly after the First World War, when the party leadership first attempted to broaden the party base.

10

TRADE UNIONS:
DIVIDE AND RULE

The Indian National Trade Union Congress was created [in 1947] to give the Congress government a foothold in the working class, and therefore it cannot be really effective in serving the interests of the working class.

> Bagaram Tulpule, a Socialist trade unionist[1]

The INTUC is the least militant in its trade union philosophy and closely identified with government and the Congress party and, therefore, the least attractive to idealistic young people who might be inclined towards trade unionism as a cause.

> Van Dusen Kennedy, an Indian-born American trade unionist[2]

As stated earlier, the First World War accelerated the process of industrialization in India. At the end of the war, the country had nearly 900,000 industrial workers employed in 2,936 factories, and many thousand more in railways, plantations, and mines. But, while the war increased job opportunities, as well as profits, it also caused a steep rise in prices which, in the absence of an equivalent increment in wages, led to a lowering of the workers' living standards. The climate was thus ripe for the emergence of trade unions, the first of which was formed in 1918, in a Madras textile mill, by B. P. Wadia, assistant editor of a local, pro-Congress daily. Dissatisfaction with their economic condition also made the industrial workers sympathetic to the call for non-co-operation with the British authorities, that the Congress gave in 1919, when the colonial government offered the country what the party considered a totally inadequate political reform.

This, in turn, engendered interest among the nationalist leaders in the welfare of industrial workers; and the Congress High Command directed its provincial committees to 'promote Labour Unions throughout the country with the view of improving social, economic, and political conditions of living and a proper place in the body politic of India'.[3] A year later, in 1920, the first session of the All India Trade Union Congress, claiming affiliation or sympathy of 107 unions, was held under the chairmanship of Lajpat Rai, the then President of the Congress.

Prominent among those who took up active trade union work were the members of the Communist groups that began to sprout throughout the country in the early 1920s. They thus established a strong foothold in the AITUC. Following the enforcement of the Trade Union Act of 1926 (modelled on the Trade Union Act of 1906 in Britain), which gave legal status to trade unions and protected them from civil or criminal liability for actions taken in pursuance of a trade dispute, the Communist trade unionists made frequent use of strikes to secure workers' demands, and became popular. Alarmed by the dramatic rise in their influence within and outside the AITUC, the British government arrested many Communist labour leaders, and simultaneously armed itself, through the Trade Disputes Act of 1929 with powers to intervene in industrial disputes – that is, apply pressure on employers, who enjoyed a powerful bargaining position *vis-à-vis* workers, on behalf of employees. This considerably damaged the Communist standing in the trade union movement.

On top of this came a split in the AITUC, in 1929, when the nationalists broke away to set up their own central organization. This weakened the AITUC, which suffered another split in 1931 when the Communists, following an ultra-radical policy, left to form their own body, leaving the AITUC in the hands of the centrists. By 1935, however, the Communists, having reversed their political line, were back in the fold; and so were the nationalists – in 1938. But this unity was disturbed when the Second World War broke out, and the three major elements within the organization took different stands on it. The conflict came to a climax when the Congress launched its 'Quit India' movement against the British, in 1942, while the Communists supported the British administration and the War effort, since Soviet Russia had, by then, joined the Allies. With the Congress trade unionists away in jail, the Communists gained full control of the AITUC which, they claimed in 1945, had the support of nearly 400 trade unions with a total membership of 500,000.

Soon after the war, the Congress leaders were released from jail and invited to form an 'interim' government in Delhi. With this, their perspective towards trade unionism changed. Agitation by workers against industrialists and the government had to give way to co-operation with both in the interests of increased production. The first step to take, therefore, was quietly to wrest control of the AITUC, the only existing central labour organization, from the Communists. The Congress leadership instructed the party's trade unionists to join the AITUC. They did; and, at the AITUC conference in February 1947, they put forward resolutions supporting labour legislation (favoured by the Congress ministries in various provinces) banning strikes, and prescribing compulsory arbitration to resolve industrial disputes. But these motions were rejected by a large majority of the delegates. Thereupon, the party hierarchy decided to establish a separate pro-Congress labour organization, committed to the ideology of class harmony and co-operation.

Within three months, the Indian National Trade Union Congress (INTUC), claiming the affiliation of over 200 unions with a membership of 575,000, was inaugurated in Delhi, with the purported objective of establishing 'an order of society which . . . goes to the utmost limit in progressively eliminating social, political or economic exploitation and inequality, the profit motive in the economic activity and organization of society, and the anti-social concentration of power in any form; to place industry under national ownership and control in suitable form in order to realize the aforesaid objective in the quickest time . . . ; to promote generally the social, civic, and political interests of the working class'![4] (Interestingly enough, the Congress leader most responsible for the founding of the INTUC was V. B. Patel, an arch-conservative, who was close to the industrialist Birla family.)

Two factors helped the Congress leadership to achieve speedily what it did. In the Hind Mazdoor Sevak Sangh (i.e. Indian Workers' Service Association), a body that had existed since the late 1930s to train the Congress workers in labour affairs on the model provided by the Textile Labour Association in Ahmedabad (founded in 1920 under the active guidance of M. K. Gandhi), it had a substantial cadre of trade unionists who believed in class harmony and the use of arbitration to settle industrial disputes; and being in office enabled it to use its power and prestige to muster support for the new organization.

Continued open favouritism by both employers and government officials, combined with repression of the Communists, helped the INTUC to claim, in 1951, that it represented 1,232 unions with a total membership of 1,548,000. What happened in the textile industry of Indore and Gwaliar, in Madhya Pradesh, was typical. 'The Communists were the first to organize industrial workers in Indore and Gwaliar [then part of princely India],' said G. M. Vaidya, an Indian journalist.

> They were repressed by the native princes before independence, but that only made them popular heroes. However, when the INTUC was formed in 1947, the employers gave money to its local organizers for maintaining full-time officials so that they could provide better service to factory workers than the AITUC could. Even then the Communist strength didn't decline. But things changed when the Communist Party went for a left-adventurist line, and invited government repression which continued until early 1952. It was thus that the INTUC was able to come up.[5]

This trend continued, and soon the INTUC was recognized by the Federal government as the largest central labour organization, a recognition which still stands.

Despite this history, leaders of both the INTUC and the Congress have always maintained that the two organizations are quite apart and independent. Some INTUC leaders even go so far as openly to criticize the Congress administration for favouring the non-INTUC unions. 'This anxiety [on the part of the government] to be impartial often ends in being partial to the non-INTUC unions', said the INTUC president in 1960. 'To treat the majority organization [such as the INTUC] and the minority organizations alike is not being impartial. . . . We want the government to give us our due.'[6] In contrast, Van Dusen Kennedy, an India-born American trade unionist, summed up the situation thus:

> Chief ministers, labour ministers, labour commissioners, registrars of trade unions, inspectors, conciliators, tribunal officials, magistrates, police officers, and all other officials who have dealings with unions and labour have been appointed by Congress governments. . . . Several management officials have told me of occasions when they were requested or pressured by government officials to assist INTUC unions to establish themselves or defeat their rival unions in their establishments.[7]

Not that employers need much pressurizing to aid the INTUC unions, since they almost invariably consider the INTUC to be the most 'reasonable' of all central trade union organizations and the CPI(M)-led Centre of Indian Trade Unions (CITU) to be the least. 'Ideally, of course, an Indian employer would much rather be without any union at all, as he regards a union to be a threat to his exclusive right of management and an impediment to his objective of maximum production at minimum cost. Often industrialists owning small or medium establishments, which dominate the industrial sector,[8] use all means, fair or foul, to hinder the formation of a union or replace an existing militant union with a non-militant one. The example of Tablets (P) Limited, a pharmaceutical company in Madras, with a workforce of 380, is typical.

The factory was established in 1967 by a Rajasthani businessman from Bombay, who appointed his 23-year-old son, N. P. Mathur, as the managing director. It began operating with a predominantly female labour force hired at the rate of Rs 2 (10p) a day (which was about 50 per cent lower than that for an agricultural worker in the countryside). Sensing a general discontent among workers regarding low wages, a 'permanent' employee (i.e. one who could not be dismissed summarily) from the accounts department approached local CPI(M) trade unionists for advice. A quiet campaign to enrol members for a union ensued. And once the majority of workers had signed membership forms, a meeting was held at the residence of an employee to elect officials. Then (in

August 1970), a letter was sent to management to arrange a meeting to discuss their demands; but nothing came of it.

N. P. Mathur described the events before and after the union's letter in August 1970 thus:

> They had done their organizing work *underground*. Suddenly there was a union. We didn't like that. The union asked for a meeting. We never replied. Instead, we dismissed ten to fifteen union-minded employees, saying that they weren't working properly. So the trouble started. There was a strike (in November). This brought in conciliation officers of the State government. They raised wage rates, from Rs 2 [10p] to Rs 4·50 [22½p] a day. We didn't like that, because the factories in this area don't pay such wages. Actually, unemployment is so high we can get workers here at Rs 1·50 [7½p] a day. Anyway, the strike ended. But now every evening they demonstrate outside the factory. These CPI(M) fellows – their tendency is to work less and agitate more. The INTUC fellows are reasonable. We wouldn't mind them at all. Actually, we tried to break up this union by bribing the leader, but it didn't work. Under this CPI(M) union, workers have got unity. Anyway, once things settle down, we'll try again to put some money into the pockets of the union leader.[9]

It can be seen that in such instances much depends on the attitude of the conciliation officers of the State government, which in this case was in the hands of the Dravida Munnetra Kazhagam, *not* the Congress. Starting with the Trade Disputes Act of 1929, the government in India has periodically invested itself with powers to intervene in industrial disputes partly to bring about some balance between the two grossly unequal forces: the politically and financially powerful employer on one side, and a body of predominantly illiterate, low caste employees, working in an environment of high unemployment, on the other.

The early commercial penetration of India by British capitalism had destroyed the indigenous craft industry and driven the once-vigorous artisan class back to the land, with the result that the manning of the factories – which were to be established later in urban centres – fell into the hands of recently arrived landless peasants, who had been forced by adverse economic circumstances, to leave their ancestral homes in the countryside. This meant that the task of organizing the rising industrial proletariat came to be performed not by the politically aware members of this class, as had happened in Western Europe, but by lawyers and social workers, who were often imbued with the ideas of nationalism or socialism or communism. In general, this development has worked to the advantage of the workers: it enables them to draw on the skills and knowledge of educated and socially conscious persons without having to pay them, something many of their unions cannot afford, while it leaves the outsiders free from pressures by the employer that the militant employees are often subjected to. Furthermore, many of these outsiders are in a position to influence government ministers when the latter have to take a decision on an industrial dispute referred to them under the provisions of the Industrial Disputes Act of 1947. This law applies nationally; and, since labour relations is a 'concurrent' subject, the Central laws automatically over-ride the State laws.

The 1947 law allows any seven employees of a firm to act collectively, register as a union, and submit demands to the employer. When these demands are not met, and a dispute ensues, either party is at liberty to approach the State government's conciliation officer. He studies the issue and proposes a solution. If this is not acceptable to the disputing parties, the labour commissioner is called in. If he too fails to get the parties to agree to the solution he offers, then the case is placed before the labour minister who decides (either singly or in consultation with his colleagues) whether to refer the dispute to an adjudicator, or an industrial court, or a specially appointed tribunal, depending on the nature of the dispute and the size of the workforce. The verdict of this body is binding on both parties. In case of certain major disputes, the dissatisfied party can appeal to the State's High Court, and finally, if necessary to the Supreme Court, where it may take as long as ten years to secure a verdict.[10] It is apparent that the government can stifle or boost a union by taking an appropriate decision in a dispute that involves a particular union. A success in a dispute helps bolster the image of a union, which may have a minority support to begin with, attract more members to it, and thus enhance its chance of becoming the majority union and securing recognition as the representative body by the employer.

Although the law does not require a management to confer recognition on one or more unions existing in its establishment, the Code of Discipline, drafted by representatives of the central trade union organizations, employers, and the government, in 1958, recommended that there be only one representative union to an establishment, and that in case of rivalry, the union with the highest number of members be recognized. This should be a fairly simple exercise, since every union is required, by law, to submit its membership records and accounts to the Registrar of Trade Unions if it wishes to retain its registered status; but it is not. Delays occur when the labour commissioner's staff, charged with the task of verifying membership lists, discover – as they almost always do – common names in the lists of competing unions, and then interview each of these members individually to establish their real choice. 'Common names occur either because the member himself has paid dues to more than one union in order to play safe, or someone from a rival union has forged his signature and paid his dues,' said V. B. Karnik, a trade unionist in Bombay. 'It takes a year to go through all this even when the total membership of the largest union is below 10,000. That's why we had to wait until January 1971 to have the final, verified figures for the central trade unions for 1968!'[11]

It would be simpler to determine the relative strength of competing unions by secret ballot, to be held every few years. Until early 1972, this method was preferred to the present one by all the central trade unions except the INTUC, whose general secretary, G. Ramnujam, argued that, 'membership fee is in itself a solid vote for the union'.[12] But the *real* reason for taking this stand was stated by Van Dusen Kennedy. 'The INTUC believes that the ballot would work to its disadvantage,' he wrote. 'The AITUC unions . . . would displace incumbent unions in a number of situations if the secret ballot method were used today.'[13]

The INTUC's stand is fully supported by the Congress Party and government, for they too are aware that, given a free choice in an election by secret ballot, workers would more often than not reject the INTUC-sponsored unions. If they had any illusions about this, these were dispelled during the period 1967–70, when the Congress lost power in many States, and the INTUC unions, stripped of their customary political and administrative backing, often failed to sustain their 'popularity' among workers, and found themselves losing recognition by employers. The case of Hindustan Steel Limited, a government-owned steel plant, in Durgapur, West Bengal, was typical. 'When Hindustan Steel at Durgapur got going [in the late 1950s] and then [Congress] government of West Bengal prevailed upon the none-too-reluctant Hindustan Steel authorities to grant recognition to an INTUC-sponsored union without any proper verification of its credentials among the workers,' noted a correspondent of *Economic and Political Weekly*. 'The workers were never reconciled to this imposition of the INTUC union. . . . Durgapur saw considerable industrial conflict as a result of this . . . and, as soon as the political weight in favour of the INTUC was lifted [following the defeat of the Congress in the 1967 general election], their recognition was successfully challenged . . . [with] a CPI(M)-led union [taking over] at Durgapur.'[14]

The INTUC's unpopularity stems from the fact that its leaders seem to care the least about the workers' lot. 'Their loyalties are to the Congress Party, then to the present [Congress] government, to the nation, and last of all to the workers who belong to their unions,' observes Myron Weiner.[15] Almost invariably, the INTUC lends its support to the Congress at the time of elections. The nineteenth conference of the INTUC in November 1971, for instance, pledged 'solid support' to the Congress at the impending elections to the State assemblies, and described it as 'a logical step arising out of the unity of purpose, plans, and programme'.[16] Not surprisingly, the INTUC was the only central trade union actively to oppose the national strike by railwaymen in May 1974 for an increment in wages to partly catch up with spiralling inflation, and the only organization of its kind not to criticize the Central government's ordinances, two months later, which amounted to a wage freeze without a corresponding guarantee to hold the price line.[17] But perhaps the most damning, albeit indirect, indictment of the INTUC came from the National Commission on Labour which stated, in its report in 1969, that, 'increases in money wages of industrial workers since Independence have not been associated with a rise in real wages, nor have real wage increases been commensurate with improvements in productivity'.[18] In short, during the generation when the INTUC had been 'officially' the largest and most important central trade union, the country's working class had suffered a *decline* in its living standards.

And yet, in the wake of the split in the Congress, in 1969, the INTUC improved its strength by attracting some of the Socialist trade unionists, who until then had been active with the Hind Mazdoor Sabha (i.e. Indian Workers Council), which had been established by Socialist leaders after they had left the Congress in 1948, and which, with 463,400 (verified) members, was the third largest central trade union in the country.[19] The AITUC was affected too, but in a different way. The already existing differences between the CPI and CPI(M) supporters within the AITUC's leadership crystallized around the issue of assessing the Congress split, with the CPI members investing the event with much political-ideological significance, and the CPI(M) supporters dismissing it as an opportunistic manoeuvre undertaken by Indira Gandhi.[20] In fact, the CPI(M) members soon left the AITUC and, in May 1970, established their own Centre of Indian Trade Unions (CITU) in Calcutta.

The animus between the AITUC and CITU was highlighted, in February 1972, when the AITUC collaborated with the INTUC and HMS to form the National Council of Trade Unions with a general policy of co-operation with the Congress administration, and announced that it no longer stood by the principle of secret ballot to determine a union's popularity but, instead, supported the idea of recognition of the majority union on the basis of verification of membership by government officials and proportional representation to other unions.[21] The CITU retaliated by forming the United Council of Trade Unions, in October 1972, in alliance with nine small national labour organizations. The rift in the AITUC was indeed a belated reflection of the split that had occurred, in 1964, in the Communist Party, and of the uneasy coexistence of the moderate and radical elements within the party that went far back.

PART III
LEFTIST FORCES

THE COMMUNIST MOVEMENT: BEFORE 1964

The Indian intellectual has perhaps suffered too long . . . from the tendency to speak and write in English, a borrowed language. When he was introduced to Marxism, instead of trying to think on his own, he again turned outward – to Moscow or Peking. The result was a craze to seek Russian or Chinese parallels in our social developments.

Sumanta Banerjee, an Indian journalist[1]

We consider that in the present historical condition, the possibility exists . . . of parties and elements, who stand for socialism, securing a majority in Parliament, and overcoming the resistance of reaction by means of mass action. And we shall try our utmost to make this possibility a reality in our country.

Ajoy Ghosh, general secretary of the Communist Party of India, in 1958[2]

The success of the Bolshevik revolution in Russia in 1917 engendered interest in Communism, and in organizing industrial workers, among many middle-class intellectuals in the Congress party, and led them to form local Communist groups in various urban centres. The establishment of two Communist journals (in English and Bengali), in Bombay and Calcutta, made these groups aware of one another's existence; and by the middle of 1922 the idea of setting up a national organization was seriously aired. Plans were made to hold the founding conference of the party in 1924. But, before the conference could be held, the British government arrested prominent Communist leaders under the charge that they had 'entered into a conspiracy to establish throughout British India a branch of the revolutionary organ, known as the Communist International, with the object of depriving the King of the Sovereignty of British India'. Consequently, the inaugural conference of the Communist Party of India was held in December 1925 with many of the party leaders still in jail. (At this conference, those of the party members who were active in the Congress movement were advised to maintain their Congress membership.)

This event was of particular interest to the Communist Party of Great Britain which, following a recommendation of the Fifth Congress of Comintern (i.e. Communist International) that close contacts be maintained between the Communist Party of an imperialist country and the Communists of its colonies, had set up a Colonial Committee in 1925. Soon after, this committee sent out three experienced British trade unionists to help the Indian Communists organize industrial workers. Partly due to this, and partly due to the enforcement of the Trade Union Act of 1926, which gave legal protection to those engaged in legitimate trade union activity, the Communists managed quickly to build up a base among the industrial proletariat. They won the employers' recognition for their textile workers' union (called the Girni Kamgar Union) in Bombay, by leading a six-month strike in 1927–8, and then went on to challenge Nehru's bid for President of the All India Trade Union Congress at its annual conference in 1928, by pitting a victimized railway worker from Bombay against him. Their candidate lost, but only by one vote. Later that year, the party's front organization, the All India Workers and Peasants Parties' Conference, met in Calcutta at the time of the biennial session of the Congress party, and led demonstrations in support of the radical group within the Congress which advocated an agitational, as opposed to constitutional, approach to the question of national independence.

These developments alarmed both industrialists and the British government; and, in March 1929, the authorities arrested thirty-one leading Communists under the charge that they had 'entered into conspiracy to wage a war against the King and to overthrow his sovereignty over India, and had with this view, organized trade unions, conducted strikes, carried on propaganda and engaged themselves in various other activities'. The conspiracy case went on for over four years, at the end of which most of the accused were released.

Meanwhile, however, the party leadership fell into the hands of younger members who, in their enthusiasm strictly to follow the resolution passed by the Sixth Congress of Comintern, in September 1928, called for a 'ruthless exposure' of the national reformism of the Indian National Congress, actively opposed Gandhi's call to the masses for passive resistance against the colonial government, broke away from the AITUC (in 1931), and generally followed ultra-leftist policies. The British administration responded to this by arresting yet more Communist activists in mid-1934, and banning the party outright, thus formalizing a situation that had existed since 1930. This brought the party membership down to 150.

The following year (1935), however, the situation changed, when, in response to the rise of fascism in Germany, the Seventh Congress of Comintern recommended the tactic of 'popular front' to the Communists in metropolitan countries, and of anti-imperialist 'united front' (including bourgeois nationalist parties) to the Communists in the colonies, and the Indian Communists followed the advice. The Communist-led Red Trade Union Congress merged with the AITUC; and individual Communists (of whom there were about a thousand then) joined the Congress Socialist Party, a ginger group within the Congress, and actively cooperated with radical Congressmen to establish the All India Kisan Congress in 1936 (later to be called the All India Kisan Sabha). The formation of a national peasant body was the culmination of the efforts of Communists and other leftists to articulate the interests of peasants who had suffered due to the fall in prices of agricultural commodities caused by the economic depression of 1929. The solution offered by the AIKS to the problem was more reformist than revolutionary: increased irrigation facilities and credit, debt relief, security of tenure, and higher prices for agricultural produce. The most radical of the AIKS's demand was for abolition of zamindari.

Such moderation in their policies, coupled with their newfound friendliness towards Congressmen, enabled the Communists to function quasi-legally in those provinces which came under the Congress rule, following the election of 1937, and publish their first (ever) national weekly in Bombay. But this situation was to prove short-lived. With the outbreak of the Second World War, in September 1939, and the subsequent resignation of the Congress ministries in protest against the British Viceroy's decision to join the Allies, without consulting any of the popular Indian leaders, the Communists lost their protective coat. Simultaneously, they stepped up their opposition to the 'imperialist' war by organizing, for instance, a strike of textile workers in Bombay, in October 1939. The British authorities retaliated by repressing the Communist movement with a heavy hand, a policy that continued until February 1942, when the Communists redefined the war as the 'people's' war in view of the fact that, following an attack on it by Germany in June 1941, Soviet Russia had by then joined the Allies.

A few months later, the government lifted its ban on the party. And, with the Congress and Congress-Socialist activists, away, behind bars – as a result of the 'Quit India' movement launched in August 1942 – its members took over the leadership of the AITUC and AIKS. The party held a national conference in 1943 (the first since its founding session in 1925), and began to widen its base, raising its membership from under 5,000 in 1942 to over 30,000 in 1945. Its involvement in helping the War effort, including the Grow More Food campaign, made it popular among middle and rich peasants in such regions as the delta area of Andhra. On the other hand, it lost influence among certain sections of the working class, such as the textile workers in Bombay, who disapproved of the party's anti-nationalist stand. Later, the Congressmen were to dub the Communists 'traitors', a label that proved a liability to those party members who contested elections, held on a restricted franchise, in 1945–6. The Communists secured about 3 per cent of the votes cast, and a total of nine provincial assembly seats.

Meanwhile, however, the end of the war in 1945 had enabled the party to resume its pre-war friendliness towards the Congress; and it had done so. Indeed, when the final plans for independence and partition of India were announced in June 1947, the party's Central Committee pledged its support to the nationalist leadership under Nehru, and called for a united front of political parties to begin the 'proud task of building the Indian Republic on democratic foundations'.

But this policy came under attack towards the end of 1947, when radicals in the party took their cue from the report submitted to Cominform (i.e. Communist Information, the successor to Communist International, which had been dissolved earlier), in September 1947, by its chief organizer, A. Zhandov, a Russian Communist leader, in which he divided the world into two hostile camps of socialism and imperialism, and warned against 'the chief danger to the working class . . . [of] under-rating its own strength and over-rating the strength of the enemy', and called on the Communists to oppose the imperialist plans for expansion and aggression.[3] The radicals in the CPI's Central Committee argued that India was a capitalist country, where the bourgeoisie had gone over to the imperialist camp, and that it was time to discard the policy of co-operation with the Nehru administration and, instead, launch an all-out offensive against it. Their viewpoint prevailed at the second congress of the party held in early 1948; and suitable action followed soon after. The Nehru government responded to this by banning the party under the Defence of India Act, a legacy of the colonial rule, and arresting many of its 89,263 members.

Despite this, the party managed to lead sporadic strikes by blue and white collar workers, and initiate or sustain militant peasant movements in Telangana and Malabar (i.e. present-day north Kerala) in the south, and parts of West Bengal and Assam. In Telangana, the party succeeded in establishing village soviets, complete with the people's courts and militia, in 3,000 villages covering 16,000 square miles, a development which brought violent reprisals from the Central government. The 50,000 to 60,000 troops deployed by the Nehru administration crushed the movement in two years, from late 1948 to late 1950, by employing the tactic of creating strategic hamlets on the model then being followed by the British in Malaya against Communist guerrillas there, and killing nearly 4,000 Communist and militant peasants, and arresting another 10,000 Communists and their sympathizers.[4] This and other setbacks, which brought the party's national membership down to 20,000 in 1950, encouraged the moderates within the party to reassert themselves.

They were helped by two other factors: the ban on the party had been successfully challenged in the High Courts of a few States as being in violation of the fundamental rights guaranteed by the new Constitution, that had been promulgated in early 1950; and a decision had been taken by the Central government to hold a general election based on a universal suffrage in the country in late 1951 to early 1952. Consequently, the party's special conference in October 1951 reversed the militant stance of the past few years.

The document, which committed the party to contest the forth-coming general elections, summed up the party's post-independence policies thus:

> For a time, it was advocated that the main weapon in our struggle would be the weapon of general strike of industrial workers, followed by a countrywide insurrection as [happened] in Russia. Later, on the basis of a wrong understanding of the lessons of the Chinese Revolution, the thesis was put forward that since ours is a semi-colonial country like China, our revolution would develop in the same way as in China, with partisan war of peasantry as its main weapon . . . [but] the Party has now arrived at a new understanding of the correct path. . . . It can . . . be seen that while the previous line of reliance on the general strike in the cities neglected the role of the peasantry, the subsequent one of partisan struggle [in the countryside] minimized the role of the working class. . . . Both the lines in practice meant ignoring the task of building the alliance of the working class and the peasantry . . . of putting the working class at the head of this [United] Front in the liberation struggle.[5]

The working class need not necessarily be guided by the Communist Party, since the party's new tactic was to forge a united front with any and every 'progressive' organization in the country in order to isolate and combat the two main enemies of the Indian people – foreign imperialist forces and their agents, the Indian monopoly capitalists.

Accordingly, the pro-Communist AITUC called for the unity of the working class and for 'one union in each industry'. To prove its sincerity, the AITUC dissolved its union among railway employees so as to strengthen the independent All India Railwaymen's Federation. 'While the initial mass battles of the working class and their trade unions were led by the Communists and their friends, it was only when the Communists and non-Communists formed a united front and main-tained the unity of the working class and trade unions irrespective of their political differences that onslaughts of the bourgeoisie could be defeated and effective gains made,' said S. A. Dange, the president of the AITUC and a prominent Communist leader.[6] The party formally called off its militant peasant movement in Telangana, and decided to restrict popular agitations in the future to those which fell within the constitutional framework.

In short, after twenty-five years of dramatic policy swings between total support to the national bourgeoisie under the overall anti-imperialist strategy (as during the periods of 1925–7, 1935–41, and 1945–7) and total opposition to this class under an anti-capitalist strategy (as during the periods 1928–34, 1942–4, and 1948–50), the party now settled for a somewhat complex policy of collaboration with it to combat imperialism abroad and monopoly capitalism at home. This meant, in effect, that the party decided to enter electoral politics on a platform of opposition to the Nehru administration in its domestic policies, and support to its foreign policy of non-alignment towards the two major power blocs, a stand which dovetailed with Soviet Russia's wish to see India do no more than stay out of the Western camp.

The election results strengthened the position of the moderates in the party since, with twenty-three seats in Parliament, the Communists and their allies emerged as the second largest group, well ahead of the Socialists. Nearly 5·5 million electors voted for the party and its allies in Parliamentary contests, and 6·2 million, constituting 7·4 per cent of the total votes cast, did so in the State assembly constituencies.[7] The Communist-led Front emerged as the single largest group in the assembly of the old (composite) State of Madras, with strong support from those parts of the State – the Andhra delta, Malabar, and Tanjore – where the Communists had, in the past, led peasant agitations.

This Front was in the process of negotiating a coalition with other non-Congress groups in the assembly with a view to forming a ministry when, at the behest of Nehru, the State governor appointed C. Rajagopalachari, a much-respected and rabidly anti-Communist Congress leader, to the State's legislative council – a manoeuvre quite within the constitutional limits – and asked him to form the ministry, even though the Congress party, like the Communist-led Front, did not have an absolute majority. On taking office, Rajagopalachari openly used bribery and nepotism to wean away some members from the ranks of those non-Congress groups which were, until then, engaged in finalizing details of a coalition with the Communist-led Front. These tactics of Nehru upset the radicals in the Communist Party, who reiterated their argument that following the path of bourgeois democracy was a futile exercise. The moderates, on the other hand, downgraded this event, and stated that the main task of the party was to counter American imperialism – which was intent on drawing India into its embrace, both militarily and economically – by supporting Nehru's foreign policy of non-alignment. In the end, the two sides compromised around the centrist position of opposition to the Nehru government in internal affairs and support to it in external affairs, that had first been adopted in 1951; and the third congress of the party, held in early 1954, endorsed it.

Later that year, America fostered two regional defence pacts, the South East Asia Treaty Organization and the Middle East Defence

Organization (later to be called the Central Treaty Organization), which included Pakistan, with whom India has had hostile relations since its creation in 1947. But before the Indian Communists could launch their propaganda against these pacts and American imperialism, and gain some popularity, Nehru and the Congress party strongly denounced the pacts and the American policy of Cold War. Towards the end of 1954, Nehru paid a state visit to the People's Republic of China, which his administration had recognized in 1950, a step which the CPI could not help approving.

On the eve of the Indian Republic Day, in January 1955, an editorial in *Pravda*, the newspaper of the Soviet Union's Communist Party, praised not only India's foreign policy under the Congress rule, but *also* its achievements at home, thus undermining the Communist propaganda in Andhra Pradesh – where the CPI was making a strong bid to win power at the forthcoming mid-term elections – and causing a drop in the Communist vote. Soon after, the Indian government signed an agreement with Russia for the establishment of a steel plant. In June, Nehru visited Soviet Russia; and in November, N. Khruschev and N. Bulganin, the highest Russian dignitaries, paid a return visit to India. The following month, Ajoy Ghosh, the CPI's general secretary, outlined a programme of 'unity with and struggle against the Congress' to build a 'national democratic front' which implied not only the concept of 'peaceful transition to socialism' (an idea which was to receive the recommendation of the Soviet Communist Party a few months later) but also that of 'national democracy'. Early next year, the CPI came out in support of the Congress government's Second Five Year Plan, covering the period of 1956–61 (whereas it had disapproved of the First Five Year Plan).

The party became more reformist in outlook when it won a majority in the legislative assembly of Kerala, in the general elections of 1957, and was allowed to form the government. The following year, the party conference adopted a new constitution which read:

> The Communist Party of India strives to achieve full Democracy and Socialism by peaceful means. It considers that by developing a powerful mass movement, by winning a majority in Parliament and by backing it with mass sanctions, the working class and its allies can overcome the resistance of the forces of reaction and insure that Parliament becomes an instrument of people's will for effecting fundamental changes in the economic, social and State structure.[8]

Reflecting the general party mood, the Communist administration in Kerala did no more than attempt to effect the agrarian reform that had been suggested by the Congress itself, ginger up the sluggish government machinery – and reform the privately managed educational institutions, most of which were run by the Nair Service Society, an influential communal organization of Nairs, upper caste Hindus, and the Roman Catholic Church, which claimed the religious allegiance of about a fifth of the State's population. Taking advantage of the feeling of unease and hysteria that the NSS and Catholic Church managed to create regarding the educational reform bill, the central office of the Congress – then run by Indira Gandhi, the party President – encouraged the formation of a united front of non-Communist forces in the State, and later encouraged it to launch a militant non-co-operation movement against the Communist administration, and thus create 'disturbed conditions'.[9] When this happened, the Central government dismissed the Communist ministry, in mid-1959, on the ground that it had failed to maintain 'law and order' in the State.

This revived the differences between the radicals and moderates in the party, with the radicals advocating rejection of the line of peaceful transition to socialism, formally adopted in 1958, and the moderates proposing a further rightward move and a seeking of allies among 'progressive' Congressmen on the plea that the reactionaries in the Congress were menacing the party's 'middle path'. Both groups prepared for a confrontation at the party's sixth conference, in April 1961, but a common desire to fight the forthcoming general elections – only ten months away – as a united party led them to adopt a compromise resolution which endorsed the tactic of 'unity and struggle' with regard to the Congress, which was now described as the 'organ of the national bourgeoisie'.

The fragile truce between the two sides, however, could not stand the pressure of the armed conflict that broke out, in October 1962, between India and China on the question of border demarcation. The moderates (who had earlier, in 1961, committed the party to the side of Russia in both the ideological and border disputes between Russia and China) were for condemning China as the aggressor, extending unqualified support to Nehru and his set of conditions for opening negotiations with China, which included China's unconditional withdrawal from the territory which India claimed to be its own, and buying arms from any country on 'commercial terms'. The radicals too were for negotiations with China, but without any pre-conditions from either side; and they were against acceptance of any 'imperialist aid' which, they felt, would endanger national independence and sovereignty.

In a showdown between the two groups at the party's National Council meeting, in November, the moderates won, and immediately began calling their opponents 'pro-Chinese agents'. Soon afterwards, forty of the 110 members of the National Council, along with hundreds of radical party leaders and activists, were arrested by the Indian government under the emergency powers acquired by it in the wake of the border clash with China. The moderates were now in a position to follow their policy of forming a united front with the Congress un-hindered, and did so, in the name of defending the country's sovereignty. S. A. Dange, their leader and the general secretary of the AITUC, offered an industrial truce to the Nehru government without bothering to consult any of the constituent trade unions.

The moderates tightened their hold over the party machine and denied the rights of 'inner democracy' to those of the radicals who were re-leased from jail and wished to express their viewpoint within the party's inner councils. Frustrated, the radicals began to press for a party con-ference to thrash out the issues of ideology and tactics, while the moderates started alleging that their opponents, following instructions from Peking, were bent on splitting the party. This went on until March 1964 when the *Current*, a Bombay weekly, published a facsimile of a letter allegedly written by S. A. Dange, in 1924, to the British Viceroy of India, offering to co-operate with the government in exchange for his release from prison to which he had been sent along with others, for 'conspiring' to overthrow the British government.[10]

Dange, now chairman of the CPI, roundly dismissed this and other letters of that period as forgery (even though the actual set of letters existed in the National Archives). At the National Council's meeting, in April, he rejected the suggestion, made by the radicals, that he should vacate the chair while the question of the authenticity of these letters was discussed. Thereupon, thirty-two (radical) members of the National Council walked out.

When their subsequent efforts to patch up differences with the moderate group which controlled the secretariat failed, these members of the National Council called a 'convention' of the Communist Party of India, in Tenali, Andhra, in August. The convention urged all mem-bers to help in 'reorganizing' the Communist Party, and declared that 'No question of being either pro-Peking or pro-Moscow shall arise whatever our enemies shout to slander the cause of Communism'.[11] This was followed by a full-scale conference, in October–November, in Calcutta – claiming to be the seventh congress of the Communist Party of India – where the issue of the ideological differences between Moscow and China was not even raised, much less discussed. In contrast, the conference held by the moderates, in December, in Bombay – also claiming to be the seventh congress of the Communist Party of India – endorsed the Russian stand in the ideological conflict. A few months later, their decision to contest mid-term elections in Kerala obliged the radical leaders to call their party the Communist Party of India (Marxist) so as to distinguish it from the Communist Party of India, which, despite the split in 1964, was allowed by the Chief Election Commission-er to retain the electoral symbol first allotted to it in 1951.

Thus the schism in the CPI which had first appeared in 1955 (much before Khruschev's denunciation of Joseph Stalin in 1956, and the

Moscow declaration of 1957 favouring peaceful transition to socialism) materialized into a fully fledged split in 1964. 'The split was over fundamental issues and programme, strategy and tactics of the Indian communist movement,' states Mohan Ram, an Indian journalist and author; 'and a number of factors hastened and formalized it – the Sino–Soviet ideological dispute, the Sino–Indian border dispute, the Sino–Soviet border dispute, and the Nehru government's anxiety to placate the pro-Moscow wing of the Communist Party and use it as a lobby to influence communist countries over the border dispute (with China).'[12]

Although the Calcutta conference in October–November 1964 signalled the birth of the CPI(M), the party leadership did not get a chance properly to formulate party policies and ideology for a year and a half. More than 900 of its leading members were arrested by the Central government in late December 1964, under the emergency powers of 'preventive detention' assumed by it, on a vague charge of promoting 'an internal revolution to synchronize with a fresh Chinese attack' – an attack which did not materialize then, in 1965, or later – and kept in jail until April–May 1966.[13]

THE COMMUNIST MOVEMENT: AFTER 1964

The CPI(M)'s work among peasants and workers is apart from and independent of fighting and winning elections.

R. K. S. Nair, an Indian journalist[1]

To Indira Gandhi, the Communist challenge today is represented not by the CPI but by the CPI(M).

Ranajit Roy, an Indian journalist[2]

The CPI's ideology is a combination of tailing behind the left wing of the Congress party and of formulating a political line which is acceptable to the government of the Soviet Union.

K. P. Karunakaran, an Indian political scientist[3]

When the CPI(M) leadership defined its policies and programme, differences with the CPI emerged on the assessment of the stage of revolution in India, the class character of the Indian state, and the strategy and tactics to be followed to create a socialist society. In the CPI's view, independence of India was a 'historic event . . . for all mankind' that had set the country on 'a path of independent development'; and, although the overall economic progress had been inadequate, the economic situation (in 1964) was one which signified 'consolidation of political independence and a step forward to economic regeneration'. In contrast, the CPI(M) document stated that the country's independence in 1947 signified no more than a 'settlement' between British imperialism and the Congress (the representative body of the Indian bourgeoisie) and the Muslim League (the chief organization of the Muslim feudal interests in the sub-continent, whose demand for a separate Muslim-majority state of Pakistan was conceded by the British). Since then, despite the introduction of economic 'planning' and the Congress Party's periodic resolutions in support of a 'socialistic pattern of society', the country had been developed along the path of capitalism – which meant transforming feudal exploiters at home into capitalist exploiters, and creating greater co-operation between the big bourgeoisie in India and the monopolistic or oligopolistic corporations in the imperialist countries. Furthermore, between two possible types of capitalist development – the conservative path taken by the indigenous big bourgeoisie with the active co-operation of foreign monopolies, and the radical path taken by the indigenous non-big bourgeoisie, concerned with preserving and consolidating its independence – the Congress government had followed more the first course than the second. The CPI held the opposite view: that is, the Congress administration had followed more the second course than the first.

As regards the class character of the Indian state, the CPI document said, 'The state in India is the organ of the class rule of the national bourgeoisie as a whole, in which the big bourgeoisie holds powerful influence. This class has strong links with landlords. These factors give rise to reactionary pulls on state power.' (This implies that, once freed of the 'power influence' of the big bourgeoisie and landlords, the ruling national bourgeoisie will follow only progressive policies.) The CPI(M) document, on the other hand, noted, 'The present Indian state is the organ of the class rule of the bourgeoisie and landlords, led by the big bourgeoisie who are increasingly collaborating with foreign finance capital in pursuit of the capitalist path of development.'

However, both parties were agreed that the time for a socialist revolution was not yet, and that, first, the current bourgeois democratic revolution, initiated in August 1947, had to be completed by forming an alliance of the anti-feudal, anti-monopoly-capitalist, and anti-imperialist elements in society so as to isolate, and then defeat, the three class enemies: landlords, monopoly capitalists, and imperialists. They were also agreed that, in the main, mass movements and actions of non-violent nature, including participation in elections, were to be the means to politicize the exploited masses, and to make them class conscious, in order to wage a struggle against their class enemies. Where they differed was on the position of the non-big bourgeoisie (i.e. rich peasants and non-monopoly capitalists) in the alliance, the leadership of the alliance, and the nature of the transient state on its way to socialism. The CPI was for forging an alliance of four classes – working class, toiling peasantry, petty bourgeoisie, and the non-big bourgeoisie – with the aim of ushering in a 'National Democratic' state, which had been defined by the international Communist conference in Moscow in 1960 as 'one that has won complete economic independence from imperialism and is ruled by a broad anti-imperialist front that includes the national bourgeoisie'.[4] The CPI(M), on the other hand, was for forming an alliance of three classes – working class, toiling peasantry, and petty bourgeoisie – with the objective of ushering in a 'People's Democratic' state. The CPI was prepared to let the non-big bourgeoisie share leadership of the alliance with the working class; but the CPI(M) was not.

The main difference, in practical terms, between the two parties boiled down to the attitude to be adopted towards the national bourgeoisie and its party, the Congress. Although claiming to be follow-ing the policy of 'unity as well as struggle' with respect to the Congress, the CPI had in effect exercised more 'unity' with the Congress than 'struggle' against it; whereas the CPI(M) had, from its inception in 1964, taken a strong anti-Congress stand. In mid-1966, it began actively to help to create a broad anti-Congress front to fight the 1967 elections. In contrast, the CPI leadership showed more interest in concentrating on defeating the CPI(M) at the polls, wherever it could, than the Congress, partly because it wished to prove that the CPI, and not the CPI(M), was the *real* and bigger Communist Party. In the end, by contesting fifty more parliamentary seats than the CPI(M)'s fifty-nine, the CPI managed to secure $\frac{1}{2}$ per cent more of the popular vote than the CPI(M) (4·8 per cent as against 4·3 per cent). (However, in the State assembly elections, the CPI trailed behind the CPI(M) by $\frac{1}{2}$ per cent of the popular vote.)

Although the CPI joined the non-Congress ministries in many of the States, where the Congress lost power, it was not too unhappy to see these coalition governments fall (often due to internal dissensions) and the tide of anti-Congressism, that had arisen in the country in the mid-1960s, subside. The rise of Indira Gandhi as the 'radical' leader of the 'progressive' wing of the Congress in the summer of 1969 gave the CPI a chance to return to its previous pro-Congress stance. It attached ideological importance to the split in the Congress. 'The alignment of the political forces on two sides of the barrier signifies rift within the class of the bourgeoisie,' stated the party's National Council in September 1969. 'The recent developments . . . signify sharpening of contradic-tions between the pro-monopoly and anti-monopoly sections of the national bourgeoisie.' The CPI(M) Politbureau, on the other hand, did not think that the exit of the Syndicate leaders – described merely as 'the most aggressive representatives of the monopolists and the extreme political reaction' – from the party had altered the essential class charac-ter of the Congress, which continued to be under the influence of the 'big bourgeoisie'.[5] Nonetheless, the CPI(M) supported the Indira Gandhi government in Parliament, where, following the Congress split, her party had lost its majority, because it believed that the other alter-native, a coalition ministry of right-wing parties including the Syndicate-Congress, would lead to the banning of both the Communist parties and a severe government repression.

This, however, did not inhibit Indira Gandhi from actively co-operating with the CPI to ease out the CPI(M) from the CPI(M)-dominated ministries in Kerala (in October 1969) and West Bengal (in March 1970). Later, this co-operation was carried a step farther when in the mid-term elections in Kerala, in September 1970, the CPI forged an alliance with the Congress with the major aim of defeating the CPI(M), which it succeeded in doing. This arrangement was extended to such major States as Uttar Pradesh, Bihar, Punjab, and Tamil Nadu when Parliamentary elections were held in March 1971; and it helped the party to win twenty out of the total of twenty-three seats, and thus manage to maintain its previous strength. By then, the party had become thoroughly respectable as far as the Indira Gandhi-led Congress was concerned. 'Indira Gandhi regards the CPI as a democratic party with a left bias and not as a Communist party in the conventional sense,' noted Ranajit Roy, an Indian journalist. 'Even the Americans have come to have the same view of the CPI. A very senior American diplomat explained to a group of Delhi journalists, soon after the Kerala mid-term elections last year [i.e. 1970], why the Americans thought so.'[6] In the most widespread electoral adjustment between any two parties in the country yet, the Congress stayed out of 130 State assembly constituencies in the March 1972 elections in favour of the CPI, thus enabling the latter to win eighty seats. This contrasted with the eleven seats won by the CPI on its own strength (versus the CPI(M)'s thirty-four).

Yet the CPI was far from jubilant, because, as its National Council put it, 'a large number of reactionary, anti-people and anti-Communist people had been elected to the State assemblies on the Congress ticket'.[7] The subsequent actions of the Congress ministries, too, disappointed the party. 'The massive victories in the elections . . . has made the national bourgeoisie self-confident,' noted the party's National Council in September 1972. 'The new prestige and power is sought to be used to effect a slideback in policies from the promises made during the elections and [this] . . . can be seen today, both in the field of agrarian reforms and in the field of anti-monopoly measures.'[8] In other words, the 'rift within the class of the bourgeoisie', and the 'leftward shift' in the Congress that the CPI analysts had perceived in mid-1969 had, by now, proved temporary. But this did not seem to materially affect the friendly relationship between the two parties. (They forged an alliance in the mid-term elections in Uttar Pradesh and Orissa, in 1974.)

On the other hand, relationship between the CPI and the CPI(M) remained as strained as ever, and that between the Congress and the CPI(M) downright hostile, especially when the CPI(M) had emerged as the dominant party in all of the three States with an effective Communist movement, namely, Andhra Pradesh, Kerala, and West Bengal, and had improved its popularity among both the industrial proletariat and the poor peasantry during the period 1966–71.

In order mainly to regain some of the lost support among peasants, due to the defection of radical cadres to the CPI(M), the CPI leadership launched a 'land grab' movement in the summer of 1970. What was to be 'grabbed', however, was limited to the cultivable waste land owned by the government, and the excess land above the legal limit, belonging to the former princes and big industrialists, but *not* to the rich peasants and non-monopoly capitalists. M. G. Vaidya, an Indian journalist, described a typical 'land grab' operation thus:

The CPI [in Madhya Pradesh] decided to occupy part of the huge farm of the Nawab [i.e. Lord] of Bhopal, which is 28 miles from Bhopal. The CPI workers said to the landless in the nearby villages, 'If you come you'll get land.' This aroused a lot of interest. But the Nawab asked for police help, and got it; and this scared a lot of people. Even then, 1,500 people turned up, on the appointed day, to occupy land. Seventy-eight of them were arrested. The police told them that if they apologized, they would be let off. Many of them did so; but some refused, and were sent to jail. But the CPI did not follow up on these militant fellows to try to politicize them. So, there was no consolidation of the gains made. The CPI got some publicity; and that was all.[9]

The continued lack of support for the party among peasants was highlighted by the fact that 'very few' of the delegates to the party's ninth congress, in October 1971, were engaged in the 'agricultural labour front'. In contrast, 25 per cent of the delegates to the ninth congress of the CPI(M), held in June 1972, were from the 'peasant and agricultural front'. However, both party conferences had a high proportion of delegates, described as 'middle class and intelligentsia' or 'middle class and middle peasantry': 55 per cent in the case of the CPI(M) and 64·5 per cent for the CPI. (These figures were not of course reflective of the class composition of the *primary* membership of these parties. Only 25 per cent of the 17,637 CPI members in West Bengal in June 1968, for instance, belonged to the 'middle class and middle peasantry'.)[10]

Both parties are meticulous about who should be allowed to join, the CPI(M), with a national membership of 105,000 in 1971, more so than the CPI, with a total membership of 243,000. An applicant for party membership must be recommended by two party members, and then serve a period of apprenticeship, ranging from six months to a year, and be accepted by the local cell or ward committee, before he or she is taken on as a member. Then the member must pay his dues and levies in time, and attend a minimum number of meetings of his cell or ward committee. The CPI(M) rules stipulate, in addition, that a member must put in a certain number of hours each week either for the party or its allied worker/peasant organizations. A small proportion of members, varying between 1 and 4 per cent, are selected by the leadership to become full-time party workers, on a nominal allowance of Rs 100 (£5) to Rs 200 (£10) a month, to maintain the party machine and work in the trade unions or peasant associations affiliated to the party's central labour or peasant organization.

Money for this and other purposes comes mainly from membership dues and levy (which varies from 1 to 3 per cent of the member's income), and donations by members and sympathizers, and peasants' and workers' organizations. Often peasant associations tell their members to maintain the party's full-time workers by giving them a small portion of their harvest. Trade unions pay allowances to party workers for their time and professional assistance. They also help the parties in raising funds for fighting elections, not by donating money from their general funds, which is forbidden by law,[11] but by asking their members, informally, to contribute, say, one day's wages to the party's election fund. 'It is reported that toddy tappers in Kerala State, who are members of the Toddy Tappers' Union, controlled by the Communists, have in their personal capacity contributed liberally to the Communist Party funds,' writes N. Pattabhi Raman.[12] In the present circumstances, these funds go to the CPI(M), not the CPI, which, having lost most of its mass base, has come to depend increasingly on donations from some of the private firms engaged in trade with Soviet Russia and East Europe, which now runs into hundreds of crores of rupees a year.[13] 'The bulk of the Soviet (and socialist bloc) trade with India is through private export–import houses, some of which have the unofficial recognition of the CPI,' reports M. R., an Indian journalist. 'The Soviet solicitude for some of the cashew-nut exporters [in Kerala] is baffling, and only the CPI in Kerala can give a credible explanation.'[14]

No wonder that the CPI has become so subservient to the Soviet Union's international interests, and that some of its leaders have been driven to protest, privately, that their party is being used as 'a post office to the Soviet embassy [in Delhi]'.[15] Whenever a conflict arises between the CPI leadership's assessment of the internal situation and the general direction of the Soviet Union's international policies, the latter takes precedence, with officials at the Soviet embassy stepping in to 'persuade' the recalcitrant CPI hierarchy. 'Soviet analysts, sensing the discontent within the CPI about its "collaborationist", "reformist" role, have been working overtime to distribute articles which emphasize the positive aspects of the "Indira Gandhi government", and what can be achieved by a collaborationist approach to economic and social policies,' reported Romesh Thapar, the Delhi correspondent of the *Economic and Political Weekly*, in September 1972.[16]

During his visit to India, in November 1973, Leonid Brezhnev, the Soviet Communist Party chief, went one step ahead. 'The ruling party, the Indian National Congress, has put forward an important democratic programme of broad socio-economic transformation designed to improve the life of its people,' he told a public meeting in Delhi. 'It [the Congress] has proclaimed socialism as its goal. Broad political and social circles in India are known to come out in favour of socialism.' Later, when the CPI delegation reportedly tried to raise the question of relations with the Congress, he reproached them. Where was the need for strikes in a developing economy when production was the main problem? he asked the delegation. And why did the CPI make so much fuss about monopolies which . . . did not exist in India?[17] In short, the CPI remains as uncritically attached to the Soviet Union as ever before.

Meanwhile, the CPI(M) has succeeded in establishing an identity of its own, ideologically and financially independent of both Moscow and Peking. After three years of silence on the subject – due to practical and other reasons – the party leadership produced, in late 1967, a document which set it apart from both the Communist Party of the Soviet Union (CPSU) and the Communist Party of China (CPC). This document rejected the Soviet position on almost all the important issues of ideology: the 'major contradictions' in the world arena; 'war and peace'; 'disarmament'; 'peaceful coexistence' ('the interpretation of the concept of peaceful coexistence between socialist and imperialist States is reduced by the revisionists to mean . . . peaceful economic competition, and thus conceals the truth that the struggle between the two systems comprises every field of an economic, political, ideological, and military nature'); and on the issue of 'forms of transition to socialism' ('there is no denying the fact that the proletariat would prefer to achieve the revolution and win power by peaceful means', but the 'modern revisionists' had neglected to apply the Marxist-Leninist method of examining the question concretely, that is, examining 'the relation of the state and its police-military apparatus', thus betraying the 'Marxist-Leninist teachings of the state and revolution'). It went on to state that 'the bankrupt revisionist line of Soviet leaders has assumed such absurd proportions that it is glaringly seen and understood . . . as more and more a line of conciliation, compromise, and collaboration between the two great powers, a line which objectively preserves and perpetuates the international status quo and which, as a line, summarily abandons the revolutionary class struggle of the international proletariat'.

But this did not lead the party to accept 'the totally erroneous idea that the Soviet Union has become an ally of US imperialism or is working for sharing world hegemony with American imperialism and for the division of spheres of influence in the world, as this is tantamount to . . . placing the Soviet Union outside the socialist camp'. That is, the party document rejected the Chinese Communist Party's analysis of the world situation as well.

Furthermore, the CPI(M) differed with the CPC on the assessment of the internal situation, namely, the class character of the Indian state, nature of class contradictions, and the tactics to be employed to isolate, and then overthrow, class enemies.[18] 'It [the CPC's analysis] is virtually negating our premise of a deepening economic crisis and the initial stages of a political crisis, and is, in its place, substituting the premise of an already matured revolutionary situation and a revolutionary crisis, demanding the highest revolutionary form of struggle,' stated a resolution by the CPI(M)'s Central Committee in 1967.[19] The establishment in 1969 of the pro-Peking Communist Party of India (Marxist-Leninist) formalized the differences between the CPI(M) and the Chinese party. The CPI(M)'s general stand was summed up by its Politbureau, in August 1971, thus: 'Each Communist Party should apply Marxism-Leninism to its problems, irrespective of the Chinese-Soviet differences, and develop its own revolutionary movement. . . . We follow an independent policy like the parties in North Vietnam and North Korea.'[20]

The 'independent policy' of the CPI(M) has been defined, aptly, by a student of Indian Communism, as 'anti-revisionism *sans* Maoism' in the ideological sphere, and 'combining parliamentary functioning with mass action, leaving the onus for peaceful transition to socialism to the class enemy' in the political-tactical field.[21] The policy of the pro-Moscow CPI, in contrast, boils down to 'revisionism' in the ideological sphere, and a commitment to the idea of peaceful transition to socialism through a series of structural reforms strictly within the present social system. Although both parties participate in the parliamentary process, they have different attitudes towards it. This is well illustrated by the manner in which they have ruled Kerala, a State where they have exercised power, alternatively, since 1967, and where the united Communist Party first secured office in 1957.

The present-day Kerala came into existence in 1956 when Malabar, the Malayalam-speaking part of the old Madras State, was merged with Travancore-Cochin, formed some years earlier by amalgamating Travancore and Cochin, two princely States which were notable for their above-average literacy rate. Literacy had been helped in these States by the long-standing Christian missions (an outgrowth of the European incursion into this part of the sub-continent dating back to the sixteenth century) and the impetus that their latter-day educational activities had given to the Nair Service Society (NSS) of Nairs, and the Sri Narayan Paripalana Sangam (SNDP) of Ezhavas, a lower Hindu caste of toddy tappers, to spread education among their caste members, in order chiefly to secure government jobs. A fairly literate and socially aware population, especially in the urban centres, had proved receptive to the nascent Communist movement, which began here in the 1930s among industrial workers.

After the vicissitudes of the 1940s, the Communist Party was able to consolidate its support, built up over the years, and show it. The party won 25 out of 108 seats in the assembly of Travancore-Cochin in the election of 1952, and emerged as the main opposition to the Congress. In the mid-term elections of 1954 the party fared equally well. By then the party had intensified its demand for 'One Kerala' to include all the Malayalam-speaking areas, including Malabar, where the party was in the hands of those leaders, who, as Congressmen in the mid-1930s, had won mass popularity by combining anti-imperialist movement with anti-landlord agitation. When the demand for 'One Kerala' was conceded, in 1956, the morale of the party soared. It entered the general elections to the State assembly in 1957 with a serious intention of winning a majority. It did. It secured 65 seats out of 126, on a popular vote of 35·3 per cent.[22]

As stated earlier,[23] the Communist government gave priority to reforming land relations and private educational institutions,[24] which aroused the ire not only of the landlords, a small minority, but also of the Catholic Church, the NSS, and SNDP, the three powerful communal bodies that ran hundreds of schools and colleges, often on commercial lines – an activity that invested them with much social and economic importance. As a result, they launched a propaganda campaign against the Communist administration. The Catholic Church had many of its followers seriously believe that what the 'Godless' Communists were really planning was nothing less than physical destruction of the church. 'Many of the schools run by the Catholic Church are within the compound of a church,' said E. M. S. Namboodripad, a present-day CPI(M) leader, who was then the chief minister. 'Our Education Bill said that if a management did not do certain things, then the government was entitled to take over a school. So church hierarchy told its congregation that the Communists were about to attack churches. And they maintained a constant vigilance!'[25]

Soon these organizations escalated their opposition to the Bill by securing the support of almost all the non-Communist parties in the State, and encouraging the students in their institutions, and others, to demonstrate against the Communist government. Finding themselves in the novel situation of having to face hostile, militant crowds in the streets, both the Communist ministry and its supporters became defensive. This, in turn, encouraged the non-Communist alliance – now being guided by such Congress dignitaries as Indira Gandhi, then the President of the party – to launch a 'non-co-operation' movement against the Communist government, which included withholding payment of taxes, with the ultimate aim of creating disorder and providing the Central authorities with an alibi to dismiss the Communist ministry for having failed to maintain 'law and order'. And, so, in July 1959, the Communists, still enjoying a majority in the assembly, found themselves stripped of power.

A common alliance by almost all the non-Communist parties at the next assembly elections, in 1960, reduced the Communist strength in the assembly by about a third, although their popular vote rose by 1·5 per cent. The split in the party, in 1964, caused only a minor decline in the total vote obtained by the two Communist parties, in the 1965 elections, when they opposed each other. The same happened in 1967, when the two parties contested elections as part of the anti-Congress United

Front, with the CPI(M) securing 24 per cent of the vote and fifty-four seats, and the CPI 9 per cent of the vote and twenty seats. They subsequently became partners in the United Front government.

This, however, did not stop the feuding between the two parties, particularly when they differed widely regarding the value of administrative power at the State level. While conceding that 'the power and resources' of a State government functioning under 'our Constitution' are 'limited', C. Achutha Menon, a CPI leader in Kerala, maintained that 'it is [still] possible to give some relief to our much suffering people'.[26] On the other hand, B. T. Ranadive, a CPI(M) leader, declared in June 1969 that:

> The task of the Marxist-dominated United Front governments of
> Kerala and West Bengal is to unleash the discontent of the people
> rather than give relief. . . . Pursuant to this tactic, the Marxist
> ministers have been told to press ahead with legislation which is
> likely to be vetoed by the Centre or the High Court. Such
> confrontations are designed to tell the masses of the impossibility
> of carrying through fundamental reform under the present
> Constitution.[27]

Robert L. Hardgrave Jr, an American political scientist, summarized the differences between the two parties thus:

> The Marxists under the United Front government sought to
> continue 'administration and struggle', popular initiative plus
> utilization of the administrative machinery for the advancement of
> the 'basic classes', [whereas the CPI's stand was] either give up
> administration and continue to struggle, or give up the struggle
> and carry on administration.[28]

Due to these and other disagreements, the CPI, along with the non-Communist partners in the United Front government, aligned with the Congress opposition, and brought about the downfall of the CPI(M)-led United Front ministry in October 1969. It then formed a 'minority' government of its own, with the Congress supporting it from 'outside', an arrangement which lasted a year, when fresh elections were held. These confirmed the previous scheme of things – with the CPI(M) in opposition and the CPI in power with the help of the Congress and a few other non-Congress groups. In other words, since the end of 1969, the CPI has been more or less free to follow its own brand of parliamentarism, and a judgment can be formed about the effect this has had on the government administration, electors, and the party.

Evidence suggests that the CPI has failed to make administration less bureaucratic or corrupt than is the case elsewhere;[29] it has come to view, consciously or subconsciously, agitations by the working people in terms of maintaining 'law and order'; it has become more dependent on administrative measures and machinery than on mass action to nurture and expand its electoral base; and it has come to place an excessive emphasis on parliamentary activity and winning elections which, in turn, has made many of its leaders vulnerable to corrupt practices.

One of the first things that the CPI ministry did, in late 1969, was to 'restore' law and order in the State – which, it claimed, had deteriorated during the rule of the previous CPI(M)-dominated government – by making an excessive use of the police force to suppress, in the main, the CPI(M)-led agitation of the landless for land. 'With dusk, the armed policemen go round the huts of villagers . . . raid huts of "suspects", beat up inmates . . . cart away men and women of their choice in police vans and dump them in lock-ups for a protracted political education, administered with *lathis* (i.e. batons), boots and bare fists,' reported Ramji, an Indian journalist. 'The policemen tell the terrified peasants that their government is no longer in power; "Your EMS (Namboo-dripad)[30] cannot save you". . . . False cases are foisted on all "suspects" who have had nothing to do with any other crime . . . except that they were either Marxists or their sympathizers.'[31]

But the return of 'law and order' to the State did not make the CPI-led ministry take kindly to a peaceful agitation in early 1971 for an increment in salaries by the government employees, whose union is barred, by law, from affiliating to any politically inclined central labour organization. 'It was strange for this correspondent to hear from the mouth of a CPI party official, who was witnessing the recent demonstration and *satyagraha* [i.e. peaceful sit-in] of the State government employees demanding Central government rates of interim relief [in salaries] that the only answer to such "unreasonable agitations and threats was to give these fellows a good thrashing",' wrote the Kerala correspondent of the *Hindustan Standard*.[32]

The prevalence of such attitudes among its leaders drives the party to rely more and more on the use of administrative patronage in order to maintain or enlarge its popular support, which, in turn, makes it obsessive about winning elections, and leads it to adopt means which are not much different from those of the Congress. 'During the recent parliamentary elections, the toddy (i.e. palm liquor) shop contractors, public works department contractors, and sea-food exporters were compelled to "donate" large sums to . . . the CPI for election expenditure,' reported Ramji. 'In return, the toddy shop auctions in the High ranges and the Alleppey coastal belt and Trichur have been given at cut rates to the favourites of the CPI.'[33]

Soon after, investigations by two senior Indian Administrative Service officers – instituted in response to vociferous demands by the opposition – confirmed the main charges of corruption and nepotism against the CPI-led ministry. One charge related to the appointment of relatives of the chief minister, C. Achutha Menon, and some other ministers, to jobs in the government-owned Travancore-Cochin Chemicals Ltd; and the other, more serious, to the acquisition of 1,000 acres of a rubber estate for a proposed agricultural university in Trichur at a grossly inflated price, allegedly in consideration of a large donation – around Rs 2,500,000 (£125,000) – to the CPI.[34]

One of the documents to point a critical finger at the party, in this field, was the Organizational Report presented to the Party Congress in October 1971 by its national leadership.

> Electioneering, and parliamentary combinations and manipulation, become the main form of activity [of the party], while mobilizing and organizing the masses for action on an even wider scale and higher level, and building and strengthening mass class organizations and the party get relegated to the background. . . . Some party cadres spend most of their time in helping individuals to get their grievances redressed or even to win favour from ministers and individuals. In such cases, the main emphasis shifts from mass work, mass campaigns, and mass activity to representation and that too for individuals. Too often, such individuals also are evaluated, not in class terms, but on the basis of their worth as election supporters.[35]

However, there is no evidence to suggest that such self-critical statements by the national leaders are reversing the party's drift towards an unqualified reformism and parliamentarism – at least not in Kerala. There, the party has become so respectable and 'democratic' that it has won acceptance of its traditional enemies – the Catholic Church and the Indian National Trade Union Congress. 'Until recently the [Catholic] Church took a stand that its congregation should not vote for the Communists, or independents supported by the Communists; and so the [Catholic] Christians generally voted for the Congress,' said Victor Z. Nariuely, the editor of *Deepika*, a Catholic daily of Kottayam, Kerala. 'During the last two elections [in 1970 and 1971], however, the church hierarchy did not send out any directive at all.'[36] The 'official' reason for this change was that there were Communist parties on both rival fronts (one led by the Congress and the other by the CPI(M)) contesting these elections, and a directive to refrain from voting Communist would have deprived many of the Catholic electors of their right to vote. But the real reason was that the Congress had forged an alliance with the CPI in both cases, and thus rendered the CPI 'harmless' and the Catholic Church had recognized the new situation and quietly altered its stand. And so had the State branch of the staunchly anti-Communist INTUC. 'The CPI is no longer a classical Communist Party,' said M. K. Raghavan, an INTUC leader in Cochin. 'Until some years ago, the party believed that changes could be brought about by revolution alone. But now it agrees that changes are possible through legislation.'[37]

The 'classical Communist Party' for these and other organizations, now, was the CPI(M), a party which, to their chagrin, had continued to lead popular agitations even while being the senior partner in the United Front government, that ruled the State from March 1967 to October 1969, and had thus increased its popularity. Summarizing the situation that existed in the State during that period, O. P. Sangal, an Indian journalist, wrote:

> The very fact of the CPI(M) emerging as the dominant political force in the State changed the psychology of the overwhelming majority of the downtrodden and oppressed masses. They felt as if they had themselves come into power. And this feeling was strengthened by their everyday experience. For example, without any legislative or executive action on the part of the government, the wages of the agricultural workers increased far above the normal market rate because of the changed political atmosphere in the State. It became possible for ordinary workers and peasant leaders to get an oppressive government official transferred from his favourite area of operation.[38]

One other 'everyday experience' of the poor people was to see police no longer acting as the protector of the propertied classes, since they had been instructed by the CPI(M)-led government not to interfere in 'mass struggles' except when there was an actual outbreak of violence. In short, the CPI(M) had succeeded in combining 'struggle' with 'administration', and heightened the class consciousness of the State's working people.

And yet, the decision of the party leadership to join the coalition ministries in Kerala and West Bengal, in early 1967, had not been an easy one. The radicals within the party had opposed the idea on the ground that participation in a non-ideological coalition, with a view to operating a bourgeois state machinery, would retard, not accelerate, the revolutionary process, and that the party might at most support such a coalition from 'outside'. The others had argued that it was only by taking up a (dominant) position *within* a coalition government that the party could apply pressure on the non-CPI(M) partners and actively help mass movements. In a way, this was the continuation of a similar argument that had developed between the two sides at the founding conference of the party in 1964.

13

EXTRA-PARLIAMENTARY COMMUNISTS

Every tendency that overestimates the strength of the enemy is a revisionist tendency; learn to recognize it as such and fight against it.

> Charu Mazmudar, chairman of the Communist Party of India (Marxist-Leninist), addressing party members[1]

We Indian Communists seem to deify foreign leaders. The practice of the Naxalites to call Chairman Mao 'our Chairman' is symptomatic. Previously, it was Stalin; now, with some, it is Mao. There is no critical appreciation of Mao and other Communist leaders, just deification.

> Utpal Dutt, a leftist playwright and actor[2]

The Naxalites did not care for a mass base; they thought they would be able to skate safely on the thin ice of popular discontent; they took themselves to be fish in water without ascertaining if the water was congenial.

> *Frontier* editorial[3]

At the 1964 conference of the CPI(M), some of the radical delegates wanted to discuss the question of the inevitability of armed struggle to achieve socialism and the need for creating an underground armed militia to work in conjunction with the overground party organization (as the Communist Party in China had done in 1922). The party leaders rejected this on the practical ground that any such move would invite government repression and make it almost impossible to maintain any overground party apparatus. They argued that the working classes would prefer to achieve power through peaceful means, but, as and when the ruling classes in India felt threatened and began attacking the democratic rights of the masses, the CPI(M) would resist this, using weapons that matched the degree of repression: armed resistance would thus emerge as a natural response to the violence perpetrated by the bourgeois state. The radicals reasoned that the bourgeoisie would use state violence against the working classes anyway, so why not get ready now rather than later. Those on the other side of the argument replied that the organization and consciousness of the working classes were still at a low level, and to prepare for an armed struggle, when the socio-political situation was far from maturing into a revolutionary crisis, would reduce the party to the status of a sectarian group, lacking a broad base. This was the end of the argument; and a united party fought the 1967 general elections, in alliance with other non-Congress parties, with the main objective of widening its mass support.

The rout of the Congress in these elections, in many of the States, made the radicals question the party's official assessment of the political situation. A revolutionary situation had already developed, they concluded; and it was time the party leadership recognized this and gave a lead to the masses to smash the bourgeois state. Instead, they found the party's leaders toying with the idea of joining coalition ministries in West Bengal and Kerala, a fatal course to follow. As stated earlier,[4] they argued against this, but were outvoted. But the matter did not rest there.

Two of the radicals – Charu Mazmudar and Kanu Sanyal, peasant leaders living in the contiguous districts of Darjeeling and Jalpaiguri in northern West Bengal – expressed their disagreement with the party's official policy by directing a group of landless peasants to occupy a piece of land near Naxalbari, a village in Darjeeling, close to the borders of Nepal, (the then) East Pakistan, and Sikkim,[5] on the day following the installation of the United Front government in Calcutta, in early March.

Although Mazmudar and Sanyal described themselves as Communist revolutionaries and declared that they had begun a guerrilla war to establish a rural 'liberated zone', what they did was no more than carry out the CPI(M)'s plans for State-wide peasant agitation, which had been formulated before the elections to be launched soon after (on the assumption that the Congress would be returned to power), and which had subsequently been postponed so as to give the CPI(M) ministers in the government time to acquaint themselves with their new job, and find ways of rendering administrative help to the landless agitators.

The non-CPI(M) parties in the United Front government advocated evicting the Naxalbari peasants from the 'illegally' occupied land; but the CPI(M) ministers persuaded the cabinet to hold off government action while they reasoned with their party dissidents. The radicals ignored the overtures of their erstwhile comrades, and intensified their movement. Between early March and the third week of May, the three police stations in the Naxalbari area, covering 250 square miles and 100,000 people, were reported to have registered sixty cases of peasants occupying or cultivating land that did not belong to them, and seizing stocks of rice and paddy from the landlords. By then, the non-Communist chief minister, who was also in charge of the police, had set up special police camps in the area, but had ordered the police *not* to attempt to move into the 'rebel' strongholds.

The uneasy peace between the two sides lasted until 23 May, when militant peasants, armed with bows and arrows, attacked a party of policemen (that had entered their village to serve arrest warrants on some of them), killing one police officer and injuring two policemen. This raised the tension in the area. Two days later, a government official, on his way to Naxalbari, ordered his police escort to fire when he found himself surrounded by a crowd of hostile villagers. The police did so, and killed ten persons, including seven women and children. With this began the phase of 'armed struggle' by peasants when, in the words of Kanu Sanyal, 'they [the peasants] armed themselves with traditional weapons, like bows and arrows and spears, as well as with guns forcibly taken away from the *jotedars* [i.e. landlords], and organized their own armed groups'. Peasant committees were formed; and they put all the landlords 'who were known for a long time as oppressors' to 'open trial', and sentenced them to death. The peasants also burnt all 'the receipts, acknowledgments, plans, deeds, and documents', and declared 'the existing bourgeois law and law courts null and void'.[6] In short, 'liberated areas' were established where 'revolutionary' peasants exercised 'state power'; and these were unmolested by the police since they were under orders from the United Front government not to enter the militant strongholds.

On 21 June the government gave an ultimatum to the militants to call off the movement or face police action. This provided the radicals within the CPI(M), and those to the left of the party, with a rallying ground. They demonstrated in Calcutta in support of the Naxalbari peasants. The Chinese Communist Party showed its sympathy through a broadcast over Peking Radio, on 28 June, which described the 'peasants' armed struggle led by the revolutionaries of the Indian Communist Party . . . in the countryside in the Darjeeling district of West Bengal' as 'the front paw of the revolutionary armed struggle launched by the Indian people under the guidance of Mao Tse-tung's teachings' which 'represents the general orientation of the Indian revolution at the present time'; and went on to state that since, 'like pre-liberation China, India is a semi-colonial and semi-feudal country', the Indian people, in order to liberate themselves, 'must proceed along the path pointed out by Comrade Mao, the path carved out by the Chinese people . . . the road of armed revolution to oppose armed counter-revolution, the establishment of rural bases, the concentration of forces in the villages, using villages to encircle the cities and then, finally, the taking over of the cities'.[7]

Peking's open approval of the Naxalbari militants' activities undermined the position of the CPI(M) ministers in the United Front government, who had until then succeeded in restraining the chief minister from taking determined action against the militants. Now, orders went out to the thousand-strong police, stationed in the area, to 're-establish' their authority in the 'liberated zones', but with the minimum possible force. The police entered the area expecting a bloody battle, only to find that the militant activists had fanned out in the adjoining areas. And none of the thousand-odd people they arrested, many of them on specific charges, offered any resistance. Within a fortnight, the 'law and order' situation was back to 'normal'; and by October (1967), there was little, if any, trace of the militant activity.

But the idea of Naxalbari-type action caught the imagination of many of the CPI(M) activists in the country, and led to the formation of the All India Co-ordination Committee of the Revolutionaries of the CPI(M), in Calcutta. At the plenum of the CPI(M), in April 1968, this committee pressed for the acceptance of the Chinese analysis of the Indian situation and the tactic of waging 'people's war', but failed. Rejecting this line of action, the CPI(M) leadership called for a simultaneous struggle against 'revisionism' and 'left sectarian deviation', and criticized both the Soviet party and the Chinese for violating the principle of non-interference in the internal affairs of other parties, 'either under the pretext of some creative Marxism of theirs or under the totally erroneous notion that they alone can think, not only for themselves, but for all other parties in the world [as well]'.[8] Thereupon the committee detached itself from the CPI(M), renamed itself, simply, the All India Co-ordination Committee of Communist Revolutionaries (AICCCR), hailed Naxalbari as 'the turning point of the Indian revolution' and 'the burial ground of parliamentarism', and resolved to launch Naxalbari-type movements 'under the banner of Chairman Mao's thoughts' in different parts of the country.

The next area to emerge as a 'liberated zone' was the tribal part of Srikakulum, the northernmost district of Andhra Pradesh. The Communist movement in the area dated back to 1959, when the party began organizing the tribals around such economic issues as restrictions on their traditional modes of cultivation imposed by the forest officers, low wages for farm work, and exploitation by (mainly non-tribal) money-lenders and landlords in terms of exorbitant interest rates (of up to 200 per cent a month) and usurping of tribal land. The split in the party, in 1964, found the local Communists solidly in the CPI(M) camp. By 1967, they could claim some tangible gains for the tribals: increase in farm wages, wresting of some mortgaged land from moneylenders and landlords, and allotment of a few thousand acres of government waste land to the tribals. A general feeling of anti-Congressism that swept the country before and after the 1967 elections encouraged the local Communists to direct the tribals to take over the lands that had earlier been usurped by the moneylender-landlords for an alleged failure, on their part, to repay the loans and excessive interest charges. The moneylender-landlords approached the State's Congress administration: it arrested nearly 1,500 tribals and set up police camps in the area. The local

CPI(M) cadres wished to escalate the conflict, but were over-ruled by the State and national leadership. Dissatisfied, they left the party in May 1968, joined the militant AICCCR, and intensified the peasant struggle, while still refraining from any violent action. The conflict between the peasant tribals on the one hand and the police and the landlords' bullies on the other reached a climax when a demonstration by the tribals was attacked by the landlords' men, in October, and the tribals retaliated by forcibly harvesting the landlords' crops.

Soon after, on the advice of Charu Mazmudar, who was then the chief tactician of the AICCCR, to go on the offensive – i.e. to annihilate both the 'class enemies' and the police – the local party cadres led a procession of 250 tribals, from twenty-five different villages, to the house of a moneylender, and seized his paddy and other grain worth Rs 20,000 (£1,000).[9] Other actions of a similar nature followed, but no deliberate attempt was made to 'annihilate' a landlord or moneylender, which was not the case as far as the police were concerned. By the end of January 1969, when the State government declared Srikakulum a 'disturbed' area, the militants claimed to have killed twenty-nine policemen.

Such actions enabled the militants to create, by March 1969, a 'liberated' zone of 500 to 700 square miles, encompassing nearly 300 villages – i.e. the area was cleared of police, and land revenue and forest officials, and the administration was taken over by the Ryotanga Sangram Samithi (i.e. Peasants' Welfare Association), the mass front organization of the party. Describing the situation then prevalent in the 'liberated' villages, Gautam Appa, an Indian academic, wrote:

> Meetings are organized by the party . . . at which the current political situation is discussed, and class enemies – landlords and their agents – are exposed. . . . Women's associations are formed to 'fight against injustices of the patriarchal system'. . . . Popular courts are held to try class enemies and to settle disputes among the people. The social background, as well as the deeds of those tried, are always considered. . . . Lastly, squads of party members, organized in guerrilla units, equipped with guns seized from landlords, operate from the mountains and jungles, fed and supported by the local population.[10]

Encouraged by this state of affairs, Charu Mazmudar, who visited the area in March 1969, expressed a hope, in an article in the party journal, that Srikakulum would become the 'Yunnan of India', the 'red fortress of revolutionaries', from which the 'flame of armed struggle' would spread to other areas.

Taking its cue from this, the AICCCR converted itself into a fully-fledged political party – the Communist Party of India (Marxist-Leninist) – in April 1969, with a well-defined assessment of the socio-political situation and a tactical line to be followed to engineer an armed revolution in the country. After declaring that 'India is a semi-colonial and semi-feudal country', and that 'the Indian state is the state of big landlords and comprador-bureaucrat capitalists', the party's Political Resolution noted that 'the world has entered . . . the era of Chairman Mao's thoughts,' and that 'Chairman Mao's theory of people's war . . . [has] charted a new path . . . that all people of colonial and semi-colonial countries like India must pursue to liberate themselves'.

The party envisaged the establishment of a socialist state in India in two stages. In the first stage, called 'democratic revolution', feudalism and imperialism were to be overthrown through armed rebellion, which was the *only* form of struggle to be employed, and which meant rejecting all peaceful forms of struggle and boycotting such bourgeois democratic institutions and processes as Parliament and elections. It felt that the time was ripe to launch an armed struggle, because the Indian government (described as 'a lackey of US imperialism and Soviet social-imperialism'), lacking popular support, survived only by virtue of its military strength, and the people were in a revolutionary mood.

Since the main force of the democratic revolution in a semi-feudal society, such as India, was the peasant mass, it was the party's immediate task to organize landless labourers, poor peasants, and the exploited middle peasants, against their oppressors: the landlords and rich peasants. This meant conducting a guerrilla warfare against the oppressing class, which was to begin with guerrilla squads physically annihilating individual class enemies. 'The annihilation of class enemy is the higher form of class struggle while the act of annihilating class enemies through guerrilla actions is the primary stage of the guerrilla struggle,' stated Charu Mazmudar, chairman of the CPI(M-L), in the party's English-language journal in late 1969.[11] A few such actions would cause the remaining class enemies either to leave the area or submit to the authority of revolutionary peasants. The area would thus be 'liberated' from feudal authority, and the repressive apparatus of the landlord-capitalist state rendered ineffective. 'Once an area is liberated from the clutches of class enemies (some are annihilated while others flee), the repressive machinery is deprived of its eyes and ears, making it impossible for the police to know who is a guerrilla and who is not, and who is tilling his own land and who tills that of the jotedar (i.e. landlord),' wrote Charu Mazmudar in the party journal, in early 1970.[12] Thus the guerrillas would be able to move about freely and the (previously oppressed) people would openly offer them their support, and help set up people's committees to run administration and dispense justice. As more and more 'liberated' zones sprang up in the countryside and began to encircle urban areas, the various guerrilla squads would merge and evolve as the People's Liberation Army, to secure the democratic revolution, and move towards socialist revolution.

While the revolutionary Communists – now commonly known as Naxalites – sharpened both their political thinking and their tactics, the Congress governments in Andhra Pradesh and elsewhere doubled their efforts to defeat their plans. Soon after declaring Srikakulum a 'disturbed' area in January 1969, and arming itself with extraordinary powers, the Congress ministry arrested hundreds of militants, and pressed into action not only its own armed police but also ten companies of the Union government's Central Reserve Police. By early August, the government had arrested over a thousand people, many of them under the Preventive Detention Act (i.e. without specifying any charge against them) while the armed police arrogated to themselves the power to dispense summary justice to those it suspected of being in the vanguard of the movement. 'The leaders of those who preach [revolutionary] violence in Srikakulum were simply picked up from their beds, taken to the forest, and shot dead,' reported a correspondent of the *Frontier*. 'A story was then invariably put out, as they did in the 1948–50 period [in the Telangana region] that they were killed in an encounter.'[13]

The Naxalites tried to enlarge their area of operation by fanning out from the tribal belt of jungle and hills, and into the plains of Sompeta; but they failed to make much headway. This area had no tradition of mass movement and agitation, and no Communist base; and the predominantly Hindu population lacked the cohesiveness and simplicity of the casteless tribal society. In order to overcome this limitation, the Naxalites abandoned their practice of linking annihilation of a class enemy with a mass movement (carefully built around such economic slogans as 'Seize the harvest', 'Take over land illegally occupied by landlords', 'Don't pay interest on usurious loans', etc.) and executing it as a form of mass action, and resorted to the murder of a class enemy by a guerrilla squad, of four to seven persons, in a conspiratorial fashion. 'The method of forming a guerrilla unit was to be wholly conspiratorial,' stated Charu Mazmudar in the party journal, in early 1970.

> The conspiracy should be between individuals and on a person-to-person basis. The petty bourgeois intellectual comrade must take the initiative in this respect as far as possible. He should approach the poor peasant who, in his opinion, has the most revolutionary potentiality, and whisper in his ear, 'Don't you think it is a good thing to finish off such and such a *jotedar* [i.e. landlord]?' This is how the guerrillas have to be selected and recruited singly and in secret, and organized into a unit.[14]

In the circumstances, individual murders of landlords did nothing more than win mild approval from the population in the plains. They did not lead the peasants to rally round the Naxalites because, in the absence of any previous exposure to party propaganda or political education, they failed to grasp the political-ideological significance of these 'annihilations'. This meant that the armed police could continue to concentrate their efforts on 'pacifying' the tribal belt. Their violent methods began to sap the militants' strength. The *Liberation*, the party's journal in English, conceded, in March 1970, that 'our losses and setbacks are heavy'. Three months later, the police succeeded in killing V. Satyanarayana and A. Kailashan, the most popular Naxalite leaders in the area; and this more or less marked the collapse of the movement.

By then (the middle of 1970) three other attempts by the Naxalites to establish centres of 'armed resistance' had also failed. One was in Musahari, a non-tribal area in Bihar, and the other two in Debra and Gopiballavpur, in the south-west tribal region of West Bengal. The main reason why Musahari and Debra were chosen by the leaders of the AICCCR, soon after its founding conference in April 1968, was that both had a history of Communist-led peasant agitation. Musahari, a block of villages with a population of 119,000, situated 40 miles to the north of Patna, was also notable for an unusually high percentage of landless labourers (39·2 per cent of the total rural workforce) and exceptionally low wages.

The Bihar Committee of the AICCCR activated the old Communist supporters in the Musahari area, and sent a contingent of young members – mainly college students – from Patna to start organizing agricultural workers around the demand of higher wages. Later, the militants encouraged the landless and poor peasants to harvest the landlords' crop and appropriate it. A hundred to two hundred peasants from a village would gather in the morning at an appointed place, and proceed to a field, shouting 'Naxalbari *zindabad*!' (i.e. 'Long live Naxalbari!'), plant a red flag in the field, and start cutting the crop. These actions reached a climax in the autumn of 1968, and, as expected, brought a large number of police into the area. Thereupon, the Naxalites left, and fanned out into other areas, only to return in the middle of 1969 to carry out the party's programme of annihilation of individual class enemies. This caused panic among landlords, and enabled the Naxalites to claim to have 'liberated' half of the villages in the area, with a population of over 50,000. Subsequently, however, the State government moved in, with its own armed police as well as the Central Reserve Police and the para-military Border Security Force, made hundreds of arrests, and severely crippled the movement.

The militant movement in Debra, an area 80 miles to the north-west of Calcutta, roughly followed the pattern of Srikakulam: that is, the local unit of the CPI(M) left the party in April 1968, joined the AICCCR, and enlarged the traditional peasant agitation for higher wages to include seizure of landlords' crops and repossession of tribal lands mortgaged with moneylenders. This continued until October 1969, when the local Naxalites, reflecting the general change in policy, committed the first of the many acts of 'annihilation of a class enemy'.

'Dangerously open, close to the railway station, and lying parallel to the Calcutta–Bombay National Highway, Debra and 150 villages under Debra thana (i.e. police station) are apparently unsafe for guerrilla action,' reported Kalyan Chaudhuri, a radical Indian journalist, in early December 1969.

> Of course, according to the CPI(M-L) leaders, the people are ably substituting hills and jungles to protect the guerrilla fighters against the reactionary onslaught. . . . The Santals and the extremely poor Kols [i.e. the predominant local tribal groups] are mobilized and ready to execute the 'annihilation *jotedar* [i.e. landlord] programme'. This most recent phase of Naxalite action excludes looting of money, ornaments, or paddy, and concentrates largely on physical liquidation of *jotedars* or their agents. This has definitely added a political dimension to the movement under the CPI(M-L) leadership. . . . Of late they [guerrilla peasants] have changed their operational strategy . . . and prefer to launch their action from underground. . . . Incidents of such lightning action are on the rise with the intensification of police measures and setting up of about twenty police camps, and mass arrests. [Many] *jotedars*, rich peasants, and big businessmen . . . have taken shelter in Midnapore town after receiving threatening letters from rebel peasants. Considerable panic is prevailing in Debra since Gunadhar Marmu, a landless Santal guerrilla leader . . . issued a 'gira', after a traditional tribal custom, by tying a knot of the bark of a sal tree, symbolizing revenge, calling upon his followers to take severe action against the *jotedars* and the district authorities. . . . [Additionally, there is] . . . a large concentration of the CPI(M-L) elements from Calcutta in Debra. . . . A good number of Calcutta University students or ex-students are reported to be working among the tribal communities in this area and trying to foment murderous attacks in keeping with the political line of the CPI(M-L).[15]

A similar concentration of university students was to be noticed in the Gopiballavpur block of 200 villages, with a predominantly tribal population of 150,000, in that forest-infested region of West Bengal where it meets Bihar and Orissa. Indeed, the militant movement there owed its existence to the pioneering efforts of two university students: Santosh Rana, a local youth, who went to university in Calcutta, and his friend Ashim Chaterjee, a brilliant student and radical Communist. Inspired by the events of Naxalbari in 1967, Rana and Chaterjee set out to identify with, and organize, the landless tribals of Gopiballavpur, most of whom eked out a living as farm workers at Re 1 (5p) a day.

The movement here followed the same pattern as elsewhere. That is, the initial stress on the economic demands of the peasants gave way to the practice of physical attacks on individual landlords and money-lenders. 'Altogether twelve big landholders were killed in October–November,' reported Kalyan Chaudhuri in early December 1969.

> Nagan Senapati . . . [who] was murdered by the CPI(M-L) poor peasants was a notorious *jotedar* and usurer. He had over 300 bighas [i.e. 100 acres] of land. . . . On 27 September, about 500 armed peasants raided the house of Baisnab Ghose . . . and seized a huge stock of hoarded rice and 400 maunds [i.e. 32,000 lb.] of paddy. The owner of 400 bighas [i.e. 133 acres] of land, Baisnab, who fled . . . was [later] killed on 10 November by rebel peasants. . . . On 30 October, some peasant guerrillas murdered Dasarath Ghorui. . . . He had 200 bighas [i.e. 67 acres] of land, twenty pieces of golden ornaments, and a huge stock of hoarded rice and paddy. The rebels attacked him when he was going from one village to another to realize interest from the poor people.[16]

Although the West Bengal government had set up police camps in Debra and Gopiballavpur areas, it had instructed the police not to undertake an offensive against the militant strongholds (a contrast to what was then happening in Srikakulum, in Andhra Pradesh), mainly because the leftist United Front was in power, and the police department was under a CPI(M) minister. However, the situation changed abruptly when the United Front ministry fell, in March 1970, and the Central government took over the State's administration. A full-scale action was launched against the militants and their strongholds by the police and para-military forces, and the movement was crushed.. Chaterjee and some of his close associates managed to escape into the 200 square miles of forest in the tri-junction area of West Bengal, Bihar, and Orissa, to carry out the party's programme; but most of the young Naxalites, who had come from Calcutta, returned to the city.

The arrival in Calcutta of young party members with some experience of 'action' in rural areas strengthened the hands of those in the party who had been advocating starting some 'action' in the city. The leadership yielded to these pressures, even though it meant deviating from the party's original plan which had visualized capturing power in urban centres as a three-stage operation: establishing a series of secure pockets in the poor quarters of a city; launching sporadic attacks on such bourgeois institutions as schools and colleges, and government establishments, the transport system, and factories, with the objectives of over-extending the police, attracting more students and youths to the movement, and damaging the economic machine of the city to the point of creating scarcity of essential goods, thus causing riots and a general sense of insecurity, and inducing a mass exodus of the middle and upper classes – all these leading to the final stage, when the party, now supported by the industrial proletariat, would obstruct the entry of more military and para-military forces into the city and fight those already inside, and overpower them, and thus capture *de facto* power in the city.[17]

Now, without first establishing pockets of support in the poor areas of Calcutta, the leadership allowed 'actions' to take place and, what is more, gave individual guerrilla squads a free hand to decide what actions to undertake and how, on the ground that a decentralized form of operation would frustrate the government's repressive measures, which were bound to follow. Exploding a bomb in a cinema showing a Hindi film with an anti-Chinese sequence, in March 1970, marked the beginning of this phase of Naxalite activity. (The film was withdrawn and re-released with the objectionable bits excised.) Then came a bomb attack on the office of the United States Information Service. These were followed by attacks on schools and colleges with crude hand-bombs, 'actions' that proved popular with students, since they caused cancellation or postponement of examinations that were then imminent. Simultaneously, some party squads took to beheading statues of leading political and literary figures of the past. Such sensational activities – reported alarmingly, and at length, in the local press – created an exaggerated impression of the strength and influence of the Naxalites; and this, more or less, dispelled (at least temporarily) any doubts that some party leaders had regarding the correctness of these tactics. Charu Mazmudar, the party's chairman, went one step ahead: he invested these 'actions', taken by individual squads on their own initiative, with much political-ideological significance. 'No revolutionary educational system or culture can develop without demolishing the colonial educational system and the statues erected by the comprador bourgeoisie,' he stated. 'There is no doubt that these raids are revolutionary actions and they are facilitating India's march forward.'[18]

Initiation and intensification of activities in urban areas, particularly Greater Calcutta, by Naxalites, heightened the conflict that had emerged between them and the CPI(M) at the time of the original Naxalbari movement, in May 1967, and had continued with the Naxalite leaders denouncing the CPI(M) as 'neo-revisionists' and the latter dismissing the Naxalites as 'petty bourgeois adventurists'. As a new, militant party with a programme of 'action', the Naxalites had won over many of the CPI(M)'s young members, which had further soured relationships between the two parties, and which, the Naxalites claimed, had made the CPI(M) leadership instruct its cadres in the party's strongholds, especially in Greater Calcutta, to hamper their militant rivals' work. Partly to overcome this handicap, and partly to establish and maintain a general presence in the city's political arena, the Naxalite leaders found it necessary to do what all other parties did – recruit some professional bullies, often with a criminal background, popularly known as *mastans*. (Later on, the party leadership was to attach ideological importance to this essentially pragmatic decision.) This, in turn, led to violent clashes between the Naxalites and the CPI(M) members, a development which was, by all accounts, welcomed by the Central government then ruling West Bengal.

Some of the *mastan* members of the CPI(M-L) found the party's programme of individual annihilation of class enemies a convenient cover to settle personal scores with particular policemen or police informers. So, attacks on individual policemen ensued. Although (according to government sources), of the 526 assaults made on policemen by the end of November 1970, only 41 proved fatal, these were considered enough by the Central government to take a series of stringent countermeasures. It armed the entire police force and trained it to 'shoot to kill', established plain clothes anti-guerrilla squads who, like the Naxalites, operated in a decentralized fashion, and promulgated the Maintenance of Public Order Act (originally designed and enforced by the British to counter 'terrorism' in the Bengal of the 1930s) and the Prevention of Violent Activities Act, laws that gave extraordinary powers of arrest and search to the police. In due course, these measures led to instances of point-blank shooting of those found writing Maoist slogans on the walls, police raids on entire localities, and wholesale arrests of residents as 'suspected Naxalites'.

'There are at least three categories of murderers carrying on a grim competition in cold blooded murders [in Greater Calcutta],' noted Ashok Rudra, an Indian academic, in November 1970; 'the urban guerrilla squads of the CPI(M-L) who have now . . . [taken] to . . . annihilating police personnel; . . . the murderers in the uniforms of the police – the police can shoot and kill with impunity anybody, anywhere, any time with *a priori* exclusion of any inquiry . . . [and] the members of the criminal underground who have taken advantage of the [temporary] absence of the Preventive Detection Act to surface and engage in murderous vendettas under the cloak of political actions.'[19]

By consciously (or subconsciously) playing up reports of violence, the local press and the government-controlled radio made it appear as if law and order in India's largest metropolis was on the verge of breakdown. This suited the Central government, because it could then continue to justify giving extraordinary powers to the police to restore 'normal conditions'. It served the purpose of the Naxalite leaders too. They were gratified by the publicity given to the violent actions of many of the party's nearly 700 'action' squads, functioning mainly in Greater Calcutta. Charu Mazmudar declared that 'chaos and confusion' were on the rise in urban centres and that this was a prelude to a revolutionary change which was also going to affect the countryside. 'Action in the cities represents the revolt of the oppressed, and through these actions will emerge the fighting cadres who will join the peasants to seize [political] power,' he wrote to the party's Bihar Committee.[20] Meanwhile, encouraged by a growing sense of insecurity among citizens, the criminal underworld enriched itself by imposing levies on businessmen and shopkeepers in certain areas of Calcutta, often in the name of the Naxalite movement. A statement by Mazmudar that collecting levies had no place in the party's programme discouraged the practice, but failed to end it.

The two groups which suffered most during this period were the CPI(M) activists – who were attacked by both the Naxalite *mastans*, or *mastans* posing as Naxalites, and the police agents[21] – and the ideologically oriented Naxalites, often middle-class youths and students, who had been the party's prime force in its early days in Calcutta, and who were the main target of the police. Many such Naxalites found themselves betrayed to the police either deliberately, by undercover agents – often *mastans* who had managed to become party members – or reluctantly, by those non-politicized members who were unable to withstand torture after arrest.[22]

The gap created by the loss of genuinely political members was filled by teenagers, mainly school dropouts, who had been attracted to the movement due to its stress on 'action', which in the early days had meant no more than smashing school furniture, writing Maoist slogans on school walls, raiding the headmaster's office, hoisting a red flag on top of the school building, and issuing a call for the boycott of examinations, a popular act. Now, these boys found themselves active members of action squads. Many of them showed remarkable daring and fanaticism, for reasons which were more psychological than ideological. 'A young boy in our society is under continued repression and domination – at home by his older relations, in his locality by older boys and at school by his teachers,' wrote a special correspondent of the *Economic and Political Weekly*, in early February 1971.

> When the same boy becomes a Naxalite, he is feared by everyone around him. He is talked about; he can order others to do what he thinks right. . . . The knowledge that these boys carry guns, knives, and bombs helps to terrorize the public and strengthen their own sense of importance. . . . Their recklessness is matched only by their lack of understanding of the ideological content of the movement. . . . With these teenagers in the forefront, the movement is assuming the form of an urban terrorist movement with few traces of Marx, Lenin, or even Mao in its programme.[23]

This apparently became a cause for concern among the party's leaders (i.e. Charu Mazmudar and a few of his close associates), especially when (as was to be revealed later) they had received, through 'underground channels', in November 1970, 'fraternal suggestions' from the Communist Party of China regarding the liberation struggle in India, which included comments on 'Annihilation'. 'Regarding the formulation that the open trade unions, open mass organizations, and mass movements are out of date, and taking to secret assassination as the only way: this idea needs rethinking,' stated the Chinese document. 'Formerly we misunderstood your word "Annihilation". We used to think that the idea is taken from our Chairman's war of annihilation. But in the July 1970 issue of *Liberation* we came to understand that this annihilation means secret assassination.'[24]

No wonder Charu Mazmudar clutched at the news of an attack by 150 Naxalites (on 9 March) on a police party in the tri-junction area of West Bengal–Bihar–Orissa – which caused the death of two policemen and resulted in the capture of nine rifles and 105 rounds of ammunition – and announced a dramatic change of policy. 'This incident has given the peasants' struggle the character of Liberation War,' he wrote in *Deshabrati*, the party's journal in Bengali, on 16 March. 'To concentrate on annihilating individual class enemies at a time when the revolutionary struggle of the peasants is about to take the shape of a Liberation War would be a sort of economism [i.e. a form of reformism].' If by this Mazmudar meant to instruct the considerably reduced body of party activists in the urban centres to cease their 'actions', and proceed to villages to help the struggle there, he was being unrealistic. The teenagers and *mastans*, who dominated the party's ranks in many of the urban areas, were neither interested in nor suitable for organizing the peasants.

Nor was the Central government in a mood to let a rifle-snatching incident be construed, then or later, as the beginning of a 'Liberation War'. Indeed, it used the event to intensify its repressive measures against the Naxalites in the area. In a joint action with the State administrations of West Bengal, Bihar, and Orissa, it pressed into action 600 armed policemen of Bihar, then supported them with the armed police force of West Bengal and Orissa, and finally deployed a whole division of the army to comb the forest-infested area. This went on until the middle of July, when the army returned to barracks.

By then the army had become an integral part of the 'seal and comb' operations that were being commonly undertaken in the urban centres of West Bengal, with the army 'sealing' a particular area, and the police 'combing' it – i.e. conducting house-to-house search – and arresting Naxalite and other leftist suspects by the hundred. While the jails were thus being filled with Naxalites, real and suspected (at the average rate of 2,000 a month in West Bengal alone),[25] those already inside were being harassed and tortured, and even fired upon. In one firing incident in Bihar, in July, the police killed seventeen Naxalite prisoners and wounded twenty-seven. In a similar incident, in August, in Asansol,

West Bengal (which was the sixth of its kind in the State since December 1970), the police killed nine Naxalites and wounded another thirteen. 'A bloody massacre of extremist prisoners' occurred in November in the Alipore jail of Greater Calcutta. 'The scale of operations against the prisoners is indicated by the fact that the number of injured Naxalites out of a total of 300 (Naxalite and non-Naxalite) prisoners was no less than 202,' reported the Calcutta correspondent of the conservative *India Express*. 'Ten of these are in a grave condition [six more had already died]. . . . All the killed and injured appear to have been victims of lathi [i.e. baton] blows inflicted by the warders.'[26]

The aggressive attitude of the police was partly due to the confident mood of the Indira Gandhi government – returned to power in the Parliamentary elections of March 1971 with a large majority – which continued to rule West Bengal, and partly due to the increasing confusion and demoralization among the Naxalites. China's opposition to the Bangladesh movement, which began in the eastern wing of Pakistan in April 1971 and which aroused a strong emotional feeling among many in the Bengali-dominated CPI(M-L), further demoralized and divided the party ranks and leaders. It heightened the differences that had arisen between Charu Mazmudar and Ashim Chaterjee, the movement's young, brilliant leader – who had all along concentrated on rural action, and who had opposed the party's policies of initiating urban action and instructing its members to withdraw from all mass organizations – and led them to part company.

Chaterjee thus joined a long line of leaders who had fallen out with Mazmudar on the matters of party organization, policies, and tactics. T. Nagi Reddy, a veteran of the Communist movement in Andhra Pradesh, was the first to leave. He subscribed to the Maoist strategy of a people's war, but did not think that the general situation in India was mature enough to warrant an immediate launching of an armed struggle. Rabbi Das, a Naxalite leader in Orissa, was the next to go: he did not agree with the tactic of secret annihilation of class enemies, since it was devoid of popular involvement. S. N. Singh and S. K. Misra – respective leaders of the party units in Bihar and Uttar Pradesh – parted company with Mazmudar, in December 1970, after they had failed to convince him that 'for a long time to come, armed struggle cannot be the principal form of struggle in urban areas,' and that such a policy in practice was merely 'helping [the government] to liquidate cadres in towns and hindering work in rural areas'. In the 'name of Mao', they said later, 'Mazmudar is carrying out the policies of Che Guevara'.[27]

But Mazmudar saw the situation differently. He considered these differences and defections as evidence that only he and his loyal supporters were pursuing a truly revolutionary path and saving the party from the corrupting influence of 'centrism'. 'We must hate centrism,' he had told the Congress of the CPI(M-L) in May 1970.

On the question of boycotting elections, Nagi Reddy said 'Yes, we accept it but it should be restricted to a certain area at a certain period'. This is Nagi Reddy's line. This is centrism. We have fought against it and *thrown the Nagi Reddys out* of our organizations. Regarding Soviet social-imperialism, some say: 'The Soviet leaders are revisionists. But how can they be imperialist? Where is the development of monopoly capital (which leads to imperialism)?' They are centrists. So we have fought against them and *thrown them out* of our Party. So the centrists raised the question of trade unions and 'working class based' party when armed class struggle is to be developed by relying on the peasantry. We fought Asit Sen and company on these issues and *threw them out* of the Party.[28]

This attitude was combined with the habit of highly romanticized reporting of 'revolutionary actions' and attaching an excessive importance to them 'For example, the front page headline of the issue of *Deshabrati*, the Bengali organ of the CPI(M-L) leadership, of 11 December 1969, was: "Fire of Naxalbari spreads over Assam State",' noted Promode Sengupta, a Maoist ideologue who did *not* belong to the CPI(M-L).

What was this big revolutionary event? It was only that 'a small guerrilla band' had killed a hated landlord in a certain village, and as a result of this, 'The CPI(M-L) has been well established in the hearts of the peasants'. . . . In its 25 December issue, *Deshabrati* gave a hair-raising account of how . . . the local committee of the CPI(M-L) organization 'finished off' a landlord in a village [in Tripura] – and concluded that 'Now the name of our beloved Tripura is joined up with the eight States which are waging terrific guerrilla warfare for the sake of establishing an exploitation-free society'.[29]

It was apparently on the basis of such reports and interpretations that Mazmudar told the Party Congress, in May 1970, that 'the Red Army can be created not only in Srikakulum [in Andhra Pradesh] but also in Punjab, Uttar Pradesh, Bihar, and West Bengal . . . [to] complete the revolution . . . that has been delayed by more than twenty years [and] brooks no further delay'.[30] Earlier, in a 'secret' circular to the students of West Bengal, he had expressed his 'firm belief' that a 'People's Liberation Army', formed by the combination of numerous 'Red Guard units' at the 'appropriate time', would be marching through the 'plains of Bengal' by the end of 1970 or early the next year (i.e. 1971).[31]

What actually happened was exactly the opposite. By the end of 1971, the party was a shambles, with thousands of its members and sympathizers in prison, and hundreds of its activists either dead or wounded in 'encounters' with the police and their agents, both inside and outside the jails. All but three of the original twenty-two members of the party's

Central Committee had, by then, been arrested or killed, or had died. (Mazmudar's arrest and subsequent death, in jail, of heart failure, came in July 1972.)

Outlining the reasons for the failure of the movement, B. G., a post-graduate student in Delhi, who was an active Naxalite in Calcutta during 1970–1, said:

> Our theory that repression by the bourgeois state will make the masses revolutionary and increase their resistance to the state failed, because our movement soon became petty bourgeois in its thinking and membership, and continued to be so. Our cadres in rural areas showed impatience and adventurism, typical of the petty bourgeoisie, and went into action without proper preparation. They launched the 'annihilation' programme without first politicizing the peasant masses, so that when the police repression came the party supporters could not withstand it, and gave in to the state apparatus. In urban areas, after finishing their actions, our cadres took refuge in petty bourgeois quarters, and not in the working-class areas, because our party had not built up a base in the working-class localities.[32]

On the other side, a high official of the Central Home Ministry attributed the movement's failure to the following factors: Mazmudar ran out of 'exciting' scenarios; ordinary people got disgusted with violence and murder; the government succeeded in infiltrating the movement; the police used their 'own methods'; and the army helped in the combing operations in both the urban and rural areas.[33]

'The undoing of the Naxalites . . . has been that while they built up . . . a fantastically efficient organization and recruited into their ranks human material of . . . high quality . . . they were completely isolated from all mass movements and mass organizations,' noted Ashok Rudra. 'Consisting almost exclusively of guerrilla squads, they moved secretively and acted terroristically, as a result of which they were incapable of doing ideological or organizational work among the masses, especially among the industrial working class.'[34] Their premature launching of 'actions' in urban areas which, in turn, intensified their hostility towards the CPI(M), made them the prime target for infiltration by the (anti-CPI(M)) police, and their decision to recruit *mastans* into the party provided an unintended opening to police agents. And once the police had established their presence, by proxy, in a party that functioned on the principle of decentralization, it made an extensive use of the infiltrated 'action' squads to 'annihilate' the CPI(M) activists. So, ironically enough, a movement which began with a programme of initiating an armed revolution found itself being used, willy nilly, by the establishment, as a tool to destroy the CPI(M), the only Communist party in West Bengal with a wide mass base.

WEST BENGAL:
REVOLUTION AND COUNTER-REVOLUTION

The fact remains that under the two successive [leftist] United Front governments [in West Bengal] the common people experienced a sense of coming into their own.

Hiten Ghosh, an Indian journalist[1]

The Congress government wishes to finish off our party, the CPI(M). But, because we are a mass party, it is difficult to finish us off politically. So the Congress government is following the policy of physical annihilation of our party cadres.

B. T. Ranadive, a CPI(M) leader[2]

It is beyond dispute that the Naxalites as well as common criminals in league with them have been utilized by the police in some areas to cut the Marxists [i.e. the CPI(M) members] down to size.

Dilip Mukerjee, an Indian journalist[3]

At least 30,000 men and women locked away without trial for political reasons; the capture of power through a *force majeure*; individual localities, including factory belts, cleansed of the turbulent leftist elements with the help of hired goons; who can doubt that West Bengal has been made safe for democracy, and for private industrial and feudal elements?

AM, the Calcutta correspondent of the
Economic and Political Weekly[4]

Geography has played a crucial role in the making of present-day Bengal. Being at the extreme eastern end of the Gangetic plain, its aboriginal settlers were left practically undisturbed by the Aryan colonizers, who infiltrated the Indian sub-continent from the (distant) north-west, until the time of consolidation of the Gupta Empire in the fifth century. This marked the introduction of Brahmin-dominated Hinduism into the region. The conquering Brahmin and other upper castes treated the indigenous population as inferior and low caste; and the latter showed their resentment by lending support to movements that challenged the hegemony of Brahmins. They leaned towards the casteless Buddhism during the rule of the local pro-Buddhist Pala kings, which lasted from the eighth to the twelfth century. Later, in the thirteenth century, when the Afghans established their rule, and Islam became the state religion, many of them became Muslims, to escape the oppressive caste system. This trend continued during the time of the Moghuls. By the time the Moghul Empire ended and British rule began, in the mid-eighteenth century, nearly half of Bengal's low caste and outcaste population had embraced Islam.

The arrival of the British introduced Western rational, liberal thought into the province; and this was at odds with orthodox Hindu thinking and practices. As a result, Bengal witnessed a number of Hindu reform movements, the last and most important of these being Brahmo Samaj. It debunked the polytheism of orthodox Hinduism and advocated puritanic monotheism; and this appealed to many middle- and upper-class Hindus in urban centres, the kind of people who formed the Indian Association of Bengal, which was to amalgamate later with similar organizations elsewhere to create the Indian National Congress (in 1885). The growing political awareness of this segment of society led it to use the Congress as the main vehicle of protest when the British partitioned the Presidency of Bengal (then consisting of Bengal, Bihar, and Orissa) in 1905.

The colonial administration annulled the partition in 1911, but decided, a year later, to carve off Bihar and Orissa from the Presidency. This considerably reduced opportunities for government jobs for the upper caste Bengalis, who had been the first to take to British education in large numbers. The subsequent resentment manifested itself in many of the politically conscious urban middle-class Bengalis rejecting the path of non-violent agitation against the imperial authority – popularized by M. K. Gandhi – in favour of violent methods. Bengal thus became a scene of political 'terrorism' in the early 1930s, and the British government took stiff measures to stamp it out. Many of these militant nationalists later became Marxists, and engaged in organizing industrial labour, an activity which enabled them to combine anti-capitalist struggle with anti-imperialist movement, because, unlike other industrial centres in India, industry in Greater Calcutta was chiefly owned by British capital.

While the Marxists, functioning chiefly within the Communist Party of India, steadily improved their standing among the industrial proletariat (and sections of the peasantry), the nationalists found themselves in disarray when, following the dispute in 1939 between S. C. Bose, a radical Bengali, and the troika of Gandhi–Patel–Nehru,[5] the Bengal unit of the Congress broke away from the national body to become part of Bose's new party, the Forward Block, thus forcing the Congress High Command to appoint an *ad hoc* committee in the province so as to preserve continuity of a sort. The elections of 1945–6 did *not* lead the

Congress to victory; and so the party could not use patronage to expand its base.

However, the situation changed when the partition in 1947 caused the eastern half of Bengal to become the eastern wing of Pakistan. The Congress assumed power in the Indian half of Bengal, now called the State of West Bengal. But the party was ill-prepared to provide the strong administration needed to tackle the enormous economic and human problems created by partition: disruption of the important jute industry in the Greater Calcutta area due to the loss of jute-producing districts to East Pakistan; and an ever-increasing flow of Hindu refugees from East Pakistan, who tended to settle in the already overcrowded southern districts of the State.[6]

Once in power, the Congress leaders – especially B. C. Roy, the chief minister, and Atulaya Ghosh, the party boss – made an extensive use of administrative patronage to build up a party base, from the top downwards, geared more to winning expensively financed elections than doing anything else. The lavish election campaigns were funded by the large Indian business houses in Calcutta, owned mainly by Rajasthani and Gujarati capitalists, that had been steadily buying up the British firms since 1947. 'The business community of West Bengal tends to give more support to the State government than business communities elsewhere,' noted Myron Weiner. 'It involves direct financial support to the Congress party organization and for the Congress candidates to the State legislative assembly and to Parliament. . . . [In return] both Bengali and non-Bengali business communities have the ear of B. C. Roy, the chief minister.'[7] In contrast, the Communists carried on their policy of building up party strength at the grass-roots level. They concentrated on organizing industrial workers and refugees from East Pakistan, and were successful. This was reflected in the popular vote they secured: up from 9·7 per cent in 1952 to 25·4 per cent ten years later.

The death of B. C. Roy in 1962 robbed the Congress of a leader who had some charisma and administrative ability. P. C. Sen, his successor, proved inept; and, for all practical purposes, political-administrative power passed into the hands of Atulaya Ghosh, the party boss, who was even closer to the business community than Roy. Administrative efficiency suffered as corruption became more rampant than before. 'There were few examples in India of such a wicked combination of the corrupt politician and the still more corrupt man of business, each concerned only with the immediate profit and each devoid of any commitment to the future of West Bengal,' wrote Pran Chopra, an Indian journalist.[8]

On top of this came war with Pakistan (in 1965), and the failure of two successive monsoons, which led to shortage of food and a runaway inflation. The people reacted to this by staging spontaneous demonstrations against the government, which replied with a brutal use of force.

This, in turn, led to a wave of strikes and general shut-downs in the spring of 1966. The Congress government in Delhi became worried, and advised the West Bengal administration to adopt a conciliatory posture. As a result, the State government took some measures to pacify the people, one of which was the release of leaders of opposition parties, chiefly the CPI(M), who had been arrested, in late 1964, as part of the joint drive against the CPI(M) by the Central and State administrations.

The support of the bulk of the Communists in the State, the able handling of the party machine by Promode Dasgupta, the State party's secretary, and the general discontent in the State's population, helped the CPI(M) quickly to establish a following among the urban working and lower-middle classes. However, its efforts to produce a single anti-Congress alliance to fight the general elections of 1967 failed, mainly because of the non-co-operative attitude of the CPI. In the end, therefore, the Congress faced two separate leftist fronts. And yet it secured no more than 127 seats out of 280. Such a strong show of aversion towards the Congress, by voters, led the two leftist fronts, commanding a total strength of 140 seats, to hammer out a common programme, and make a bid for power. They adopted an eighteen-point programme and formed the government in March.

Although the CPI(M) had the largest contingent of members in the Assembly – forty-three – it considered it prudent not to press the point and accepted the three seats offered to it in a ministry of eighteen. The party's main objective was to tailor its administrative role to build up its mass organizations and party membership. 'The particular immediate task is that of educating, reorganizing, rebuilding, consolidating, and expanding the party organization . . . of proper selection, promotion, and grading of cadres, and their proper deployment in different class and mass fronts,' stated the party's Central Committee in April 1967.[9]

At the same time the CPI(M) ministers prodded their colleagues to effect a series of progressive measures, and soon. As a result, within the first fifty *days*, this government had decided to reduce municipal taxes on slum houses; vest refugees from East Pakistan, staying in squatter colonies, with legal rights; increase dearness allowance of teachers and State government employees; fix minimum wages in thirteen important industries; instruct the police not to interfere in the 'legitimate trade union movement'; impose a moratorium on taxes and cesses in drought-stricken areas; and grant proprietorial rights over homestead land to landless labourers and poor peasants.[10] The pace slackened a bit later on. But before the United Front government, enjoying a precarious majority in the assembly, fell in November 1967, it had distributed 248,000 acres of surplus land, illegally held by landlords and tea-garden owners, to poor peasants.[11]

In the subsequent election, held in February 1969, eleven leftist and centrist parties combined to form the United Front, and adopted a thirty-two-point programme, which promised action in the fields of land reform, industrialization, unemployment, education, social inequalities, and administrative efficiency. The United Front won 214 seats, the Congress only 55. The CPI(M) nearly doubled its strength (to eighty), and managed to secure such important ministries as land revenue, police, labour, education, and refugee rehabilitation. Its leaders could claim that their twin policy of 'administration *and* struggle' had indeed paid off: the party had improved its strength, and the masses had become more politically conscious than before. They therefore pressed on with the same policy with an added vigour, particularly when they had an intuition that, despite the massive majority enjoyed by the United Front ministry, the Congress administration in Delhi would not let it finish its full term of five years. (Indeed, they reckoned that the ministry would last about two years.)[12]

H. K. Konar, the CPI(M) minister in charge of the land revenue department responsible for the enforcement of land reform laws, concentrated on implementing the land ceiling legislation passed by the previous Congress administrations. During its brief life of thirteen months, this department succeeded in placing nearly 300,000 acres of surplus land in the hands of the landless and poor peasants.[13] This was done either by the department taking over the landlords' excess land, an unprecedented act, or by detecting *malafide* transfers of land (by utilizing both the government machinery and information passed on by farm workers to the CPI(M)'s peasant organization) and then encouraging the rural poor to occupy these lands. 'For the first time in their life, thousands of poor peasants took an initiative, *and* it was successful, a truly electrifying experience for them,' said H. K. Konar.[14]

'In the course of the drive for recovery of *benami* [i.e. *malafide*] lands, the State government and the United Front parties have succeeded in unleashing a massive force in the countryside, which has not only brought direct benefits to a section of peasantry, but has also dealt a heavy blow to the social base of conservatism and reaction in the rural areas,' reported a correspondent of the *Economic and Political Weekly* in September 1969.[15] The landlords were unable to retaliate, because they were denied the customary help of the police, who had been instructed by Jyoti Basu, another CPI(M) minister in the government, not to interfere in landlord–peasant disputes unless violence erupted, and because the violence perpetrated by the bullies in the landlords' pay was effectively countered by the defence squads of poor peasants, formed under the guidance of the CPI(M) and other leftist parties. Meanwhile, the rural poor were encouraged to consolidate their hold over land by cultivating it, as the CPI(M)-controlled ministry hastened to legalize these occupations.

A similar change occurred in industrial relations in the State. Emboldened by the existence of a leftist ministry, in 1967 workers had designed and applied a new tactic of *gherao* (literally, surrounding) – i.e. restricting the movements of management or managerial staff – to have their demands accepted. Between March and October 1967, more than 1,300 *gheraos* had occurred in 800 establishments, often to the benefit of workers, since the police had been ordered by the State government to contact the leftist labour minister before taking any action concerning a *gherao* in an industrial establishment. The success of *gherao* had not only helped workers economically but had also made them sufficiently self-confident to urge their traditional trade union leaders to get their long-standing grievances redressed. The overall spirit fostered in the industrial proletariat by the incidents of *gherao* was described by Nitish R. De, an Indian academic, as one of 'liberation' and 'fusion'.[16]

The return to power by the leftists, particularly the CPI(M), in 1969, boosted the morale of the working class. Nearly 300,000 employees in jute and tea industries went on strike for better wages and working conditions, and secured substantial gains within two weeks, and without any violence (except once in a tea-garden), an unprecedented event in the century-old history of these industries.[17] Later, workers in textile and engineering first followed suit, and won better terms for themselves. All told, nearly 750,000 employees in these four major industries of the State secured a total wage increase of Rs 50 crores (£25 million) a year. The labour minister, a CPI(M) nominee, played a crucial role in this. He exerted the considerable influence of his office to further the interests of workers, thus dramatically reversing the pro-employer policies of his Congress predecessors. Furthermore, the minister piloted a Bill which stipulated a secret ballot to determine the most popular trade union in an establishment and compulsory recognition of it by the management.[18]

This series of events during the two successive United Front governments put capitalists on the defensive. The change in their attitude was illustrated by L. R. Dasgupta, secretary of the Bharat Chamber of Commerce, thus:

> Before 1967, businessmen did not even bother to read the resolutions of the All India Congress Committee. They knew that most of these were for public consumption, and were not to be taken seriously. But now [in 1970] it is all changed. In our *Monthly Newsletter*, we make sure to include not only the resolutions of the CPI(M) and CPI, but also the Forward Block [a small leftist party]. And our members read these carefully.[19]

While the propertied classes became demoralized, the poorer sections of society began to assert themselves by joining the mass organizations of the CPI(M). The party received as many as 400,000 applications for membership in 1969. But, only 7,000 of these were accepted (thus bringing the total membership in the State to 23,000), with another

92,000 given the status of 'sympathizers', i.e. they could support the party without participating in its policy-making process.

Encouraged by the dramatic upsurge in the party's popularity, the CPI(M) leaders initiated a policy of dislodging the small leftist parties from their bases by making an adroit use of their administrative and police powers, the party's defence squads, and its considerable skills in agitprop. The small leftist parties reacted to this by banding together and fighting back. The divisive repercussions of the violent clashes that developed between the two sides were soon felt at the ministerial level. The situation was further exacerbated by developments in the national arena, when, following the fall of the CPI(M)-dominated government in Kerala, in October 1969, the CPI began co-operating with the Congress led by Indira Gandhi. By early 1970, the United Front ministry had become too riven by internal divisions – with one group of parties lining up behind the CPI(M) and the other behind the CPI – to function efficiently. The government finally fell in March 1970; and the State's administration was taken over by the Centre.

This gave the Congress government in Delhi the opportunity to curb both the CPI(M) and the Naxalites, who had just then begun their urban actions. It increased the powers of the police to apprehend real and suspected 'extremists', and engaged *mastans* and police agents to infiltrate the Naxalite movement to collect information about the party's ideologically orientated cadres, and use the party's programme of annihilation of 'class enemies' to murder individual CPI(M) activists, and thus intensify animosity between the two parties.[20] Indeed, the police authorities soon began to label all those who attacked the CPI(M) members as 'Naxalites'. 'What are often dubbed as Naxalites are antisocial elements owing allegiance to various political parties,' stated the *Frontier*. 'The Congress and the CPI must have been using their *mastan* following for anti-CPI(M) ends; and it suited the police and the Centre to describe every group as a "Naxalite" group.'[21]

The CPI(M) leadership tried to withstand this pressure by making use of its defence squads, and maintaining the morale of its party cadre by instructing it to concentrate on work in the party's mass organizations, and keep up the demand for return to popular rule in the State. The dissolution of Parliament, in December 1970, raised the possibility that voters in the State would get the opportunity to elect their assembly as well. But the non-CPI(M) parties, fearing defeat at the hands of the CPI(M), argued that due to 'disturbed conditions' in the State, 'free and fair' elections could not be held. They did not consider the 61,000-strong police force – supported by a further 24,000 members of the Central Reserve Police, the Border Security Force, the Eastern Frontier Rifles, and the National Volunteer Force – sufficient to ensure 'law and order' during elections. More radical measures had to be taken to instil 'confidence' among electors, they insisted, when they realized that it would most probably be unconstitutional for the Indira Gandhi government to withhold elections to the national Parliament in one State – namely, West Bengal – and holding these elections while *not* holding elections to the assembly simply could not be justified. This provided the rationale to the Centre to assign 50,000 troops to the State authorities, to be posted at district and sub-divisional headquarters, to undertake nothing more than 'routine flag marches'.

But soon after the troops arrived in West Bengal, in early February 1971, they were drawn into the 'comb and search' operations that were launched by the State administration (under the direction of the Centre) in Greater Calcutta, ostensibly to rid the area of the 'Naxalite menace'. Not many Naxalites were caught, however, because the official tipping off of the police agents who had infiltrated the movement caused the other party members too to leave an area before it was cordoned off and combed. In the end, the party which suffered most due to these operations was the CPI(M), many of whose workers, then engaged in an election campaign, found themselves rounded up by the police as 'extremists'.

And yet, since Greater Calcutta accounted for only 8 per cent of the assembly seats, these arrests did not materially affect the overall electoral chances of the CPI(M)-led alliance. Opposition to it was divided. The Congress was fighting on its own, and some leftist and centrist parties had lined up behind the CPI. The reports of the Central government's Intelligence Bureau predicted the CPI(M)-led alliance winning 150 to 160 seats in a house of 280. The anti-CPI(M) forces therefore needed something drastic to happen to reserve the pro-CPI(M) trend; and it did.

On 20 February, barely two and a half weeks before the polling day, Hemanta Kumar Basu, a candidate of the CPI-led alliance for an assembly seat, was attacked by a few young men in north Calcutta, and killed. The president of the Forward Block, a small leftist party, H. K. Basu, an old man of 70, was a much-respected public figure; and the news of his murder shocked many of the urban dwellers. Within half an hour of the event, the Police Commissioner of Calcutta told the press that the two young men arrested as suspects (for the murder) were 'connected' with the CPI(M). An important Congress functionary declared that he had 'authentic information' that the cadres of the CPI(M) had murdered H. K. Basu.[22] The leaders of the Congress and the CPI-led alliance turned the condolence meeting held in honour of H. K. Basu into an anti-CPI(M) rally, and passed a resolution which openly accused the CPI(M) of murdering Basu.

This put the CPI(M) leadership on the defensive. All it could do was to repudiate the allegation, while its opponents, aided by the press and the government-controlled radio, launched a shrill campaign to depict the CPI(M) as a party wedded to violence and murder. 'The urban middle class in particular was sought to be aroused against the CPI(M) as it had never been aroused (before),' noted AM, the Calcutta correspondent of the *Economic and Political Weekly*. 'The All India Radio chimed in: every quarter of an hour, it would call upon the good citizens to come out on election day and fulfil their noble obligation for voting against the cult of violence.'[23]

These tactics were effective in swaying a substantial section of the urban and suburban middle-class voters away from the CPI(M). In Greater Calcutta, for instance, where the CPI(M) in its less popular days had won half the seats in the town hall, it now secured less than a quarter of the assembly seats. All told, it is estimated that the propaganda concerning Basu's murder cost the CPI(M)-led alliance thirty-five seats, each of which was lost by a margin of less than 2,000 votes – enough to rob it of a majority in the assembly, but still leave it as the largest group, commanding the support of 123 members, well ahead of the Congress's strength of 105.

At the behest of Indira Gandhi herself, a coalition of the Congress and the CPI-led front was formed, and installed in office, in mid-March 1971, even though its total strength of 134 (in a house of 277) fell short of a majority. (Soon after, the Calcutta police withdrew charges against the suspects arrested at the time of Basu's murder. And, in early May, it was reported that some of the suspects on the new list of 'wanted men' were 'connected' with the Congress.[24]) This ministry managed to survive for a brief period of three months. While in office, it concerned itself almost exclusively with intensifying repression against the CPI(M) and genuine Naxalites. The launching of the Bangladesh movement in neighbouring East Pakistan, in April, provided it with a rationale to retain the 50,000 troops brought into the State earlier with the specific purpose of ensuring 'free and fair' elections, and assume extraordinary police powers under the provisions of the recently promulgated Maintenance of Internal Security Act, passed by the Congress-controlled Parliament. As a result, there was an upsurge in the government-directed violence against the leftists. The average number of 'political murders' per month went up from 53 a year ago to 137, with two-thirds of the victims belonging to the CPI(M). 'The impunity with which criminal gangs are allowed to terrorize certain pockets of the CPI(M)'s influence, the open co-ordination between gang attacks and police violence in certain zones – these are some of the clear indications of a new *modus operandi*, which emerges from reports even from the conservative Press in Calcutta,' reported a correspondent of the *Economic and Political Weekly*. 'Literally, thousands [of CPI(M) supporters] have become refugees in the sense that they have had to change their area of residence.'[25]

The fall of this ministry, and the subsequent dissolution of the assembly, enabled the Central government to conduct the anti-leftist campaign directly. Now, the members of the Youth Congress, the youth wing of the Congress, were instructed to collaborate openly with the police – that is, point out the CPI(M) activists to them, and man the 'Resistance Squads', formed in various urban localities and villages to counter the 'violence of the CPI(M) and Naxalites'. Simultaneously, these Congress elements were armed with a set of pseudo-leftist slogans – such as 'The decade of the seventies will be the decade of liberation [of Bangladesh]' (a parody of a Naxalite slogan), 'Down with American imperialism in Vietnam, Chinese imperialism in Tibet, and Soviet imperialism in Czechoslovakia', and 'Socialism will come to India in India's own way, and not through Karl Marx's writings' – which they splashed on the walls of localities which had until recently been leftist strongholds. The final 'securing' of these areas was then formalized by holding a public meeting – something neither they nor the Congress, their parent organization, had dared to do only a few months earlier – where local Congress functionaries showered praise on Indira Gandhi, hailed the Bangladesh movement, and vehemently decried the 'cult of violence' preached by the CPI(M) and Naxalites, stressing all along that the latter were the result of the former (but not stating that the CPI(M) was the offspring of the now respectable CPI). In short, this phase of the repression of the CPI(M) and genuine Naxalites was marked by the introduction of a set of radical-sounding slogans and political attitudes, which were voiced, in the main, by the young supporters of the Congress.

It was ironic for the Youth Congress to be playing a leading role in the political events of the State: it had been reinvigorated by the Congress hierarchy in Delhi only because the split in the party, in the summer of 1969, had found Atulaya Ghosh, the powerful party boss in West Bengal, and most of the party apparatus in the State, in the camp opposed to Indira Gandhi. Until then, the Youth Congress and Chhatra Parishad (i.e. Students' Association), both established in 1964, had done nothing more spectacular than provide volunteers to Congress candidates during election campaigns. The 1971 elections offered a chance to the freshly revived Congress youth and student bodies to prove their mettle. They made a moderate contribution to the victory of some Congress candidates in the Greater Calcutta area. But this was not enough to win them a noticeable popularity. It needed a series of virulent actions against the leftist forces by the Congress-dominated government in the State to engender an atmosphere in which these organizations could grow.

And when such actions finally happened, three diverse elements swelled the ranks of the Youth Congress and Chhatra Parishad. The young *mastans*, who, following the defeat of the Congress in 1967, had taken to 'diversifying' their political loyalties, noted the re-emergence of the Congress as the ruling party, and rushed to the fold of the Youth Congress. The children of the lower-middle-class parents, forming a majority in high schools and colleges, realized the grave consequences of pursuing leftist politics and, in addition, saw in the membership of the Chhatra Parishad a chance of finding an increasingly elusive job. The progeny of the urban and rural rich joined these organizations out of sheer class interest, and in large numbers. No wonder, by the end of 1971, that the Chhatra Parishad could claim a membership of 117,000 (as against 8,000 in 1965), and the Youth Congress, 75,000. What is more, by then, these organizations had managed to initiate pro-Congress and anti-CPI(M) actions in the countryside. The case of Sahajapur, a village described earlier,[26] was typical.

Soon after the Congress-dominated coalition assumed power, in March 1971, one K. K. Sengupta, a Youth Congress leader from the (nearby) town of Bolpur, visited Sahajapur, and sought the help of the local Youth Club – formed a few months earlier by the sons of a few well-off peasants – to counter the widespread support for the CPI(M) in the village. He had fifty to fifty-five posters of the Chhatra Parishad pasted on the village walls. These carried such slogans as 'We will not commit crimes and will not allow crimes to be committed', 'Wage a revolutionary struggle against price rise', 'Why should there be no proper treatment of the poor in hospitals?', 'Why is there no milk distribution for the poor?', 'We should try our best to establish law and order', and 'Spread the idea of nationalism to counter the machinations of the CPI(M)'. (Some of these slogans, meant to appeal to the urban population, were quite meaningless to the villagers.)

Then, in July, came the idea of forming a 'Resistance Squad', originally introduced to the Congress leaders of Bolpur by the State government's Intelligence Bureau inspector, and carried to the village by one S. K. Gupta, a Youth Congress leader. As expected, he sought and secured the help of the local landlord – the Mandals – and rich farmers. Then a public meeting was held where the idea of establishing a 'Resistance Squad' was aired and volunteers were sought. As a result, such a squad came into existence; and the fifty men armed with staves and spears who constituted it drilled in the village every so often. Its self-assigned job was to keep the peace; and it did so by having seven of its men patrol the village at night. The Bolpur police, who had the final responsibility for sustaining the squad, maintained their interest by sending an official to the village every week to assess its progress.

The villagers were divided in their attitude to the squad. This was illustrated by the way they described its emergence and functions. Ramranjan Mistri, a rich peasant, who owned 50 acres (but publicly admitted only 12), said, 'The Resistance Squad was formed because of the Naxalite menace which the police could not tackle on its own. The idea came from outside the village, but its supporters are from here. People from the Youth Congress in Bolpur and the police came here in July. They held a public meeting. Two hundred people came, both rich and poor. I joined the Resistance Squad. Our job is to maintain peace, see that no dacoity occurs, and nobody steals paddy. If the CPI(M) or Naxalites try to break up meetings we try to stop them. The Resistance Squad is like the police.'[27] On the other hand, Netai Majhi, a landless labourer, said, 'There are only *bhadra lok* (i.e. gentlemen) in the Resistance Squad. We [the landless] volunteered to join, but they turned us down. The same happened at the public meeting. There were no poor people there. I wanted to attend, but was warned to keep away. The truth is that the Resistance Squad is against the CPI(M).'

Majhi then described as to how the local CPI(M) members were being harassed. 'The CRP [i.e. Central Reserve Police] came to the village last month [i.e. December 1971],' he said. 'They came at two at night. They picked up twelve men, all CPI(M) members or sympathizers, took them to the police station in Bolpur, and beat them up. They beat one so badly that he had to be taken to hospital. The villagers say that it was the *jotedars* (i.e. landlords) who got the police to arrest these people. That is the difference between now and the United Front government's rule. In those days the police were neutral between the rich and the poor. Now, the police are being used to beat up poor people.'

The harassment by the police and CRP had reduced the support for the CPI(M) in the village, he added. 'But, even then, a majority of them would vote for the CPI(M). At the last elections [in March 1971] three-quarters of them had voted for it. On the other hand, *jotedars* remain bitterly opposed to the CPI(M) and will hit it hard whenever they get the chance.'[28] Actually, Deepapada Mandal, the oldest of the local landlord family, had said earlier, 'If the CPI(M) is voted back to power, I'll take poison.'[29] References to elections were in order then (January 1972); because it was most likely that in view of the upsurge in her popularity, especially in West Bengal, due to India's victory over Pakistan on the issue of Bangladesh, in December 1971, Indira Gandhi would add West Bengal to the list of States where elections were due in March. She did.

This time, various political parties lined up behind the two main contenders for power: the CPI(M) and the Congress. Sheer instinct for survival led the small leftist parties – except the pro-Congress CPI – to ally with the CPI(M) to form the United Left Front. The CPI(M) leadership needed this co-operation, if only to counter the demoralization among the party workers, who had, since March 1970, seen 650 of their comrades murdered, and some 40,000 party members and sympathizers chased out of their homes, in areas that were once CPI(M) strongholds, by strong-arm brigades of the Youth Congress in collusion with the police, and who could see no sign of the Congress pressure on their party easing off. Indeed, their party was forced to write off thirty-four constituencies, because it found it almost impossible to conduct an election campaign there. Describing the conditions prevailing in Kalna, one such constituency, Biplab Dasgupta, an Indian academic wrote: 'No form of campaigning was possible [for the CPI(M)], no posters could be posted, no person approached for campaigning, no campaign office could be opened, and no polling agents could be sent to the booths'.[30] (The veracity of this statement was provided by the election results: the CPI(M) secured 929 votes, as against 31,896 in 1971; and the Congress 62,336, as against 24,930.)

In contrast, the Congress had all the advantages, administrative, political and financial, and used (and misused) them to the hilt. It had been ruling the State, directly or indirectly (through the Union President) since March 1970, and had the police as well as the bulk of the *mastans* on its side. It had the unqualified backing of the rich and powerful business community of Calcutta, which was determined, more than ever before, to keep the CPI(M) out of power.[31] It had the almost unanimous support of the press and the government-controlled radio. And it squeezed the maximum possible electoral dividend out of India's success in getting Bangladesh established as an independent country:[32] Indira Gandhi had Sheikh Mujibur Rahman of Bangladesh, then riding an unparalleled wave of popularity in West Bengal, address a vast Congress election rally in Calcutta from the same platform as herself.

Yet neither independent political analysts nor the Central government's Intelligence Bureau was prepared to concede the Congress anything more than a 'slight' victory. This fell short of Delhi's objective of giving West Bengal a 'stable' Congress government for the next five years so as to undo all the 'damage' caused by the twenty-two-month rule of the CPI(M)-dominated ministries during the previous five years. And so, to quote a correspondent of the *Economic and Political Weekly*, 'well prepared contingency plans' of the Central government, 'providing for open and bold tampering with the election process', were put into effect.[33]

The execution of these 'contingency plans' was so thorough that it boosted the Congress strength in the assembly from 105 to 216, and reduced that of the CPI(M) from 113 to 14! 'There has been widespread intimidation of voters coupled with false voting on a truly gigantic scale,' reported Ashok Rudra. 'It is true that in many areas CPI(M) [election] agents could not go near the booths and [that] Congress "volunteers" went from house to house warning people known to be CPI(M) sympathizers not to go out on the election day. It is true that election officers had been carefully selected to collaborate with Congress *goondas* (i.e. bullies). It is [also] true that armed ruffians entered [polling] booths and cast false votes before the very eyes of the guardians of law and order.'[34] A full list of election irregularities, prepared by the CPI(M), included: occupation of polling booths by the Congress and CPI cadres; driving away of the election agents of other parties; forcing presiding

and polling officers at gun point to initial ballot papers and stamp on
the Congress and CPI election symbols; filling ballot boxes with false
votes by about 1 p.m.; threatening voters in some areas on the previous
night not to go out to vote; using duplicate ballot papers; replacing
ballot boxes; and invalidating ballot papers cast in favour of the leftist
parties by putting a second stamp on them.

As expected, the Congress denied these allegations. But the truth was
revealed in a confidential memorandum, concerning the party's organization in the State, that some local leaders wrote to the party's High
Command in Delhi.

> The manner in which all opposition parties in the State were
> exterminated [in the elections] cannot be ascribed as a good
> precedent in a democratic country. . . . The victory resulting from
> the rigged election has not brought glory to the Congress. It would
> have been much more honourable for the Congress to come back
> to power with a strength of 150 to 160 in a house of 280 in a free
> and fair election. . . . *It would not be possible to prove the rigging of
> the election in a court of law.* Still, it can be said without hesitation
> that the politically conscious people of West Bengal are hanging
> their heads in shame for being deprived of the right of franchise by
> terroristic and various unfair means.[35]

It seemed that the election-rigging operation had been masterminded
by the same organization in Delhi which had been generally planning
and co-ordinating government actions to counter the Naxalite and
CPI(M) 'menace' over the past few years – namely, the innocuous-
sounding Research and Analysis Wing (RAW) of the Union cabinet
secretariat, which worked under the direct supervision of the Prime
Minister Indira Gandhi.[36] In this case, apparently, it concentrated on
those 113 constituencies in the State which had elected the CPI(M)
candidates in the 1971 poll. What was needed to ensure the defeat of
the CPI(M)-led alliance candidates now were reduction in the CPI(M)
vote, and boosting of the vote for the Congress-CPI alliance. The first
objective was to be achieved by keeping the CPI(M) supporters away
from the polling stations through intimidation and/or having their votes
cast by impersonators early in the day. And the second objective was to
be attained through massive impersonation and stuffing of the ballot
boxes with forged ballot papers, with the CPI(M) election agents evicted
from the polling stations, and the protesting polling officers silenced by
the flashing of guns, if necessary, by the Congress-CPI bullies, while the
policemen on duty looked away. On the other hand, the 105 constituencies which had returned the Congress candidates to the assembly in
1971 were to b left unmolested. The election results provided the
evidence of this strategy and the thoroughness with which it was carried
out.

In Baranagar, a working-class constituency which had voted CPI(M) in the past three elections, for instance, the CPI(M) vote declined from 43,340 (in 1971) to 32,287, while that for the major anti-CPI(M) contestant rose from 30,158 to 69,145. Similarly, in Dum Dum, another working-class area which had elected a CPI(M) candidate in the last three elections, the CPI(M) vote plummeted from 40,750 to 15,023; whereas support for the major anti-CPI(M) candidate shot up from 31,423 votes to 91,423! Interestingly enough, in the 105 pro-Congress constituencies, which had been allowed the privilege of 'free and fair' elections, the total CPI(M) vote actually went *up*. Partly due to this, and partly due to the absence of opposition from the small leftist parties, which in 1971 had joined the CPI-led alliance, the overall decline in the CPI(M)'s popular vote was only 6 per cent – down from 32 per cent to 26. (In contrast, the Congress vote went up from 28 per cent to 49 per cent!) But the resulting loss of nearly 100 seats in the assembly was a shattering blow to the party's morale. What was worse was that the CPI(M) leaders realized that beyond instructing the party's fourteen assembly members to boycott the house, and demanding an inquiry into the election rigging, which had no chance of being conceded by the Congress administration, they could do no more. Indeed, they feared a major governmental attack on their party's base in the working class; and their fears were soon to be realized.

The Congress administration and industrialists together used a variety of tactics to reduce the CPI(M)'s influence among the industrial proletariat: large-scale dismissals of the CPI(M) members and sympathizers from their jobs; arrests of the party's trade unionists under such all-embracing laws as the Prevention of Violent Activities Act; and physical assaults on them and their families by the police and Youth Congress members. The scale of such actions could be gauged by the fact that in one department of the government-owned steel plant alone, some fifty activists of the CPI(M)-led trade union were summarily dismissed. 'The CPI(M) trade union cadres are being terrorized, many have been and are being arrested on this or that pretext, their offices have been captured and [their] families turned out from the [company] quarters,' reported the Calcutta correspondent of the *Economic and Political Weekly* in August 1972.[37]

In short, now, in mid-1972, West Bengal was being pushed in a direction which ran counter to the one it had experienced, intermittently, during the past five years, when the policies of the CPI(M)-dominated United Front governments *and* agitations by the urban and rural poor had put the business community and landlords on the defensive. After a period of 'revolution', within the limited parameter of the Congress-type 'parliamentary democracy', had begun a period of 'counter-revolution'.

Summing up the situation prevalent in the State, in the autumn of

1972, R. P. Mullick, an Indian academic, wrote:

> The slightest growth of agitational, far less militant, struggle in industrial areas is met with immediate punitive response, and squashed. The strategy . . . [and] tactics [of the Congress government] are: submerge the mass and class organs of economic and political struggle under the wave of preventive detention, arrests, search-warrants . . . ; utilize the administrative machinery to bear upon public opinion through a gigantic demonstration of state power . . . and a subtle interference in public life through mass propaganda . . . ; create an army of *mastans*, drawn from the anti-social fringe elements of the lumpenproletariat as well as from the rural sections of decadent middle-class 'intelligentsia' of political illiterates, encourage them to be aggressive towards left-party cadres, thereby giving a false impression among the uninformed as though the ruling [Congress] party is gaining popularity. Also draw upon left ideology, distorting the call of the repressed have-nots for struggle, and lead them towards social conservatism, economic anarchy, and political confusion – in short, towards counter-revolution.[38]

The Congress provided the main political thrust to the virulent campaign against the CPI(M) and Naxalites in West Bengal, partly because it was the most right-wing of the parties existing in the State, and partly because the leftist influence was so widespread that only an organization of the stature and resources of the Congress – working in conjunction with the police, army and local *mastans* – could have expected to succeed in turning the leftist tide. Elsewhere, the role of militant, even violent, opposition to the Communist movement has often been assumed by small, overtly right-wing parties or groups, such as the Shiv Sena (in Bombay), Rashtriya Swayamsevak Sangh (i.e. National Volunteer Union), Jan Sangh, and the Swatantra Party.

PART IV
RIGHTIST FORCES

RIGHTIST FORCES:
POLITICAL

Contempt for democracy and glorification of [right-wing] dictatorship has been, from the beginning, a part of the political education of the activists in the Shiv Sena.

Ram Joshi, an Indian academic[1]

I believe that the Sangha [i.e. Rashtriya Swayamsevak Sangh] ideology can act as a corrective to the Communist mode of thinking in Bharat [i.e. India].

M. S. Golwalker, Supreme Leader of the Sangha[2]

Logically and inevitably . . . a socialist state becomes a slave state; and if socialism brings about equality, it is equality in slavery and serfdom.

D. P. Ghosh, President of the Jan Sangh, in 1956[3]

The total evil is the Communist evil, whether it is in the Communist Party or whether it has infiltrated the Congress.

Minoo R. Masani, a Swatantra Party leader[4]

In recent years, the Shiv Sena (literally, Army of Shivaji, a hero of Hindu Maharashtrians, who successfully fought the Muslim rulers in the seventeenth century) has played a leading role in eradicating Communist influence among Bombay's industrial and lower-middle classes, a task in which it has received the covert and overt support of the Congress Party and government, and some of the leading industrialists. This, however, was not the original purpose of the organization when it was formed, in 1966, by Bal Thackeray, the founder-editor of *Marmik*, a Marathi cartoon weekly. The main objective then was to fight for the rights of Maharashtrians in the city (constituting 42 per cent of its population and engaged mainly in menial, clerical, and semi-skilled jobs) by proclaiming 'Maharashtra for Maharashtrians', a slogan which attracted thousands of young, jobless Maharashtrians, who had, by then, become disappointed by the lack of progress made by their community in the six years since Maharashtra State, with Bombay as its capital, was carved out of the old bilingual State of Bombay, comprising Maharashtra and Gujarat. This had happened, partly because the local unit of the Congress, led by S. K. Patil, was too close to the predominantly non-Maharashtrian business community to pay much attention to the legitimate Maharashtrian grievances and aspirations, and partly because of the inability of the leftist parties, for both ideological and tactical reasons, to raise the slogan of 'Maharashtra for Maharashtrians'. These factors, coupled with economic recession, which began in 1966, helped Thackeray to launch a campaign that Bombay's South Indian residents (whom he once described as 'criminals, gamblers, illicit liquor distillers, pimps, goondas (i.e. bullies), and Communists')[5] be sent back to their respective States. (Oddly enough, he refrained from attacking the Gujarati residents of the city, who are twice as numerous as South Indians – 19 per cent as opposed to 9 per cent – and own most of the metropolis's wealth.)

The general election of 1967 provided the Shiv Sena with a perfect target: V. K. Krishna Menon, a South Indian, a Keralite, and a 'crypto-Communist', who stood as an independent to retain a Parliamentary seat from Bombay that he had won in the previous two elections as a Congress nominee. The Shiv Sena volunteers joined the campaign against him, and received support not only from the staunchly anti-Communist S. K. Patil of the Congress but also the Jan Sangh, the Swatantra Party, and some leading industrialists. Together they succeeded in defeating Menon, an event that endeared the Shiv Sena to local industrialists, and led Thackeray to publicly describe 'Tatas and Birlas' – both non-Maharashtrian business houses – as 'annadatas (i.e. breadgivers)' to Maharashtrians.

Having secured a base among the city's Maharashtrian lower-middle class, on the basis of a sustained campaign against the South Indians – who are the Maharashtrians' main competitors for white collar jobs – Thackeray tried to build up support among the industrial workers. He glorified the Maharashtrian past, revived the idea of Shivaji as the pioneer of Maharashtrian nationalism, preached ultra-nationalism, and singled out the Communists as 'foreign agents' who had to be fought. This delighted the Congress and local industrialists. They saw the value of the Shiv Sena as an effective anti-Communist organization, and helped it financially and politically.[6] In the 1968 local elections, the Congress abstained from contesting seats in predominantly Maharashtrian working- and lower-middle-class areas in order to help the Shiv Sena candidates defeat their Communist rivals. They did. With forty-two seats to its credit, the Shiv Sena emerged as the second largest group in the town hall, and left the Communists – i.e. the CPI and CPI(M) – trailing far behind.

A few months later, the Shiv Sena established its own trade union wing, the Bharatiya Kamgar Sena (i.e. Indian Workers' Army). Summarizing its ideology, Thackeray said, 'I am against strikes and go-slow tactics. The most important thing is production. Management and labour are two wheels of industry; and they must move smoothly. A trade union should work as a lubricant. Actually, there is no need for a trade union if management behaves sensibly.'[7] No wonder employers welcomed the new trade union organization with open arms. When faced with strikes, many of them, especially those dealing with a Communist-led trade union, turned to Shiv Sena, pointing out the 'unpatriotic' act of the workers. Thereupon, the Sena, openly committed to the policy of 'breaking up red unions',[8] provided strike-breakers to employers and set up a trade union under its own aegis, with the Congress government and the police lending it their support as well.

By the middle of 1970, the Bharatiya Kamgar Sena had acquired the affiliation of forty unions with a total membership of 60,000.[9] And a year later, Thackeray made an unverified claim that the BKS then had the affiliation of unions with a total membership of over 100,000.[10] These gains were no doubt made at the cost of the Communist-led trade unions. For, in June 1972, the general secretary of the CPI-led Maharashtra State Trade Union Committee publicly admitted that 'workers in Bombay . . . have lost all respect and liking for the leftist trade unions, particularly the CPI-led unions', and attributed this loss of influence to, among other things, 'the anti-Communist activities of the Shiv Sena and other independent unions'.[11]

An environment where even the CPI found itself on the defensive was hardly conducive for the growth of the CPI(M) or the Naxalites. Indeed, the Naxalite movement never got off the ground in the city. 'If nothing else,' said Ram Joshi, a Maharashtrian academic in Bombay, 'Thackeray has saved the young generation of Maharashtrians in the city from the Naxalite movement.'[12]

In Punjab, where both the CPI and CPI(M) have pockets of strength, the task of 'saving' the young generation from the Naxalite influence was assumed, by design or accident, by the Jan Sangh, a party which has substantial support in many urban areas. 'According to me,' said L. C. Sabharwal, vice-president of the Jan Sangh in the State, in mid-1970, 'the only way to end the Naxalites is to follow a "tit for tat" policy and kill those who kill others. The government must act firmly to curb the activities of the CPI(M-L). If it waits till the grievances of the people are removed, it will wait for ever.'[13] When, a year later, the police intensified their campaign against the Naxalites, and began to kill them in 'encounters' – some of them occurring when the suspected Naxalites were in police custody – the Jan Sangh sided with the police and roundly criticized those who condemned the illegal actions of the police, which, in this case, included the State unit of the CPI.

After reporting (in early December 1971) that police action in various districts of the State had caused the 'surrender' of 'a large number of Naxalites' and death of 'several of them' in 'encounters', the Punjab correspondent of the *Organizer*, the national organ of the Jan Sangh, attacked the CPI's Punjab unit for launching 'a campaign of vilification' against the police. 'It is known that a section of the extremists [i.e. Naxalites] forms a card-holding cadre of the party which spearheaded the "land grab" movement in the State [in the summer of 1970 – i.e. the CPI],' he added. 'This movement had provided a common cause to the CPI, CPI(M), and the extremists to sow the seeds of lawlessness in the rural areas of the State which, later, exploded into ugly violence.'[14] This was a reference to the essentially ineffective 'land grab' campaign launched nationally by the CPI in the summer of 1970,[15] which had, nevertheless, aroused the ire of the rural rich, whose sympathies lay with the police and such right-wing parties as the Jan Sangh.

The pro-Jan Sangh bias of the rural rich is understandable, because the party has traditionally sided with the big and middle-sized land-owners rather than the smaller ones, and concerned itself with the problems of landowners rather than the landless. Its 1967 election manifesto, for instance, criticized 'the manner in which an unending series of land reform laws have been enacted' for engendering 'a feeling of uncertainty in the mind of the peasant with regard to his cadastral rights'. And its 1971 election manifesto opposed lowering the land ceiling on the ground that this would deny benefits of the 'green revolution' to those farmers 'who had worked for it'. 'The move to lower the maximum size of holdings might create uncertainty in rural areas,' said S. S. Bhandari, the party's general secretary, in November 1971.[16]

It was not until the State assembly elections, in March 1972 (when the Jan Sangh's total strength nearly halved, from 197 to 105) that the party leadership paid any attention to the landless. The party's General Council, meeting in May, threatened a countrywide agitation if the surplus land, already acquired by the government, were not distributed to the landless by the middle of August. However, nothing came of this: the Congress administrations took no action, and the Jan Sangh launched no agitation. Nonetheless, this was an example of the growing realization by the party leaders of the need to widen the party's support by extending its appeal beyond the groups that had helped it initially.

In fact, this awareness had begun a year before, in 1971, when the party had experienced its first reversal in the popular vote, as well as Parliamentary seats, since its inception in 1952 – down, respectively, from 9·3 per cent to 7·4 per cent, and from thirty-five to twenty-two. The party hierarchy had then tried to tone down the 'upper caste Hindu' image of the organization by including an Untouchable and a Muslim in the reconstituted Working Committee: the party's highest committee. Earlier, the party's ideology of 'Hinduization' had been refurbished as 'Indianization' so as to make it less unpalatable to religious minorities. And 'Indianization' was defined, simply, as 'an unalloyed nationalism based first and foremost on allegiance to the Indian soil and its age-old heritage and culture'. 'We [in the Jan Sangh] require Indianization of not only a good section of Muslims but also of all Indians who place their loyalty to caste, religion, linguistic or political group to which they belong, over loyalty to the nation,' stated Balraj Madhok, a party ideologue.[17]

The concept of 'Hinduization' goes back to the origins of the Jan Sangh's parent body – the Rashtriya Swayamsevak Sangh, a Hindu volunteer organization – founded by K. B. Hedgewar, a doctor in Nagpur, Maharashtra, in 1925, soon after he came under the influence of V. D. Savarkar, a militant Hindu leader. Savarkar, who argued that the Hindus in the Indian sub-continent constituted a nation, defined a Hindu as a person who loved the land that stretches from the Indus river to the 'seas on the east', and considered it as both fatherland *and* holy land. To be a Muslim or Christian, he stated, meant having a religion that draws its cultural resources from outside this holy land; and this caused a division of loyalties and weakening of the Hindu nation. It behoved the militant Hindu to undertake the task of minimizing, and then eliminating, this division, and rejuvenating the Hindu nation. (In practical terms, it meant having Muslims and Christians adopt Hindu/Indian names and participate in such Hindu/Indian festivals as *holi*, festival of colour, and *divali*, festival of light. Hedgewar set out to do so by forming a volunteer corps, whose members met daily, wearing a uniform, drilled and played games, and had a session of political discussion and indoctrination.

Over the years, the RSS gained recruits from among the urban, upper caste, middle-class Hindus in the Marathi-speaking area, and more importantly the north-western region of the sub-continent, where Hindus, forming a minority, felt threatened as (from 1940 onwards) the Muslim League, increasingly supported by Muslims – then constituting a quarter of the sub-continent's population – began agitating for a separate state of Pakistan, consisting of the Muslim majority provinces.[18] The establishment of Pakistan in 1947, preceded and followed by large-scale inter-religious violence, with Hindus and Sikhs on one side, and Muslims on the other, mainly in the undivided Punjab, gave an added strengh to the RSS. The subsequent exchange of population, across the borders of (Western) Pakistan and India, caused the RSS members to spread out widely over the northern and western parts of India and establish new branches. This continued until the assassination of Mahatma Gandhi, in January 1948, by N. R. Godse, a Hindu fanatic, when the Central government banned the RSS, and arrested its Supreme Leader, M. S. Golwalker, and many of his followers.

However, once Golwalker had agreed, in the summer of 1949, to have his organization adopt a written constitution (which it had not done before) and declare its loyalty to the new Indian Constitution, soon to be promulgated, he and his followers were released and the ban on the RSS lifted. 'The aims and objects of the Sangha [i.e. RSS] are to weld the diverse groups within the Hindu *samaj* [i.e. society] and to revitalize and rejuvenate the same on the basis of its *dharma* [i.e. ethics] and *sanskriti* [i.e. culture] so that it may achieve an all-sided development of Bharatvarsha [i.e. India]', stated its constitution. In a little over a year, the RSS was able to re-establish nearly 5,000 of its old branches, with an estimated strength of 600,000 members and active sympathizers.[19]

This attracted the attention of S. P. Mookerjee, a prominent Bengali Hindu politician who, after his resignation from Nehru's cabinet, in 1950, in protest against what he considered to be the government's 'weak-kneed' policy towards Pakistan, and a 'suicidal policy of appeasement' towards Muslims (in India), wanted to form a new party with the primary objective of countering the pro-Muslim bias of the Congress. He held a series of meetings with Golwalker to explore the possibility of converting the RSS into a political party. In the end, Golwalker decided against changing the 'cultural' nature of his organization, but instructed some of his most trusted lieutenants to help Mookerjee establish a political party, to be known as the Bharatiya Jan Sangh, essentially in the image of the RSS, but open, theoretically speaking, to all Indians, including non-Hindus. It came into existence in late 1951, and contested the first general election, held in 1952.

The party advocated 'hard' policies towards Muslims at home and Pakistan abroad; and this endeared it to a large segment of Hindu refugees from West Pakistan, now forming an important section of the urban petty bourgeoisie in northern and western India. Its lack of interest in land reform made it attractive to many of the feudal lords of the former princely states – mainly in Madhya Pradesh and Rajasthan. As the party's candidates for election, they were successful in attracting a considerable section of voters in rural areas. These factors enabled the party to increase its popular vote from 3·3 per cent in 1952 to 6·44 per cent in 1962.

The events of the early and mid-1960s made the party more popular. Wars with China (in 1962) and Pakistan (in 1965) added weight to the party's view that these countries are the 'arch enemies' of India, and that the government should 'Militarize the Nation' and 'Modernize the Military'. Its agitation, in 1965, that Hindi be made the *sole* official language for all-India purposes (instead of Hindi and English continuing to enjoy an equal status) increased its popularity among the urban middle classes in the north-central region, since they stood to gain by it. The corresponding loss in popularity in non-Hindi areas did not matter, because the party lacked a base in the south and east. Its agitation, in 1966, often headed by holy men, for a blanket ban on cow slaughter in the country, through an amendment in the Constitution, gained it support among women. Consequently, the party's claimed membership jumped from 275,000 in 1960–1 to 812,000 in 1964–5. The situation improved further when, following the 1967 elections, it shared power with other parties in the non-Congress ministries that assumed power in some States; and its nominees in the government used their administrative powers to help raise the strength of both the Jan Sangh and the RSS. By 1970–1, the party's leadership was claiming a membership of 1·3 million.

And yet this could not mask an outstanding weakness of the party: it lacked any coherent socio-economic ideology. For a long time, its leaders continued to downgrade economic issues, and dismissed both capitalist and socialist modes of economic development as, simply, 'foreign' to the Indian soil. But as the Congress persisted in flaunting first its 'socialistic pattern of society' and then its 'democratic socialism', they had to take a stand. They rejected both socialism and capitalism, and opted for 'Integral Humanism'. 'The capitalistic system of economy which accepts the "economic man" as the central point of all its activities is inadequate,' stated A. B. Vajpayee, a party ideologue, in 1967.

The selfish desire to acquire more and more profit is the motivating force in this system, with competition as its regulator. This does not conform to Bharatiyan [i.e. Indian] philosophy. . . . Socialism's objectives are commendable, but in its end-result it has failed to profit mankind. The reason is that analysis of society and individual by Karl Marx, the propounder of scientific socialism, is basically materialistic and so it is inadequate. The concept of class conflict cannot give rise to a spirit of spontaneous and permanent cooperation. . . . Integral Humanism must necessarily make a balanced appraisal of both Bharatiyan as well as Western ideologies. . . . There can be no spiritual salvation without material prosperity.[20]

However, a balanced stress on 'spiritual salvation' and 'material prosperity' was discarded, in late 1971, when the party hierarchy emphasized the need to create 'a psycho-cultural environment' in which the 'social evolution' of an individual will be based upon the extent of 'cultural elevation' and 'aparigraha (i.e. spiritualism)' and not upon the size of 'material wealth'.[21]

While the party's economic ideology continues to be muddled, its loyalty to the initial emotive slogan of 'One country, one nation, one culture' remains steadfast. The oneness here is that of militant Hinduism. 'What is wanted [by the Jan Sangh] is a unified, disciplined, militant, and militarized Hindu community, bound together as far as possible in a full-fledged Gemeinschaft by its ties of blood, culture, language, religion, and the like, capable of taking a leading place among the nations of the world as a consequence,' notes Howard L. Erdman.

'The preferred policy is a highly centralized and if necessary a highly authoritarian state.'[22]

Although right-wing in its orientation, the Swatantra Party differed from the Jan Sangh in more ways than one. Firstly, unlike the Jan Sangh, the Swatantra outlined its economic policy in the list of Party Principles, adopted at its founding convention in 1959. 'The Party holds that the progress, welfare, and happiness of the people depend on individual initiative, enterprise, and energy,' stated the Party Principles. 'The Party stands for the principle of maximum freedom for the individual and minimum interference by the state . . . and to create the conditions in which individual initiative will thrive and be fruitful.' Secondly, unlike the Jan Sangh, which came into being, essentially, as the political arm of the already existing RSS, a Hindu revivalist volunteer organization, the Swatantra was established at the initiative of two recently formed conservative lobbies which wanted to safeguard the economic interests of their members. One was the Forum for Free Enterprise, established in Bombay in 1956, by a group of businessmen and industrialists, to foster the growth of free enterprise in the country; and the other was the All India Agriculturists' Federation, a body of large landowners, formed in 1958 primarily to oppose land ceiling legislation. They were appalled by the Congress's Nagpur Resolution, in January 1959, recommending co-operative farming, and reacted by securing the support of C. Rajagopalachari, well known for his anti-Communist views, and Minoo R. Masani, an anti-Communist intellectual who was close to the industrial house of Tatas, and establishing a political party some months later.

Thirdly, instead of concentrating initially on creating a hard core of dedicated party workers to build a strong base for future growth, as the Jan Sangh leadership had done, the Swatantra leaders followed the expedient strategy of securing the support of rich and influential people, either as individuals or as leaders of local conservative parties. They persuaded the Maharani Gayatri Devi of Jaipur, the most important of the twenty-two princely States that had been amalgamated to form Rajasthan, to join the party. They also had the Raja of Ramgarh, in Bihar, merge his Janata Party – formed in 1950 mainly to oppose the abolition of zamindari – with theirs. Similarly, they succeeded in getting the leadership of the Ganatantra Parishad (a party formed on the eve of the 1952 elections by some of the former princes) to merge with the Swatantra. In addition, they won the support of many of the feudal lords in north Gujarat.

The short-term impact of this strategy was quite impressive; and the result of the 1962 elections showed it. Thanks to the vote-pulling power of the former princes and feudal lords in Rajasthan, north Gujarat, the large tribal belt of Orissa, and parts of Bihar, the party emerged as the main opposition group in these States, and won twenty-five seats in

Parliament on a popular vote of 8·3 per cent. Its leadership took this to be evidence of the correctness of its strategy, and visualized a rosy future for the organization. But this was not to be so.

The Congress, never too serious about implementing the resolution on 'co-operative farming', gave the idea a quiet burial, and thus robbed the Swatantra of its most emotive rallying cry. The business community although approving of the Swatantra's strident propaganda for 'private enterprise', proved less than generous in its donations to the party. Anxious not to alienate the powerful Central administration, which was in the hands of the Congress, most businessmen continued to treat the Congress favourably as far as donations were concerned. 'The heart of the rich is with us but their money is with the Congress,' wrote C. Rajagopalachari, a Swatantra leader.[23] The death of Nehru in 1964 made the conservatives in the Congress stay on in order to steer the whole party to the right; and this frustrated the Swatantra leaders' hope of causing a split in the Congress and attracting its conservative wing. Finally, periodic attempts to bring about a merger of the Swatantra and the Jan Sangh proved unsuccessful.

The two parties realized that the differences between them were far too acute to be reconciled. The Swatantra, enjoying some support in the southern States of Andhra Pradesh and Tamil Nadu, disapproved of the fanaticism of the Jan Sangh in regarding Hindi as the only official all-India language. It was committed to creating amity between India and Pakistan; whereas the Jan Sangh was militantly anti-Pakistan and had not yet reconciled itself to what it called the 'vivisection' of *Akhand Bharat* (i.e. Indivisible India). Its leaders feared that, in case of a merger, the 'anti-Muslim' image of the Jan Sangh would destroy its influence among non-Hindus who regarded it as both militantly anti-Communist *and* secular. On the other hand, the Jan Sangh leaders felt that the image of the Swatantra as a 'rich man's party' would weaken their support among the urban lower- and middle-middle classes in the north-western region. In any case, they considered the Swatantra as a 'personality-based' party, and therefore one without much staying power.

However, this did not stop the two parties from joining a broad anti-Congress alliance (which often included both right- and left-wing opposition to the Congress) that was forged, in various States, on the eve of the 1967 election. And this arrangement benefited them both, separately. It enabled the Swatantra to improve its Parliamentary strength to forty-four, without either having to increase its popular vote (of about 8·5 per cent) or broadening the composition of its electoral base. As a study of election results showed, the party continued to have 'a predominantly rural base', with its support confined 'more to the land-owning cultivators and their "clients" among the landless labourers' than to the middle strata.[24]

Whatever support the party had acquired among the middle peasants in Gujarat and the delta area of Andhra Pradesh faded, when the Congress, following the split in 1969, began to woo this section of peasantry by offering it credit facilities and 'miracle' seeds. Its popularity in Rajasthan and the tribal belt of Orissa declined as more and more young electors – lacking any memory of the paternalistic attitude of the former princes, and finding themselves unable to share the awe that their parents had for the old rulers – voted differently from their elders. At the same time, the former princes found it increasingly difficult to bestow material or other benefits on a large number of their erstwhile vassals, and realized the meagreness of their resources in comparison to the powers of patronage that can be exercised by a present-day government minister.

The cumulative effect of these trends manifested itself in the Parliamentary elections of 1971. Although the Swatantra contested these elections in alliance with the Jan Sangh, the Syndicate-Congress, and the (politically insignificant) Samyukta Socialists, the party's popular vote slumped to 3·1 per cent, and its strength in Parliament to eight. The party's performance in the State assembly elections of 1972 was even worse. Its total strength plummeted from 109 seats to 16, with Andhra Pradesh registering a sharp fall from 29 to 2, and Rajasthan, once its stronghold, from 48 to 11. For all practical purposes, the Swatantra had collapsed by early 1972. Its formal disbandment occurred in August 1974, when its leaders chose to merge it with six small parties to form the Bharatiya Lok Dal (i.e. Indian People's Union), with a view to creating an all-India party committed to 'right-of-centre' policies.[25]

The Jan Sangh, on the other hand, continues to function separately and hold its ground fairly well. It contested the 1974 elections in Uttar Pradesh on its own, and managed to improve its strength in the assembly from 49 to 61 while maintaining its popular vote at 17 per cent (as in 1969). But this does not preclude the possibility of the party co-operating with other 'like-minded' parties at the next election, or the one after. It seems the three right-of-centre parties – the Syndicate – Congress, Bharatiya Lok Dal, and Jan Sangh – will continue to exist separately, co-operating and competing with one another. 'In the future,' notes Howard L. Erdman, 'there should be ample scope for both moderate and militant rightism . . . although it is impossible to specify what the balance will be. . . . The social forces which have supported various rightist positions will continue to work through diverse channels.'[26]

In any case, shifting combinations of various rightist elements in the political arena leave undisturbed the nature of the state's most powerful institutions, namely, the police, intelligence, and the military. Because of historical reasons, these institutions in India are rightist. They evolved in their modern form during the time of the British, and their single most important function was to enable the imperialist power to maintain its hold over the sub-continent. The ultra-conservatism of their mainly Indian officers seems, in retrospect, to dismay even some of their British contemporaries. 'I [now] find it odd to recall that between the wars it was not unusual in military circles [in India] to hear both Mahatma Gandhi and Pandit Nehru referred to as traitors,' wrote John Morris, a retired British officer in the Indian Army, in 1974.[27] Political independence has brought little, if any, change in these attitudes: the Gandhis and Nehrus of yesteryear have given way to the Communist leaders of today. At the same time, it has brought, in its train, an enormous increase in the size of these institutions.

16

RIGHTIST FORCES:
INSTITUTIONAL

As a rule, we [Indian Army officer-cadets] are conservative in
our attitudes. We do not like socialism because we see it as one
form of communism.

An officer-cadet at the Indian Military Academy,
Dehra Dun, Uttar Pradesh[1]

The British organized their police in India almost as an adjunct
to the army.

Brig. S. K. Sinha of the Indian Army[2]

Long used to absolute power, it is impossible for the new
[police] recruits to adhere to the needs of a changing society. The
police still believe in third degree, torture, and terrorization.

Surrinder Khullar, an Indian journalist[3]

The Watergate scandal reminds me of the time I was attached to
the [Union] Home Ministry. Bugging the place [in Parliament
House] where an opposition party would hold its meetings was
normal practice. . . . Verbatim reports of what transpired behind
closed doors were available to the Ministry. . . . Tapping
telephones of important persons . . . was also a rule rather than
an exception.

Kuldip Nayar, an Indian journalist and author[4]

The main prop of the British rule in India was the army. The British
created it, piecemeal, as they went along, conquering more and more
territory in the sub-continent, and reorganized it after the anti-British
uprising of 1857, making sure to keep the ratio of Indians to Britons at
no more than two to one, sharply down from the ratio of nine to one,
prevalent before the uprising. They succeeded in maintaining it as a
united and powerful force by following an adroit combination of
policies, which included substantial material benefits and security to
recruits, restricting recruitment to politically reliable groups, under the
guise of 'martial races', and engendering a healthy rivalry among them
in regard to service to their impartial and beneficent rulers, and, most

importantly, by fostering a sense of intense loyalty to individual regiments, consisting almost exclusively of such 'martial' races as Rajputs, Dogras, Pathans, Sikhs, Gurkhas, and Mahrattas.

The British labelled a particular group a 'martial race' more out of geo-political reasons than racial. They were more interested in the group's historical attitude towards them, its geographical location, and religious affiliation, than in its 'innate' fighting qualities. The Sikhs, living mainly in Punjab, for instance, were classified 'martial' principally because they had supported the British in quelling the anti-British uprising by other Indians in 1857. The (Muslim) Pathans in the North West Frontier Province and the Muslims in Punjab were considered 'martial' chiefly because they lived in areas that were nearest to Russia, which was then considered the major threat to India, and because it was regarded as politically wise to maintain parity between Muslims and Hindus in the army.[5] Among Hindus, it was mainly such castes as Rajputs, Dogras, Jats, and Ahirs, who lived in the north-western region, who were classified 'martial'.

The policy of limiting recruitment to martial races served the British interest well. 'The very fact that the army was drawn from particular castes and classes set these classes well apart,' notes Stephen P. Cohen, an American political scientist. 'This status brought them into a close relationship with the British and the government, and some groups were encouraged to think of themselves as above the rest. . . . Each class was encouraged to develop particular attributes which set it apart from other recruit classes and from the mass of Indian peasantry.'[6] Along with this went a policy of *not* deploying a unit of the army, recruited from a certain part of the sub-continent, locally. It was, for instance, a party of Gurkhas, recruited from the neighbouring Nepal into the Indian Army, that was ordered by Brigadier-General Reginald Dyer to fire on a crowd of nationalist Indians in a park in Amritsar in April 1919 – an event that caused the death of 379 persons and injuries to over 1,200.

No wonder, then, that as nationalist consciousness grew, particularly after 1919, the Congress came to regard the British policies and practices concerning the army as divisive and undemocratic, implying thereby that the situation would change with independence. But it has not. The units of the army continue to be posted and deployed away from their areas of recruitment; and the old regiments and their composition have changed but little.

'The army continues to recruit from the same groups as in the days of the British,' said Colonel R. Rama Rao, a director of the Indian Institute of Defence Studies in Delhi.[7] Sikhs continue to be favoured as before; and so do middle caste Hindus from Punjab and Haryana. Though only 2 per cent of the national population, Sikhs form 11 per cent of the Indian Army today. Similarly, Punjab, accounting for only 2·4 per cent of the country's population, provides 15·3 per cent of its soldiers.[8] Haryana, too, makes an above-average contribution to the army. According to a correspondent of *Link*, in half of the State's districts 'almost every household has one family member in the army or the Border Security Force'.[9] This means that, as in pre-independence days, such areas as West Bengal continue to be almost totally un-represented in the army. Furthermore, the traditional alienation of the average soldier from the common people remains as marked as before. 'A soldier here is made to feel that he is a class by himself, and is superior to others,' said Lieutenant-General B. M. Kaul. 'This feeling is reinforced by the fact that he lives apart from society, in barracks.'[10]

A similar situation prevails among the officers. They are taught to keep themselves aloof from the ranks; and the region of Punjab–Haryana–Delhi–north Rajasthan is over-represented in the officer corps. In 1971, for example, this region provided nearly 40 per cent of the cadets at the Indian Military Academy in Dehra Dun, Uttar Pradesh, which is a 'rounding off' institute for army cadets,[11] and corresponds to the Royal Military Academy in Sandhurst, England. Interestingly enough, of the Indians who passed the entrance examina-tion to the Royal Military Academy in Sandhurst, during the period of 1918–26, 42 per cent were from the (undivided) Punjab – which then included present-day Punjab and Haryana, in India, and West Punjab in Pakistan.[12]

The Indian Military Academy draws its cadets from the 'general purpose' National Defence Academy, near Poona, Maharashtra; the Army Cadet Corps; the élitist schools and military colleges; and the ranks. Since selection to the National Defence Academy is based on open competition, and since the ranks qualify for selection to the IMA (once they have passed certain examinations), the cadets with a poor or lower-middle-class background should be expected to be the dominant group at the IMA. But the actual situation is quite the contrary. In 1971, at the IMA, for instance, the cadets from the ranks were only a third of those from such élitist institutions as the St Paul's (Private) School in Darjeeling, West Bengal, and the Prince of Wales Royal Military College, in Dehra Dun, as from the ranks. 'There is a tradition of the princely class and landed aristocracy being trained to become army officers,' said General R. Prasad, commander of the IMA.[13]

This tradition dates back to 1918, when the Indians were first given the King's Commission and accepted at Sandhurst. Describing the social background of the 126 Indians who underwent training at Sand-hurst during the following fourteen years, Cohen writes: 'They were almost all sons of Indian princes, wealthy zamindars, planters, or they came from military families. . . . Collectively, they were the most reliable, politically inert, aristocratic, and conservative group the

British could select.'[14] Since then, the social base from which the army draws its officers has widened marginally, to include the high-income urban professional class. A typical gathering of cadets at the IMA, in 1972, for instance, showed that 63 per cent of them were sons or nephews of army or police officers – all of them landowners; and 18 per cent were sons of urban professionals.[15]

Although training of Indian cadets in England ceased in 1932, when the IMA was established in Dehra Dun, the impact of the Sandhurst style persists. 'The Sandhurst model is still very much alive in the upper echelons of the [armed] service,' noted André Beteille, an Indian sociologist, in 1967.

> Officers tend to be primarily English-speaking. . . . An officer who comes from an upper-middle-class family and has been to a public school has an advantage over one who is lower-middle class in origin and a product of a vernacular school. One can get a fair idea of the styles of life of officers . . . by observing their behaviour in the various messes. . . . The Central Vista Mess for the air force, situated on Janpath in the heart of New Delhi, may prove a good example. There is much to remind one of the glories of the British Raj: the silver, the cut glass, and the linen remain the same. Officers spend their evenings playing billiards or poker, and drinking beer, whisky, or rum. . . . The tone of social life in an officers' mess is in many ways highly anglicized, and parties and dating are important elements in it.[16]

Colonial attitudes persist in other aspects of army life as well. 'A classical example [of the continued British influence in the Indian Army today] is the continuance . . . of regimental march-pasts like "Scotland the Brave",' states Lieutenant-Colonel S. K. Sinha.

> Similarly, it is strange that battalions of the Rajputana Rifles should continue to be known after foreign military officers of any consequence like Napier or Outram, instead of carrying the illustrious names of our own Rajput heroes, like Rana Pratap or Rana Sangha. . . . Yet another facet of our military traditions is our mess customs. In our officers' mess today, we continue to ape a way of life foreign to our culture and background. Besides the change in the toast from the King Emperor to the President and with it [the change] of the national anthem, the ritual in our messes continues in every respect to be what the British officers practised when not a single Indian, other than the mess servants, was allowed in these messes. . . . The band plays English tunes as it did in British days, notwithstanding the fact that over 90 per cent of the officers have not the faintest idea of these tunes! . . . These mess customs to which we cling so passionately,

as our cherished traditions, tend to alienate us from our men.
They convey to them the image of a brown sahib (i.e.
gentleman) who has replaced the old white sahib and not of
military leaders, sprouting from a common soil with them – the
national soil of India.[17]

But alienation between soldiers and officers goes much farther and
is, indeed, a result of the training imparted to the officers. 'There are
officer games and soldier games; and we keep them separate', said
General R. Prasad. 'Officer games are tennis, squash, golf, riding. And
troops games are basket ball, hockey, football. An officer should know
just enough of soldiers' games to be able to act as a referee, no more.'[18]
Cadets are constantly exposed to such attitudes, held by their superiors,
and soon begin to reflect them. When asked, by an outside interviewer,
what kind of relationship they should have with their soldiers, a group
of cadets at the IMA replied, almost unanimously, 'We should keep our
distance' or, 'We should mix with them *only* during sports time'. Not
surprisingly, none of the cadets could tell the average salary and
allowances of a soldier![19] This attitude is justified on the ground that
only by keeping his distance from the men can an officer enforce
discipline. But the fact is that it is the exceptionally harsh system of
punishment for disobedience or insubordination, conceived and
codified by the colonial government, which helps, in the main, to
maintain a high degree of discipline in the Indian Army. There are
thirty-five sections of military offences, and some of the most serious
are punishable by death. Each year, no less than 3,300 members of the
army are court-martialled for purely military offences and some
3,200 convicted.
    The officers are also instructed not to discuss politics in the mess.
Such a policy is expected to help maintain the tradition of non-
involvement of the armed forces in the political affairs of the country,
originally conceived and enforced by the British, chiefly because in
those days, 'politics' often meant, to them, 'sedition'. However, there
have been lapses in this code of conduct, especially in late 1962, when
an armed conflict broke out between India and China on the issue of
border demarcation, and these have been overlooked, even condoned,
by the senior officers. This revelation was made by no less a person
than General J. N. Chaudhuri. 'In 1963, when I was the Chief of Staff,
Prime Minister Nehru discussed with some of us the desirability of
officers talking politics in the mess,' he stated. 'It had been reported to
him [Nehru] that many young officers were referring in a critical
manner to the events leading up to the Indo-Chinese clash of 1962.
This was true . . . [but the Army commanders, present at the meeting,
argued that] if a political topic came up [in conversation in the mess],
suppressing such discussion by order would only drive it harmfully

underground.'[20] Such tolerance towards anti-Communist attitudes contrasts sharply with reports of many Keralaites, serving in the Indian Air Force, losing their job for the mere 'crime' – detected by the Central government's intelligence – of attending, during their leave at home, a public rally by the CPI(M).

Their social background, economic interest, professional training, and the general milieu in which they live and work make the vast majority of officers, inertly or overtly, anti-Communist. This can be seen clearly in the articles written by the past and present officers, and published in the quasi-official *United Services Institute Journal*. 'It [Communism] is a new and dynamic creed promising plenty to the "have nots",' states Flight-Lieutenant K. R. Nambiar. 'It matters little if the promises are empty . . . if the promised utopia turns out to be a cheerless society of regimented monotony. Communism will continue to appeal to the needy and the gullible. How then are we to counter subversion? A vigilant watch is to be kept on the subversive factions, and their nefarious activities nipped in the bud.'[21]

The idea that India may go Communist disturbs the officers, many of whom offer their own solutions to abort such a possibility. 'The subjugation of India would be the greatest gain possible for Communism short of capitulation of the United States,' writes Lieutenant-Colonel M. R. P. Varma. 'Communist ideology permits ways and means that are repugnant to our way of life. We know from the experience of other nations what these methods are, how to arrest and defeat them.'[22] The implication is that there is an inherent conflict between the Indian 'way of life' and Communism, which cannot be resolved. And yet preserving this way of life is sought to be achieved by securing a 'democratic and *secular*' society on one hand, and having *religious* education imparted to the ranks on the other. 'Not nearly enough is done to educate the soldier about the new democratic and secular society we are trying to create and his mission to secure it from aggression,' writes Major G. S. Kapur. 'The importance of this advantage [of religion] we have over our latest and Godless enemy [i.e. Communist China] has not yet sufficiently been realized.'[23] Outlining the methods to 'thwart the Communist tactics of exploiting officer–man, rich–poor relationship in our country,' Major P. S. Anand suggests that 'greater stress should be laid on religious education of our troops, particularly the officers'.[24]

The clash with China in 1962 increased the anti-Communist sentiment in the upper echelons of the military, and caused a dramatic expansion in the armed forces and their hardware. The annual defence expenditure jumped from Rs 312·5 crores (£156·25 million) in 1961–2 to Rs 816·10 crores (£408·05 million) in 1963–4, an increase of 261 per cent. During the same period, the strength of the army went up from under 550,000 to 825,000, three times its size on the eve of independence in 1947. A rapid expansion of the air force continued throughout the 1960s so that, by 1970, with its 2,000 aircraft and 90,000 personnel, the Indian Air Force had emerged as the world's fifth largest. By then, the country had also become self-sufficient in the manufacture of rifles, RCL guns, howitzers, anti-aircraft guns, medium tanks, frigates, helicopters, and aircraft. All this had cost enormous sums of money. Within a decade – from 1961 to 1971 – the annual national defence expenditure rose by four and a half times.

During the same period, the annual budget of the Central Police Department of the Union Home Ministry, shot up six and a half times, from Rs 18·76 crores (£9·38 million) to Rs 118·82 crores (£59·41 million). By then (1971) the State governments were spending more on the police, Rs 244·33 crores (£122·17 million), than on general administration, Rs 210·67 crores (£105·34 million).[25] The Congress administration in Delhi had not only expanded the already existing para-military and central police forces, namely, the Territorial Army, the National Cadet Corps, and the Central Reserve Police – but had also established such new organizations as the Border Security Force, for routine patrolling of borders, and the Central Industrial Security Force, for protecting the Central government's industrial undertakings in the country, under the aegis of its Home Ministry. The result was that, by the early 1970s, the Central Police Department had become a multifarious organization, encompassing such intelligence, security, and police forces as the Central Intelligence Bureau (concentrating mainly on political intelligence), Central Bureau of Investigation (for investigating inter-State crimes), Director General of Security, Central Industrial Security Force, Railway Protection Force, Border Security Force, and the Central Reserve Police Force; and its budget had shot up nearly forty times in a little over a generation, from Rs 3 crores (£1·5 million) in 1950 to Rs 119 crores (£59·5 million) in 1971.[26]

Furthermore, by then, organizations like the Territorial Army, functioning within the Defence Ministry, and the Border Security Force, created, in essence, to help secure the country against external threat, were being increasingly used to establish law and order *within* the country. By the Central government's own admission, in 1973–4, the over-100,000-strong BSF was used for 'maintenance of internal security' in as many as thirteen States.[27]

Both the BSF and Territorial Army are also being used to break up strikes, especially those by other Central government employees like the railwaymen and postmen. 'According to the Territorial Army Act, the Territorial Army . . . can be employed in a national emergency only, viz., in a war or near war situation; or when a general mobilization is ordered by the government,' states S. N. Antia, a retired Major-General. 'Yet, some of the Territorial Army units have been "embodied" (without the existence of national emergency), as was the case during the recent Railway strikes in Dhanbad and Tatanagar [in Bihar]. This is usually done by the government without the approval of Parliament. It is later published in the *Government of India Gazette* to give it legal sanctity.'[28] A similar pattern was repeated on a national scale, in May 1974, when a large majority of the railways' 1·7 million workers went on strike, with one difference: this time the Central administration acted 'constitutionally', since the country was under a state of national emergency which had been declared in December 1971 on the eve of war with Pakistan, and had not been lifted. 'The Territorial Army and other para-military organizations were pressed into service to make up for mass absenteeism at several crucial [railway] centres like Delhi, Bombay, and Moghulsarai,' reported Sarwar Lateef, an Indian journalist.[29] The 'other' para-military organizations included the Border Security Force. Indeed, the change in its role had been indirectly acknowledged earlier, when the Home Ministry had disclosed, in its report for 1973–4, that attempts were being made to 'broadbase' the training of the BSF personnel.[30]

Similarly, the Research and Analysis Wing (RAW) that had first been established within the Union Cabinet Secretariat by Indira Gandhi in 1967, to take over the functions of gathering and analysing foreign intelligence, from the Central Intelligence Bureau, was drawn into the domestic affairs of the country two years later. This happened, because, following the split in her party – when her adversaries frequently attacked her as 'pro-Communist' – she began doubting the loyalty of the arch-conservative Central Intelligence Bureau, and instructed the RAW to research and analyse political trends *within* the country. The RAW soon proved itself superior to the Central Intelligence Bureau. For instance, contrary to the Intelligence Bureau reports, the RAW informed Indira Gandhi that she was popular with the electorate, and that she would be best advised to dissolve Parliament before its term ran out in March 1972, and seek a fresh mandate. She did; and the election result proved the RAW right. This endeared it to the Prime Minister, who had earlier brought the organization under her direct supervision and removed recruitment to it out of the purview of the Union Public Service Commission. Shortly after, the head of the RAW, R. N. Kao – a retired police officer and, like Indira Gandhi, a Kashmiri Brahmin – was accorded the status of a departmental secretary; and this gave him complete freedom to spend the budgeted amount as he saw fit.[31] In 1974, he was appointed secretary of the newly formed National Security Department of the cabinet secretariat, a development which marked the formal amalgamation of the 'external' and 'internal' aspects of the country's security.

The RAW was also drawn into another domestic matter – countering the 'left adventurist' trends in West Bengal – and began to play an important behind-the-scenes role after March 1970, when the Centre took over the State's administration. It worked in conjunction with other Central and State intelligence and police forces. Together, they seemed to have masterminded a plan which combined such tactics as infiltration of leftist parties, accentuation of differences between these parties, especially the CPI(M) and Naxalites, and between ideological and non-ideological Naxalites, and cloak-and-dagger killings: activities which, at their peak, reportedly involved as many as 29,000 government agents of one kind or another,[32] and caused the deaths of some 2,000 Naxalites and CPI(M) members, and the arrest (often followed by beatings and sometimes by torture) of many thousands of them.

Some of the tactics, devised apparently by the RAW officials, were extraordinarily clever and effective. While an off-duty policeman in plain clothes would follow the instructions of his superiors and kill a pro-CPI(M) colleague, the police authorities would announce, as a matter of routine, that 'Naxalites' had killed a policeman. This kind of (supposedly Naxalite) 'action' yielded rich dividends to the Congress government: (a) it demoralized the small pro-CPI(M) minority in the police force; (b) it exacerbated relations between the CPI(M) and Naxalites; (c) it made policemen clamour for more training and more arms; and (d) it made the police force, as a whole, more anti-Naxalite than before. Such ingenuity on the part of Government Intelligence was ascribed by many to the training received by some of the Intelligence officers at the International Police Academy in Washington DC – an institution which specializes in training officers of the non-Communist world in the ways of fighting Communism at home. 'The activities of the Research and Analysis Wing (RAW) are as much clothed in secrecy as those of the CIA,' noted the *Frontier*, 'but very few people doubt that some of the officers have had foreign training in the art of creating inter-party and intra-party strife, infiltration, and annihilation. Perhaps some day some official of the International Police Academy in Washington DC will be able to throw some light on this fascinating subject.'[33]

Having thus engendered a militantly vengeful attitude in the police, the top officers let the ranks indulge in open violence against the Naxalites in order to terrorize the public and discourage young people from joining the movement. The degree of terrorization can be gauged by the fact that, between 30 October and 9 November 1970 alone, twenty-one Naxalites were killed and another seven injured by the police in the Greater Calcutta area. (The official story, invariably, was that the police had been attacked with 'bombs' and had had to fire in 'self-defence'.) 'On the night of 20 November, four Naxalite youths in Beliaghat [in Calcutta] were dragged out of their beds and shot,' wrote T. Goswami, an Indian journalist.

The same night eleven Naxalites were shot dead and their bullet-ridden bodies thrown along a highway in the Barasat area. . . . Bullets of service revolvers found in the bodies of the youths in the Barasat area, and other reports published in conservative papers like *Ananda Bazar Patrika*, as to how they were rounded up in the Maidan [open ground in central Calcutta] area while holding a secret meeting, left hardly anybody in doubt as to the 'mystery' of the massacre. . . . The next big success of the police was at Beliaghat again when five men were killed in broad daylight.[34]

There was, however, a danger that constant repetition of such acts by the police could prove counter-productive; and so it was time to call for some restraint. 'The Government of West Bengal has directed the police to eschew extra-legal methods in dealing with Naxalites,' wrote a staff reporter of the pro-Congress *Hindustan Standard* on 20 December 1970. This did not mean that 'extra-legal' behaviour of the police ceased altogether, only that there was to be a temporary cooling off. Given the traditional function of the police, as the arm of a foreign ruler to maintain 'law and order' in the country, it was not surprising that the police, especially the top and middle-rank officers, took up the task of crushing the 'left adventurist' movement in West Bengal with such enthusiasm.

In contrast, they had felt uneasy at being denied their customary role of intervening in disputes between workers and management, and peasants and landlords, in favour of management and landlords, as had been the case during the two leftist United Front governments. The senior officers, in particular, had found the situation almost unbearable. An incident in a village in the district of 24-Parganas in July 1969, when a policeman was killed in a clash with members of a leftist party, provided them with a chance to vent their feelings. They did so by, covertly, diverting a funeral procession of some 3,000 members of the State's armed police force, in Calcutta, in honour of their dead colleague, away from the crematorium and to the State assembly house. On arrival there, the police demonstrators attacked leftist ministers and assembly members, while the officers at Calcutta's police headquarters, situated nearby, took half an hour to arrive on the scene.

An official inquiry into the incident confirmed the widely held belief that many of the State's senior police officers were involved in causing the violent incident. But the leftist administration could not take any action against them, since, as members of the Indian Police Service, an all-India service, they were, legally speaking, on loan to the State government, and therefore beyond its disciplinary powers. Commenting on the police violence in the assembly hall, Jyoti Basu, the CPI(M) minister for the police, said:

The role that the police were made to play by the alien rulers of India did not undergo any change when they transferred the mantle of government to the Congress. The police were used before [independence], as also during the past two decades [of independence], for serving the interests of the few against those of the many . . . for the suppression of the democratic movements, and other legitimate aspirations of the people.[35]

Among those who have noted a lack of change in the Indian police after independence is an American academic, David H. Bayley, the author of *The Police and Political Development in India*.[36] 'The most surprising feature of the contemporary Indian police is that its activity remains so largely colonial in its mould', he writes.' Reference, here, is not to overall organization of the police . . . [but to] the persistence of [their] behaviour patterns and philosophy. The primary function of the police continues to be containment of trouble once it occurs. . . . They react to threats to law and to government, but they do not actively seek to serve the peculiar security needs of individual citizens.'[37] The organization and duties of the police continue to be guided by the Police Act of 1861. This had its origin in the Madras Police Act of 1857, a law which – to quote *The Report of the Working Group of Police Administration*, published in 1970 – made no reference whatsoever to 'the nature or the incidence of crime to be dealt with' but put all the emphasis on 'the repressive function of the police for the preservation of the peace and control of disturbances'.[38]

No wonder, then, that over the decades of British rule the police came to be considered by the public as a 'protective, detective, and repressive' arm of the government – a fact which was acknowledged by the Police Commission of 1902–3 which stated in its report that 'It [the police force] is generally regarded as corrupt and oppressive,' and that 'it has utterly failed to secure the confidence and co-operation of the people'. Interestingly enough, an exhaustive survey of 2,400 people in one rural and two urban areas of the country, conducted more than sixty years later, led the researchers to conclude that 'the Indian public is deeply suspicious of the activities of the police', and that 'a considerable proportion expect the police to be rude, brutal, corrupt, sometimes in collusion with criminals, and very frequently dealing unevenly with their clients'.[39] The following incident, narrated by Sunanda K. Datta-Ray, an Indian journalist, sums up the popular feeling about the police: 'Most telling, perhaps, was an encounter with a village lad on his way to market with a basketful of chickens. The car had broken down and, before venturing across the country for assistance, I asked him if it was safe. In all simplicity, the lad replied: "Oh yes! There are no policemen here now." '[40]

Not only have the Congress governments in the States and at the Centre failed to alter the traditionally oppressive behaviour of the police but also they have vastly increased both its size and fire-power. Between

1950 and 1970, the total strength of the police in the States rose from under 380,000 to over 800,000.[41] During this period, the proportion of the armed wing in the force – which is organized like the army infantry but with less officering and fire-power – jumped from 15 per cent to 56 per cent. That is, more than half of the Indian policemen today are trained in the use of firearms, live away from the community, in cantonments, and function only in groups.

The strength of the Central Reserve Police – the armed police force established by the Union government in 1949 (just a year before the enforcement of the new Constitution which includes the police in the 'State List') – has risen astronomically. It went up from 1 battalion at the time of its inception to 60 battalions in 1973, with the major increase concentrated in the quinquennial period of 1965–70, which registered a near fivefold growth in the force's budget.[42] The latter half of the 1960s witnessed a series of mass agitations, rooted in both economic and non-economic (i.e. linguistic, religious, and ethnic) issues, and the loss of power by the Congress in many of the major States. And the Congress administration in Delhi responded to this by boosting the size of its armed police.

The deployment pattern of the force, which draws nearly three-fifths of its ranks from the Hindi-speaking areas,[43] in the early 1970s, showed the continued apprehension of the Indira Gandhi government. According to the unconfirmed press reports, in early 1972, one-sixth of the CRP force was posted in West Bengal and Kerala, where a large minority of voters support the CPI(M). A little over 50 per cent of the force was stationed in those border areas where religious and ethnic minorities dominate local politics: 43 per cent in the north-eastern States and sub-States, with large numbers of non-Hindu, non-Aryan inhabitants, and the remainder in the Muslim-majority State of Jammu and Kashmir.[44] In other words, the Congress government in Delhi has come to rely increasingly on its armed police and the army to check the political aspirations of the masses in left-orientated States, and of the religious and ethnic minorities inhabiting the country's border areas.

PART V
RESILIENCE OF THE SYSTEM

17

THE INTERNAL STRAINS

In the final analysis, stability of Kashmir does not depend on the political prowess of this or that personality in the Congress or in the Plebiscite Front: it depends upon the might of the Indian military machine.

Economic and Political Weekly editorial[1]

We are about to see re-enacted for the nth time the elaborate farce of a 'free' election in the Kashmir Valley.

Rasheed Talib, an Indian journalist, in February 1972[2]

Our demand for State autonomy arises because the State governments are closer to the people, and only after the State governments take over these [administrative and financial] powers from the Centre would they be able to serve the people in a manner expected of them.

Election manifesto of the Dravida Munnetra Kazhagam in Tamil Nadu[3]

It may be a long way before an average Naga can call himself an Indian.

Sachin Barooah, an Indian journalist[4]

Ideologically, Hinduism and Islam are quite antithetical to each other.

Imtiaz Ahmad, an Indian social scientist[5]

The status of the people of Jammu and Kashmir, which has been a bone of contention between India and Pakistan since 1947, and the cause of two wars between them, has an important bearing on the position of Muslim minority in India and on the wider issue of division of power between the States and the Centre. The roots of the Kashmir problem lie in the fact that the British law, granting independence to India, and creating two Dominions of India and Pakistan, gave rulers of the 'native' states an option to accede to one or the other, or remain independent, and that while Maharaja Hari Singh, the ruler of Jammu and Kashmir, was a Hindu (a Dogra, by caste), three-quarters of his subjects were Muslim.

The state of Jammu and Kashmir came into existence in 1846, when Raja Gulab Singh, the Dogra ruler of Jammu, amalgamated the newly acquired territories of (predominantly Muslim) Kashmir and (Buddhist) Ladakh with (marginally Hindu-majority) Jammu. The attitude of the inhabitants of this polyglot state to the Dogra dynasty varied from region to region. Buddhist Ladakhis, living mainly in inaccessible areas, were indifferent to the Hindu chief. The people of Jammu, particularly the Hindus, held their ruler in high esteem, whereas the predominantly Muslim populace of the Kashmir Valley, which accounted for nearly half of the state's population, disliked the feudal authority of their Dogra overlords. But it was not until the 1930s that a democratic movement for political reform got under way in the Valley; and it was not until the mid-1940s that the Kashmir National Conference, led by Sheikh Mohammed Abdullah, launched the 'Quit Kashmir' campaign against the Maharaja, a step that was actively supported by Nehru.

When independence came, in August 1947, the Maharaja offered 'standstill agreement' to both the Dominions. Pakistan accepted; India did not. Instead, India's leaders urged the Maharaja to release Sheikh Abdullah and other leaders, then in jail, and consult them regarding the State's future. The Maharaja did so a few weeks later. On his release, Sheikh Abdullah sent two of his emissaries to Pakistan, but their talks with the Pakistani authorities proved unfruitful. Soon after, the predominantly Muslim inhabitants of Poonch-Mirpur area, outside the Kashmir Valley, adjoining Pakistan, revolted against the Maharaja, set up their own Azad (i.e. Free) Kashmir government, and sought the help of both the Pakistan authorities and Pathan tribals, in Pakistan's North West Frontier Province, to 'liberate' the rest of the State.

In mid-October, these tribals launched an attack on the Kashmir Valley. On 25 October, when the tribals were within a few miles of Srinagar, the State capital, the Maharaja conveyed his wish to Delhi to accede to the Indian Union, and asked that Indian troops be sent forthwith to repulse the aggressors, a decision which was endorsed by Sheikh Abdullah. In accepting the accession, Lord Mountbatten, the Governor-General of India, added the proviso that 'as soon as law and order have been restored in Kashmir and its soil cleared of the invader, the question of the State's accession should be referred to the people'. (Simultaneously, the Indian government lodged a complaint with the United Nations Security Council that Pakistan had armed and abetted the tribals from their country to attack Kashmir, and that it should be asked to vacate 'gains of aggression'. It was thus that Kashmir became an 'international' problem.)

The Indian troops arrived in time to save the capital from the invaders. But the fighting in the State went on for more than a year, as the tribals were first supported, and then replaced, by the regular forces of the Pakistani Army. The ceasefire agreement signed between India and Pakistan, with the aid of the United Nations, on 1 January 1949, left Pakistan with nearly 32,000 square miles of the State's original 86,000 square miles.

The Indian government had the unpopular Maharaja first go into voluntary exile and then abdicate in favour of his son, Karan Singh (in mid-1949), with the effective administrative power passing into the the hands of Sheikh Abdullah, who became the Executive Head of the State. Like other princely States, Jammu and Kashmir was invited to send its representative to the Indian Constituent Assembly; and it did so. But, whereas the representatives of all other princely states – which had earlier signed the Instrument of Accession, submitting the rights of defence, foreign affairs, and communications to the Indian Union – decided to vest their residuary rights in the Union Parliament, the representatives of Jammu and Kashmir did not. Indeed, an Article (number 370) in the Indian Constitution formalized the special status of Jammu and Kashmir by stating that the powers of the Union Parliament are to be limited to only those subjects as were covered by the Instrument of Accession, signed in October 1947. Thus, the people of the State were formally reassured that they had a free hand to run their internal affairs the way they saw fit.

This meant that a separate constitution had to be framed for the State. It was therefore decided by Sheikh Abdullah's administration to convene a Constituent Assembly elected on the basis of universal suffrage. The State was divided into seventy-five constituencies and electoral rolls were prepared. In the end, however, elections took place in only four constituencies, because those opposing Sheikh Abdullah's National Conference, concentrated mainly in the Jammu region, were told by the returning officers that they had (all) filled in their nomination papers 'incorrectly' and could not therefore contest the election. (Evidently, the State officials, acting as returning officers, were carrying out (verbal) instructions given to them by their political superiors, an event which did not augur well for democracy in the State.)

By thus pre-empting all opposition in the Constituent Assembly, through misuse of his popularity and administrative powers, Sheikh Abdullah accentuated the traditional animosity that had existed between the Hindus in Jammu (then comprising 60 per cent of its population),[6] who in the past had identified with the Dogra ruler, and the Muslims in Kashmir (constituting 95 per cent of its population), who had always detested the Maharaja. Now, the Hindus in Jammu began protesting against 'Kashmiri domination' and agitating for closer ties with India. Responding to the pressure from Jammu, and the Indian leaders in Delhi, Sheikh Abdullah made certain concessions, in July 1952. These gave the Indian President power to declare a 'state of emergency' in the

State in case of external aggression, and the Indian Supreme Court jurisdiction in certain matters. However, this did not satisfy the pro-accessionist elements in Jammu, who launched an agitation, in late 1952, under the auspices of the Jan Sangh, for 'One Constitution, one flag, and one President'. This caused apprehension among Kashmiri Muslims, who saw in this a threat to the 'special status' conferred on them through the Indian Constitution.

It was in this atmosphere of rising tension and suspicion in the State that a plan to arrest Abdullah was conceived – in Delhi, under the supervision of Nehru – by a cabal of R. A. Kidwai, a Muslim colleague of Nehru in the central cabinet, Bakshi Ghulam Mohammad, deputy to Sheikh Abdullah, D. P. Dhar, a Hindu colleague of Sheikh Abdullah, and Karan Singh, the head of the State.[7] In August 1953, on the order of Karan Singh, Sheikh Abdullah was arrested under the State's Public Security Act, and, except for a brief spell of four months in 1958, kept in jail until April 1964.

Meanwhile, the Indian government continued to stall the efforts of the United Nations Security Council to make arrangements for holding a plebiscite in the State to determine whether the people wished to accede to India or Pakistan, by arguing that Pakistan must vacate the 'gains of aggression' *completely* before the question of a plebiscite was discussed. This was unacceptable to Pakistan which feared that evacuation of any area would lead to its occupation by India – for good. When, in 1954, Pakistan signed a Mutual Security Pact with America, Nehru stated that that changed the whole context of the Kashmir problem and freed India from its earlier commitment to hold a plebiscite in the State.

With Sheikh Abdullah in jail, Bakshi Ghulam Mohammad, the new prime minister of the State, co-operated wholeheartedly with the Indian government to help it consolidate its position through a variety of means – economic bribes, repression, and election-rigging. Balraj Puri, a Hindu journalist and author of Jammu, describes the 'artful blend of corruption and tyranny' employed by Bakshi Mohammad:

> Appointments to government jobs, promotions and transfers, admissions to educational institutions, grants of licences, quotas, and loans and contracts for business, were invariably made by him. Through the use of such patronage he created a cadre of thousands of men who were personally loyal to him. He created a private army, paid from the State funds, called the Peace Brigade, which was used to disrupt political meetings of opponents.[8] He had the State assembly pass a Preventive Detention Act with a proviso for detention of a person for up to five years without trial.[9]

Simultaneously, he tried to win popular support by increasing the supply of cheap rice (subsidized by the government to the extent of 75 per cent of its price), enlarging educational and health facilities, and instituting easy credit schemes for agriculture and industry. All this was possible because of the excessive generosity of the Indian government: its per capita grant-in-aid to the State for the period of 1958–62, for instance, was seven times the national average.[10]

When, following the promulgation of the State's Constitution in 1956, it became necessary to hold elections in 1957, Bakshi Mohammad combined bribery with harassment of his political opponents, and thus secured a massive majority for his party, the National Conference. 'Prospective opposition candidates were offered cash or a job,' said Shamim Ahmed Shamim, an independent member of Parliament from Kashmir, in 1971. 'But if the candidate still persisted, he was kidnapped so that he could not file his nomination papers in time, or he found that he had arrived at the wrong place on the wrong day fixed for the scrutiny of nomination papers. Or, the returning officer refused to accept that the candidate's proposer was one Mohammad Ali or whosoever he actually was. And so the nomination papers of the opposition candidates were rejected.'[11] Similar tactics were used in the 1962 elections as well, but to a slightly lesser extent. As a result, the number of constituencies where contest was allowed went up from thirty-two in 1957 to forty-one in 1962. Significantly, most of these were in the Hindu majority region of Jammu, where opposition to the National Conference was from the elements who were even more pro-India than Bakshi Mohammad.

Over the years, the corruption and tyranny of Bakshi Mohammad's regime became unbearable; and Nehru, using the device of the Kamraj Plan, conceived in late 1963, to invigorate Congress by drafting many of the State and Central ministers into the party work, persuaded Bakshi Mohammad to resign.[12] G. M. Sadiq, who succeeded Bakshi Mohammad after a brief interval, liberalized the regime somewhat. He disbanded the much-hated Peace Brigade, and made the provisions of the oppressive Preventive Detention Act less harsh than before. Responding to the pressure from Nehru, whose attitude towards Pakistan had softened as a result of the armed conflict with China in late 1962, Sadiq released Sheikh Abdullah, and his loyal lieutenant, M. A. Beg, in April 1964. Sheikh Abdullah had a series of meetings with Nehru to find a solution to the Kashmir problem, and then went off to Pakistan, in May, to confer with President Ayub Khan. But Nehru died while Sheikh Abdullah was still in Pakistan.

With this died any chance there was of an amicable settlement with Pakistan on this issue. L. B. Shastri, who succeeded Nehru, had neither the charisma nor the popularity needed to win the approval of Parliament for an agreement with Pakistan, which would have inevitably involved some concessions to Pakistan and/or the idea of letting the State's people exercise their right of 'self-determination'. Realizing this, Sheikh Abdullah openly called for a plebiscite, something he had never done before. This had an unsettling effect on Sadiq, who had simultaneously to cope with the manoeuvres of Bakshi Mohammad in the State assembly against his recently formed government. He therefore found it necessary to rely even more heavily on the Indian administration than Bakshi Mohammad had done, in order to stay in power: he actively co-operated with Delhi to further integrate the State into the Indian Union.

Towards the end of 1964, the President of India acquired powers (hitherto denied him) to take over the State's administration if he felt that the constitutional machinery had broken down. He abrogated the special status of the head of the State and made him merely the governor, as was the case with all other States. (And so, too was the office of *Wazir-e-Azam*, the prime minister, abolished, and that of chief minister introduced.) He also extended the jurisdiction of such Indian institutions as the Supreme Court, Election Commission, etc. to the State. In short, the main features of the 'special relationship' that had existed all along between the State and the Indian Union were annulled. On top of this, in early 1965, the National Conference, the leading political organization of the State, was dissolved and then re-established as the State unit of the Indian National Congress.

Sheikh Abdullah protested against these changes, and advised his followers to conduct a 'social boycott' of all those who had joined the Congress party. Then, accompanied by Beg, he went off on a foreign tour, during the course of which he had an unscheduled meeting with Chou En-lai, the Chinese Prime Minister, in Algiers. Chou En-lai reiterated his support for 'the right of self-determination for the people of Kashmir', and Sheikh Abdullah thanked him for this – an action, which landed him, and Beg, in jail as soon as they returned to India in May 1965. They were in prison when a war broke out between India and Pakistan on the issue of Kashmir in September 1965, and when general elections took place in the State in early 1967.

The war between India and Pakistan ended, after three weeks, in a virtual stalemate on both sides of the front line. But the temporary ceasefire was not formalized until January 1966, when Prime Minister Shastri and President Ayub Khan had a successful meeting in Tashkent, USSR, where top Soviet leaders played a mediatory role.[13] The curtailment of civil liberties in the State during and after the war, including the arrest of 1,200 opponents of the regime, under the Defence of India Rules, and the banning of their publications, paralysed the opposition forces.[14] This, and the failure of Pakistan to achieve a military solution to the Kashmir problem, demoralized the pro-Pakistani elements in the State, and engendered a general feeling of resignation among the people. And yet the Indian government clung to its old policy of not letting a multi-party democracy emerge in the State. During her tour of the area, in October 1966, the Prime Minister Indira Gandhi said that there was no need for 'another party' in Kashmir, because 'the danger of formation of a separate party [other than the Congress] was that one did not know which direction finally it would take.'[15] This was a clear hint that the forthcoming elections were not going to be free and fair. And they were not.

There was the customary rejection of the nomination papers of the opposition candidates, especially in the Muslim majority constituencies in the Kashmir Valley. In all, 140 nomination papers of the non-Congress candidates were declared invalid. 'The wholesale rejection of the nomination papers of the opposition candidates was pre-planned,' said Balraj Madhok, a Jan Sangh leader. 'The rejection on the ground that they were not accompanied by the Oath of Allegiance [to the Indian Constitution] was preposterous – because the Oath papers had been deliberately removed from the nomination papers.'[16] With twenty-one seats – all in the Kashmir Valley – to its credit, even before a single vote had been cast, the Congress went on to 'win' thirty-nine more, leaving a meagre fifteen for the opposition parties.

The methods used by the ruling party to guarantee itself a massive victory at the polls were summarized by R. R. Parihar, an Indian academic, thus: offering jobs to prospective opposition candidates; kidnapping a few opposition party leaders to prevent them filling nomination papers in time; using government machinery for electoral purposes; a lavish use of money; making duplicate ballot papers available to the Congress candidates in the Kashmir Valley; police harassment and arrest of the polling agents of opposition candidates; last-minute opening of polling booths, thus denying time and opportunity to opposition candidates to send their polling agents; and marking of ballot papers by the Congress polling agents in collusion with presiding officers when voters did not turn up.[17]

Like the previous election, this one too was boycotted by the Plebiscite Front, an organization established originally by Beg, during his brief spell of freedom in 1955, and then revived by him and Sheikh Abdullah in 1964–5, only to be left leaderless by their subsequent incarceration, which ended in early 1968. With this, the Plebiscite Front once again became active; and the following year, its leadership decided to end the election boycott and strive to achieve its objective of having the State's people exercise their right of self-determination in a plebiscite, through the ballot box. When Parliament was dissolved in late December 1970, Sheikh Abdullah and Beg announced, during their visit to Delhi, that they would contest two of the three Parliamentary seats allotted to the Kashmir Valley. The State government reacted to this by serving externment orders on them and barring their return to the State, and followed this up with a ban on the Plebiscite

Front and the arrest of nearly 400 of its activists, and the disqualification of all of its present and *past* members *and* sympathizers from contesting the forthcoming election.

In the circumstances, Sheikh Abdullah and Beg could no more than lend their moral (and distant) support to some independent candidates *after* their nomination papers had been accepted. They did so; and this was enough to enable these candidates to win majority or near-majority votes in twenty-eight of the forty-two State assembly constituencies, comprising the three Parliamentary areas in Kashmir,[18] with one of them, Shamim Ahmed Shamim, actually defeating his Congress rival by a large margin.

This meant that the Congress hierarchy in Delhi could not afford to hold free and fair elections in the State and still win. Any hope that the electors might be given a chance to make their choice freely, while voting for the State assembly in March 1972, was dashed by the events in the eastern wing of Pakistan during the period March–December 1971. It was the decisive victory at the polls won by the Awami League, led by Sheikh Mujibur Rahman, in a genuinely free and fair contest in Pakistan under the military regime of Yahya Khan in March 1971, that had made its demand for internal autonomy irresistible. This was realized by the top policy-makers in Delhi, in early 1972, who dreaded the possibility of the Kashmiri people voting overwhelmingly for Sheikh Abdullah's party at the polls, so soon after the Indian government had given active moral and material help to Sheikh Mujib's forces to establish an independent Bangladesh. They therefore decided to stick to the old familiar ways of tampering with the wishes of the Kashmiris in the March 1972 elections,[19] and thus enabled the Congress, now led by Mir Qasim, to win fifty-seven seats. 'Indira Gandhi talks of the will of the people of Bangladesh while she has blatantly suppressed the aspirations of the people of Kashmir,' said Sheikh Abdullah in March 1972.[20]

However, once elections were out of the way and the political fate of the State settled for the next five years, Sheikh Abdullah and Beg were allowed to return to their native State. Later, in September, they formed the United Front, consisting of their followers from the now outlawed Plebiscite Front and members of the Awami Action Committee – another organization committed to securing the right of self-determination for the Kashmiri people – to contest local elections in the four leading towns of the Kashmir Valley. The Front won fifty-six out of fifty-nine seats on a popular vote of 70 per cent. Fearing a rout at the hands of the Front, the State's Congress party had desisted from fighting these elections (the first to be held since 1954!) on the ground that it did not wish to introduce 'politics' into civic affairs, a transparently unconvincing argument since the party contested these elections in the Jammu region.[21] These results showed that, despite sustained efforts by the Congress hierarchy in Srinagar and Delhi, since 1953, to undermine Sheikh Abdullah's standing in Kashmir, he continued to be the single most popular leader of the Kashmiris.

A begrudging acceptance of this fact by the Congress leadership, and Sheikh Abdullah's public statements that he did not dispute the legality of the State's original accession to India in 1947, created an atmosphere of mutual tolerance between the two sides. The State government did not renew its ban on the Plebiscite Front when it lapsed at the end of two years, in January 1973. Soon, dialogue got under way between Sheikh Abdullah and Beg on one side, and Mir Qasim and Indira Gandhi on the other, to find a lasting solution to the 'Kashmir problem'.

To underline his moderation, Sheikh Abdullah pointed out, in April 1974, that while demanding a plebiscite to determine the will of the people of the State, the Plebiscite Front had 'also' maintained that it would accept a 'reasonable alternative' to the idea of a plebiscite,[22] a statement that was reiterated by Beg, the president of the Front, at its first (ever) conference in July 1974. Where Sheikh Abdullah and Beg were insistent was on the question of the constitutional relationship between the State and the Indian Union, which, they said, must be brought back in line with Article 370 of the *Indian* Constitution, by annulling all the steps taken towards integration of the State within the Indian Union after their removal from office, and imprisonment, in 1953.

Serious negotiations then began between Beg and G. Parthasarthi, the respective emissaries of Sheikh Abdullah and Indira Gandhi; and agreement was reached between them in November 1974. This was ratified later by the principals, and led, in February 1975, to the installation of Abdullah as the *Wazir-e-Azam* (i.e. prime minister) of Jammu and Kashmir after he had been unanimously elected the leader by the State's Congress legislature group, even though he did *not* join the party.

On the other hand, in a letter to Indira Gandhi, Sheikh Abdullah said, 'The accession of the State of Jammu and Kashmir is not a matter in issue. It has been my firm belief that the future of Jammu and Kashmir lies with India because of the common ideals we share.' Also, the details of the agreement between the two sides showed that he and Beg had settled for much less than what they had demanded in the beginning. Their proposals that the jurisdiction of the Indian Supreme Court in relation to the State be curtailed and that the supervision and control of elections to the State assembly by the Election Commission of India be ended, were both rejected. Even the compromise proposal that the power of the Indian President to take over the State's administration be made conditional on the concurrence of the State governor was turned down. There was of course no question of returning to the situation, prevailing before 1964, regarding the office of the head of the State, and the institution of the governor was to continue in the same way as in other States. The only concession made by Delhi was that in case the State government came with any proposals to alter a Central law made after 1953 on subjects in the 'concurrent list' such as social welfare measures, cultural matters, social security, procedural laws, etc., these would be considered 'sympathetically' by the Centre.

On their part, Sheikh Abdullah and Beg could claim that they had secured a reiteration by the Indian government that the State of Jammu and Kashmir 'shall in its relations with the Union, continue to be governed by Article 370 of the Constitution of India'. But then the existence of this Article had not in any way impeded the State's integration into the Indian Union during the period of 1953–74. The two leaders could draw some comfort from the fact that the State continued to have its own constitution, and that the agreement reached with Delhi stated clearly that 'the residual powers of legislation shall remain with the State'.

In that sense the State remains unique, even though the events of the period of 1953–74 have shown that Kashmiri Muslims are not the only minority to feel a special need to protect their cultural and religious identity. Sikhs, Dravidian Tamils, and the Mongoloid Nagas and Mizos feel likewise, and have expressed this feeling by lending their support to such regional parties as the (Sikh) Akali Party in Punjab, Dravida Munnetra Kazhagam, Naga National Council, and Mizo National Front. But, unlike the National Conference of Kashmir, these parties have had to operate in areas that have been considered integral parts of India since 1947, and have been governed, since 1950, by the Constitution of India, which – to quote Mohan Ram – is 'federal in form and unitary in spirit, with the Centre's writ running all over the document'.[23] Furthermore, successive Congress governments in Delhi, enjoying overwhelming majorities in Parliament, have consistently increased the powers of the Centre – both administrative and financial – at the expense of the States.

The decline in the party's strength in Parliament, in 1967, did not arrest or reverse the process. On the contrary, when faced with the situation of having to deal with a non-Congress government or a large non-Congress opposition, offering a viable alternative to an existing Congress ministry in many of the major States, the Congress administration in Delhi used the Constitutional provisions in a way that increased the already considerable powers of the State governor – an appointee of the Centre and responsible to it – and thus further eroded the powers of a State. In most cases, the State governor tailored his action (or inaction) to suit the interests of the Congress group in the assembly. Due to this, and other reasons, none of the parties favouring greater autonomy for the States managed to stay in power long enough to do

something tangible about it. The only exception was the Dravida
Munnetra Kazhagam (DMK), a party which has ruled Tamil Nadu
since 1967, first in coalition with a few other small parties, and then –
following the general election of 1971 – on its own.

In 1969, the DMK-led government in Tamil Nadu appointed a
committee to study the subject of State–Centre relations. In its report,
published in 1971, the committee recommended, in general, 'fullest
autonomy' for the States 'within the general framework of the Constitution and without in any way impairing the integrity of the country'
– and, in particular, transfer of residuary powers of legislation, at
present vested in the Union Parliament, to the States, and deletion of
Article 356, which empowers the Centre to suspend a State government
(through the governor) and rule it directly. The DMK government
accepted the report whereas, not surprisingly, the Congress administration in Delhi ignored it altogether. This led M. Karunanidhi, the DMK
chief minister of Tamil Nadu, to warn that 'The Central government
[in India] should avoid the mistakes of Pakistan (in dealing with the
demand for autonomy by its eastern wing), and concede autonomy to
the States'.[24]

Such a statement from a DMK leader was not unexpected because,
until 1963, when an amendment to the Constitution made it illegal for
a party or an individual to demand secession of any territory from India,
both the DMK and its parent body, Dravida Kazhagam, were committed
to the idea of creating a separate, sovereign state of Dravida Nadu –
comprising the Dravidian States of Andhra Pradesh, Tamil Nadu,
Karnataka, and Kerala – or, at least, a separate Tamil Nadu.

The alienation of Dravidians, especially those living in the southernmost Tamil Nadu, from the Aryans of the north is rooted in ancient
history. The invading Aryan tribes, entering the sub-continent from
the north-west, first pushed the indigenous Dravidians southwards,
and then subjugated them there. Over the centuries, the Dravidian
languages came under a varying influence of Sanskrit, the language of
the ruling Brahminical order, with the Tamil-speaking people, proud
of their own ancient heritage and imperial glory, emerging as the most
resistant to Sanskritization of their language. Indeed, in Tamil Nadu,
the language came to distinguish the ruler from the ruled. The former,
taking their cue from the Brahmins, spoke Sanskrit, while the latter –
non-Brahmins all – stuck to their native Tamil. This division has
continued. In modern times, it is mainly the Brahmins who cultivate
Sanskrit, and the non-Brahmins who cultivate Tamil.

The arrival of the English, in the wake of the British rule in the
south established in the last quarter of the eighteenth century, reinforced the traditional cleavage. The Brahmins were the first to learn the
new language, and in due course acquired a near-monopoly in civil
service, law, teaching, and political life. The non-Brahmin business

and landowning castes, who emulated the Brahmins in learning English nearly a century later, failed to make much headway in the civil service and professions due to the resistance of the already entrenched Brahmins. Later, the economic conflict between the two groups took on a political turn, with the Brahmins, in general, supporting the moderate wing of the Congress, and the educated non-Brahmins forming their own Justice Party, in 1917, in what was then Madras Presidency – consisting of present-day Tamil Nadu, the coastal districts of Andhra Pradesh, and northern Kerala.

The Justice Party contested the elections of 1920, held on a limited franchise – which kept out the generally poor lower castes and Untouchables – and won, chiefly because the non-Brahmin business and landowning castes favouring it were six times more numerous than Brahmins, who formed a meagre 3 per cent of the population. It won the subsequent elections until 1936, when it lost to the Congress. The following year, when the Congress ministry, containing a majority of Brahmins, prescribed compulsory teaching of Hindi in schools, it seized upon the issue to bolster its popularity. It found an ally in the Self-Respect Movement, led by the charismatic E. V. Ramaswamy Naicker, which opposed the caste system and the hegemony of Brahmins and the north. Together, they launched an agitation against the teaching of Hindi in schools, something that caught the imagination of many townspeople. A year later, the Justice Party elected Naicker its president. Under his leadership, the party became increasingly militant, and adopted a demand, in 1940, for a separate Dravida Nadu. Four years later, it changed its name to Dravida Kazhagam.

Differences arose in the party, in 1947, when Naicker instructed party members to boycott the independence celebrations, since 'independence' did not signify any change in the condition of the Dravidian people, who, he said, would continue to suffer the mal-effects of 'Hindi imperialism'. A group of young activists in the party, led by C. N. Annadurai, disagreed with him. 'It would not be right either to ignore, or to measure merely by the standard of our own principles, a great event that is being keenly watched by the entire world,' wrote Annadurai in his paper *Dravida Nad*.[25]

Two years later, Annadurai and many other young leaders left the Dravida Kazhagam to form the Dravida Munnetra Kazhagam. Its aims and objects were basically the same as those of its parent organization; but its tone of propaganda was less vehement, and its tactics less aggressive. However, it was not until the mid-1950s that the DMK decided to end the boycott of elections, a policy that the DK had followed since 1947. It fought the 1957 elections on the platform of opposition to 'Tata-Birla capitalism' and commitment to nationalization of 'banks, big enterprises, cinemas, etc.', and won fifteen assembly seats on a popular vote of 13 per cent. In the 1962 elections, it combined popular leftist slogans with Tamil nationalism and the establishment of Dravida Nadu, and secured fifty seats in the State assembly on a popular vote of 25 per cent.

After 1963 – when a Constitutional amendment made it illegal to demand secession of any territory from the Indian Union – the DMK whittled down its demand for a separate, sovereign Dravida Nadu to greater autonomy for the States, in general, and for Tamil Nadu, in particular. However, the party maintained its total opposition to the policy of teaching Hindi in schools, and the use of Hindi as the *sole* official language for all-India purposes after 26 January 1965, as had been specified by the Constitution. In fact, the DMK greeted the day with anti-Hindi demonstrations, in which students played an important role. Unnerved, the Congress administration in the State used excessive police violence against the demonstrators. This, in turn, led to students' strikes and widespread public disturbances, resulting in immense damage to public and private property, and the arrest of nearly 5,000 DMK supporters. The situation calmed down only after Prime Minister Shastri stepped in to promise a Central law embodying Nehru's (earlier) assurance that English would continue to enjoy the status of the official language for all-India purposes, along with Hindi, for as long as any *one* of the States of the Union wished it.

The DMK capitalized on the anti-Congress feeling, engendered, among other things, by the Congress government's mishandling of the anti-Hindi agitation, and led an alliance of non-Congress parties to a massive victory in the 1967 elections, increasing its own strength in the Assembly to 138 seats on a popular vote of 41 per cent. The DMK-dominated government stopped the teaching of Hindi in schools and raised the status and importance of Tamil, and, in general, created an environment in which the DMK could expand. The result was that by the time the next general election was held, in 1971, the party had established 9,600 branches with a claimed membership of 784,700.

While the DMK had, by the early 1970s, established itself as the single most important political force in Tamil Nadu, it had failed to win support in the remaining States of the south. This had happened partly because none of these States had a strong nascent separatist impulse in it, to be developed by a party, and partly because other parties had, in essence played the role that the DMK did in Tamil Nadu. In Kerala, for instance, the Communists had supported the anti-caste social reform movement, and had adroitly guided it into the channels of class struggle. They had also led the agitation for One Kerala, which was established in 1956, as a result of a major reorganization of the States along linguistic lines. The demand for the formation of Visalandhra (i.e. Greater Andhra) for the Telugu-speaking people, on the other hand, had come from a section of the Congress party in the old Madras State, and was realized in two stages – in 1953 and 1956. As for the

Kannada-speaking people, they saw little need for agitation for One Karnataka, since most of them were already concentrated in Mysore, a 'native' state governed by a comparatively liberal ruler. Morever, the Telugu and Kannada-speaking peoples, living in areas contiguous to the Sanskritized part of India, do not feel the isolation and alienation that the Tamils feel. 'The Tamil-speaking people stand to the rest of India in relation somewhat different from that of any other linguistic group,' notes P. Spratt, an Indian journalist and author.

Geography nurtures their feeling of isolation: far from the land frontiers, they have little sense of danger from abroad or of the need for unity in the defence of India. . . . The Kingdoms of the extreme south, those of the Chola, Chera, and Pandya dynasties, are mentioned in northern works as early as the fourth century BC, but were never incorporated into any of the early empires. Tamilnad thus cherishes an ancient tradition of political independence.[26]

So do the Nagas – a family of Mongoloid tribes living along India's north-eastern borders with Burma – cherish a long tradition of independence. They are believed to have travelled originally from the Malayan archipelago in ancient times, and settled in the forest-covered hill ranges of the area. As highlanders, they led a secluded life, making periodic forays into the nearby Brahmaputra valley (in Assam) either to trade or, as was often the case, rob and kill the plainsmen. Over the centuries, the plains-dwellers came to dread them. When, in the mid-1820s, the British replaced the Ahom kingdom in Assam, they inherited the hostile relationship that had existed between the Nagas and Ahom kings.

At first, the British reacted to the Naga practice of raiding the plains by sending punitive expeditions against them into the hills. Later, from 1866 onwards, however, they began establishing their own posts in the Naga Hills, taking care not to cover all of the Naga area, and to limit their 'administration' of the area to the nominal ritual of an annual tour by a British official. At the same time, they protected the Naga economic interests and cultural identity by banning the entry of Indians and foreigners beyond the 'Inner Line', defined by the foot of the Naga Hills, the only exception being the American Baptist missionaries, who first arrived in 1872.

The gradual spread of Christianity and literacy (in English) lessened the traditional hostility between the sixteen Naga tribes inhabiting the area, and engendered among them a sense of Naga nationalism, which, in turn, heightened their historical alienation from the predominantly Hindu plainsmen. They were untouched by the politics of the plains and the nationalist movement. In a memorandum submitted to the Simon Commission, in 1929 – appointed by the British government to recommend constitutional reform in India – the Naga Club, originally formed in 1910, stated, 'You [the British] are the only people who have ever conquered us, and when you go we should be as we were [before].' This sentiment was noted; and the Government of India Act of 1935 classified the Naga Hills district, first formed in 1881 (as well as the Mizo Hills district and the North Cachar Hills district) as an 'excluded' area within Assam, with the administrative responsibility vested directly in the hands of the governor, and not the popularly elected State legislature, dominated by the plainsmen.

The Second World War had a profound effect on the Nagas, since part of the Naga Hills fell into the hands of the Japanese advancing from Burma, and thousands of Nagas joined the (British) Indian Army, to fight the Japanese, and thus became well-versed in the handling of modern arms, a skill many of them were to use, later, against the authority of the Congress government in Delhi. Shortly after the war, in 1946, the Naga Hills District Council, a representative body of the Nagas, originally fostered by the British, enlarged itself and renamed itself the Naga National Council. In early 1947, the NNC sent a delegation (led by Angami Zapu Phizo) to Delhi, to suggest that the Nagas should be ruled by an interim government of their own for ten years, during which India should act as the 'guardian power', and maintain a defence force in the Naga Hills, in consultation with the NNC, and that at the end of this period the Nagas should be given a chance to decide their future. The delegation was told to submit this proposal to the Advisory Committee on the Aboriginal Tribes when it visited the Naga Hills district. It did so in May 1947; but the Advisory Committee made no such recommendation to the Indian Constituent Assembly – a body the NNC considered irrelevant to the Nagas since, they said, they already had a constitution of their own.

The following month, however, the NNC succeeded in reaching a nine-point agreement with the governor of Assam, who then had the direct responsibility for the affairs of such 'excluded' areas as the Naga Hills district. This agreement acknowledged the NNC as the principal political and administrative force. 'The general principle is accepted that what the Naga National Council will pay for, it will control,' stated the agreement. 'The Naga National Council will be responsible for imposition, collection, and expenditure of land revenue and house tax and of such other taxes as may be imposed by the Naga National Council.' Article 8 stated:

The governor of Assam as the Agent of the Government of the Indian Union will have special responsibility for a period of ten years to ensure due observance of this agreement; at the end of this period, the Naga National Council will be asked whether they require the above agreement to be extended for a further period, or a new agreement regarding the future of the Naga people be arrived at.[27]

But the Constituent Assembly in Delhi, which the NNC continued to boycott, seemed to take no notice of this agreement, while the Assam government, ignoring the NNC's protests, extended its administrative control to Tuensang, a Naga area that the British had left unadministered. The NNC, now led by the militant Phizo, reacted to this by reiterating that the new Indian Constitution, promulgated in January 1950, did not apply to the Nagas, and that it wanted nothing less than complete independence for the Naga people.

The following year, the NNC organized a plebiscite which showed that almost the entire adult population supported the idea of independence. This was confirmed when the Nagas carried out a total boycott of the general election of 1952. Not a single Naga cast his vote. Phizo had a meeting with Nehru; but nothing came of it. Then the NNC gave a call of non-co-operation with the Indian government. The Nagas refused to pay taxes; teachers and students withdrew from schools; and the government officials resigned *en masse*. 'It was the Indian independence movement over again, on a tiny scale – and the Indian government reacted in rather the same way as at first the British had,' writes Neville Maxwell, a British journalist and author. 'Several leaders of the NNC were arrested. . . . The sixteen tribal councils . . . under the leadership of the NNC were abolished. Reinforcements of armed police were moved into the area in service of a "get tough" policy.'[28]

The NNC retaliated by offering armed resistance. It did not take it long to mobilize men and materials to do so. The arms were either collected from the arms dumps left behind by the Allies during the War, or bought from the Karen rebels of Burma from across the border. And demobilized Naga soldiers from the old Indian Army provided the core of the NNC's fighting force – called the Naga Home Guard – estimated, then, to be five to six thousand strong.[29]

As the Naga resistance increased, the Indian authorities reinforced the Assam government's armed police force with the para-military Assam Rifles and later, in August 1955, the Indian Army, but to little avail. Finally, in March 1956 – when the NNC formally inaugurated the independent state of Nagaland, with its own Naga Federal Government and Parliament (called Tatar Hoho), and the Naga Federal Army – the Indian government handed over the whole 'pacification' operation to the army. Soon well over a division of Indian soldiers, supported by various ancillary forces, Assam Rifles, and armed police battalions from different parts of the country, were active in the Naga Hills. The consequent intensification of fighting brought much suffering. 'Retaliating against villagers for the action of the [Naga] guerrillas, the Indian forces set fire to villages and granaries and destroyed crops,' writes Neville Maxwell. 'Some villages were burned, rebuilt, and burned again. Reports of torture and massacre of villagers by the Indian forces accumulated.'[30]

The army's repressive powers were further augmented by the Armed Forces (Special Powers) Regulations Act, passed in 1958, which enabled an army officer to arrest anybody on suspicion and search any person or premises. And the army's strength was increased progressively so that by the end of the 1950s some 100,000 troops, forming about a fifth of the *total* Indian Army, were engaged in 'pacifying' an area measuring 6,370 square miles and having no more than 350,000 Naga men, women, and children.

Meanwhile, shocked by the escalating violence and brutality, the Naga church leaders decided to act. They called a conference of delegates of various Naga tribes, in 1957, to consider ways of ending the conflict. The conference demanded that, to begin with, all Naga areas be placed under the Indian government's External Affairs Ministry. (The NNC, committed to the goal of total independence, boycotted the conference.) Nehru agreed to this readily in order to give the non-NNC Nagas some political weight. These Nagas then went on to hold conferences, in 1958 and 1959, and finally to demand that a separate State of Nagaland be formed *within* the Indian Union. At first, Nehru publicly disapproved of the idea, and then gave in *after* he had received the non-NNC Naga delegation, in Delhi, in July 1960, a tactical move designed to make it appear that the idea had originally come from the Nagas (which was not the case) and that the Indian government had agreed to it reluctantly. But it was not until three years later, in 1963, that the State of Nagaland was actually established. The intervening period was used by the Indian Army to intensify further its campaign against the guerrillas by employing such tactics as 'village grouping' and calling in the Indian Air Force to strafe and bomb the camps of the guerrillas, estimated to be 12,000 strong in the early 1960s.

It was under such circumstances that elections to the State assembly were held. The pro-India Naga Nationalist Organization encountered no difficulty in putting up candidates in all of the forty constituencies, whereas the independent Democratic Party of Nagaland could manage to do so only in eighteen constituencies. No wonder the NNC won a comfortable majority, which was bolstered further by the addition of six government-nominated members from Tuensang, an area which was officially admitted to be too 'disturbed' to have elections.

Once the elections were over and a new government formed, the church leaders pursued their peace-making efforts with renewed interest. As a result, the Indian government and the NNC's Naga Federal Government signed a ceasefire agreement in May 1964, under which the Indian Army agreed to suspend its operations and restrict patrolling to areas within a thousand yards of its fixed posts, cease searching villages, imposing political fines, and using forced labour; and the Nagaland Federal Government promised to suspend its actions of sabotage and ambush, and recruitment to its army. A condition was thus created in which the next step – negotiations between the two sides to bring about a 'political' solution to the Naga problem – could take place. But this expectation was not fulfilled, because, whereas the Nagaland Federal Government representatives were prepared to sit down and talk without any pre-conditions, the Indian side insisted that talks could be conducted only within the framework of the Indian Constitution. A series of attempts, made in 1966 and 1967, to develop dialogue between the two sides proved abortive. This led the NNC to seek active support for their cause from neighbouring countries such as Pakistan and China. The help from China was to be in terms of guerrilla training to Naga partisans and the supply of small arms to them. This infuriated the Indian authorities, and soured the relations between the two sides. Nonetheless, the ceasefire lasted, at least nominally, until 1972.

While the Congress government in Delhi remained adamant in its attitude towards the dissidents in Nagaland, it showed over-indulgence towards its protégé, the Naga Nationalist Organization ministry, and used it as a funnel through which to pour vast sums of money into the State so as to impress on the Nagas the economic advantage of staying within the Indian Union and create a large body of Nagas with a direct, personal stake in the *status quo*. In 1968–9, for instance, while the State's treasury collected only Rs 1·03 crores (£515,000) in taxes and levies, it spent Rs 24·39 crores (£12,195,000), the difference being covered by grants and loans by the Centre.[31] Such massive expenditure of money caused the number of students in educational institutions to double in a decade, and that of hospitals and dispensaries to treble. The State bureaucracy was expanded to the point where one out of ten Naga adults was employed as a civil servant; and the police force was enlarged to the extent that the ratio of policemen to civilians (at 19 per 1,000) became ten times as high as in the neighbouring Assam.

Yet the Nagas continued to remain aware of their 'political' problem. And election results showed it. The pro-India NNO, enjoying all the administrative and financial advantages of a ruling party, managed to win no more than twenty-two of the forty elective seats in the assembly elections of 1969, with Tuensang district, containing a third of the State's population, once again denied the right to vote. Two years later, in the contest for the only Parliamentary seat in the State, the NNO candidate lost to an independent, A. Kuvichusa – who advocated negotiations between the two sides without any pre-conditions – by 54,000 votes to 84,000. The NNO government thought it prudent to acknowledge the political reality, and allowed its members in the assembly to support the opposition's resolution, submitted in September

1971, that 'Political talks should be resumed immediately between the Government of India and the Underground Nagas in association with leaders of public confidence [i.e. church leaders]'.

But the Centre took no notice. In fact, following the establishment of Bangladesh as an independent country in December 1971, and the subsequent loss of sanctuaries to the Naga rebels provided to them by the (previous) East Pakistan regime, the General-Officer-Commanding of the Indian Army in Nagaland warned the Home Minister of the Federal Government of Nagaland, 'While it took fourteen days to complete the war in Bangladesh, it would take less time to complete the work in Nagaland.'[32]

The Indian government's chance to 'complete the work' came in August 1972, when an unsuccessful attempt to kill Hokishe Sema, the State's chief minister, was made by Nagas of unknown political loyalty. Using this incident, the Indian authorities unilaterally terminated the ceasefire agreement, and outlawed the NNC, and its government and army. 'Any opposition member [of Nagaland Assembly] who continues to advocate the case of the "Underground" will be brought to trial,' warned Sema.[33] The strength of the army and para-military forces was raised to nearly 100,000, and the 'final drive' to solve the Naga problem once and for all was launched. It reached a peak in February–March 1973, a period that produced seventy-nine allegations of atrocities – rape, beatings, torture, and desecration of churches – by the Indian forces.[34] By September, enough 'progress' had been made by the Indian side to enable the junior Minister for Home Affairs to Delhi to tell Parliament confidently that the 'Naga problem' no longer existed.[35]

To prove that 'normalcy' had been restored to all parts of the State, it was announced by the authorities that the residents of Tuensang district would be allowed to elect their representatives to the assembly at the next election to be held in February 1974. Simultaneously, however, thousands of non-Naga road and construction workers, labourers, rickshaw-pullers, and traders – who had been allowed to live and work in the State on a *temporary* basis – were also enfranchised. Nagaland thus found itself, almost overnight, with nearly 100,000 non-Naga voters, forming a quarter of its total electorate! This was evidently meant to help the pro-India NNO at the polls. To ensure that all non-Naga voters supported the NNO – which faithfully echoed the Indian view that the 'Naga problem' no longer existed – a rumour was set afloat that if the opposition United Democratic Front – which stood for 'a final negotiated settlement of the Naga political problem' through constitutional means – were voted to power, all non-Nagas would lose their residential permits and be driven out of the State.

Despite all this, the NNO won only twenty-three seats, whereas the UDF secured twenty-five. Of the twelve independents elected to the assembly, seven decided to join the UDF, and thus made it the majority party in a house of sixty. This deeply embarrassed the Congress government of Delhi, since the UDF was led by Rano Shaiza – a niece of Phizo, the NNC president living in exile in England – and Vizol, who had until 1967 sided with the 'Underground'. The State governor, acting on instructions from the Centre, held back the swearing-in ceremony of the new government while efforts were made to persuade some independent members to leave the UDF and support the pro-India NNO. These failed; and the UDF ministry was finally sworn in.[36]

Shortly after assuming power, Vizol, the UDF chief minister, declared that his government wanted to see a peaceful settlement of the 'Naga problem' – which was 'very much alive' – through talks between the Indian authorities and the 'Underground', the Naga National Council. He and his government were willing to tell the 'Underground' that their demand for complete independence was 'unrealistic', and that the Central government, which continued to have the responsibility for the maintenance of law and order in the State, through the application of the Armed Forces (Special Powers) Regulations Act of 1958, should help to engender the right atmosphere by ceasing its 'military operations'.

The Centre ignored this advice on the ground that the Naga 'hostiles', encouraged by the victory of the UDF at the polls, were stepping up their activities. This was hardly the case. Indeed, the rebel Nagas showed their willingness to talk to the other side by refraining from firing near towns on 15 August, Indian Independence Day, something they had been doing since 1956, when they established their own Naga Federal Government. Later, the Central administration rejected the UDF government's advice not to renew the ban on the Naga National Council and its allied organizations when it expired in early September. It reimposed the ban for another two years under the Unlawful Activities (Prevention) Act of 1967, which empowers the Indian military and para-military forces to shoot, arrest, or punish anyone they may suspect of being a sympathizer of the proscribed organizations. Apparently, the Congress government in Delhi wished to be as non-co-operative with the UDF administration as possible, and thus pave a way for its fall and the return of the pro-India NNO to power, or an imposition of Presidential rule in the State. 'The NNO is . . . conspiring with officialdom to create conditions for the imposition of President's rule in Nagaland and the toppling of the present UDF government,' reported Harish Chandola of the *Economic and Political Weekly* in late September.[37]

And this is precisely what happened in March 1975. A dozen assembly members of the UDF were lured to join the NNO, and the party was installed into office. But this did not last, as most of the defectors – unable to face the anger of their constituents at their switch-over –

returned to the UDF fold. Thereupon, the governor asked the Centre to take over the State's administration; and it did.

A similar attitude has been adopted by the Centre towards the independence movement by the Mizos – a 300,000-strong, Mongoloid, overwhelmingly Christian tribe, wedged between Bangladesh and Burma – led by the Mizo National Front. A proposal by the Mizoram's Congress Chief Minister, Chal Chhunga, in December 1974, that a dialogue be initiated between the Central government and the Mizo National Front, without any pre-conditions, was rejected by Indira Gandhi, who insisted that Mizo 'hostiles' should first surrender their arms and agree to work within the present Indian Constitution before talks were begun. Later, following the assassination of three senior police officers in Aizawl, the capital of Mizoram, in January 1975, the Indian government declared the territory a 'disturbed area', and extended the application of the Armed Forces (Special Powers) Regulations Act of 1958 for a further six months.

Unlike the Nagas, who had first hinted at their desire to be independent in 1929, and made a formal demand in 1949, the Mizos had come up with this proposal only in 1961, when the Mizo National Front was formed. But, like the Nagas, the Mizos' political consciousness and expertise in handling modern firearms dates back to the Second World War, when the Japanese and Allied forces fought bitterly along the Indo-Burmese border, and thousands of Mizos joined the (British) Indian Army.

The immediate post-war period witnessed the formation of two political parties: the Mizo Union and the United Mizo Freedom Organization. The Mizo Union, supported by most of the demobilized Mizos, stood for the abolition of the system of rule by tribal chiefs, in the Mizo Hills district, under the tutelage of the British. The United Mizo Freedom Organization, supported by the tribal chiefs and their personal followers, on the other hand, raised a demand for a merger with Burma. The Mizo Union favoured inclusion of the district in the Indian Union, and associated itself with the Congress Party in Assam. It proved its popularity by winning all the three assembly seats, allotted to the district, in the 1952 general election. The abolition of the chieftain system, in 1954, however, caused its support to decline. In the 1957 election, it won one of the three assembly seats. Its mis-handling of the famine relief for the district, in 1959–60, led to the establishment of the Mizo National Famine Front to render voluntary help to the famine-stricken populace, and fight the 'half-hearted policies' of the Assam government towards the Mizos. Later when the famine ended, this organization converted itself into a fully-fledged political party, the Mizo National Front, and committed itself to achiev-ing an independent Mizoram. Simultaneously, unknown to the Indian authorities, the Front began training an armed volunteer force.

On 1 March 1966, hundreds of armed Mizo National Front volunteers over-ran police posts and administrative centres, and held Aizawl, the district capital, for six days. The Indian Army moved in large numbers, and captured the main centres, leaving the insurgents in control of the thousand-odd villages and hamlets. Later, the army launched a massive counter-insurgency drive, which lasted more than a year. 'Guerrilla warfare in the 8,000 square miles of mountains [of the Mizo area] has claimed more than 500 lives in a little over a year,' reported Peter Hazelhurst, a British journalist, from Delhi, in September 1967. 'About 3,500 Mizos – hillmen – who have drawn their political aspirations from the Naga struggle for independence have been arrested or have surrendered to the Indian forces. Villages have been regrouped on the Malayan pattern to isolate the guerrillas of the militant Mizo National Front.'[38]

Following the punitive military action, the Indian government began making political concessions to local aspirations for autonomy. Finally, in January 1972, it separated the Mizo Hills district from Assam, named it Mizoram, and gave it the status of a Union Territory – just short of Statehood – under the direct supervision of the Centre. This was, indeed, part of a major reorganization of the north-eastern region of the country, to meet the persistent demand of hill tribes for maximum political-administrative autonomy, which created five fully-fledged States (in place of the previous two) and two Union Territories. 'This may be seen as India's fall-back position, adopted because the provisions of the Sixth Schedule of the Constitution, giving local autonomy to the hill districts and tribal areas, did not satisfy the particularist demands of their inhabitants,' writes Neville Maxwell.[39]

It was more the geo-political considerations than genuine respect for different racial-cultural identity of the hill tribes, living along the border areas in the north-east, that had made the Indian Constitution-makers pay some attention to tribal sentiments. For the hill tribes living away from the borders had received no special treatment from them. The Adivasis (literally, Original Inhabitants), tribes of Australoid and Dravidian stocks, living in southern-Bihar–western-Orissa, are a case in point. As inhabitants of the forest-covered hills of the region since ancient times, they led a secluded life, which was not to be disturbed until the latter half of the sixteenth century, when the Mughal rulers – in the process of consolidating their conquests in the area – sent their forces into the hitherto unexplored forests. However, it was only after the arrival of the British that the Adivasi life was materially affected by the intrusion of non-Adivasis. The British rule, which brought money, government officials, and moneylenders into the area, caused the loss of most of the Adivasi land to outsiders. Simultaneously, Christian missions, established under the benevolent eye of the British, educated the Adivasis as well as proselytized them.

Education made the tribals conscious of their identity as Adivasis, and resentful of the economic domination by the 'outsiders' – i.e. Hindus from north Bihar and eastern Orissa. Some of the educated Adivasis formed the Chhotanagpur Unaati Samaj (i.e. Chhotanagpur – the name of the region – Welfare Society), in 1920 to work for the social and political welfare of the community. Soon, however, it was realized by them that the best way to preserve an Adivasi identity *and* make economic progress was by having a separate State of their own. A demand for the creation of such a State was, therefore, made before the Simon Commission by Adivasi leaders in 1929, but it was not conceded.

Later, in 1937, a political organization called Chhotanagpur Adivasi Mahasabha was formed; and the following year, Jaipal Singh, an Oxford-educated Adivasi, was invited to become its president. Under his leadership, the formation of Jharkhand (literally, the Land of Forests), consisting of six districts of south Bihar and three districts of west Orissa, became the main objective of the party. During the war, the party co-operated with the British government in its War effort; and this alienated it from the Congress, which was popular among Bihari Hindus, and which, following its assumption of power in 1946, tried to win support of the Adivasis. In 1949, the Chhotanagpur Adivasi Mahasabha changed its name to the Jharkhand Party, and opened its membership to non-Adivasis.

The general election of 1952 provided the Jharkhand and the Congress with a chance to measure their popularity in south Bihar – the Chhotanagpur region – where the State's Adivasis are concentrated. The Jharkhand trounced its rival by winning forty-five assembly seats out of the sixty-one allotted to this region. And yet its plea to the States Reorganization Commission, in 1955, to recommend the formation of the State of Jharkhand on 'linguistic, cultural, geographical, administrative, and economic' grounds, was rejected. This had a depressing effect on the party's leadership, particularly Jaipal Singh. The party's popular vote began to decline. And, in 1963, Jaipal Singh – feeling that the objective of creating the separate State of Jharkhand might better be served by working from *within* the Congress – announced the merger of his party with the Congress, and advised his followers to join the latter. But only a minority did so.

Many of the erstwhile Jharkhand members joined hands with militant Adivasis; and together they formed the Bisra Seva Dal (i.e. Bisra Service League), named after Bisra, the first Adivasi to lead an armed rebellion against both landlords and the British during the late 1890s. The Dal combined the demand for an Adivasi State with a call for militant action by tribal peasants against moneylender-landlords who, in contravention of the law, had been usurping Adivasi land, charging extortionist rates of interest on loans, and often holding the Adivasi borrowers as bonded servants.

This movement reached a peak in 1968, when repeated demonstrations by the Adivasis kept the city of Ranchi, in southern Bihar, in
turmoil for nearly three months. The government reacted to this with
characteristic duality. It arrested the leaders of the Bisra Seval Dal, and
then issued an ordinance which nullified all transfers or sales of Adivasi
land to non-Adivasis over the past thirty years. But the *actual* impact
has been marginal. 'The whole process is so slow that, over the past
eighteen months, only a hundred cases have been disposed of,' said
P. D. Dasgupta, a Hindu journalist in Ranchi. 'What makes the situation
worse in this case is that Adivasis have to deal with lawyers and bureaucrats who are all non-Adivasi.'[40] This sums up the predicament of
Adivasis aptly. They are caught in a vicious cycle: because they are a
minority and are also economically and educationally backward, they are
handicapped in their dealings with the comparatively advanced majority
– the caste Hindus. And this, in turn, severely limits their chance of
progress. The only redeeming factor is the Constitutional provision
which allows the government to stipulate that a certain percentage of
jobs in the civil service, and places in institutions of higher education
and legislatures, be reserved for them – and the outcaste Hindus.

But no such provision exists for Muslims, the country's most widely
distributed minority, who also lag far behind the majority community,
economically and otherwise. Muslims form 11·2 per cent of the national
population, but their share in public and private life 'of any significance'
is estimated to be about 3 per cent.[41] In the mid-1960s, only 5·3 per cent
of the IAS officers and 3·6 per cent of the IPS officers were Muslim; and
less than 1 per cent of the Central civil servants were Muslim.[42] In
the present Parliament, Muslims account for only 5·5 per cent of the
total; and the figure for the State assemblies is often lower. In Andhra
Pradesh, for instance, they are 8 per cent of the population; but they
occupy only 2·4 per cent of the assembly seats. And yet the question of
reserving seats for them in legislatures or government departments has
never been seriously considered in independent India.

The subject is taboo. It brings up bitter memories of the past, since
most caste Hindu politicians and historians, in India, believe that the
single most important factor that led to the creation of the Muslim state
of Pakistan, in 1947, was the system of 'separate electorate' – i.e.
Muslims to vote for Muslims only, and non-Muslims for non-Muslims –
introduced by the British, in 1909, in response to a demand by the
Muslim leaders. The latter had demanded this, as a safeguard, out of a
genuine fear that Muslims would be overwhelmed by the sheer size of
the Hindu community, then forming 70 per cent of the country's
population, as the right to vote, first accorded in 1892 in local elections,
came to be conferred on an ever-increasing number of Indians. The
prospect was doubly unpalatable to them, because until only a century
earlier, they had been ruling the Hindus, and they had found it difficult

enough to adjust to the reality of being subjects themselves – of a new ruler, the British. The Hindus, on the other hand, had had no such experience: for them it was simply a change of masters. Indeed, the literary castes among them had readily discarded Persian, the official language of the Muslim rulers, for English, and secured most of the higher administrative posts in the new government as well as learnt the skills of modern political organization. When, at last, the Muslim educated classes overcame their antipathy towards the British, and learnt English and the English Common Law, they found themselves a poor match for their already established Hindu counterparts in both the civil service and political organizations. Something needed to be done to redress the situation. It was this consideration that drove the traditional Muslim leaders – princes, landlords, and intellectuals – to form a separate Muslim body, the All India Muslim League, in 1906, in Dacca (in the then undivided Bengal). One of the first acts of the League was to demand a 'separate electorate' for Muslims, and reservation of seats, commensurate with their numerical strength, in legislatures. Both these demands were conceded by the British.

The Congress leaders, claiming to represent both the communities, resented the emergence of the Muslim League, and interpreted the British decision as an example of the infamous policy of 'Divide and Rule' that the imperialist powers customarily used to maintain control over their colonies. They wished to show the colonial government that, despite their divisive policies, it was possible to have Hindu–Muslim accord. Their chance came when the First World War broke out in 1914 – with Turkey, then the leading Muslim power in the world, siding with Germany and Austria–Hungary against the Allies – and Muslim opinion in India turned anti-British. With this, the Muslim League softened its attitude towards the Congress; and the latter reciprocated. In 1916, the two parties reached an agreement, whereby the Congress accepted the arrangement of a 'separate electorate' and reservation of seats for Muslims in legislature. By the mid-1920s, however, this accord had come to an end. The rise of Kemal Ataturk in Turkey, and his abolition of the office of the Holy Caliph altogether, in 1924, removed the ground for animus against the British among Indian Muslims. And the emergence of M. K. Gandhi – who used the religious idiom and imagery of Hindus to win support for the Congress among Hindu masses – as the leading figure of the Congress alienated Muslims from the party.[43]

Among those to be disenchanted with the party was M. A. Jinnah, a Muslim barrister from Bombay who, as a member of the Congress, had played a leading role in creating the Congress–Muslim League accord of 1916. He left the Congress, in 1921, but did not join the Muslim League. Indeed, as the leader of the thirty-member Independent Party in Bombay's legislative assembly, in the early 1920s, he often co-operated with the Congress group. But growing fears of Muslims as a result of a greater degree of self-rule by Indians – which, to them, meant more power to the dominant Hindus – reinforced by inter-communal riots, caused the Muslims to close ranks, and led Jinnah to drift farther away from the Congress. A continual wrangle over communal safeguards soured relationship between the two communities, and strengthened the Muslim League. In 1934, Jinnah was asked by Muslim leaders to end his three-year self-exile in England, and lead the Muslim League. He did so. Under his leadership, the much-strengthened League demanded an extension of the principle of communal representation in the civil service, and a federal set-up, with a comparatively weak centre and a strong government in the provinces.

As regards relations with the Congress, Jinnah was not averse to reaching a formal understanding with it. Indeed, in the 1937 elections, which followed the enforcement of the Government of India Act of 1935, granting greater autonomy to the provinces, the Muslim League in United Provinces (i.e. the present-day Uttar Pradesh) formed an alliance with the Congress with a view to forming a coalition ministry. But, when the Congress found itself the majority party in the assembly, with 135 seats out of 228, it insisted (on instructions from Nehru, the then Congress President) that the Muslim League should merge itself into the Congress before its members were included in the ministry. The League refused to do so, and found itself denied of its share of power. This incident finally convinced Jinnah that it was next to impossible to reach a genuine understanding with the Congress leaders. From then on, he pursued anti-Congress policies. For instance, he instructed his followers to greet the *en bloc* resignations of the various Congress ministries, in October 1939 – soon after the outbreak of war – with demonstrations to celebrate their 'Deliverance Day'. In contrast to the Congress policy, his party supported the War effort.

In March 1940, the League passed a resolution that 'The North-Western and Eastern zones of India should be grouped to constitute "Independent States" in which the constituent units shall be autonomous and sovereign'. Within a few years this resolution came to mean a demand for the creation of a Muslim-dominated state of Pakistan, consisting of Sind, Baluchistan, North West Frontier Province, Punjab, and Bengal. The League contested the elections to the Central Legislative Assembly, in December 1945, in the separate Muslim constituencies, on the platform of a demand for the establishment of Pakistan; and won them all. This strengthened its case for a separate Muslim state. And, eighteen months later, after a period of intense negotiations between the British government and the Indian political parties, the League and Congress leaders agreed to a plan of partition of India, according to which Sind, Baluchistan, North West Frontier Province, the Western half of Punjab, the eastern half of Bengal, and the Sylhet district of Assam were to constitute the new state of Pakistan, on 14 August 1947.

Soon after partition, communal violence of major proportions broke out in the two Punjabs (of India and Pakistan), with Hindus and Sikhs on one side and Muslims on the other. It is estimated that up to half a million people were killed, and in the course of the official exchange of population that followed, some 8 million people left their ancestral homes. This emptied West Pakistan of almost all the Hindus and Sikhs, and India's East Punjab of almost all the Muslims. But this still left some 9 million Hindus in East Pakistan, and 40 million Muslims scattered all over India.

The Muslims in post-partition India faced a dilemma, which is described by Imtiaz Ahmad, an Indian social scientist thus:

> The Indian Muslim had to learn to regard his brothers-in-faith in Karachi or Lahore, whom he had supported in the demand for Pakistan, as foreigners. He had to learn to view his Hindu neighbours, with whom he has never had much social intercourse, as fellow-citizens. And, he had to reconcile himself to the fact that political power [now] lay in Hindu hands. . . . These were difficult emotional adjustments in themselves. . . . [on top of that] the vast majority of Hindus blamed the Indian Muslims for the division of the sub-continent and doubted their political loyalty to the country.[44]

In short, following the establishment of Pakistan, Muslims in India felt more threatened about their political status and cultural identity than the larger Muslim community in pre-partition India had.

The situation worsened for the Muslims as Hindus – realizing that they had at last become masters of their homeland after centuries of subjugation by non-Hindu foreigners, namely, the Muslim tribes and the Christian British – began to reassert their identity, while ostensibly recreating an 'Indian' personality, with the two notions getting inextricably mixed up.

There was the inevitable rewriting and rehashing of history, now to be taught to tens of millions of young Indians; and almost invariably the resistance offered by the Hindu 'natives' to the invading or trading non-Hindu 'foreigners' was glorified. Hindi, the official language, was 'purified', that is, words of Persian origin were replaced by those of Sanskrit. Slowly, subconsciously, the distinction between being Indian and being Hindu was made less and less, while 'officially' both the government and the Congress reiterated their commitment to 'secularism', a term popularized by Nehru and repeated endlessly by the lower echelons of his party and administration. 'Indians regard the River Ganges as sacred,' stated the new Basic Hindi Reader for the fifth class, prescribed for use in *all* the state-supported schools, edited by the director of education of Uttar Pradesh. 'It is said that emerging from the feet of Lord Vishnu, the Ganges came to the thick hair of Lord Shiva and from there to the Himalayas. . . . The Ganges is believed to wash away all sins.'[45] The fact that this is clearly a *Hindu* myth, and that it offends the religious susceptibilities of Muslims who, unlike the pantheistic, idol-worshipping Hindus, are monotheistic and do not believe in gods and goddesses, seemed to have escaped the minds of the education authorities of the 'secular' government of Uttar Pradesh, a State with a population of over 10 million Muslims. 'With few exceptions, non-communal Hindus are ignorant, and therefore indifferent, to the militant communalism within their own midst,' writes M. R. A. Baig, a former Indian Muslim diplomat. 'It is the apathy of secular Hindus that is the Muslims' despair.'[46]

The subtle, but potent, injection of Hindu religious values and symbols into textbooks and the government-controlled mass media has been accompanied by overt exhortations by some Hindu revivalist leaders that Muslims should give up their Arabic and Persian names and their traditional language, Urdu. In the political sphere, the Muslims' sense of insecurity has been aggravated by the continuing cool to hostile relations between India and Pakistan, with a record of three wars in twenty-five years of their existence, and with Pakistan considering the Kashmir problem still unsolved; the increasingly militant tone of the anti-Muslim propaganda employed by the Jan Sangh, Rashtriya Swayamsevak Sangh, and Shiv Sena in order to gain popularity among Hindu masses; and the rising frequency of communal riots in which Muslims are, almost always, the major sufferers.

The number of communal riots per year shot up from seventy-four, during the period of 1954–9, to 462 during 1968–70.[47] At the same time, riots became bloodier. Whereas the total death toll for the eight-year period 1954–62 was 314, the figure for 1967 alone was 301. And this was surpassed during the first half of the following year, with 84 per cent of those killed being Muslim.[48] The total for 1969 ran well into four figures since in one riot alone – in Ahmadabad – over 1,000 people, mostly Muslim, were killed and nearly 6,300 dwellings and shops burnt down.

A series of events over the previous four years had led to the violent orgy against Muslims in Ahmadabad. The outbreak of war between India and Pakistan, in September 1965, had intensified the traditional ill-will against Muslims, with every Muslim suspected of being a saboteur, or a spy for Pakistan. This was accentuated by the Jan Sangh agitation for a ban on cow-slaughter and a popular misconception among Hindus that the Congress administration had desisted from imposing the ban in order to please Muslims. However, the fact was that the State government had already enacted a ban on cow slaughter, and that the Muslims in the State, particularly in Ahmadabad, its capital, had by then been disappointed with the Congress for its failure to ameliorate their grievances. They expressed their feelings in the 1967 elections by deserting the Congress, a party they had supported overwhelmingly since the first general election, and going over to an alliance of the opposition parties, which, however, failed to win power.

The next year, in June, Jamait-ul-Ulema, a Muslim body sympathetic to the Congress, tried to give vent to Muslim opinion by holding a large meeting in Ahmadabad and passing a series of resolutions, including one which demanded special facilities for Muslim government officers to offer their Friday prayers. This upset many Hindu intellectuals, some of whom wrote articles in the local press deploring such communal demands. Some months later, the Rashtriya Swayamsevak Sangh held a massive rally in Ahmadabad, where their Supreme Leader, Golwalker, called for the establishment of 'Hindu *Rashtra*' – i.e., 'Hindu Nation' – a concept which many urban Hindus in the State seemed to consider synonymous with Indian nationalism.

In July 1969, the Muslims in Gujarat protested against the attack on Al-Aqsa mosque in Jerusalem – regarded as the third most sacred Muslim shrine in the world – by holding processions in various parts of the State, including Ahmadabad. This caused much resentment amongst the local Hindus, who considered it as a threat to themselves. Soon after, Balraj Madhok, a prominent Jan Sangh leader, played on this fear, and in a speech at a public rally, in Ahmadabad, taunted the Muslims for protesting about a mosque that was 'thousands of miles away'. By now the city was taut with communal tension. It only needed a minor incident – such as a scuffle between a group of Hindu holy men from a temple on the outskirts of a Muslim-dominated area of the city, and a group of young Muslims, that occurred in mid-September – to trigger off a violent outburst. And once started, it went on for three days, non-stop.

What was worse was that after the bloody riot, which caused widespread killing of Muslims and destruction of their property, local Hindus expressed no remorse, but, instead, a triumphant pride. 'Among the Hindus, there was a feeling of jubilation over their "victory over Muslims",' noted Ghanshyam Shah, a Gujarati Hindu academic. ' "For the first time," a social worker and Congressman said, "Hindus were able to teach a lesson to Muslims". These attitudes are reflected [even] among the educated and prosperous sections [of Hindus]. . . . They thought of various propositions: either Muslims should become Hindu, or go to Pakistan, or some other Islamic country. Not all Hindus had turned communalist, although there was no doubt that a vast majority had.'[49] Neither such attitudes nor their overt expression seemed to surprise or dismay the Muslims. For a Muslim leader, reflecting the general feelings of his community, told Shah, 'You

[Hindus] want 'to drive us out or convert us to Hinduism. You want that we should not live according to our way of life. Well, you may do so. But, then, please do not talk about secularism.'[50]

The only weapon Muslims have possessed to overcome their predicament in independent India, has been the right to vote. And they have tried to use it judiciously Following independence and partition, they almost totally withdrew their support from the All India Muslim League – renamed, in March 1948, the Indian Union Muslim League[51] – and lent it to the Congress. They remained faithful to the Congress in the first three general elections, partly because it was the ruling party, and partly because Nehru, its unchallenged leader, was a genuine secularist. The events of the mid-1960s – the death of Nehru; an emotional agitation for a ban on cow-slaughtering by the Jan Sangh-led Hindus; war with Pakistan, which was accompanied by a spy scare that landed many a loyal Muslim in jail; and the failure of many Congress administrations in the States to put down communal riots firmly – led Muslims to reappraise the situation. In the 1967 elections, many Muslims chose to vote for other secular parties, from the right-wing Swatantra Party in Tamil Nadu and north Gujarat to the left-wing CPI and CPI(M) in West Bengal. This was not to the liking of the local Congress leaders, and made them even more apathetic to the Muslim cause than before. The Congressmen's behaviour in Ahmadabad, and other towns in Gujarat, during and after the riots in September 1969, was typical. 'No Gujarat Congressman had come out to stop the frenzy [against Muslims],' noted Ghanshyam Shah. 'Congress House . . . did not refute any rumours or provide any information to its workers. . . . The District Congress Committee of Baroda [in fact] . . . blamed the Muslims for such riots. Responsible Congressmen criticized Muslims . . . and suggested that they should go to Pakistan. . . . A few Congressmen even took a direct or indirect part in the riots.'[52] And yet, most of the Muslim voters returned to the fold of the Congress, led by Indira Gandhi, in the 1971 parliamentary elections, since the alternative – the Grand Alliance – included the much-hated Jan Sangh.

The break-up of Pakistan, in late 1971, with its eastern wing re-emerging as an independent Muslim-majority but secular state, with the active help of India, had an important bearing on Hindu–Muslim relationships in India. The Hindus, in India, were pleased to see the power and importance of Pakistan reduced dramatically, and therefore became less aggressive towards Muslims in their midst. This situation continued for as long as the relationship between Pakistan and Bangladesh remained strained. Normalization of relations between these two countries, which occurred, in August 1975, after the assassination of Sheikh Mujib and a coup in Bangladesh, displeased many of the Hindus in India and caused a revival of anti-Muslim feeling. In other words, Muslims will continue to provide an easy target to Hindus to express their anti-Pakistani sentiments, which is likely to persist for at least as long as Pakistan maintains that the Kashmir problem exists, while India insists that it is an 'internal' issue, and that, in any case, it was finally solved through *rapprochement* with Sheikh Abdullah in February 1975.

Even otherwise, as a widely dispersed minority, Muslims will continue to be an easy quarry for any frustration or stress that the majority community may feel, from time to time, on matters that have little, or nothing, to do with religion or culture. In that sense, the Muslim problem will remain for at least the next few decades, unless the historical Hindu–Muslim animosity is replaced by a militant conflict between the rich and the poor in the psyche of the masses (something the CPI(M) managed to achieve, to a substantial extent, in West Bengal during the late 1960s) on a national scale. But since the Congress, the only truly national party, is committed to blunting class consciousness and creating class co-operation, this is not likely to happen. The best that can therefore be expected is that the Congress will try to contain the Muslim problem through the combination of administrative, institutional, propagandistic, and political tools, that it has employed, successfully, since 1947, to preserve its political supremacy in the country while holding India together as one administrative-political unit.

18

INTERNAL STRENGTH AND EXTERNAL SUPPORT

Evidence shows that a high Intelligence Quotient or talent is not the only basis of success in competitive examinations. To enter the Indian Administrative Service, one has to be 'talented' plus socially above par.

C. P. Bhambhri, an Indian political scientist[1]

Self-imposed censorship by newspapers and government's anxiety to manage the mass media seem to mark the general pattern in our part of the world.

Nireekshak, an Indian journalist in 1972[2]

Over the past few years there has been a marked tendency to turn the All India Radio into All Indira Radio.

Patrakar, an Indian journalist in 1974[3]

Henry Kissinger, the American Secretary of State, said . . . that the United States would not be hurt by the development of friendly relations between India and the Soviet Union and hoped that 'the Soviet Union would not be offended either by friendly relations between India and the United States'.

News item in the *Overseas Hindustan Times*[4]

Russia has taken over the function, once assumed to be America's, of developing in India a counterpoise to the Chinese might in Asia.

C. L. Sulzberger, an American journalist[5]

During the immediate post-independent period, when India's unity came under considerable strain, the following factors helped to hold the polity together: Nehru's popularity with the masses throughout most of the country; the existence of an able, experienced, and, on the whole, honest body of officers of the Indian Civil Service; the government's control of radio, the only means of mass communication; and the loyalty of the armed forces' hierarchy to the new regime. These cohesive factors – aided by a vast fund of experience in political manipulation and compromise acquired by the Congress since 1947 – continue to be operative today, the only difference being that Nehru has been replaced by his daughter, Indira Gandhi.

The origins of the Indian Civil Service date back to 1793, when the Charter Act, passed by the British Parliament, stipulated that government jobs carrying salaries of £500 a year or more were to be assigned only to members of the 'covenanted service'. To guard against the possibility of a covenanted officer becoming corrupt or tyrannical, Lord Cornwallis, who was then British Governor-General in India, excluded Indians – whom he considered corrupt – from the service. and concentrated on recruiting Englishmen of ability and integrity. This continued until 1853, when the introduction of competitive examinations (to be held in England) for recruitment to the covenanted service opened the doors to Indians. But since very few young Indians could afford to travel to England to take the examinations, the progress made by the Indians was tardy. By 1909, they formed only 10 per cent of the service, which, two decades earlier, had been renamed the Indian Civil Service. It was not until the 1930s that the Indians were recruited into the ICS to an appreciable degree – about thirty a year. However, like the entry into the army officer corps, induction into the ICS too was limited to the top echelons of Indian society. 'The majority of the ICS men came from rich and professional families,' notes K. S. Nayar, an Indian academic. 'The similarity of social and, very often, educational background helped the ICS to make a homogeneous team.'[6] The ICS formed the 'steel frame' of British rule in India, co-ordinating administration at various levels: district, provincial, and central. An ICS member in charge of a district was its virtual ruler, with authority to collect taxes, keep the peace (through the police force), *and* administer justice; while his fellow-members of the service occupied all the important positions in the Provincial and Central secretariats.

With independence and partition, in 1947, the ICS became smaller (451-strong versus 1,064-strong, just before independence), but more homogeneous, since almost all the British and Muslim members opted out of it. Its name was soon changed to the Indian Administrative Service, and the service's existence was sanctified, a few years later, by the new Constitution.

Since then, its strength has been augmented dramatically (it was 2,725 in 1969–70); but its élitist character has remained, essentially, unchanged. A study of the IAS, covering the periods 1947–56 and 1957–63, by V. Subramaniam, an Indian researcher, revealed that the salaried and professional middle class is over-represented, and peasants and workers are grossly under-represented.[7] A breakdown of the social background of the IAS probationers, in 1970, by C. P. Bhambhri, showed that two-thirds of them belonged to higher (Hindu) castes, and that 69·4 per cent were from families with fathers who were 'high level' professionals (namely, doctors, lawyers, high grade civil servants), and 9·4 per cent 'low level' professionals (such as teachers and clerks).[8] 'When to all this is added a need for proficiency in English as the main all-India language for mutual communication among the educated, it is clear that one has a public service which is hardly more representative than it was in British days,' states W. H. Morris-Jones, a British political scientist.[9] However, the value of the top administrative service to the contemporary rulers, the Congress politicians, does not lie in its representativeness, but in its social homogeneity, which, in turn, provides the much-publicized coat of national unity to the present polity, and the officers' ability to work smoothly with politicians of centrist and rightist hues. On both these counts, the IAS, and its sister organization, the 1,560-strong[10] Indian Police Service, have showed themselves to be valuable and reliable.

The other institution, established during pre-independence days, which has proved extremely useful to present-day rulers in India in engendering a certain feeling of national unity, is the broadcasting service. Ironically enough, the colonial government stepped into this area in 1932, not as a matter of policy, but only because a private company which had initiated the service in 1927 had gone bankrupt a few years later. It was the outbreak of the Second World War, however, that led the British administration to develop the broadcasting service – by then named the All India Radio – as a major tool of official propaganda. Since then, there has been no change in this policy: the Congress regime has continued the colonial tradition.

What helped the Congress during the crucial first decade of independence was the fact that it was the only party that mattered both at the Centre and in the States, and playing up the achievements of the government meant, in effect, boosting the Congress image. Later, as the opposition parties began to gain ground, they shared some of the limelight, simply because their agitational activities were too newsworthy to be totally ignored by the AIR. Their capture of the legislative assemblies in some States, during the period 1967–70, however, did not affect the near-monopolistic hold of the Congress on the All India Radio, since broadcasting is a Central subject. Indeed, Indira Gandhi, who had first joined the Central government in 1968 as Minister of Information and Broadcasting, went on to make full use of the AIR in her battle with her rivals *within* the Congress in 1969. Two years later, in the parliamentary elections, she utilized the AIR as a medium of propaganda for herself and her party. And, as stated earlier, the AIR played an important role in denying the CPI(M) a majority in the 1971 State assembly elections by playing up the murder of H. K. Basu, and the allegations that his murderers were 'connected' with the CPI(M), and repeatedly exhorting the electors to go out to vote *against* the 'cult of violence'.[11]

At the time of the national strike by workers of the government-owned railways in May 1974, Indira Gandhi openly stated that the purpose of the government information media, *including* the AIR, was 'propagation and projection of the government policies',[12] and her administration pressed the AIR into service to conduct a virulent propaganda campaign against striking workers, denouncing them, among other things, as 'enemies within', and broadcasting news about the strike which was full of distortions, half-truths, and lies. This was clearly an abnormal situation; but even in the course of their normal duties, the AIR's civil servants – cautious to the extent of being servile – are only too willing to toe the line of their political superiors. 'The hundreds of so-called [radio] journalists waited for the official directive before they set out to discover (a six-month old) drought,' noted Sanjaya, an Indian journalist. 'You just don't expect the All India Radio to discover drought and distress [in nearly a third of the country] before the Prime Minister has discovered it [during her tour].'[13] In short, the nearly 13 million owners of radio receivers,[14] and another estimated 50 million, who listen fairly regularly to the AIR news broadcasts, have no choice but to put up with its pro-Congress bias.

This is of course not the case with a little under 9 million Indians who buy a newspaper, since, theoretically speaking, they have some 800 dailies to choose from. In practice, however, nearly half of them buy the top 42 newspapers, 31 of which are owned by four major private companies – Express Newspapers, Hindustan Times, Bennett Coleman, and Statesman – respective publishers, among others, of the English-language *Indian Express, Hindustan Times, Times of India,* and *Statesman.* These dailies, with 13 editions published from 6 different cities, consume about a third of *all* the newsprint allotted by the Central government to nearly 2,500 dailies and periodicals, which are published fairly regularly and have a viable circulation.[15]

'Lumped together, they certainly represent what may be called a "sectoral monopoly",' notes Rasheed Talib, an Indian journalist. 'For, between them, they claim the large bulk of the total English daily circulation in India. What is more damaging, they are all owned by the same sector of society: big industry. Consequently, they represent the interests of a very limited section of .even the capitalist class – the larger industrial houses whose investments are spread out in various basic industries and to which the newspaper investment is ancillary.'[16] The Goenkas, who control the Express Newspapers, for instance, have interests in tea, chemicals, automobiles, cement, and sugar; the Birlas, who own the *Hindustan Times,* are in tea, jute, textiles, automobiles, aluminium, and consumer goods; Bennett Coleman's owners are in cement, coal, mining, and paper; and the owners of the *Statesman* have interests in steel, heavy engineering, textiles, coal, mining, paper, chemicals, and consumer goods.

The owners exercise fairly tight control over the editorial policies of their papers. And those editors who have, in the past, strayed from these have ended up with dismissal, or threat of it. Pran Chopra, editor of the *Statesman*, in Calcutta, for instance, lost his job in the late 1960s, when he refused to reflect fully the management's attitude towards the CPI(M)-dominated United Front government in West Bengal. And a dismissal notice was served on B. G. Verghese, editor of the *Hindustan Times*, in Delhi, in late 1974, when he persisted in following a fairly independent line in the paper's editorial column that he had initiated in the early 1970s. K. K. Birla, the chairman of the newspaper's board of directors, was reported to have acted in this way as a result of advice offered to him by 'numerous friends, including ministers, members of Parliament, and politicians'.[17]

The ruling party is particularly sensitive to criticisms in these (comparatively) large-circulation English-language dailies, partly because they set the bias, tone, and style for the more numerous Indian language papers, and, more importantly, because they play a substantial role in creating and moulding political consciousness of the only section of society that *really* counts – as far as day-to-day politicking during the inter-election period is concerned – the urban middle classes.

In theory, the press is free to criticize; but, in practice, its industrialist-owners take care to see that criticism against the Congress administration remains fairly restrained and 'issue-orientated'; for – as Pran Chopra points out – 'the press baron is sensitive to the government's industrial policy in which free enterprise and regulation are two phases of the same game'.[18] No wonder, then, that the relations between the press, led by the English-language dailies, and the Congress regime in the past have been generally correct to cordial. The strains that developed between the Congress, led by Indira Gandhi, and the conservative *Indian Express* and *Statesman* at the time of the split in the party, in mid-1969, ended when Indira Gandhi emerged as the clear victor at the polls in March 1971.

From an ideological viewpoint, the industrialist-owners of the press would prefer a party committed, unambiguously, to helping free enterprise; but as pragmatists, who understand the implications of a parliamentary system based on universal suffrage in a poor country such as India, they consider the Congress to be the best bet. They also realize that it is the only truly all-India party, and that it is committed to countering any and all divisive tendencies in the country no matter how high the cost. This policy is beneficial to their larger economic interests, since, as industrialists, they do not wish to see the size of their market diminish. Indeed, besides the members of the top administrative services and armed forces officer corps, the large industrialists, with their capital dispersed throughout the country, are the only group of people who think of themselves as Indians, in the real sense of the word.

The political framework within which these administrative and propagandistic institutions function is provided by the Congress, a party which has shown a remarkable instinct for self-preservation and self-perpetuation, and an unusual degree of flexibility. The way in which it has tackled opposition from both right and left is illustrative of this. It has countered the Communist movement by combining the tactics of repression, harassment, infiltration, propaganda, and active encouragement to militantly anti-Communist organizations with concessions to certain exploited sections of society. And it has tried to contain the conservative, right-wing forces, existing outside its fold, by either drawing them inside or making concessions to their viewpoint.

For example, while conducting an annihilation campaign against militant Communists in the Telangana region, in 1948, the Congress regime abolished landlordism in the State, and passed a law giving security of tenure to the tenants. A few years later, C. Rajagopalachari, the Congress Chief Minister of Madras, followed up his diatribe against communism and the Communists, who formed the second largest group in the State assembly, with an ordinance which reduced rent on agricultural land from the customary 70 per cent of produce to 40 per cent.

Summing up the Congress's policy towards the Communist party of India during the decade of 1947–57, Marshall Windmiller and Gene D. Overstreet, American political scientists, wrote:

It [the Congress government] has pursued a policy which has included: close police surveillance of the CPI, its auxiliary organizations, and their foreign contacts; restrictions of travel of Communists going to and from India; restriction and limitation of delegations to international Communist front organizations; prompt prosecution when Communists break the law, and extensive use of preventive detention when it is anticipated they might; control and sometimes limitation of public meetings held by Communists; intensive anti-Communist propaganda by government and Congress Party leaders; creation of mass organizations to compete with Communist-controlled mass organizations; infiltration by government and Congress Party personnel of some front organizations to such an extent that the Communists are unable to control organizational policy; stringent repressive measures when the CPI adopts a policy of armed struggle . . . [and] extension of full constitutional rights to Communists including office holding, thus giving the party a vested interest in the existing governmental system.[19]

It was the intent to give the Communists a 'vested interest' in the present political system that led Nehru to resist pressures from the conservative wing in his party to deny the CPI power in Kerala, after it had won a majority of seats in the State Assembly in the 1957 election.

But when the Communists initiated, among other things, land reform legislation, which was no more radical than what the Congress itself had recommended, the national leadership of the Congress encouraged its State unit to employ extra-parliamentary tactics – labelled 'Liberation struggle' – to hinder the working of the elected government, and thus provide an alibi for the Centre to dismiss the Communist ministry for having failed to maintain 'law and order'.

Later, in 1965, the Centre went one step further to keep the CPI(M) out of office in Kerala. It instructed the State governor not to convene the assembly, simply because the CPI(M) had emerged as the largest single group in the assembly in the mid-term elections, even though many of its candidates had contested the election from under 'preventive detention' imposed on them by the Congress regime a few months earlier. In the 1967 poll, however, the CPI(M)-led alliance (which included the CPI) won such a massive victory – capturing 117 seats out of 134, with the CPI(M) securing 54 – that it could not be denied power. Feeling too demoralized to mount a frontal attack on the CPI(M)-dominated ministry in the form of a popular agitation, as it had done nearly a decade ago, the Congress concentrated on creating a division among the coalescing parties. Its efforts succeeded in October 1969, when the CPI and a few small non-Communist groups in the assembly allied with it to defeat the leftist government. Soon after, it supported the minority government, formed by the CPI and a few non-Communist parties, from 'outside'.

A similar use was made of the CPI, by the Congress hierarchy, to bring down the CPI(M)-dominated government in West Bengal in March 1970. Later, the Congress administration (in Delhi and Calcutta) exploited the differences between the CPI(M) and Naxalites, and used infiltration and cloak-and-dagger tactics to cause the deaths of hundreds of activists of both parties. At the same time, it built up a private force, consisting mainly of urban lumpenproletariat with criminal backgrounds, under the banner of the Youth Congress, and armed them with both weapons and pseudo-radical slogans to terrorize the (genuine) Naxalites and CPI(M) members. A few years earlier, in Greater Bombay, the Congress government had quietly encouraged Shiv Sena, a local party (which posed no threat whatsoever to the Congress at the State or national level), to pursue its policy of terrorizing the supporters of both the CPI(M) *and* CPI, in the city's working-class areas – a policy which continues.

The Congress has also had considerable success in countering right-wing forces operating both within and outside the Jan Sangh and the (now defunct) Swatantra Party. But it has done so without ever resorting to violent or terroristic tactics. Indeed, in some cases, the party has shown much concern for the conservative sections of society. Soon after the termination of the hereditary powers of the princes, in 1949, the

Congress leadership went out of its way to welcome the former rulers into the party. Some of them joined the party right away; others, after a while. By the mid-1950s, they formed a substantial section of the Congress leadership in such States as Rajasthan, Orissa, and Madhya Pradesh. But this was not enough to arrest the slow drift of the party – facing a serious challenge from the Communists in the south – towards a commitment to impose a ceiling on agricultural land. This, and the party's adoption of resolution for 'co-operative farming', in early 1959, led many of the feudal lords, within and outside the Congress, to go over to the newly established Swatantra Party or the steadily growing Jan Sangh. When this happened, the Congress compromised. It discontinued any reference to 'co-operative farming', and prolonged the actual passage and enforcement of land ceiling legislation, already made practically ineffectual by a long list of exemptions. Finally, in the mid-1960s, the Congress began showering large landowners with monetary and other incentives on the plea that raising production, by whatever means necessary, should be the first priority.

Furthermore, in order to make the Swatantra party less attractive to businessmen, and to retain the Congress's position as the leading beneficiary of businessmen's contributions to political parties, the Congress government in Delhi deviated from its publicly stated policies on industrial development. 'The Industrial Policy Resolution has been violated and industries which were supposed to be reserved for the public sector have been increasingly opened to the private sector, the licensing system has been relaxed, the import control policy has been liberalized to facilitate freer imports by the private sector,' noted Ashok Rudra in 1969.[20]

In the same way, the Congress has made adroit use of its policy of 'non-alignment' with either of the two power blocs, in foreign affairs, to counter both left- and right-wing opposition at home. It protested vehemently when Pakistan signed a Mutual Security Pact with America, in 1954 (and later joined the South East Asia Treaty Organization), and launched a countrywide campaign of denunciation of both Pakistan and America, thus stealing a march against both the (anti-American) Communists and (anti-Pakistani) Jan Sangh. Nehru, the architect and executor of the party's foreign policy, also used the occasion to back out of the commitment to hold a plebiscite in Kashmir, and, in the process, robbed the Jan Sangh of a chance to build up its strength on this highly emotional issue.

By then, Nehru's foreign policies had won the formal approval of the Indian Communists as well. After all, he had recognized the Communist government in China within a few months of its establishment in Peking, in October 1949, accepted the Chinese suzerainty over Tibet, and later, in 1954, signed an agreement with it on 'Trade and Intercourse between the Tibet Region of China and India', which, in its preamble, included

the famous *Panchsheel* – the Five Principles of Peaceful Co-existence –
'Mutual respect for each other's territorial integrity and sovereignty;
mutual non-aggression; mutual non-interference in each other's internal
affairs; equality and mutual benefit; and peaceful co-existence'. And,
following Joseph Stalin's death, in March 1953, relations with Soviet
Russia too had improved, resulting in a signing of a trade pact between
India and Soviet Russia later that year. However, the growing friendliness between the two countries cost the CPI dear. When, for instance,
Pravda, the Soviet Communist Party paper, praised (in January 1955)
not only the Indian government's foreign policy of non-alignment but
also its domestic achievements, the Congress made an extensive use of
the statement in the closely contested mid-term elections in Andhra
Pradesh, and defeated the CPI, its main rival.

Although unhappy at the increasing warmth between India and
Russia, the American government continued to give India economic aid,
including foodgrains under Public Law 480 – a law which allows the
American administration to sell agricultural commodities at concessional rates and accept the bulk of payments in the recipient country's
currency – first begun in 1950. Of the sums received for foodgrains, the
American government returned all but 20 per cent (to be used for the
maintenance of its embassy and consulates in the country) to the Indian
authorities in outright grants (amounting to about a quarter of the sum)
and loans to be used for development projects. The prime reason for all
this was the American administration's desire to see India win the
economic race against Communist China and thus establish the sup-
eriority of the Western-style democracy to communism to the rest of
the Afro-Asian world.

Unable to match the American economic aid to India, Russia made
it a point to support India on the sensitive and emotional issue of
Kashmir. It vetoed a discussion on the subject in the United Nations
Security Council, in 1957, thus lending its weight to the Indian position
that Kashmir was a purely 'internal' problem. This proved doubly
advantageous to Russia: it embarrassed America, which stood by
Pakistan on this issue; and blunted the militantly anti-Russian attitude
of such Indian political parties as the Jan Sangh and Swatantra. Actually,
in a few years' time, Communist China was to emerge as the chief
villain for these parties as well as the Congress and even a substantial
section of the CPI at home, and America *and* Russia abroad.

Present evidence suggests that the Nehru administration's hostility
towards Communist China dates back to the time when it was, ostensibly, negotiating an agreement with the Peking authorities regarding the
new status of Tibet. The formal signing of the agreement, in 1954, did
not lead Nehru to discontinue the policy of keeping 'in touch' with, and
helping in every possible way, Gyalo Thendup, the anti-Communist
brother of the Dalai Lama (spiritual leader of Tibet), and other Tibetan

refugees, then living in and around Kalimpong on the Indo–Sikkimese border, that his Central Intelligence Bureau had initiated in 1953. 'Regarding the spirit of resistance in Tibet, the Prime Minister was of the view (after the 1954 agreement with China) that even if these refugees helped their brethren inside Tibet, the government of India would not take any notice and, unless they compromised themselves too openly, no Chinese protest would be entertained,' wrote B. N. Mullik, the then director of the Central Intelligence Bureau in his memoirs.[21]

By 1956, knowingly or unknowingly, secret agents of America and Taiwan, operating mainly from Kalimpong, were engaged in the same activity as their counterparts from India and Russia – recruiting and arming Tibetan *émigrés* to organize a separatist rebellion in Tibet against the Peking administration, with the Khamba tribes in eastern Tibet providing the initial thrust. They succeeded in this. The rebellion, which began modestly in the east in 1956–7, spread to the west; in the fighting that broke out in Lhasa, the capital, in early 1959, the Dalai Lama sided with the rebels. Later, however, as the Peking authorities re-established control, the Dalai Lama fled, and sought asylum in India, which was granted to him readily. 'We have no desire whatever to interfere in Tibet, but at the same time we have every sympathy for the people of Tibet, and we are greatly distressed at their helpless plight,' said Nehru in Parliament, in March 1959.[22]

These events soured relationships between India and China which had, by then, become strained on the issue of border demarcation, something that the previous regimes – the British in India and the pre-revolution governments in China and Tibet – had not carried out fully and properly. In August 1959, and again in October, there were shooting affrays between the forces of the two countries in the border areas. The second skirmish, which occurred near Hotsprings in Ladakh, led to the death of nine members of the Indian Central Reserve Police party sent there by B. N. Mullik, the director of the Central Intelligence Bureau, which was then responsible for both border security and foreign intelligence (and which had earlier been involved in fomenting rebellion in Tibet).[23] This incident, and its one-sided reporting, shocked and angered most Indians, and dissipated whatever goodwill then existed between the two countries.

The growing animosity between India and China pleased not only America, but also Russia, which was developing its own border dispute with China, and which was later to be put off by China's refusal to subscribe to the concept of 'peaceful co-existence' between socialism and capitalism that Nikita Khrushev and President Dwight Eisenhower worked out during their talks in Camp David, America, in late 1959. In fact, Russia went on to encourage India to believe that, if attacked, China would not fight back,[24] and, starting in the middle of 1960, began supplying it with military hardware, including heavy transport planes and helicopters. These were particularly useful to the Indian government in the execution of its 'Forward Policy' along the borders with China, which began in the winter of 1961–2 and which, finally, led to large-scale hostilities between the two countries in October 1962 on two fronts – east and west (in Ladakh).

The Chinese fought with vigour; and in less than a month, their forces over-ran the Indian positions along the border and, in the case of the eastern sector, began advancing into the plains of Brahmaputra in Assam. At this point, Nehru's policy of 'non-alignment' broke down. 'Late that night [20 November 1962] Nehru made an urgent, open appeal for the intervention of the United States with bomber and fighter squadrons to go into action against the Chinese,' states Neville Maxwell. 'This appeal was detailed, even specifying the number of squadrons required – fifteen. . . . In response an American aircraft carrier was dispatched from the Pacific towards Indian waters; but the crisis passed twenty-four hours after Nehru had made his appeal (when the Chinese declared a unilateral ceasefire and began withdrawing immediately to their borders), and the aircraft carrier turned back before it reached Bay of Bengal.'[25] As such, and because he made his appeal to America in secret, without consulting or even telling any of his colleagues, Nehru could continue to proclaim that India was still wedded to the principle of 'non-alignment' in world affairs. In any case, Nehru asked for, and promptly received, a squadron of big turbo-jet transport aircraft from America. And the special government missions from America and Britain that arrived soon after laid the groundwork for military assistance to India, worth $120 million, spread out over the next three years. (Interestingly enough, by then – 1963, the Indian government owed America $2·32 billion, or more than half of the *total* Indian money then in circulation.)[26]

Nehru's actions were supported not only by the right-wing opposition but also by the moderate section of the CPI, which saw nothing wrong in India buying arms from 'any country' on 'commercial terms', a stand that tied up neatly with that of the Russian leadership which – as George Hilsman, a former member of the Kennedy administration in America, points out – had been informed by Nehru of his imminent request to America for military assistance, and had expressed its 'understanding' of the situation.[27] Later, Russia itself increased both military and economic aid to India. And since the mid-1960s, with minor exceptions, the two super-powers have followed complementary, rather than competitive, policies towards India.

When war broke out between India and Pakistan, in September 1965, America helped to shorten it by suspending military supplies to both countries, and thus denying them the vitally important spare parts to repair their American military equipment. The Soviet Union supported America's restraining efforts and later, in January 1966, had the two parties meet in Tashkent, USSR, and formalize their earlier ceasefire agreement. During the following two years, 1966–8, when India faced acute food shortage, America supplied it with the bulk of the 20 million tonnes of foodgrains needed, under the concessional terms of Public Law 480. Meanwhile, America's continued embargo on arms supply to India (and Pakistan) enabled Russia to sell India more and more of its military hardware. The result was that, by the late 1960s, Russia had become India's largest supplier of arms. A similar trend had developed in trade relations between the two countries. In fact, in 1970–1, Russia became the biggest single buyer of Indian goods, a shade ahead of America.[28]

It was against this background that India and the Soviet Union signed a friendship treaty, valid for twenty years, in August 1971. 'Each of the High Contracting Parties' declared that it will maintain 'regular contacts with each other on major international problems affecting the interests of both the states', and that 'it shall not enter into or participate in any military alliance directed against the other Party', and that 'In the event of either Party being subjected to an attack or a threat thereof, the High Contracting Parties shall immediately enter into mutual consultations in order to remove such threat and to take appropriate effective measures to ensure peace and the security of their countries'. This was clearly a departure from the traditional 'non-alignment' policy that the Congress administration claimed to be following. But the timing of the treaty – when India was actively helping the independent Bangladesh movement in East Pakistan – and its implied warning to China to keep out of any armed conflict that might erupt in the subcontinent, on the Bangladesh issue, were such that even the Jan Sangh supported the treaty.

However, the Soviet Union did not wish to spoil its friendly relations with Pakistan, which it had been cultivating since the Tashkent conference in 1966. It, therefore, took the position that the conflict in East Pakistan was an 'internal problem' of Pakistan – until early November, when the military regime in Pakistan sent an official delegation headed by Z. A. Bhutto, well known for his cordial relations with the Chinese leaders, ostensibly to seek an assurance of material help in case of war with India. Although no guarantee of support seemed to have been given by the Chinese, the initiative taken by Pakistan was enough to upset Russia. Soon the Soviet Union took an openly partisan stand on the Bangladesh issue, and supported India all the way through its war with Pakistan, which lasted a brief two weeks in December 1971, and left India victorious and the strongest military power in South Asia, from Iran to Indo-China. 'Only because of the support of social imperialists [i.e. Russia] did the Indian reactionaries dare to launch a war of aggression against Pakistan and thus become insolent': this is what Chou En-lai, the Prime Minister of China, is reported to have told a visiting dignitary.[29]

A genuine fear of disintegration of Pakistan – a breakaway of its eastern wing and a break-up of its western wing – had made America take a pro-Pakistan stance on the Bangladesh issue. But when the war broke out, it did not go to the rescue of Pakistan. Instead, it concentrated on securing a quick ceasefire by working through diplomatic channels. Its pressure on Russia, however, went no further than issuing a threat that Russian failure to co-operate in securing an immediate ceasefire would lead to the cancellation of President Richard Nixon's scheduled visit to Moscow in the summer. And its steps against India itself amounted to no more than instructing (belatedly, as it turned out, due to the quick end to the war) one of its aircraft carriers in the Pacific to proceed to the Bay of Bengal, and suspending part of its economic aid to the country. Nonetheless, these measures were enough to cause diplomatic coolness between the two governments.

But this did not last long. Following President Nixon's trip to Moscow, in June 1972, John Connally, his special envoy, visited Delhi to 'mend fences',[30] and some months later, Indira Gandhi, faced once again with the prospect of food shortage in the country, quietly sent her emissaries to Washington DC to 'sound [out] the grain market' there.[31] In any case, the diplomatic strain between India and America had no effect whatsoever on the sympathetic attitude towards India of the America-dominated World Bank (officially known as the International Bank of Reconstruction and Development) and its soft loan affiliate, the International Development Association, or the Aid-India Consortium, consisting of twelve Western countries and Japan – the institutions which together had, until then (March 1972), provided nearly as much economic aid (Rs 3,450 crores, £1,725 million) to India as America had (Rs 3,760 crores, £1,780 million).[32]

The second Nixon administration, inaugurated in January 1973, initiated talks with the Indian authorities to find ways of reducing the burden, borne by India, of $3·2 billion worth of rupees that the American government then held in India. In the end, the American administration decided to write off $2·2 billion worth of rupees altogether, and leave the rest to cover the expenses of maintaining its embassies, consulates, and information centres in India and Nepal. The financial importance of the American gesture was underlined by an Indian official who said, 'If we were to pay back all the American rupees, it will take us . . . [up to] about year 2050.'[33]

The Russians too were doing their best to provide economic aid to Indira Gandhi's government, which they regarded – to quote the *Economic and Political Weekly* – as 'politically stable, temperamentally cautious, ideologically "progressive" enough'.[34] During his week-long visit to India, in November 1973, Leonid Brezhnev signed a fifteen-year agreement on 'further development of economic and trade co-operation' between the two countries which, among other things, visualized a 15 per cent annual increase in Indo–Soviet trade,[35] then amounting to about Rs 500 crores (£250 million) a year – an event that was applauded by Daniel P. Moynihan, the American ambassador in Delhi. Welcoming the 'development of relations' between the Soviet Union and India, Moynihan said that 'The United States shares the Soviet desire to help the sub-continent in its development ventures'.[36] Not to be left behind, during his visit to Delhi, in October 1974, Dr Henry Kissinger, the American Secretary of State, signed an agreement with the Indian government to constitute 'a joint commission on economic, commercial, scientific, technological, educational, and cultural co-operation' to promote, among other things, 'possibilities of increased investment consistent with the investment policies of the two countries'.[37]

Some months earlier, the World Bank, headed by Robert McNamara, a former Defence Secretary of America, had taken one step further in engendering East–West co-operation to help sustain the present system in India. In a 'confidential' memorandum to the members of the Aid-India Consortium – which made a pointed reference to the growing shortages of oil, fertilizers, electric power, and food – it enclosed an appeal to the Soviet Union to 'bail India out of a critical economic crisis that could lead to political chaos'.[38] But Russia was fully aware of the situation. It had already 'loaned' India 2 million tonnes of wheat, that it had itself bought abroad and had signed an agreement to supply India with 350,000 tonnes of fertilizers, and help it expedite its programme of oil-exploration. As for the Aid-India Consortium, many of its members overcame their feeling of unease at the Indian government's extravagance in developing and exploding (in May 1974) a 'nuclear device' at an estimated cost of $1·5 billion, spent over the previous decade,[39] and went on to sanction, at their meeting in June, a loan of $1·4 billion – the largest sum ever in the Consortium's life – to India.

Meanwhile, Russia had pressed on with its programme of supplying India with aircraft, missiles, naval vessels, and armoured fighting vehicles. Its total military aid to India, standing at $1·1 billion in 1971, was the second highest to any country.[40] This is likely to go up considerably as Russia concedes the Indian demand for sophisticated military equipment following America's decision, in February 1975, to lift its embargo on arms supplies to Pakistan. Actually, a beginning had been made in this direction, in early 1974, when Russia agreed to supply India with SAM-6 missiles, which had proved effective in the Middle East War in October 1973, and which were expected to dramatically improve the efficiency of the Indian air defence.[41]

And a few weeks earlier had come the announcement that America had lifted its embargo on the Project Peace Indigo, a military communications system designed to tie up air defence radar sites along the

Sino–Indian frontier. The project had been conceived in 1965, begun a few years later, and suspended during the Indo–Pakistan war of 1971. When completed, it will link up the American equipment – that had been left in the border areas after the joint air exercises by the Air Forces of India, America, and Britain, in 1963 – with radar stations subsequently supplied by Russia. 'The lifting of the embargo [by America] on the Project Peace Indigo should be most welcome to the Soviet Union,' wrote a correspondent of the *Economic and Political Weekly.* 'In this context, the reported Soviet offer made during the recent Brezhnev visit [in November 1973] to develop sheep breeding in the Ladakh heights is all the more intriguing. It could ensure a Soviet presence in the most strategic sector of the long Sino–Indian border.'[42] This is a good example of the super-power understanding to build up India as a military 'countervailing force' to China.

The Congress administration in Delhi has been actively pursuing this policy since the early 1960s. It was the Chinese explosion of a 'nuclear device' near Lop Nor, Kansu, in October 1964, that seems to have led it to decide to develop its own nuclear bomb. When it exploded a 'nuclear device' in the Rajasthan desert, in May 1974, its spokesmen said that further experiments would be conducted to perfect 'nuclear devices', but that it was all for 'peaceful purposes' – an unconvincing statement. 'There is little question about the ultimately military purpose of the Indian explosions,' stated Edward Cochran, a British expert on nuclear technology. 'The conspicuous absence of any credible Indian projects for civil exploitation, and the economically nonsensical insistence on Indian self-sufficiency in all facets of nuclear technology, are only two of the many indicators. . . . These eventual nuclear weapons are intended to deter China.'[43]

This, and the launching of an Indian unmanned satellite from a Soviet 'cosmodrome' in April 1975 (with a Soviet-supplied launcher rocket and American-supplied space grade components),[44] and the Indian government's statement a few months later that it proposed to carry out new underground nuclear tests,[45] all indicate that the long-term plan is to build up a stockpile of nuclear bombs, and acquire a delivery system of long-range bombers, or missiles, to be stationed along the border with China.

The speed and determination with which India acted, in collusion with Russia, in the case of the Bangladesh movement in the eastern wing of Pakistan (a country friendly with China), and with which it has since then been consolidating its position along the north-east border – particularly Sikkim – provide further evidence of the pursuit of this strategy.

In a series of moves that were initiated in April 1973 and concluded two years later, with a referendum – that was announced and held within three *days* – the Indira Gandhi administration transformed

the protectorate of Sikkim first into an Associate State of the Indian
Union, and then into a fully integrated State. In the process, it stripped
the Chogyal (i.e. ruler) of Sikkim, Palden Thondup Namgyal, of all
authority, and ended the separate identity of his kingdom, which had
been underlined by the fact that since 1947 the Indian government
had maintained relations with Sikkim through its Ministry of External
Affairs. And it did so despite the existence of a treaty signed between
the two governments in 1950, which placed Sikkim's defence, external
affairs, communications, and currency into Indian hands, and formalized the practice, begun a year earlier, of the Indian authorities
appointing the kingdom's *Dewan*, the Chief Administrator; and despite
the consistently co-operative attitude by the Chogyal towards Delhi.
At the first sign of tension between India and China, in 1959, he had
closed the high pass of Nathu La to the Chinese, and allowed the size
of Indian troops stationed in his kingdom to be increased dramatically.
The result was that by September 1974 (when the Indian Constitution
was amended to make Sikkim an Associate State of India) this tiny
kingdom of 2,700 square miles and 200,000 people held some 20,000
to 40,000 Indian troops.[46]

Significantly enough, when criticisms were made abroad, particularly
in China and Nepal, against Delhi's actions in Sikkim, Tass, the
official Russian news agency, described these as an 'interference in the
internal affairs of India'.[47] A few months later, the *Sovetskaya Rossia*,
a Moscow newspaper, reported that China was 'plotting' to set up a
separate state, comprising parts of India and Burma, as a 'buffer'
between itself and its neighbours to the south – a report which,
according to a correspondent of the *Overseas Hindustan Times*, could
not be corroborated by the 'Indian intelligence sources'.[48]

The policy of competition with China, in the military field, is proving
expensive and distorting India's fragile economy. And yet the Congress
administration continues to spend ever-increasing sums on its military
establishment even when it means having to prune the country's already
modest economic development plans. Between 1971–2 and 1974–5,
for instance, India's annual military budget went up by 41 per cent,
but its development expenditure rose by only 10 per cent, which, allowing for a high inflation rate, was a considerable *decline* in real terms.
The annual sum spent on economic development, which, until 1971–2,
used to exceed the military expenditure, now lags behind it, the respective figures for 1974–5 being Rs 1,573·1 crores (£786·6 million) and
Rs 1,679·7 crores (£839·9 million).[49]

The mal-effects of this policy on the populace were all the greater
because it continued to be pursued during a period when prices were
rising fast while production and personal income declined or remained
static. Between 1971–2 and 1973–4, for example, per capita availability of foodgrains fell by 11 per cent,[50] and industrial production

stagnated,[51] whereas the wholesale price index rose by 33 per cent[52] and per capita income declined by 4·2 per cent.[53] Large sections of society, particularly in the urban areas, blamed the ruling party for this, and began to express their discontent by participating in anti-government rallies, demonstrations, and general business and industrial shutdowns. This put the Congress governments in the States and at the Centre on the defensive. Unable, or unwilling, to stop the downward slide in the living standards of the masses, they made an increasing use of the police, para-military forces – and even the army – to meet the situation.[54] This only turned more and more people against the ruling party. In one State, Gujarat, the protest movement initiated and led by university students in early 1974 spread so quickly and widely that it finally caused the downfall of the Congress ministry.

Encouraged by this, the students in Bihar launched a similar movement against the corrupt and inefficient Congress administration. The ruling party reacted with an excessive show of force; and this led Jaya Prakash Narayan (a native of Bihar and an old stalwart of Indian public life, who had given up active politics in 1957 to devote himself to the non-partisan Sarvodaya – i.e. Universal Welfare – movement) to enter the political arena with a long-term programme of creating, in India, a democracy emanating from the grass-roots upwards.

By the end of 1974, all the opposition parties except the CPI had rallied round Narayan; and the protest movement, now sponsored by a united opposition, had been widened to include demands for eradication of corruption in political life and government bureaucracy, and an overhaul of an inequitable electoral system which had been corrupted by the Congress. By early June 1975, the opposition parties in West Bengal had resolved to launch a joint protest movement – with the CPI(M), actively participating in the exercise, showing signs of revival – a development that deeply disturbed the Congress hierarchy.

On top of this, the Congress was delivered two severe blows: the election of Indira Gandhi to the Lok Sabha was declared null and void by a High Court judge; and the party lost the mid-term election in Gujarat. A jubilant opposition prepared to launch a national campaign to secure the resignation of Indira Gandhi, when – suddenly – the Congress government in Delhi declared an emergency due to a threat of 'internal disturbances', jailed thousands of political opponents, suspended basic human rights of citizens, and imposed a strict press censorship.

This was an admission, albeit implicit, by the Congress Party that the strains on the political system that it had devised and operated with reasonable success since 1950 had become unbearable, and that extraordinary steps had to be taken to save both itself and the system – either as they had existed in the past or in a modified form.

THE 'INTERNAL' EMERGENCY: PRELUDE TO CONGRESS DEFEAT

India has declared states of emergency before now [June 1975] but never before have members of Parliament been hauled out of bed before dawn; never before has a total censorship been imposed upon the press.

The Times editorial[1]

You called me a dictator when I was not. I am a dictator now, you will see.

Indira Gandhi in the lower house of Parliament on 22 July 1975[2]

A citizen has absolutely no recourse to any redress or legal or constitutional remedy through courts to safeguard his right to personal liberty during the period of emergency, even if he is totally innocent and is illegally and wrongfully detained on wrong and false information and material, or non-existent grounds.

V. P. Raman, Additional Solicitor-General of India, to the Supreme Court, on 9 January 1976[3]

The powerful issues of this election [in March 1977] are forcible sterilisations and official harassment under the umbrella of emergency.

Chanchal Sarkar, an Indian journalist[4]

The [March 1977] election to the Lok Sabha has been a truly astounding event. There is a fairy tale quality about the way the people rose to overthrow their tyrannical rulers.

Economic and Political Weekly editorial[5]

The anti-Congress movement in Gujarat grew out of hardship suffered by people due to spiralling prices and growing scarcity of the basic necessities of life. Between the summers of 1972 and 1973, prices of foodgrains, edible oil, vegetables and meat rose by 30 to more than 100 per cent. Such essential commodities as wheat, rice, paraffin (used as fuel for cooking and lighting) and cooking oil became scarce.[6]

Several voluntary organizations as well as political parties protested against this.

But it was not until December 1973 – when resident students at an engineering college in Ahmadabad, the State capital, were asked to pay a 41 per cent higher mess bill the following month – that the protestors turned violent, and burned public property. The Congress government sent in a large contingent of police to the campus. The excessive force used by the police further alienated the students and other sections of society from the government. Popular protest broke out in various parts of the State in the form of processions, demonstrations, general shut-downs, and sacking of foodgrains godowns, groceries, and cloth shops. 'Prohibitory orders, arrests, tear-gassing, baton charges, and even firings could not stem the tide of the people's wrath against the government,' noted Ghanshyam Shah, an Indian sociologist.[7]

By the middle of February, 52 of the State's 63 towns, with a population of over 20,000, had experienced mass protest and police firings, which had claimed more than 100 lives.[8] The situation became so unbearable that first the Congress ministry, and then the majority of the State assembly legislators, resigned, so that the Congress government in Delhi was forced to dissolve the assembly. This brought a sense of relief to the State. (By then 223 people had lost their lives mainly as a result of the police firings.)

The example of students in Gujarat was emulated by the United Students and Youth Front in Bihar, who organized demonstrations against rising prices, food shortages, high unemployment, and government corruption. This brought the police, para-military forces, and the army to the streets and caused the death of 22 demonstrators due to firings by these forces.[9] The brutal handling of the demonstrators by the Congress government was condemned by, among others, J. P. Narayan – who emerged, over the months, as the leading spokesman of the opposition parties (except the CPI), as they prepared to challenge, more and more, the misrule of the Congress.

The Congress administration in Delhi proved even more repressive than its counterparts in the State capitals, when it came to handling such matters as demands for higher wages by its employees in order to partly compensate for the dramatic increase in prices. The methods it used to crush the railwaymen's strike in May 1974, in support of their claim for a wage rise,[10] were summarized by a correspondent of the *Economic and Political Weekly* thus:

> Organized brutality, spearheaded by the minions of law and order; the vicious bayonet thrust at the bodies of the striking railwaymen waylaid by the police; the bundling into prison of thousands who refused to act as blacklegs; the terrorization in the employees' quarters; the deployment of hired goons to beat up

workers and their families; the harassment of women and children; the brusque ejectments [from railway quarters]; the summary dismissals.[11]

Along with this went arrests of over 30,000 railway workers and their trade union leaders under the Maintenance of Internal Security Act 1971, and the Defence of India Rules 1971 (framed under the Defence of India Act 1971).

The Defence of India Rules 1971 – a carbon copy of the Rules, under the same title, that were enacted by the colonial regime during the Second World War – came into force when, on the eve of the war with Pakistan in December 1971, the President declared a state of emergency due to a threat of 'war or external aggression' against India. Among other things, these Rules authorize the government to arrest any person on suspicion and detain him without trial for as long as the emergency lasts, not that the Central or State governments had lacked power of 'preventive' detention before.

Within a few weeks of the promulgation of the Constitution, in January 1950, the Congress government in Delhi had passed the Preventive Detention Act, as a temporary measure, meant to last a year. But it kept renewing the Act year after year until the end of 1969. Then, the Indira Gandhi administration, lacking a Parliamentary majority on this measure (due to the opposition of the leftists), let it lapse. However, within a few months of being returned to power with a large majority, in March 1971, the Indira Gandhi government passed the Maintenance of Internal Security Act. Like its predecessor, the Preventive Detention Act, this law empowers the Central and State governments to arrest any person on a mere suspicion of his attempting to disturb public order, or disrupt essential services, or endanger security of the country, or damage its relations with a foreign country. He can be held without trial for up to one year, with no restrictions on his being re-arrested if 'fresh facts' arise. While piloting the Bill through Parliament, the government spokesmen had stated that this law would be not used against political opponents or legitimate trade union or other activities. But this was not to be, as the Central government's actions in dealing with the railway strike amply showed.[12]

Its success in breaking the railway strike emboldened the Indira Gandhi government to impose a virtual freeze on wages and salaries in both public and private sectors, through a Presidential ordinance, issued in July, while leaving prices and the price mechanism undisturbed. This caused further economic distress to a large section of the politically sensitive urban populace, and increased the anti-Congress sentiment in the country.

Reflecting the bitter mood of the people, the opposition parties became militant in their statements and programmes. George Fernandes, a leader of the Socialist Party, proposed intensification of popular agitation against the Congress governments 'all over the country'; and so did E. M. S. Namboodripad of the CPI(M). In a paper, published in September, A. B. Vajpayee, a leader of the Jan Sangh, wrote of a 'confrontation between the government and the people' to be conducted 'in the streets, in the Chambers and Legislatures, in the corridors of power, in all sensitive centres of the establishment'.[13] In November, five opposition parties met in Delhi under the chairmanship of J. P. Narayan and formed a National Co-ordination Committee to harmonize their plans and actions for giving expression to popular discontent.

The anti-Congress forces received a further boost to their morale when scandals concerning the issue of import licences by L. N. Mishra–a confidante of Indira Gandhi and a senior minister in her cabinet, and a leading fund-raiser of the Congress – broke out during the winter session of Parliament. It was alleged that, as Minister of Foreign Trade, Mishra had issued (or ordered to be issued) import licences to a 'deregistered' firm in Bombay, and to a group of seven individual businessmen in Pondicherry – with the latter deal involving a recommendation signed by twenty-one Congress members of Parliament; and that large sums of kick-back money were involved. Despite repeated demands by the opposition, the Congress government refused to place before Parliament a report of inquiry by the Central Bureau of Investigation, or to hold a Parliamentary inquiry into the matter.

The Congress administration stonewalled again, when Mishra died – as a result of a bomb explosion at a public meeting in Bihar, in January – and the opposition demanded a 'high power' inquiry, presided over by a Supreme Court judge. This strengthened the suspicion of many people that Mishra had been allowed to be 'sacrificed' so as to abort the possibility of further exposures of corruption prevalent in the top echelons of the Congress government. 'The credibility of Mrs Gandhi's administration has sunk so low in popular estimation that many ordinary Indians are quite ready to believe that Mr Mishra was liquidated by the government itself,' reported Michael Hornsby of *The Times*.[14]

The opposition parties harnessed this sentiment by organizing rallies and demonstrations, against corruption and Congress misrule, in various district towns and State capitals. The peak of this wave of protest was reached in March, when Narayan, leading a peaceful procession of many hundreds of thousands in Delhi, presented a 'Charter of Demands' to the Speaker of the Lok Sabha and the Chairman of the Rajya Sabha. This charter demanded dissolution of the corrupt and repressive Congress ministry in Bihar and the holding of fresh elections in Gujarat and Bihar, sweeping electoral reform including introduction of proportional representation, and an end to the power of money in elections and the Congress practice of using administrative powers and government-controlled mass media for partisan ends in elections.

As it happened, that very month – March – the issue of electoral corruption came under judicial scrutiny in the High Court of Uttar Pradesh, in Allahabad. Making use of the services of State and Central government officials and facilities provided by them, at public cost, to further her election prospects, were two of the fifty-two charges of electoral malpractices levelled against Indira Gandhi by Raj Narain, her Socialist rival at the Parliamentary election of 1971,[15] in the Rae Bareli constituency of Uttar Pradesh.

The wider question of electoral tactics came up a few months later, when elections to the legislative assembly in Gujarat were announced. The Congress regime in Delhi – then ruling Gujarat through the State governor – used its immense resources to bribe the voters along the lines it had followed the previous year in Uttar Pradesh.[16] 'Jeep-loads of government officials have been making frequent rounds of the hundreds of relief works [in the country-side], which have suddenly sprung up,' reported a correspondent of the *Economic and Political Weekly* in May 1975. 'Train-loads of grain and fodder have begun to move fast to [various towns and cities] . . . for distribution around these centres. Fleets of watertank trucks have overnight begun to speed around carrying water to villages and to relief works so that [relief] workers need not trek 2 to 5 miles for their drinking water. . . . Contractors and petty clerks are suddenly sufficiently flush with funds to pay full wages [to relief workers] once in two days, if not daily – and they are paid even for those days when they attend the "correct" election meetings.'[17] Indira Gandhi took personal charge of her party's election campaign, and toured 150 of the 182 constituencies.

In both these cases, however, Indira Gandhi and her party lost. The voters in Gujarat preferred the Janata Morcha (i.e. People's Front), an alliance of five opposition parties, to the Congress. They elected 87 members of the Janata Morcha and only 75 of the Congress – a severe blow to a party which had held 140 of the 168 seats in the previous assembly.

This news almost coincided with the verdict, delivered on 12 June, by the High Court judge in Allahabad that Indira Gandhi was guilty of two (above-mentioned) charges of corrupt electoral practices, as defined in Section 123(7) of the Representation of the People Act, and that that made her election to Parliament null and void, and disqualified her from contesting a seat to Parliament or State assembly for the next six years. Thereupon, the counsel for Indira Gandhi petitioned that the court order be stayed for twenty days so as to give time to the Congress Party in Parliament to elect a new leader. The judge accepted the petition.

But the Congress members of Parliament never got a chance to elect a new leader. Indira Gandhi refused to resign on the grounds that her party and the 'people'[18] wanted her to continue in office, and that she planned to appeal to the Supreme Court against the High Court's verdict.

The opposition leaders pointed out that the High Court had issued the stay order only to enable the Congress Parliamentary Party to choose a new leader before Indira Gandhi ceased to be a member of Parliament, and thus avoid the damaging possibility of a break in normal government in Delhi; and that in similar circumstances, Chenna Reddy, Indira Gandhi's one-time colleague in the central cabinet, had resigned and appealed to the Supreme Court as an ordinary citizen. 'The proper course in the circumstances would be for the Prime Minister to resign her office pending disposal of the appeal to the Supreme Court,' wrote the *Overseas Hindustan Times*. 'The alternative of having Mrs Gandhi remain would be further to coarsen politics and invite bitter political controversy which will not be easily stilled even in the event of a favourable revision judgment [by the Supreme Court].'[19] But such advice was brusquely spurned.

On 21 June, Indira Gandhi filed her appeal with the Supreme Court and simultaneously petitioned it for an 'unconditional' stay of the High Court order. Three days later, the vacation judge of the Supreme Court allowed her a 'conditional' stay of the lower court's order: she could continue to hold office and attend Parliamentary sessions, but she could not vote or draw a member's salary. The proper hearing of her appeal was postponed to 14 July.

Her failure to secure an 'unconditional' stay order from the Supreme Court encouraged the opposition leaders to announce the next day a programme of action, scheduled to begin on 29 June and last eight days. It consisted, mainly, of plans to hold rallies in State capitals and district centres to 'educate the people on the need for Mrs Gandhi to step down (during the pendancy of her appeal to the Supreme Court) on the grounds of political propriety and democratic convention'.[20]

The Indira Gandhi government reacted to this fast – and hard. In a pre-dawn swoop, it arrested hundreds of prominent opposition and other political leaders (including some dissident Congressmen) under the powers invested in it by the emergency that had been declared, due to an external threat, in December 1971, and had not been lifted, and imposed strict pre-censorship of news. A few hours later on 26 June, President F. A. Ahmed, acting on the advice of Indira Gandhi,[21] declared a state of emergency on the ground that 'a grave emergency exists whereby the security of India is threatened by internal disturbances'.[22]

Outlining the reasons for the imposition of emergency, in a national broadcast, Indira Gandhi mentioned 'the deep and widespread conspiracy that has been brewing', 'the forces of disintegration . . . in full play', 'communal passions . . . threatening our unity', and 'new programmes challenging law and order throughout the country', and referred to 'certain persons' going to the length of 'inciting' the police and army to 'rebel'.

'These are abstractions that tell us very little, certainly nothing that can justify the action that has been taken, 'wrote *The Times*. 'If . . . there are within this opposition [to the Congress] those who have been inciting mutiny among army and police then action should be taken against them without such sweeping gestures as will now inhibit the country's political life.'[23]

A few days later, in another national broadcast, Indira Gandhi announced a twenty-point economic programme. This included implementing land reform laws 'with redoubled zeal';[24] abolishing bonded labour; liquidating rural indebtedness; fixing minimum wages for agricultural workers; increasing irrigation facilities and power generation capacity; supplying 'better quality' clothes to the public through a 'controlled cloth scheme'; imposing ceiling on the ownership and possession of vacant land in urban areas;[25] setting up 'special squads' to undertake valuation of 'grossly undervalued' urban property; intensifying the campaign against smugglers;[26] simplifying procedures for issuing industrial licences; introducing schemes for workers' participation in industries;[27] raising the exemption limit for income tax from Rs 6,000 (£300) a year to Rs 8,000 (£400); supplying all 'essential commodities' to student hostels at 'controlled' prices; and amending the Apprenticeship Act to increase job opportunities for educated young people. There was very little in this programme that was new or radical or controversial.[28] Indeed, the DMK government in Tamil Nadu was quick to point out that it had *already* implemented fifteen of the twenty points mentioned in the broadcast.

Meanwhile, the Congress governments in the country went about vigorously implementing their programme of silencing opposition. Within a week of the proclamation of emergency, they had jailed some 3,000 political opponents while the Union President had suspended the three Articles in the Constitution which normally guarantee the citizen 'equal protection of the laws' (Article 14), protection of 'life and personal liberty' (Article 21), and protection against unwarranted arrest and detention (Article 22), and had so amended the Maintenance of Internal Security Act as to exempt the authorities from stating the reason(s) for which a person had been arrested.

The number of political detainees went up sharply, to 5,000,[29] when a few days later, the Central government banned twenty-six organizations, including the Rashtriyaswayam Sevak Sangh (RSS); the Jamaat-e-Islami, an association of orthodox Muslims; fifteen branches of Anand Marg, a politico-religious sect of Hindus; and nine factions of the Communist Party of India (Marxist-Leninist).

It can be seen that, when faced with a political crisis situation, the Congress party reacted in the same way as it had done in the past: it came up with a composite policy of reform and repression.[30] The only difference was that this time its reform package, although large, was the least inspiring, while the scale and degree of repression undertaken by it was the widest and harshest yet.

The Constitution proved no bar to the repressive plans of the Congress; because it has a string of extraordinary provisions (Articles 352 to 360) that can be used to throttle democratic processes. Article 352 authorizes the Union President to declare a national emergency if he is 'satisfied', on ministerial advice, that a grave threat to India, or any part of it, exists. Once this happens, the executive acquires immense powers. It can enact legislation and issue orders which infringe upon any or all of the fundamental rights listed in Part III of the Constitution: Articles 14 to 35, including Article 19 which lists the seven fundamental freedoms (*vide* Articles 358 and 359). It can direct State governors as to how they should exercise their powers (*vide* Article 353). And it can legislate on subjects included in the State list either directly, through Parliament, or by conferring this right on the Union President (*vide* Articles 356 and 357). 'The closest parallel to the emergency provisions of the Indian Constitution can be found in the Weimar Constitution of Germany's Third Republic,' notes Mohan Ram. 'Compared to Article 48 of the Weimar Constitution, the provisions of the Indian Constitution are actually more drastic!'[31] Furthermore, there is no limit to the existence of emergency, once it has been approved by Parliament, by simple majority, within two months of its declaration. (And while emergency is on, the normal duration of five years of the lower house of Parliament can be extended by Parliament by law for a period not exceeding a year 'at a time': a self-perpetuating situation.)

Now, as Parliament prepared to meet, the Indira Gandhi administration prohibited the press from publishing accounts of the forthcoming session of Parliament *and* barred it from publishing the latest censorship rules. When Parliament met on 21 July, the government suspended the normal procedures of business, and disallowed such items as questions, 'call attention' motions, and private Bills by members. These steps were taken partly to thwart the opposition's plans to use the Parliamentary forum to attack the government's repressive actions, and partly to black out the anti-emergency stance of the CPI(M) members, which, if publicized, would have undermined the Congress-CPI propaganda that the government had acted, as it did, in order to frustrate the attempt by right-wing reactionaries, in collusion with the American CIA, to take over power through 'extra-constitutional means'.[32]

Angered by these tactics of the ruling party, the entire opposition (except the CPI) – consisting of 59 members in the Lok Sabha and 33 members in the Rajya Sabha – voted against the resolution approving emergency, and then walked out. 'News censorship and suspension of members' rights to put questions to the government and submit motions on important public matters cut at the very root of parliamentary democracy,' said the statement issued jointly by seven opposition groups and four independents in the Lok Sabha. 'We are satisfied that no useful purpose will be served by our further participation in the proceedings of the house.'[33]

The government then introduced an amendment to the Constitution which makes the emergency declaration by the President 'non-justiciable' – that is, above challenge in the courts. This was passed in the Lok Sabha by 342 votes to 1, and in the Rajya Sabha by 164 votes to none. (All along the speeches of the government supporters in Parliament were widely and lengthily reported, whereas those of the opposition were totally blacked out.)

Having done this, the Congress government turned its attention to the problem of Indira Gandhi's election. It introduced the Election Laws (Amendment) Bill to be applicable retrospectively to 'any election held before the commencement of this Act to either house of Parliament or either house of the legislature of a State'. One of the provisions of the Bill states that 'any act or thing' done by a government officer in the discharge or 'purported discharge' of his official duty shall not be deemed to be assistance for the furtherance of a candidate's election; and the other divests courts of their right to disqualify legislators and transfers it to the President.

During the course of debate on this Bill, a Congress backbencher suggested amending the Constitution to make election of a person who is, or subsequently becomes, the Prime Minister 'non-justiciable'. This suggestion was immediately accepted by the government. Within two days, it presented to the Lok Sabha a long and comprehensive Bill: the Constitution (39th Amendment) Bill. Clause 4 of this Bill stated that 'no law made by Parliament before the commencement of the Constitution (39th Amendment) Act, 1975, in so far as it relates to the election petitions and matters connected therewith, shall apply or deemed ever to have applied to or in relation to the election of any such person as is referred to in Clause 1 (namely, the President, Vice-President, the Prime Minister, and the Speaker of the Lok Sabha) to either house of Parliament'.

In less than an hour and a half, the Lok Sabha passed the Bill by 366 votes to 1. The next day, a Friday, the Rajya Sabha passed it unanimously; and the day after, seventeen of the country's twenty-two State assemblies ratified it. The following day, a Sunday, the President signed it; and the Act came into effect immediately. The intent of the ruling party was clear: to present the Supreme Court, meeting the next day (11 August) to consider Indira Gandhi's appeal, with a declaration that no matter what its final decision, the election of Indira Gandhi would stay.

As it turned out, there was no need for the Congress legislators to have bent the Constitution to keep Indira Gandhi in office:[34] mere changes in the election law, applied retrospectively, were enough. Accepting these amendments to be valid, the Supreme Court judges, in a verdict delivered on 7 November, upheld Indira Gandhi's appeal and set aside her disqualification from holding an elective office for six years.

'No one should expect a judiciary to persevere at odds with the political facts of life [in India] for too long,' wrote the *Guardian* on 8 November.[35] 'What Mrs Gandhi did in the panicky wake of the Allahabad [High Court] judgement . . . was to scrap democracy. She denies that, of course; and she has her Congress party majority to back the assertion. But a land where thousands, including prime political adversaries, are rounded up and imprisoned without trial, a land where the press is muzzled, cannot truly be called democracy.'

By then – late 1975 – the number of people jailed without trial was believed to have soared to 100,000,[36] and the Maintenance of Internal Security Act had been made non-justiciable and amended four times to make its provisions retroactive and increasingly more repressive. In December the existing censorship guidelines, imposed under a section of the Defence of India Act 1971, were buttressed by a set of Presidential ordinances.

One of these repealed the Parliamentary Proceedings (Protection of Publication) Act 1956, and ended the immunity given to the press regarding reporting utterances in Parliament or Parliamentary committees. Another – the Prevention of Publication of Objectionable Matter Ordinance – put crippling restrictions on the freedom of the press. The definition of 'objectionable matter' included anything that might 'bring into hatred or contempt or excite disaffection towards the government . . . (or) promote disharmony or feeling of enmity, hatred, or ill will between different religions, racial, language, or regional groups or castes or communities . . . (or) cause fear or alarm to the public or to any section of the public.'

The following February these ordinances were replaced by legislation passed by Parliament; and three months later they were included in the Ninth Schedule of the Constitution, and thus made non-justiciable.

Some examples of what was censored, after the above Act came into force in February 1976, were:

9 March 1976: the Finance Minister rested for a while in the course of his budget speech – not to be mentioned (banned).

17 March: answers to Parliamentary questions on censorship, court case on censorship and the press, and the Prevention of Publication of Objectionable Matter Act (banned).

1 April: no criticism of family planning programme; this includes letters to the editor.

16 July: Mr Jaya Prakash Narayan's movements not to be published in the interest of law and order (banned).

17 July: all news, comments, and editorials on the price situation (pre-censorship).

26 August: Prime Minister's intervention in Parliament on foreign intelligence and any reference to CIA activities on that question not to be used (banned).

5 October: kindly do not publish any news about the strike in Dhariwal Mills.

10 December: kindly do not publish any report on the supply of US jet fighters (Skyhawks) to India.

20 December: all stories, comments, reports relating to rivalries within the Congress, and between the Youth Congress and the Congress, should not be used.

23 December: stories and articles on insurgency in the northeastern region should not be published without clearance from the censor.[37]

By then, news control had been facilitated further by the merging of four news agencies, at the behest of the government, into one unit – Samachar – in May 1976; and by the fact that only 45 of the 830 publications had the resources to post full-time reporters away from the head office.

No wonder then that, within a year of emergency, all but a few of the publications submitted to the government's will. The dissenting ones were subjected to pressures of all kinds. When, for instance, the *Indian Express* and *Statesman* refused to yield day-to-day management to the government nominees, or their agents, they were harassed through such actions as disconnection of electricity and the withdrawal of government advertisements.

To maintain a tight, centralized control over the press, two senior police officers were attached to the Ministry of Information and Broadcasting to oversee its working, with powers to bypass the Ministry's highest civil servant, and liaise directly with the Prime Minister's secretariat. The then all-powerful Prime Minister's secretariat was itself being run mainly by police and intelligence officers,[38] with R. N. Kao, the head of the RAW – now engaged not only in large-scale surveillance of judges, academics, political opponents, journalists, State and Central ministers, and top civil servants and armed forces officers, but also supervising other intelligence agencies[39] – conferring daily with Indira Gandhi and/or her son Sanjay.

Nonetheless, some of the government actions were challenged – sometimes successfully – in courts of law by the publishers of small circulation journals. Upholding an objection raised by a Delhi-based periodical against a decision by the Chief Censor, in May 1976, the judges of Delhi High Court criticized the censorship rules for completely choking 'the pipeline of democracy', and seeking to create a special group who 'wire fenced' the Indian people.

The censorship rules, said the judges, imposed a 'mask of suffocation and strangulation' by banning reports of Parliament, the courts, and peaceful demonstrations, by forbidding newspapers to indicate that material had been censored, and by banning publication of the names of political prisoners.[40]

Although there was no internal disorder, or any possibility of it; and although Indira Gandhi herself said in June that 'India was never before more united, stronger, and more stable than today',[41] the number of political prisoners remained as high as, if not higher than, that prevailing six months earlier. Peaceful protest rallies and marches on 26 June 1976, to mark the first anniversary of emergency, led to the imprisonment of tens of thousands of people, and brought the total of post-emergency political prisoners to about 100,000 to 125,000.[42]

The unremitting repression drove the opposition forces to close ranks. The rightist opposition, consisting mainly of the Jan Sangh, Bharatiya Lok Dal, and Syndicate-Congress began functioning as a single entity in Parliament, and actively considered the idea of forging a united umbrella organization, with a common set of policies and programmes. The leftist forces, hitherto splintered into the CPI(M) and various Naxalite groups, were also driven to consider adopting mutually tolerant attitudes. In that sense, one of the major purposes of emergency – namely, to stem the tide of extremism, both right and left – was far from being achieved.

Nor was the situation any the better as far as other purposes of emergency, conjured *after* the proclamation, were concerned: toning up of administration, curbing inflation, and improving the economy. Addressing a conference of government officials in Delhi in May, Indira Gandhi herself said, 'I have a feeling, confirmed by many visitors, that the initial alertness has slackened, even in the railways.'[43]

By then, the spring of 1976, the downward trend in prices – which had first been noticed in the autumn of 1974 due to good crops – had come to a halt, with an upward trend manifesting itself. The record annual foodgrains production of 114 million tonnes for 1975–6, caused mainly by favourable monsoons,[44] was only 5·5 per cent higher than that in 1970–1 (whereas the population increase during those five years had been 11 per cent, or twice as much).

Though the overall growth in industry in 1975–6, at 4 to 5 per cent, was better than that in the previous two years, the consumer industries in general were in a poor state. 'Textiles, tobacco industries, paper industries, rubber products, metal products, electrical machinery, apparatus and appliances, and transport equipment showed an absolute reduction in output or at least a lower growth rate in 1975–6 [than before],' noted the *Economic and Political Weekly* after a perusal of the Industry Ministry's latest annual report.[45] Lack of demand for consumer goods was due to reduced purchasing power of the masses, a situation created, in the main, by the government's anti-labour policies followed vigorously after emergency, in the name of creating a body of workers imbued with a sense of 'discipline'.

While the workers were denied the right to strike, the industrialists were given a free hand to dismiss employees and did so, laying off 479,327 workers, during the first six months of emergency.[46] In September 1975 the President issued an ordinance curtailing the workers' minimum bonus from 8·33 per cent of the earnings to 4 per cent. Even the pro-emergency INTUC and AITUC found this unpalatable, and said so. The anti-labour and pro-capital bias of the ruling party was amply illustrated by the decisions of the Central government to let the Dividend Restrictions Act, enforced in July 1974, lapse when its two-year term ended in July 1976,[47] but to extend by a year the Additional Emoluments (Compulsory Deposit) Act – a virtual freeze for millions of wage- and salary-earners – when it expired in July 1976.[48]

Little wonder then that the post-emergency actions of the Congress government were applauded by the industrialists at home and the World Bank abroad, and that the Western-dominated Aid India Consortium promised it aid of $1,600 million, a record.[49]

Taken as a whole, all this fitted in well with the historic behaviour of the Congress: radical-sounding words combined with conservative actions. What the 'radical' Indira Gandhi did, in the mid-1970s, in the industrial sector of the economy, was no different from what the 'conservative' L. B. Shastri had done ten years earlier in the agricultural sector. When faced with a choice between increasing production *per se* or taking steps to create an egalitarian society, they had both opted for the former course. Led by Shastri, the ruling party had poured vast government resources into the hands of rich farmers in the name of increasing agricultural output. Now the party, led by Indira Gandhi, was all set to boost private enterprise in the cause of raising industrial production. It could thus be seen that, emergency or not, neither the policies nor the socio-economic biases of the Congress had changed. All that had changed was the style of its operation. Increasingly afraid of losing power at the Centre, due to a steady decline in its popularity, the party had come to use repression and coercion more frequently against its political opponents, and had become less inhibited in the use of administrative resources and mass media – both publicly and privately owned – for its partisan ends.

But this did not go unchallenged. The non-Congress ministries in Tamil Nadu, Gujarat, and Jammu and Kashmir, for instance, refused to toe Delhi's line on emergency. The DMK, then running the State administration of Tamil Nadu, publicly condemned the imposition of emergency, and held anti-emergency rallies. The People's Front government in Gujarat disregarded the existence of emergency and held local elections in towns and villages when they became due in the winter of 1975.[50] And Sheikh Abdullah, the chief minister of Jammu and Kashmir, resisted pressures on him to join the Congress. Instead, he disbanded the Plebiscite Front, re-formed it as the National Conference – a party he had led since its inception in 1931 until his arrest in 1953, and which had been merged into the Congress in 1965[51] – and joined it.

A section of the lawyers and judges too resisted the growing authoritarianism of the Congress government by challenging some of its actions. In this they were occasionally successful. In December 1975, for instance, two judges of the Maharashtra High Court upheld a petition of the Democratic Lawyers Association in Bombay against a government order banning an indoor meeting to discuss 'civil liberties and the rule of law'.[52]

The members of the public were not idle either. They responded in their thousands to the periodic calls given by the underground version of the People's Action Committee – which, before emergency, had co-ordinated support for the anti-Congress movement led by J. P. Narayan – to insist on their fundamental right of peaceful assembly, and to court arrest, if necessary, to uphold it.

The ruling party, however, was in no mood to respond to such protests. By the first anniversary of emergency, in June 1976, it had resolved to institutionalize the restrictive features of emergency by changing the Constitution. The Constitution (42nd Amendment) Bill, presented to Parliament four months later, confirmed the party's authoritarian intentions. The 59-clause Bill included amendments to thirty-six Articles, substitution of four existing Articles with new ones, and thirteen altogether new Articles.

These amendments were designed to (a) end the power of courts to rule on the validity of these or future Constitutional amendments; (b) deprive courts of authority to compel the executive to produce 'documents' (meaning thereby: the rules framed by the executive in the conduct of its business); (c) make the President 'expressly bound' to act on the advice of the Prime Minister, thus robbing him of his discretionary powers; (d) authorize the President (i.e. the Prime Minister, by virtue of (c) above) to amend the Constitution himself (initially for the next two years), without even having to secure subsequent Parliamentary approval; (e) empower Parliament to pass laws for the prevention or prohibition of a wide range of 'anti-national' activities, including 'creating internal disturbances or disrupting public services' (terms open to such wide interpretation as to cover most of the traditional forms of Indian political and trade union activities); and (f) authorize the Centre to send security forces into any of the States without the invitation of the State's government.

In early November, this Bill was passed by 366 votes in favour and four against, with the Congress and the CPI members of the Lok Sabha supporting it, and the opposition – consisting of the right-wing parties, the Socialists, the CPI(M) and the DMK – boycotting the session. The opposition argued that the continued enforcement of emergency and press censorship had inhibited a full and fair discussion of the radical changes being effected in the Constitution, and that the then Lok Sabha lacked the moral authority to alter the Constitution, since its normal term of life had expired many months ago.

The Indira Gandhi government responded to this by introducing a Bill that extended the life of the Lok Sabha by one more year – that is, up to March 1978. The Bill was passed. But, significantly enough, of the 330 Congress members present, only 180 voted for it, with the rest abstaining[53] – a clear sign of dissension within the party on this issue. The reason for discontent lay as much with the leadership of Indira Gandhi as with her 30-year-old son, Sanjay, who, within a year of being co-opted into the National Committee of the Youth Congress in December 1975, had emerged as the second most powerful politician in the country.

'I firmly believe that the best ideology for the people is my ideology,' he had declared in April 1976.[54] This consisted of a programme of tree planting, eradication of illiteracy, an end to caste distinctions, abolition of the dowry system, and birth control. To popularize his five-point programme, he undertook widely-publicized tours of the country, and was received by local dignitaries with triumphal arches, bands and red carpet, and was described as, among other things, 'the beacon of hope of awakened India', and 'the rising sun in the political horizon'.[55]

Sanjay Gandhi took particular interest in 'popularizing' birth control, since this was the one item in his five-point programme which could be quantified, to the last digit, and where statistics could be used to show that, thanks to his energetic leadership, dramatic progress was being made.

In this he was zealously supported by many of the State chief ministers and health ministers, who felt that by jumping on the recently started bandwagon of Sanjay Gandhi they could advance their own political careers. When, therefore, a national target of 4·3 million sterilizations was announced for the period April 1976–March 1977 (at more than twice the figure achieved during the past twelve-month period), many of the chief ministers vied with one another in raising the quota fixed for their respective States. The chief minister of Uttar Pradesh, for instance, unilaterally changed the State's target from 400,000 to 1,500,000.[56]

These ministers then pressurized the civil servants, health and family planning workers, teachers and the police to help achieve the extraordinarily high targets by imposing quotas on individual employees and giving the matter wide publicity in the mass media. When the government employees failed to meet their quotas they found themselves deprived of their salaries or regular increments, or served with dismissal notices. In Bihar alone, some 50,000 government employees had their salaries withheld for three months and 600 more were sacked on this ground.[57] Under the circumstances, many of the public employees were compelled to use repressive and corrupt means to meet their targets.

Sometimes they approached the commission agencies which grew up to provide 'volunteers' for sterilization: old men, unsuspecting villagers, and teenage boys, lured to the operating table by middlemen working for the agencies. Other times they abused their own authority to get results. The district collectors would often mobilize government staff, school teachers and the police to descend on the weekly market fairs in larger towns and villages to 'persuade' the people to get sterilized.[58] The police in such cities as Delhi and Bombay would periodically arrest people in the streets and drive them straight to the sterilization clinics, with the rich among the catch bribing their way out.[59]

None of these actions was challenged in courts, because emergency had given the executive arm of the government unlimited, unchecked authority. 'Even if an executive officer were to deprive a citizen of life or personal liberty by way of settling some personal score, the citizen would not have any remedy so long as the emergency and the Presidential proclamation under Article 359 of the Constitution lasted,' the Attorney-General had submitted to the Supreme Court in December 1975.[60] No wonder then that, by the end of 1976, the implications of the mass sterilization drive had permeated almost all areas of contact between the citizen and the government.

Summarizing the findings of his field researchers in the villages of various States during the period of October 1976 to January 1977, Professor D. Banerji of the Centre of Social Medicine and Community Health, Jawaharlal Nehru University, Delhi, stated:

> The issue of licence for guns, shops, sugarcane crushers and vehicles; issue of [government] loans of various kinds; registration of land; issue of ration cards [for food]; exemption from payment of school fees or land revenue; supply of irrigation canal water; submission of applications for any job; any form of registration; obtaining bail, and facilitation of court cases: all these were linked up with the procurement of cases for sterilisation.[61]

Despite this situation, and despite the general feeling of fear that stalked the country, many of the villages and urban localities resisted the government's sterilization drive. When this happened, the police and family planning personnel retaliated by carrying out organized raids on the recalcitrant community, and bundling off its 'eligible' men for vasectomy. This practice created such fear in the minds of rural people that, in some parts of the country, the entire adult population of a village would often flee at the sight of an approaching car or jeep.[62]

In the urban centres, however, when the situation reached an unbearable stage, the people sometimes demonstrated openly. This led to brutal police retaliation. In two known cases of popular demonstrations against forced sterilizations, in the towns of Muzaffarnagar and Sultanpur in Uttar Pradesh in October 1976, more than seventy people were killed.[63]

None of these events was allowed to be publicized. The press censorship in general and the order of 1 April 1976 – 'No criticism of family planning programme; this includes letters to the editor' – in particular[64] were used to kill all news about forced sterilization and its disastrous consequences.

But the fact that prices were rising rapidly again could not be hidden from the public. During April–November 1976 the level of retail prices in Greater Bombay, for example, rose by 9·7 per cent as against an increase of 0·6 per cent during the corresponding period of the past year.[65] This happened while wages remained frozen. Under the circumstances, despite the heavy risks involved, workers began resorting to strike action.[66]

While the popular mood in the urban areas was turning sour, the dissensions within the ruling party were becoming increasingly difficult to paper over. The censorship order of 20 December 1976 – 'All stories, comments, reports relating to rivalries within the Congress, and between the Youth Congress and the Congress, should not be used'[67] – was indicative of the seriousness of the situation.

One way to solve the ruling party's pressing problem was to hold fresh elections, and use the occasion to purge the Congress of all those of doubtful loyalty to Indira Gandhi – and more particularly her son, Sanjay. Indeed, by early December, it was widely known that Sanjay Gandhi had prepared a list of the Congress candidates for the next election, and that it excluded all but 100 of the sitting members.[68] The only question was *when* exactly to hold the election.

The answer was provided primarily by the favourable intelligence report in January (forecasting electoral victory for the Congress), and secondarily by the decision of Z. A. Bhutto, the Prime Minister of neighbouring Pakistan, to hold a general election in early March, and gentle pressure reportedly applied by the about-to-be-installed Jimmy Carter administration in America. Consequently, on 18 January, Indira Gandhi announced fresh elections to be held in mid-March under conditions of 'relaxed' emergency.

The circumstances favoured Indira Gandhi and her party. The opposition forces were divided and demoralized, and lacked resources to fight the election. In contrast, the ruling party had all the advantages of political power, control of the mass media, and the immense funds collected over the past many months.

But the despondency of opposition ended dramatically when, on 2 February, Jagjivan Ram – the most senior minister in Indira Gandhi's cabinet and a Congress leader of long standing – resigned from both the government and the party. He did so, because Indira Gandhi rejected his advice to lift emergency and dispel the 'fear psychosis [that] had overtaken the whole nation'.[69] In this he was joined by other Congress leaders, including H. N. Bahuguna and Nandini Satapathy, the former chief ministers respectively of Uttar Pradesh and Orissa.

These resignations boosted the morale of the opposition, and encouraged ordinary people to shed fear and speak their minds. They put Indira Gandhi and her son, Sanjay, on the defensive, forcing them to cancel their plan to deny the party tickets to 250 Congress members of the dissolved Lok Sabha, and instead to stem the tide of defections by renominating most of the old Congress members of the House, and sparing only a dozen tickets for the Youth Congress followers, including Sanjay Gandhi.

Meanwhile Ram, after naming his dissident group as the Congress for Democracy, aligned himself with the Janata (i.e., People's) Party, which had been formed earlier by the merger of the Jan Sangh, Bharatiya Lok Dal, Syndicate-Congress, and Socialist Party, and which had initiated talks with the remaining opposition parties – the CPI(M), the (Sikh) Akali Dal, and the DMK – for making electoral adjustments. This unprecedented closing of the ranks by most of the opposition forces was a bad omen for the Congress.

In the end, the Congress nominated candidates for 492 seats, leaving the remaining fifty for its allies: the CPI, and the All India Anna-DMK, a breakaway group of the DMK in Tamil Nadu. The Janata Party contested 394 seats, and made electoral adjustments for 134 seats with Ram's Congress for Democracy, the CPI(M), the DMK, and the Akali Dal.

The Congress election manifesto made many references to the gains made during emergency and repeated the 1971 election slogan: 'Poverty must go'; Disparity must diminish; and Injustice must end.'[70] The Janata Party's manifesto considered it 'possible' to 'eliminate destitution within a decade by raising every family above the poverty line', and promised to replace the constitutional 'right to property' with 'right to work'. It also promised to end emergency, restore civil liberties, and repeal the latest and most radical amendment to the Constitution.

For all practical purposes, the election was fought on the single issue of emergency: its merits and demerits. The Congress, led by Indira Gandhi, conducted its campaign along the familiar lines, following well-tried tactics of the past. The party made an open and unashamed use of the state-run radio[71] and television, reinforced this time by Samachar, the (sole) government-directed news agency; its control of other government machinery; the unprecedently large election fund, estimated to be Rs 40 crores (£250 million) to Rs 90 crores (£562 million), collected as usual from numerous business houses;[72] and its ability to offer economic bribes, to the tune of Rs 200 crores (£1,250 million), to important sections of the electorate.[73] The eve-of-poll concessions offered by the various Congress governments in the States included: lowering land taxes; reducing electricity and irrigation water rates; exempting house and professional taxes; lowering various licence fees; and improving pay scales of, and awarding additional dearness allowances to, the government employees.

But, for once, these familiar tactics failed. As the stories of arrogance, brutality, and corruption of the police, intelligence, and bureaucracy (particularly in regard to the sterilization campaign and the arbitrary bulldozing of the slums to 'beautify' the cities)[74] gained currency, the majority of the electorate turned decidedly against the Congress.

The result of the election, in which more than 193 million voters participated, showed this clearly. In northern and central India, where the sterilization campaign had been pursued vigorously, the Congress was routed. Of the 245 Parliamentary seats in these regions, the party won a total of four! Among its defeated candidates were *both* Indira Gandhi and her son, Sanjay. The popular vote of the Congress in the individual States and Union Territories of north-central India varied between 18 per cent and 36 per cent, while that of the (barely two-month-old) Janata Party, and its allies, did not fall below 58 per cent.[75]

The Congress strength in Parliament plummeted from 357 to 153, with its total vote going down from 43·7 per cent to 34·5 per cent. In contrast, the Janata Party won 271 seats (out of a total of 539) on a popular vote of 43·2 per cent – an improvement of nearly 20 per cent on the vote secured by the Grand Alliance, its forerunner at the previous election.[76] With the help of twenty-eight members of the Congress for Democracy, and eight members of the Akali Dal, the Janata Party formed a coalition government under the premiership of Morarji Desai.[77]

Within weeks of taking office, the Janata government lifted the (external) emergency imposed at the time of the Bangladesh war in 1971, the (internal) emergency having been withdrawn by Indira Gandhi immediately after her defeat at the polls. It appointed commissions of inquiry into the business dealings of Sanjay Gandhi since 1966, when he was awarded a monopoly licence to manufacture a 'people's car' which failed to materialize, and into 'the excesses, malpractices, and abuses of authority' during the twenty-one-month-long emergency, involving not only compulsory sterilizations and punitive demolition of entire urban colonies on the pretext of 'change of plans', but also arbitrary arrests at the instigation of the Youth Congress members, and torture or harassment in jails.[78]

Also, the new government passed Bills to repeal the Prevention of Publication of Objectionable Matter Act and restore the Parliamentary Proceedings (Protection of Publication) Act; announced plans to end the

Samachar news-agency monopoly and to convert the state-run radio and television services into autonomous corporations; and lifted the ban on the twenty-six organizations proscribed soon after the emergency of June 1975.

However, it could not realize its intention to re-amend the Constitution so as to 'restore the balance between the people, Parliament, the judiciary and the executive', that had been destroyed by the Constitution (42nd Amendment) Act of 1976. It could muster a two-thirds majority in the lower house of Parliament, but not in the upper house, where the Congress was the predominant group. It also lacked the support of a majority of the State governments needed to effect a change in the Constitution.

The result of the Parliamentary election was considered enough of a reason, by the Janata government in Delhi, to warrant dissolution of the assemblies in those States where the Congress had fared badly. This was done in late April.

By the time fresh elections were held in eleven States, in mid-June, the Janata Party had emerged as a single unit, with its four constituents *and* the Congress for Democracy formally dissolving their individual identities, in May. Excepting the Punjab, the Janata Party entered the assembly election battles with intent to win on its own. It did so in seven of the States – covering the entire Hindi-speaking belt, from Bihar to Himachal Pradesh, and Orissa. In the remaining States of Tamil Nadu, Punjab, West Bengal, and Jammu and Kashmir, victory went either to a regional party or the CPI(M)-led leftist front. In almost all cases the victors had one thing in common: they had defeated the Congress.

The elections of March and June 1977 thus signalled the end of a thirty-year-long era. They marked the end of one-party dominance of Indian politics at the Central and State levels. Equally significantly, they marked the beginning of a period when the nationally victorious Janata Party has had to concede defeat in three major States, and share power in the fourth (Punjab), with a regional group (the Akali Party) as a junior partner.

20

THE FUTURE: PROSPECTS AND POSSIBILITIES

Morarji Desai's Janata Party is even more beholden to gentleman farmers [than the Congress]. . . . Disregarding danger signals [for the future], Desai suggests that the land ceilings should be *raised* so that a decent income is guaranteed to educated farmers.

Sunanda Datta-Ray, an Indian journalist[1]

Earlier I had disliked the idea of organizing the Harijans and the landless on class lines. But now I am in favour of class organizations. Class struggle is inevitable. The Sarvodaya movement [based on persuasion] went up to a point. After that it failed.

J. P. Narayan, a former Sarvodaya leader[2]

It is true that the police and army [in India] . . . are strong enough to snuff out local agrarian agitations. But unless a long-term strategy is devised, it seems unlikely that a bush-fire approach can indefinitely forestall more extensive conflagrations.

Francine R. Frankel, an American AID (Agency for International Development) official[3]

As many as 84 per cent of the urban dwellers [in Gujarat] felt that their children would have to face greater hardship than they.

Ghanshyam Shah, an Indian sociologist[4]

Naxalism is not finished, and will reappear.

V. Srinivasan, a former Joint Secretary of the Union Home Ministry, in 1971[5]

Will loss of office cause total disintegration of the Congress within the next few years? Or will it be able to survive long enough to stage a comeback either by winning the next general election or, more likely, by forging an alliance with one or more of the constituents of the still disparate Janata Party in the Lok Sabha? The answer will be determined by the following developments: the findings of the commissions of inquiry into the excesses of emergency and the business dealings of Sanjay Gandhi's companies; the government investigations into the

277

instances of administrative corruption by Indira Gandhi and her close advisers, and massive misappropriation of the Congress election funds by them; the status that the Congress Party accords to Indira Gandhi; and finally, the general stance that the Janata government adopts towards the Congress.

By early October 1977, investigations by the Central Bureau of Investigation had revealed enough evidence to enable the government to initiate proceedings in three major cases of corruption and abuse of official position, under the Prevention of Corruption Act (1947), and the Indian Penal Code. These cases concerned (a) awarding a contract to a French firm, Cie Française de Petrol, even though its tender was four times higher than that of its nearest competitor; (b) securing, through corrupt means, 104 jeeps, worth Rs 4,000,000, (£250,000), for election purposes; and (c) obtaining large sums from businessmen for advertising in souvenirs published (or promised to be published) by the All India Congress Committee, at the time of the 1977 general election and before.[6] Singly or jointly, they led to the arrests of Indira Gandhi, four of her former cabinet colleagues and three of her former aides, and a group of businessmen close to her.[7]

In addition, the initial hearings of inquiry into the excesses of emergency, headed by J. C. Shah, a retired Supreme Court judge, had brought to light highly damaging evidence against Indira Gandhi's administration, most of it coming from top civil servants and former cabinet ministers. This included such actions of Indira Gandhi as demoting and maltreating independent-minded judges; harassment (by way of, say, ordering house raids by the Central Bureau of Investigation) of those officials of the Industry Ministry who had been asked, by their own minister, to collect information about Sanjay Gandhi's group of companies;[8] promoting grossly under-qualified persons as heads of the nationalized banks;[9] and using the Chief Censor's office, the Press Information Bureau, the All India Radio and television, and other media for 'slanting news in favour of the government', and portraying Indira Gandhi as 'the supreme and beloved leader of the country', and Sanjay Gandhi as 'an up and coming leader in his own right'.[10]

In his evidence to the Shah commission, S. C. Bhatt, the director of the news services of the All India Radio (AIR), said: 'My impression was that All India Radio, a department of the government, was being used as an agent of the then ruling party. The difference between the state and the party was eliminated.'[11] He referred to a speech by Indira Gandhi to the AIR station directors' conference on 9 September 1975, when she said, 'Being a government department, there was no question of AIR or television adopting an attitude of neutrality or to be concerned about credibility.'[12]

Meanwhile neither Indira Gandhi nor her party has regretted the imposition of internal emergency, the single most important reason for the Congress's electoral defeat. After a brief period of ostracization of Indira Gandhi, both Y. B. Chavan, the new leader of the Congress opposition in Parliament, and K. Brahmananda Reddy, the Congress president (who was the Central Home Minister during and before emergency), drafted her into the inner circle of the party hierarchy. And, following her arrest and unconditional release, in early October, they called a session of the All India Congress Committee to express 'solidarity' with her and other arrested Congress leaders.

However, when Indira Gandhi and her staunch supporters tried to use the occasion to jettison Reddy and install her as the party president – in a move to secure her 'political' protection against a further set of criminal and other charges expected to be preferred against her in the coming months – they failed. The delegates to the AICC session reiterated their earlier resolution upholding the concept of 'collective leadership', and rejecting, by implication, the attempt to reintroduce the practice of 'a single national leader'. They did so partly to draw a line between the party and its now fallen 'supreme leader', and partly to reinforce the working relationship that had developed between their party and the Janata government in Parliament. They were uncannily aware that electing Indira Gandhi as the party president would drive the Janata government and party into a posture of extreme hostility to their party, and strengthen the hands of those in the Janata hierarchy who wish to see both the Congress and Indira Gandhi politically decimated. (This wish, incidentally, is shared by the leftist forces outside the Janata, particularly the CPI(M) and the various Naxalite groups.)

By refusing to rally behind Indira Gandhi, the Congress delegates implicitly supported that section of the Janata leadership which wants the Congress to survive, and function as strong and responsible opposition, thus heralding an era of two-party democracy in India. Among those who share this wish are many of the leading businessmen. They visualize the prospect of the demise of the Congress with alarm, fearing that that would hasten the emergence of the CPI(M)-led leftist front as a national alternative to the Janata. They base their apprehension on the sweeping victory of the leftist front in the West Bengal assembly election of June 1977, and the subsequent 'softening' of the CPI(M) coupled with its overtures to various regional leftist groups to form a united leftist front, independent of both the major 'bourgeois' parties.

Business interests in general were quick to patronize the Janata once it had secured power in Delhi. 'The same people, who were dancing before the Congress government and Mr Sanjay Gandhi with their black money, are now seen coming to the Janata Party,' observed N. Sanjiva Reddy, a Janata leader (who was later to be elected the President of India), a few weeks after the Parliamentary elections.[13] The industrialists of West Bengal were lavish in their contributions to the Janata fund for the State assembly elections.[14] Many of the landlords and rich farmers, who supported the Congress in the Parliamentary election switched their loyalty to the Janata in the assembly election. 'We voted for the Janata [in June] because that was our only hope to be saved from the Marxists,' said Satish Kumar Mandal, a landlord in Sahajapur, West Bengal.[15] A similar pattern was to be noticed in other States as well.[16]

This was not unexpected, because the first action of the Janata government in the agrarian sector was to offer high procurement prices for foodgrains, a step designed to benefit rich farmers and landlords, the ones with surplus to sell. In contrast, its policy on land reform could only be described as lukewarm to negative. Charan Singh, the Central Home Minister (and leader of the 'dissolved' Bharatiya Lok Dal, a party mainly of the rich and middle peasants) told Parliament in early April: 'I want to make it clear that agrarian reforms should have come twenty years ago, and that many legal complications have entered them now, so that however good the intentions of the government may be, I have doubts about it completely succeeding.'[17] Some months later he was to describe land reform as 'a wicked Moscow-inspired conspiracy to ruin Indian agriculture'.[18]

Not surprisingly, Singh's statement went more or less unchallenged by other Janata leaders. After all, disregarding the small Socialist bloc of 27 MPs (i.e. members of Parliament), the Lok Sabha Janata Party consists of members who are either conservative (the Syndicate-Congress's 60 MPs), or right-of-centre (the Bharatiya Lok Dal's 74 MPs), or right wing (the Jan Sangh's 87 MPs).[19] Likewise, only four of the 44 junior and cabinet ministers are former Socialists.[20] 'Much of the Janata Party consists of former Congressmen, and the rest is dominated by the right-wing Jan Sangh,' states Walter Schwarz, a former Delhi correspondent of the *Guardian*. 'A profound failure of the Congress regime was the party's alliance with the dominant classes in both town and country. This alliance, which frustrates reform, promises to be continued by the Janata government.'[21]

The Janata has tried to present its commitment to encourage decentralization of industry and help labour-intensive small and cottage industries as something 'revolutionary'.[22] This is not so. The Industrial Policy Resolution of 1956, passed by the Congress-dominated Parliament, states, 'The government of India would . . . stress the role of cottage and village and small-scale industries in the development of the national economy. . . . They provide immediate large scale employment; they offer a method of ensuring a more equitable distribution of national income; and they facilitate an effective mobilisation of resources of capital and skill which might otherwise remain unutilised.'[23]

But these aspirations remained unattained, because the large business houses, with their control of the Congress, willed it so. Some small-scale industries were certainly allowed, but *not* as competitors to the large-scale ones – only as suppliers to them. The big industrialists consider small-scale manufacturing as basically wasteful and inefficient, and are unmoved by its potential to solve the country's massive unemployment. In any case, centralized production is encouraged by the largely centralized market for manufactured goods, concentrated as it is in the urban centres – and to a small, well-off section of society (not exceeding a tenth of the population),[24] due to extremely uneven distribution of wealth and income.

Unless the Janata Party produces a blueprint for lessening income disparities, particularly in the countryside, and breaking up the political power of the large industrial houses (which are as much its paymasters as they were, and still are, of the Congress), the party cannot successfully implement its policy of encouraging small and cottage industries.

Meanwhile the process of politicization of the Indian masses, accelerated by emergency and the subsequent overthrow of the oppressive Congress regime, continues apace. The Janata Party's (expected) failure to reverse the trend towards greater inequality and growing pauperization of the masses, coupled with a rising political consciousness in the country, can only lead to a series of economic-political crises – each one more severe than the one before – and discredit the new party. The disenchanted voters may then find themselves with no choice except to give a second chance to the Congress, if it is still intact as a national body. Or they may find themselves with two alternatives: the Congress and a national leftist alliance.

Whether or not the second alternative materializes will depend on how well the leftists – both parliamentary and extra-parliamentary – are able to close ranks, and widen their support in the areas where they have had some standing in the past, and strike roots in such traditionally non-leftist regions as the vast Hindi belt, in the coming years. Given a marked decrease in animosity between the Marxists and Naxalites (of various hues), and the participation of certain sections of the Naxalite movement in the assembly election of June 1977, a broad understanding between national and regional leftist organizations cannot be ruled out.

One of the features of the March 1977 poll was that it established the CPI(M) as the dominant parliamentary Communist party in terms of both seats (twenty-three) and popular vote (4·3 per cent). The CPI did badly. It lost 16 of the 23 seats it had won in the previous general election, and its popular vote fell to 2·8 per cent. Its poor performance was mainly due to its close co-operation with the Congress, its support of emergency, and its almost total neglect of organizational work among peasants and workers.

The assembly elections of June 1977 confirmed the relative strengths of the two Communist parties, with the CPI(M) winning 178 of the 293 seats in West Bengal assembly – and its leftist allies gaining another

50 – and the CPI securing only 3. The result was all the more remark-able because, unlike the Parliamentary poll, the CPI(M) did not contest the assembly election in alliance with the Janata.

It seemed the CPI(M) and other leftist groups were the beneficiaries of the popular revulsion against emergency, and the Congress party's dictatorial ways – which, significantly enough, had originated in the West Bengal of the early 1970s, and had been directed primarily at the Marxists and Naxalites.[25] Later such tactics as recruiting criminal elements into the Youth Congress and giving them the backing of the local police, to browbeat *all* opponents of the Congress, were to be extended to other parts of the country.

There were other, positive reasons why the West Bengal electors had preferred the CPI(M) and its allies to either the Janata or Congress. A large majority of the poor voters remembered the actions and policies of the two brief United Front governments of 1967 and 1969 (in which the CPI(M) played a leading role) that had benefited them at the expense of the rich.[26]

Interestingly enough, some of the Naxalites canvassed for the CPI(M) and other leftists in the assembly elections of West Bengal. Their main interest lay in the release of all Naxalite and other political prisoners, a subject of much import in West Bengal, which had the largest segment of such detainees in the country, and a matter on which the Naxalites and Marxists were in agreement. Earlier, at the time of the Parliamentary elections, the Delhi unit of the central organizing committee of the Communist Party of India (Marxist-Leninist), led by S. N. Singh, had urged 'the people in general and our members in particular' to vote for the opposition parties – including the Janata, Congress for Democracy, the CPI(M), and Akali Dal – and to 'build a powerful movement for democratic rights and the release of all political prisoners'.[27] Three of the party members in West Bengal fought assembly elections, and one of them, Santosh Rana (contesting from jail), won a seat from his native Gopiballavpur.[28]

S. N. Singh represented one of the two major Naxalite groups that had disputed Charu Mazmudar's leadership of the CPI(M-L), and the tactics of individual annihilation and urban 'actions', the other such group being represented, among others, by Kanu Sanyal, who was one of the two original organizers of the militant peasant movement in Naxalbari in 1967.

Though the Charu Mazmudar group was subdivided among those who supported the theories of Lin Piao, a radical Chinese Communist leader, and those who did not, its members upheld the tactical line of Charu Mazmudar. They had been concentrating on their work in villages in a few districts of West Bengal and five contiguous districts of western Bihar and eastern Uttar Pradesh, generally known as the Bhojpur region. Following the pattern of the early stages of movement in

Srikakulum,[29] they had been organizing the poor and landless peasants – often low-caste Hindus and Outcastes – around economic demands, and resisting, by force if necessary, the social and economic oppression to which the peasants were subjected by their upper-caste landlords.

After a slow start in the early 1970s, the Naxalites in the Bhojpur region engaged in 48 militant actions between January 1974 and July 1975,[30] including armed encounters with the para-military Central Reserve Police, which was posted in the area in August 1974. Some of these incidents involved long and bloody battles between the armed forces and peasant guerrillas. A skirmish in early June 1975 in the Musahari section of Patna district – an area which had been the scene of Naxalite activity a few years earlier[31] – led to injuries to 24 policemen, including three members of the CRP, and the death of fifteen Naxalites. Significantly enough, the dead Naxalites (some of whom died as a result of the fire that enveloped their place of hiding) included an ex-serviceman of the army and a former member of the Bihar Military Police.[32] A few weeks later, an armed encounter between the Naxalites and the troopers of the CRP in Bahuara village led to the death of eight Naxalites and four troopers.[33] The following month, another armed skirmish near Arrah, a town 60 miles west of Patna, resulted in the death of four guerrillas and two troopers.[34]

The imposition of emergency failed to cripple the Naxalite movement effectively. While referring to 'the disturbing signs of armed rebellion in 14 out of Bihar's 37 districts', Sunanda Datta-Ray reported in late February 1977: 'Officials in Patna, the capital city, admit that 200 landowners, fifty Outcastes and thirty policemen have been murdered, and that 500 Outcastes [peasants] are in jail. Eleven aridly remote pockets are claimed as "liberated zones".'[35]

The development of a militant peasant movement in parts of Bihar and Uttar Pradesh was particularly worrying to the Congress leaders. These States form a major part of the Hindi-speaking region – the heartland of the Indian polity – which contributes the largest single bloc of members to Parliament, and which has hitherto been almost untouched by a leftist ideology or action.

Of the two States, Bihar is the more vulnerable. (Not surprisingly, it had the second largest contingent of political prisoners during and before emergency.) It is bounded in the north by Nepal, a country having friendly relations with China. The flat countryside on both sides of the border, which is minimally guarded, is ideal for those engaged in subversive activities: they can criss-cross the border without much difficulty. Its southern and south-western parts are hilly and forest-infested, and inhabited, in the main, by tribals who feel alienated from the mainstream of Hindu society, and who are more receptive to subversive ideas than non-tribals. Most of Bihar's industry and mining are concentrated in an area contiguous with West Bengal – a State which, from the Centre's viewpoint, has been the most problematical of all.

The leftist leanings of a large section of Bengali society are considered, by the non-leftist forces, to be a threat to the stability of the eastern zone in particular and the country in general. This was apparent from the fact, among others (outlined earlier),[36] that even *before* the emergency of June 1975, according to Amnesty International, West Bengal had 15,000 to 20,000 political prisoners, most of them real or suspected Naxalites, and many of them held without trial since 1970–1; and that repeated demands by various groups and individuals, within and outside the country, either to release them or bring them to trial had gone unheeded by the administrations in Delhi and Calcutta.

The Congress leadership seemed uncannily aware that, despite the introduction of a stable Congress government in the State, from March 1972 onwards, and its apparent success in muzzling opposition, consisting of the CPI(M) and other leftist groups, the masses remained sullen and dissatisfied. This became apparent when J. P. Narayan's mass rally in Calcutta, in early June 1975, drew the largest crowd the city had seen in a long time; and the crowd cheered the loudest when Jyoti Basu, the CPI(M) leader, rose to address it. This alarmed the Congress leadership, and was one of the main, albeit unstated, reasons for Indira Gandhi to declare emergency a few weeks later.[37]

The swift and violent changes in Bangladesh during the latter half of 1975 – the assassination of Sheikh Mujibur Rahman, the pro-India President, two coups in quick succession, and a rebellion by soldiers – caused grave concern in Delhi. Earlier in the year, the fall of the pro-Western regimes in Cambodia, South Vietnam, and Laos to the Communist and pro-Communist insurgent forces had shaken the regimes of neighbouring Thailand and Malaysia, and encouraged the outlawed Communists and other insurgents to intensify their movements. Burma too had experienced an increase in the activities of the armed Communist rebels. In the spring of 1975, the pro-Peking Communist Party of Burma – which had moved its base to the mountainous north-east, adjoining Yunnan province of China, in 1969 – had reaffirmed its commitment to the path of armed struggle to achieve the overthrow of the ruling military junta and establishment of socialism,[38] and to its strategy of concentrating its main effort in the areas populated by such mountain tribes as Chins, Kachins, and Shans.

All this was disturbing news to Delhi, only too aware of the fact that India's mountainous and forest-infested north-eastern frontier is populated mainly by tribals, and of the danger that this presents to the stability of the region. Tribals form 95 per cent of Mizoram's population, 86 per cent of Nagaland's, 80 per cent of Meghalaya's, 75 per cent of Arunachal's, 32 per cent of Tripura's, and 30 per cent of Manipur's. For geographical, historical, racial and cultural reasons, many of these tribes – Idus, Wanchos, and Nactes in Arunachal; Nagas and Kukis in Manipur; Cacharis and Mikirs in Assam; Khasis and Garos in Meghalaya; Tripuris and Naotias in Tripura; Nagas in Nagaland; and Mizos in Mizoram – feel alienated from the predominantly Hindu society of India.

Despite its best efforts, the Congress failed to gain much support among the tribals. The Janata Party's attempts to build up a base in the area are also proving futile. This is most apparent in the case of the Nagas and Mizos. The independence movements in Nagaland and Mizoram, which have tied down a large body of Indian military and para-military forces for the past many years, still do not show signs of dying down.

It was hoped by the Indian government that the emergence of a friendly Bangladesh, in place of a hostile East Pakistan, in December 1971, would deprive the rebel Nagas and Mizos of sanctuaries in a neighbouring country, and finish their movement;[39] and that elevating Meghalaya, Manipur, and Tripura to the status of States, and Mizoram and Arunachal to Union Territories, in early 1972, would satisfy the particularist demands of the peoples of this region, and pre-empt secessionist aspirations. But this has not been so.

Rejection of the pro-Indian Naga Nationalist Organization at the polls in early 1974 showed that the rebels continued to enjoy the support and sympathy of a large section of the Naga population.[40] The fall of the pro-rebel United Democratic Front government in March 1975, instigated by the Congress regime in Delhi, and imposition of the President's rule in the State soon after, were followed by intensive operations by India's security forces. This led the Underground Nagas to turn more and more to China for training and supply of small arms, and to an increasing stress on the political-ideological (as against racial-cultural) aspect of the Naga struggle for independence. They intensified their practice of sending some of their followers to China for guerrilla training, with nearly 200 young Nagas doing so in early 1975.

The anticipated return of the trained Naga rebels to Nagaland, around August–September, was met with a 'massive operation' by the Indian Army, including a thousand arrests, and imposition of a twenty-four-hour curfew in border areas, mainly to prohibit villagers from harvesting their rice crop, and thus demoralizing them.[41] The general aim seemed to be to pressurize the Underground leaders to negotiate a settlement.

In November, the Indian government announced that it had reached an accord with some Underground leaders, who had accepted the Indian Constitution 'without any condition' and promised to deposit their arms 'at appointed places' to be named, while it had agreed to suspend the operation of the Unlawful Activities (Prevention) Act, that had been in force since August 1972; and that these Underground leaders had consulted Z. A. Phizo – the 'father of the Nagas', living in exile in

England – while negotiating the agreement. This was promptly denied by Phizo, who told the London correspondent of the *Overseas Hindustan Times*, among others, that he would continue 'the struggle'.[42]

Hopes that change of administration in Delhi would finally break the impasse between the rebel Nagas and the Indian government were dashed when a meeting between Phizo and Morarji Desai in London, in June 1977, ended in a disaster. While Phizo said that he had come to see the Prime Minister of India, because 'we must find a way out to end the trouble', Desai maintained that 'there is no problem', and that 'I will exterminate all Naga rebels'.[43] Some days later, Phizo was quoted by a British newspaper as saying, 'If our voice cannot be heard without fighting then we shall have to fight more seriously.'[44]

A similar stance was announced in July by Laldenga, the Mizo National Front leader. He repudiated the peace accord he had signed with the Indian government a year earlier, during emergency, and asked his followers to boycott the next election in the territory.[45] While most of the Mizo rebels remained in Mizoram, some of them led by Biakvela, the 'adjutant general' of the MNF, crossed into the Chittagong Hill Tracts of Bangladesh, to harass India's security forces from there.[46] The change in the MNF's stand was caused primarily by the local administration's introduction of the identity card system in the territory[47] and the terroristic activities of the 'special force' of the Mizoram Armed Police.[48]

The earlier loss of sanctuaries in East Pakistan, towards the end of 1971, had weakened, but not destroyed, the rebel Mizo movement. The secessionist MNF had transferred its base to the Chin Hills and Arakan Hills region of Burma, and established contacts with the Naga Underground. By late 1974, the MNF had also succeeded in infiltrating the administration *in* Mizoram – particularly the police and intelligence – a fact that was discovered by the Central Bureau of Investigation, which had been assigned the task of investigating the murder of three senior police officers in Aizawl, Mizoram's capital, in January 1975. It was found that the members of the Mizo Underground, employed in the sensitive departments of the administration, had, in the past, kept the rebels informed of the plans and counter-plans of the Indian authorities, and had thus sabotaged the Indian attempts to track down and destroy rebel camps. This, in turn, had caused frustration among the Indian forces, who had taken to the practice of dispensing 'summary justice' to innocent Mizos, which had only driven more Mizos to the side of the Underground and intensified anti-Indian feelings. 'The image of the Indian Army has reached its bottom as far as the general public in Mizoram are concerned,' stated Thenphunga Sailo, a retired Mizo brigadier of the Indian Army, in early May 1975.[49]

By then, the impact of the rebel Mizo activity had been felt in neighbouring Tripura. There were reports of 'collusion' between the Mizo guerrillas and militant tribals in northern Tripura for what seemed to be a nascent movement for territorial independence as well as elimination of (non-tribal) moneylender-landlords. Once before, in 1948–9, the tribals in Tripura – many of them with experience in handling firearms, acquired as recruits in the (British) Indian Army during the Second World War – had taken up arms in response to a call given by the Communist Party, then, to launch an armed struggle against the Congress regime, and held out in the forest-infested areas of the State until the army launched an all-out attack against them in 1950. In those days, the tribals formed two-thirds of the State's population of about 600,000. This began to change, as an increasing number of Hindu refugees arrived from the then East Pakistan, so that by 1971 the *non*-tribals constituted two-thirds of the State's population of 1·57 million, with the tribals largely expropriated of their hereditary land, and squeezed into an ever-decreasing area. 'To us, tribals, progress means growth of towns and loss of our land to the non-tribals, and an increase in our sense of insecurity,' said a tribal leader in Agartala, the State's capital, in early 1972.[50]

But neither this change nor the bitter memory of the military repression of their militant movement in 1950 seems to have diminished their loyalty to the Communists – i.e. the CPI(M). By and large, they continue to vote CPI(M). It was this factor which enabled the party to win a quarter of the assembly seats in March 1972 election, despite a strong pro-Congress sentiment created by India's victory over Pakistan in the Bangladesh war. The situation improved further for the CPI(M), when following the electoral defeat of the Congress at the Centre, in March 1977, the local Congress split, causing the downfall of its Congress ministry, and the installing of a coalition government of the local Janata and the CPI(M). The chances of the Marxists winning an outright majority of their own in the next assembly election remain high; and the Janata leaders, at the local and national levels, view such a prospect with a certain foreboding.

The possibility that the deeply rooted particularist aspirations of the tribal masses might combine with a newly acquired awareness of their exploitation by landlords, moneylenders, and merchants – almost invariably non-tribals – and emerging as a militant anti-establishment movement throughout the sensitive north-east alarms the Janata hierarchy as much as it did the Congress. The contrary seems to be the case with the leftist forces in general. The popularity of the CPI(M) in Tripura and West Bengal, and its advocacy of greater powers to the States and Union Territories, mean that the leftist views on the subject cannot be ignored altogether.

Taken as a whole, the leftist forces in the country are now less divided than they have been for a decade. The relentless repression of the Naxalites and Marxists by the Congress administration, which reached its peak during emergency, had the effect of blunting the feelings of animosity and competitiveness that had existed between them since the late 1960s.

The adoption of a document by the Naxalites led by S. N. Singh and C. Pulla Reddy, in early 1975 – which described the attempt in the past of building a people's army by 'killing indiscriminately landlords and other exploiters in a conspiratorial manner, through a campaign of annihilation of "class enemies" ' as 'disastrous', creating not a people's army but 'terrorist bands' – was a pointer in this direction.[51] Their party's directive to its cadres to 'wholeheartedly participate in the [March 1977] election by mobilizing people to vote for the opposition parties' was a further evidence of this trend.[52] The other major Naxalite group, led by Kanu Sanyal, is also reportedly moving closer to the CPI(M): a party which is now committed to forming a broad left front, encompassing even the CPI, if its leaders were to sever all connections with the Congress, and publicly admit the incorrectness of their pro-emergency stand. (The CPI's inclusion in the broad front could help the leftist cause in Bihar, a strategically placed Hindi-speaking State, where the party has many pockets of strength.)

The refusal of the Charu Mazmudar group of Naxalites, committed to total boycott of parliamentary processes, to join a united left front, under the leadership of the CPI(M), need not be viewed in antagonistic terms. In the present Indian circumstances there is room enough for a Marxist-Leninist group to devote itself exclusively to sharpening class struggle, preferably in areas that have hitherto been untouched by a Communist movement. Likewise, there seems no basic conflict between the strategy that emphasizes creating fairly strong bases of support in the north-eastern and eastern regions, and the one that stresses establishing bases that are scattered around the country. The two strategies could in fact be seen as complementary.

The task of creating and strengthening a broad left front will need to be pursued with urgency and vigour, because the threat to the democratic rights of the Indian people is not over yet, and will persist for the next few decades. There is no guarantee that, when faced with a grave economic-political crisis, the Janata government will not turn as repressive as did the Congress under Indira Gandhi.[53] After all the Janata represents the economic interests of the same classes – industrialists and large landowners – as does the Congress, the only difference between the two parties being that the Janata is *at present* committed to upholding democratic rights and civil liberties. The long-term factors that caused the downfall of the Congress apply equally to the Janata.

By the late 1960s, the Congress had played out its historically progressive role: a successful challenge to the foreign, imperialistic capital on behalf of the indigenous capital; and substitution or supplanting of the large absentee, feudal ownership in agriculture with directly managed landlordship or 'self-cultivating' ownership by rich peasants. And, given its class composition, and its commitment – reiterated publicly by Indira Gandhi in early 1975 – to a policy of 'holding all economic classes together',[54] it could not initiate, let alone accomplish, the next progressive step in the economic evolution of Indian society: combating landlords and rich farmers for the benefit of the landless, and the poor and middle peasants.

Yet any political dogma aside, this is the *only* way to arrest the continuing increase in the relative and absolute size of the country's poor. It means effecting an equitable distribution of what is produced – that is, in practical terms, putting more money into the pockets of the poor *at the cost of the rich* – curbing the superfluous consumption of the rich; and mopping up their excessive income through an honest and efficient system of tax assessment and collection, and investing it as capital for the economic development of the country. This is the only means of assuring a rapid and sustained industrialization (whether large-scale, or small) of the economy, without which it is almost impossible to underwrite a steady rise in popular living standards and, more importantly, political stability. (Nothing illustrates the dismal failure of the Congress in the field of industrialization better than a statement made by the Central Minister of Industry, in October 1975, that 'Market for industrial goods, apart from textiles, hardly exceeds 50 to 60 million people, or hardly 10 per cent of the population'.[55] (And this at the end of *four* Five Year Plans!) The alternative method of industrialization – whereby foreign capital is pumped into an under-developed economy on a massive scale to enable it to reach the 'take-off' stage – which has worked well in such countries as Taiwan and South Korea is out of the question for India. Its needs for developmental capital are so astronomical that no single country or bloc of countries can possibly meet them.

The failure of the Congress to effect the desired change in class and property relations that is needed for the simple and pragmatic reason of keeping the economy in good health meant that the Indian polity under its rule faced an economic crisis every so often, with the most severe one emerging in 1973–4. Given the class nature of the Janata Party, it seems set for a course followed earlier by the Congress – a prospect that offers unprecedented opportunity to the leftist forces to gain ground, particularly in the crucial Hindi belt, the present strong-hold of the Janata.

There is as yet another alternative which might enable the Indian economy to reach a self-regenerative stage in the not-too-distant future, and thus remove pressure on the ruling party (either the Janata or Congress) to institute some basic social changes. This consists of the country finding itself possessing enormous oil reserves, and/or gradually becoming an important part of the prosperous and rapidly expanding economies of Iran and the Middle-East, and/or attracting the capital of the many thousands of its affluent expatriates living in various parts of the world. A healthy economy, thus engendered, would mean a much higher investment in the non-agrarian sector than has been the case until now, and an accelerated capitalization of agriculture. These developments, if realized, can only aid, not weaken, the leftist movement.

An expanding industry will create a larger working class, and offer greater opportunities for the establishment of leftist-led trade unions.[56] And growing capitalization of agriculture will transform more and more of the traditional peasants and tenants into wage labourers, and thus introduce economic and political militancy into the rural areas. The extent of the change that could occur in the country, as a whole, can be gauged by the fact that progressive modernization of agriculture in the Punjab-Haryana region, during the period 1953–68, reduced the number of tenants by 85 per cent,[57] and caused a dramatic rise in the number of wage labourers.

In the short run, the introduction of modern inputs and such farm implements as tractors – which replace bullocks, *not* human beings – and the subsequent increase in the number of crops and yield, engender demand for labour and an increase in wages. But, as Wolf Ladejinsky points out, 'Additional employment (due to the labour intensive nature of new technology) and better wages are not for ever, because farm practices are bringing in a host of labour-saving devices (such as threshers). . . . Thus, the outlook is for an overcrowded low-wage farm market regardless of the scope of the green revolution.'[58] Such conditions can only give impetus to leftist politics. And an indication of this is already available. As Rajni Kothari states:

A factor analysis of social, economic, and political variables for all the districts [in India] shows that the appeal of the extreme left (i.e. the CPI(M) is by and large limited to areas characterized by high degrees of urbanization, literacy, the growth of secondary and tertiary sectors [of the economy], unemployment, and population density, as also a high proportion of voter turnout in elections. These are still few and scattered. But it must be remembered that it is precisely these indicators that will be on the upswing in the process of [economic] development.[59]

In short, in either case – whether the country's economy improves or deteriorates – the leftist movement in India has a promising future in the coming decades. However, the path to such a future will not be straight. Periods of leftist advance will follow periods of repression and setback, as the dominant classes manipulate the political form of the state from liberal democratic to authoritarian or semi-authoritarian – each democratic interregnum, however brief, providing fresh chances to the leftists to expand their base.

POSTSCRIPT

By the spring of 1979, the debate among the Janata leaders on the stance to be adopted towards the Congress opposition had been settled.[1] Those who wanted the government to take a tough stand against the Congress, and prosecute Indira Gandhi on various charges of misuse of power, during and before emergency, prevailed over those who wished to let bygones be bygones. But the resolution was slow to come about, since many in the Janata hierarchy saw no political threat in Indira Gandhi, who had been reduced to leading a party considerably weakened by a split she herself had inadvertently caused.

Following her failure to win the presidency of the (undivided) Congress — after her arrest and unconditional release in October 1977 — Indira Gandhi called a convention of her supporters in Delhi, in December. This convention elected her president of the party: an act that led to an open division in the parliamentary group, with a little over half of the 150-odd Congress members of the Lok Sabha backing Indira Gandhi's Congress, and the remainder staying with the (official) Congress led by Y. B. Chavan.

The trial of strength between the two factions came in February 1978, when elections were held to the assemblies of Andhra Pradesh, Assam, Karnataka, and Maharashtra — the states where the (undivided) Congress had done well in the March 1977 parliamentary poll. The official Congress did poorly while Indira Gandhi's Congress did well, winning comfortable majorities in the Andhra Pradesh and Karnataka assemblies, and emerging as the third largest group in Maharashtra. (The results confirmed the continued weakness of the Janata in the southern states of Andhra Pradesh and Karnataka, with Maharashtra and Assam reflecting a favourable picture.)[2]

A further boost was given to Indira Gandhi's Congress in May, when it won a parliamentary by-election in Uttar Pradesh, considered a stronghold of the Janata. The climax came four months later, when Indira Gandhi herself got elected from Chikmagalur, a constituency in Karnataka, after a member of her party had dutifully resigned his safe seat to make way for her.

Indira Gandhi's return to Parliament improved the chance of the two factions of the Congress party uniting under her leadership, and challenging the Janata government, which was then practically immobilised by a running feud between Prime Minister Desai and Charan Singh (leader of the Bharatiya Lok Dal group) who had been made to resign his post as Home Minister in July 1978. While Charan Singh claimed that he had been eased out of the cabinet mainly because he had been pressing for urgent governmental action against Indira Gandhi, the Prime Minister justified his move on the grounds of restoring discipline in the party.

However, Desai's firm action failed to win him the status of the supreme leader of a united party that he aspired to. The leaders of the five major factions within the Janata—the rightwing Jan Sangh, the right-of-centre BLD, the conservative ex-Congressmen, the radical ex-Congressmen, and the Socialists — continued to be more interested in strengthening their individual groups, under the umbrella of the Janata, than building up the party as a unified political entity. In fact, by then, public rhetoric to the contrary, the wish to create a united party with a cohesive socio-political ideology had been quietly abandoned in favour of a tacit understanding to run the government on the basis of consensus reached between the leaders of different factions.

By the summer of 1978, the logic that had caused the defeat of the Grand Alliance in the 1971 election — the liability of each of the constituents rubbing off on the whole conglomerate[3]—had begun to work against the Janata government. The increasingly violent attacks on the outcaste landless peasants by the pro-BLD upper- and middle-caste landlords in northern India had largely alienated the outcastes from the Janata. The communalist actions and speeches of the Jan Sangh-Rashtriya Swayamsevak Sangh group within the Janata had a similar effect on the Muslims. The initial attempts to forge a national economic policy and a five-year plan to better the socio-economic condition of the masses had yielded little; and no fresh effort was being made.

The only area of tangible achievement was the restoration of civil liberties. The much-hated Maintenance of Internal Security Act of 1971 was repealed. The authoritarian elements of the Constitution (39th Amendment) Act and the Constitution (42nd Amendment) Act of 1975 were nullified by the Constitution (45th Amendment) Act of 1978. The new law restored to the courts the power to adjudicate on the disputes arising over the election of the President, the Vice-President, the Prime Minister, or the Speaker of the Lok Sabha. It also restored to the Supreme Court its authority to judge whether or not an emergency proclamation was justified.

It removed the threat of 'internal disturbance' from the emergency clause of Article 352, and substituted it with 'armed rebellion.'[4] It specified that the Central cabinet must submit advice in writing to the President that an emergency declaration is essential, and that such a proclamation must be ratified within a month by a two-thirds majority in both houses of Parliament.

In contrast the Janata government had been tardy in implementing its promise to punish all those who were responsible for imposing the emergency of 1975-77, and taking the law into their hands during that period. This had happened despite the fact that the reports submitted by the Shah commission, in May and September 1978, had confirmed many of the allegations made against Indira Gandhi, her son Sanjay, and their close aides.

Rejecting the reasons for declaring emergency offered by Indira Gandhi in her broadcast of 26 June 1975 (outlined on pp. 262-63), the Shah commission concluded, 'The one and only motivating force for tendering the extraordinary advice to the President to declare an "internal emergency" was the intense political activity generated in the ruling party and the opposition by the decision of the Allahabad High Court declaring the election of the Prime Minister of the day invalid on the ground of corrupt practices.'[5]

The Shah commission was equally unambiguous about the slum clearance and the sterilization programmes carried out during emergency. Regarding the demolition of 150,015 structures by the local authorities in Delhi during emergency (an 83-fold increase in demolitions over an equivalent period before emergency), it concluded: 'The prime mover for most of these demolitions was Sanjay Gandhi. . . . The manner in which the demolitions were carried out in Delhi during emergency is an unrelieved story of illegality, callousness, and of sickening sycophancy by the senior officers of Sanjay Gandhi . . . [a person] who held no position in the administrative or constitutional set-up of Delhi, or of any other place.'[6]

The commission confirmed that coercion and intimidation were employed first by the ministers and top bureaucrats on the civil servants, and then by the latter on ordinary citizens (as described earlier on pp. 271-73), to implement the sterilization programme. The prime source of this human misery and degradation was unmistakably Sanjay Gandhi — described euphemistically as 'an extra-constitutional power' by Karan Singh, the Central Health Minister during emergency, in his evidence to the commission. 'The chief ministers who owed special allegiance to this authority vied with one another in raising their sterilization targets in order to gain favour,' he said.[7]

Furthermore, the commission found that Indira Gandhi was responsible for 'the institution of criminal proceedings against the four officers (of the Industry Ministry) concerned, having their houses searched and subjecting them to humiliation, merely because they were responsible for collecting information in the discharge of their duties, which would have been prejudicial to the interests of Maruti Limited, a concern in which Sanjay Gandhi, her son, was vitally interested.'[8]

Since these civil servants were collecting material for the Industry Minister, to prepare a reply to a parliamentary question, the Parliament's privileges committee decided to punish Indira Gandhi for tampering with the working of Parliament. Its decision, in mid-December, to expel her from the Lok Sabha (to which she had been elected only the previous month), and to send her to jail until the end of the session, about a week later, was endorsed by the House.

This governmental action — enthusiastically supported by that majority of the Janata members of Parliament who wanted to mete out some punishment to Indira Gandhi — helped Desai to consolidate his leadership. It also mollified Charan Singh, who when invited to head the Finance Ministry, some weeks later, rejoined the cabinet, thus restoring the badly shaken unity of the Janata party.

In contrast the talks between the two factions of the Congress to unite, under the overall direction of Indira Gandhi, reached an impasse and were finally discontinued in March, with the anti-unity section in the official Congress charging Indira Gandhi with 'continuing dictatorial tendencies.'[9]

As a result, the official Congress backed the government's Special Courts Bill — designed to try expeditiously all those who had committed offences during and before emergency — in the Rajya Sabha, and thus pave the way for a swift prosecution of Indira Gandhi, and her son Sanjay. This support was crucial since out of the 250 seats in the Rajya Sabha, the Janata held only 71, whereas Indira Gandhi's Congress held 66 and the official Congress 45. The Bill, which had earlier received a large majority in the Lok Sabha, secured 119 votes in favour, and 98 against, in the Rajya Sabha.[10]

What was significant was that the CPI's nine members in the Rajya Sabha sided with the government, and against Indira Gandhi's party: a decision that was related to the public admission made by the CPI's National Council, in December 1977, that its support to emergency had been 'wrong,' and that the party should have waited to 'grasp the implications of emergency.'[11]

Such an admission by the CPI leadership laid the ground for cooperation between the CPI and the CPI(M) on specific issues.

About a year later, for instance, the two parties decided to cooperate on the trade union front and oppose the Janata government's Industrial Relations Bill, presented to Parliament in August 1978. They were joined in this by the non-Communist trade unionists as well.

'A strongly suspicious, if not outright anti-union, attitude is discernible in the various provisions of the Bill,' noted Bagaram Tulpule, a veteran Socialist trade unionist. 'The Bill seeks to perpetuate, no extend, the policy of the government control and compulsory adjudication of labour-management disputes, along with its corollary of wholesale ban on strikes and other forms of direct action by workers in defence, and pursuit, of their interests.'[12]

An attempt by the Janata government to curtail the trade union rights of the workers did not come as a surprise to the CPI(M), which had extended conditional support to the Janata since its inception. The party's draft political resolution had stated, in early 1978, that 'The antecedants of the main constituents of the Janata party have been anti-democratic and reactionary.'[13]

The most anti-democratic and reactionary constituent of the Janata is the Jan Sangh, closely allied as it is with the ultra-nationalist, fascist Rashtriya Swayamsevak Sangh (RSS), open only to the Hindus. It is the Jan Sangh-RSS which has been the most successful in dovetailing its policy of rapid expansion with a vigorous infiltration of the various state institutions since the Janata came to power in March 1977. The disarray caused by the six-month long rupture between Morarji Desai and Charan Singh—when the Jan Sangh steadfastly backed the Prime Minister—enabled the Jan Sangh-RSS to expand even faster than before.[14] This development alarmed not only the leftist parties but also the democratic and secular forces inside the Janata and outside; and rightly so.

Despite the success that the anti-authoritarian elements in the country have had in finally bringing Indira Gandhi and her close aides to court, with a strong possibility of conviction and imprisonment, they remain well aware that the long-term danger to Indian democracy lies in the strength of such anti-democratic organizations as the Jan Sangh and the RSS, and that the task of countering such forces is better undertaken now, rather than later.

30 April 1979

NOTES

CHAPTER 1: VILLAGE INDIA

1 *Monthly Commentary*, February 1971, p. 36.
2 *Amrita Bazar Patrika*, 29 November 1970.
3 Interview, in Dusi, 7 February 1971.
4 Interview, in Dusi, 8 February 1971.
5 *Seminar*, December 1969, p. 21.
6 Zamindar means, literally, owner of land; and *jagirdar*, owner of a *jagir*, a country estate.
7 Kajha was visited, by the author, in March 1971; Nihal in January 1972; Dusi in February 1971; and Sahajapur in January 1971, and again in January 1972.
8 See Chapter 8.
9 See p. 6.
10 See Chapter 7.
11 *Studies in Indian Agriculture*, University of California Press, Berkeley, 1968, p. 93.
12 In 1969 these two States, comprising only 4 per cent of the national population, accounted for 33 per cent of the country's tractors.
13 *India's Green Revolution*, Princeton University Press, Princeton, 1972, p. 48.
14 Literally, 'Child of God', a term coined by Mahatma Gandhi, popular nationalist leader, in the 1930s to describe an Untouchable.
15 Cited in *Economic and Political Weekly*, 26 March 1973, pp. 926–7.
16 At 1960–1 prices.
17 Gradual alienation of small peasants from land is a State-wide phenomenon. Between 1961 and 1971, the proportion of land-owning cultivators in West Bengal decreased from 38·5 per cent of the total workforce to 31·7 per cent – a decline of nearly 18 per cent. *Amrita Bazar Patrika*, 24 March 1976.

CHAPTER 2: URBAN INDIA

1 *Economic and Political Weekly*, 28 March 1970, p. 567.
2 Cited in *Link*, 13 February 1972, p. 12.
3 31 January 1976.
4 The density of population in Calcutta, in the early 1960s, was 102,012. The corresponding figure for Ahmadabad, the second most crowded city in India, was 56,540; and that for New York was 27,900. Geoffrey Moorhouse, *Calcutta*, Penguin Books, Harmondsworth, 1974, p. 103.
5 S. N. Sen, *The City of Calcutta*, Bookland, Calcutta, 1960, p. 121.

6 *Statesman*, 19 June 1972.
7 Interview on 7 January 1971.
8 A detailed survey of a *bustee* by M. K. A. Siddiqui, in the mid-1960s, showed that 90 per cent of the residents were either manual or semi-skilled workers – printing-press workers, machine operators, sanitary workers, bus and tram drivers and conductors, rickshaw pullers and taxi drivers, book-binders, and tailors – or small traders, hawkers, clerks, peons, and night watchmen. *Indian Journal of Social Work*, July 1968, pp. 173-82.
9 This *bustee* was investigated, by the author, in January 1971.
10 Between 1965 and 1968, the number of jobs in registered factories in West Bengal went down from 910,191 to 850,287; and the trend has continued since then. Sankar Ghosh, *The Disinherited State*, Orient Longman, Calcutta, 1971, p. 34.
11 Cited in *Frontier*, 16 March 1974, p. 8.
12 *Statesman*, 19 June 1972.
13 Ibid.
14 *New Statesman*, 8 May 1970, p. 649.
15 Interview, 14 December 1970.
16 *Observer Magazine*, 11 October 1970, p. 57.
17 Interview, 10 December 1970.
18 Interview, 13 March 1971.
19 *Economic and Political Weekly*, 2 November 1972, p. 1818.
20 *Statistical Outline of India, 1972-73*, Tata Services Limited, Bombay, p. 28.
21 Ram Joshi, 'Maharashtra', in Myron Weiner (ed.), *State Politics in India*, Princeton University Press, Princeton, 1968, p. 182.
22 5 June 1971.
23 *Economic and Political Weekly*, 3 August 1974, p. 1219.
24 This slum was investigated, by the author, in July–August 1971.
25 This was so until August 1972 when prohibition, that had existed in the State for more than a generation, was lifted.
26 See p. 27.
27 Interview, 6 August 1971.
28 *Economic Times*, 8 September 1971.
29 Between 1958 and 1962, employment in registered factories rose by 40·9 per cent. *Radical Review*, April–June 1970, p. 5.
30 *Hindu*, 5 September 1971; and *Times Weekly*, 2 January 1972.
31 This slum was investigated, by the author, in February 1971.
32 See p. 22.
33 Interview, 30 January 1971.
34 *Times Weekly*, 22 August 1971.
35 Ibid.
36 *Statesman*, 14 November 1971.
37 *Indian Express*, 22 December 1971.
38 22 January 1972.
39 31 December 1971.
40 *Overseas Hindustan Times*, 24 January 1972.
41 13 May 1972, p. 960.

CHAPTER 3: A CORRUPT SOCIETY

1 Cited in *New Wave*, 13 February 1972, p. 1.
2 *Statesman*, 21 November 1971.
3 *Hindustan Standard*, 11 January 1972.
4 *Overseas Hindustan Times*, 28 December 1972.

5 Ibid., 9 August 1973. Some three years later, the estimate for black money in circulation varied between Rs 10,000 crores (£5,000 million) and Rs 30,000 crores (£15,000 million). *Overseas Hindustan Times*, 9 January 1975.
6 *India Weekly*, 22 August 1974, p. 4.
7 *Times of India*, 30 July 1971.
8 *Times Weekly*, 26 September 1971. There was a noticeable decline in this practice when, following the declaration of national emergency in June 1975, the government tried to put a stop to it.
9 Publications Division, Government of India, New Delhi, 1964, pp. 9–10.
10 *The Illustrated Weekly of India*, 10 October 1971, p. 12.
11 Electric cash registers are as yet uncommon in India.
12 Interview, 13 March 1971.
13 Op. cit., p. 13.
14 A check-up by the Uttar Pradesh government revealed the existence of 700 bogus industrial units, established mainly to obtain scarce raw materials for resale at higher prices. *Hindustan Times*, 18 November 1971.
15 Op. cit., p. 10.
16 Interview, in Mandar, 23 April 1971.
17 *The Illustrated Weekly of India*, 10 October 1971, p. 15.
18 *Link*, 8 March 1971, p. 17.
19 17 May 1971.
20 Interview with I. M. Jha, a local journalist, 17 April 1971.
21 *Hindustan Times*, 17 May 1971.
22 Ibid.
23 *Overseas Hindustan Times*, 10 June 1972.
24 *Hindustan Times*, 7 June 1971.
25 Cited in the *Journal of Tamil Chamber of Commerce*, Madras, December 1970, p. 13.
26 Interview, in Trivandrum, 12 September 1971.
27 *New Statesman*, 9 June 1972, p. 789.
28 Interview, 7 January 1971.
29 *Times of India*, 12 August 1971.
30 *Hindustan Times*, 15 November 1971.
31 24 May 1971.
32 23 September 1972, p. 1949.
33 *Bureaucrats Under Stress*, University of California Press, Berkeley, 1969, pp. 163–4. Author's italics.
34 5 April 1974.
35 23 September 1972, p. 1949.
36 *Overseas Hindustan Times*, 11 January 1973.
37 *Sixth Annual Report of the Central Vigilance Commission*, Publications Division, Government of India, New Delhi, 1970, pp. 5–6.
38 *Asian Drama: An Inquiry into the Poverty of Nations*, vol. 2, Penguin Books, Harmondsworth, 1968, p. 952.
39 Op. cit., p. 180.
40 *Mail*, 3 February 1971.

CHAPTER 4: PRESENT POLITICAL-ADMINISTRATIVE STRUCTURE

1 *India's Democracy*, Weidenfeld & Nicolson, London, 1972, p. 25.
2 Cited in Hugh Tinker, *India and Pakistan: A Political Analysis*, Frederick Praeger, New York, 1963, p. 48.

3 See Chapter 18.
4 Interview with J. S. R. A. Shastri, a village leader, 23 August 1971.

CHAPTER 5: ELECTORAL POLITICS

1 *Economic and Political Weekly*, July 1968, p. 1087.
2 *Overseas Hindustan Times*, 22 August 1974.
3 Interview, in Madras, 4 February 1971.
4 'One Party Dominance' in Rajni Kothari (ed.), *Party System and Election Studies*, Allied Publishers, Bombay, 1967, pp. 49–50.
5 George Rosen, *Democracy and Economic Change in India*, University of California Press, Berkeley, 1966, p. 3.
6 Cited in *Mainstream*, 9 May 1970, p. 10.
7 *Economic and Political Weekly*, 7 January 1967, p. 23.
8 This will be discussed later.
9 Interview in Vijaywada, Andhra Pradesh, 22 August 1971.
10 *Overseas Hindustan Times*, 21 February 1974.
11 Duncan B. Forrester in *Economic and Political Weekly*, July 1968, p. 1087. He points out that he obtained this information indirectly, as part of a general discussion on election campaign with individual legislators, and that the figures mentioned by them were on the low side since they were all along aware of the existence of the law.
12 Debate in Rajya Sabha, 28 July 1971.
13 *Overseas Hindustan Times*, 17 October 1974, and *Economic and Political Weekly*, 26 October 1974, p. 1795.
14 Kuldip Nayar in *Statesman*, 9 March 1971.
15 The insignificance of this source of income is apparent from the fact that during the four-year period of 1959–63 the All India Congress Committee received a mere Rs 554,646 (£27,700) as membership dues. Gopal Krishna in Rajni Kothari, op. cit., p. 40.
16 See Chapter 9.
17 Gopal Krishna in Rajni Kothari, op. cit., p. 43.
18 Kuldip Nayar, *India: the critical years*, Vikas, Delhi, 1971, p. 364. All the ninety-one commercial undertakings run by the Central government were asked to find some means of contributing funds to the Congress, and reportedly managed to do so.
19 Op. cit., p. 363.
20 *Indian Express*, 22 February 1971.
21 Interview, 21 December 1970. The following example further illustrates the affinity that exists between the Congress and the business community. An appeal by the Congress president for funds to construct a new office for the All India Congress Committee in Delhi, at the cost of Rs 1 crore (£500,000), brought pledges of Rs 37 lakhs (£185,000), mainly from businessmen, within an *hour*. *Economic and Political Weekly*, 3 June 1972, p. 1099.
22 Interview, 5 August 1971.
23 *The Illustrated Weekly of India*, 28 February 1971, p. 48.
24 11 February 1971.
25 The Dravida Munnetra Kazhagam, in Tamil Nadu, expressed its belief in 'establishing a Socialist Society suited to the Age of Science'.
26 *Times of India*, 28 February 1971.
27 *Statesman*, 7 March 1971.
28 He died on 2 October 1975.
29 *Elections and Political Consciousness in India*, Meenakshi, Meerut, 1967, p. 82.

30 *The Indian Political System*, Houghton Mifflin, Boston, 1961, pp. 218-19.
31 *Economic and Political Weekly*, 20 May 1972, p. 1027. A study of an urban constituency in Gujarat, in 1962, led the researchers to conclude that money is an important part of bargaining between certain (mainly poor) sections of electorate and the candidates. Rajni Kothari (ed.), *Party System and Election Studies*, p. 134.
32 This was one of the two charges of electoral malpractices on which Indira Gandhi was found guilty, in June 1975. See Chapter 19, p. 261 and pp. 265-6.
33 *Statesman*, 12 January 1971.
34 See Chapter 18.
35 *Economic and Political Weekly*, 14 August 1971, p. 1779.
36 *New Statesman*, 8 March 1974, p. 320.
37 'The co-operatives often contribute, directly or indirectly, to the [Congress] party funds,' states B. S. Baviskar, an Indian academic. *Economic and Political Weekly*, 23 March 1968, p. 493.
38 Interview, in Bombay, 26 July 1971.
39 *Economic and Political Weekly*, January 1971, p. 239.
40 Rajni Kothari, *Politics in India*, Orient Longman, Delhi, 1970, p. 204.
41 *Economic and Political Weekly*, January 1971, p. 258.
42 Op. cit., p. 239.
43 Op. cit., p. 241.
44 Op. cit., p. 239.
45 Op. cit., p. 242.
46 Op. cit., p. 235.
47 Op. cit., p. 245.
48 Rajni Kothari, *Politics in India*, p. 212.
49 See Chapter 6.
50 *Economic and Political Weekly*, 27 March 1971, p. 705.
51 *Statesman*, 14 October 1970.
52 Interview, 31 January 1971.
53 *Party Building in a New Nation*, University of Chicago Press, Chicago, 1967, pp. 208-9.

CHAPTER 6: THE CONGRESS PARTY: FACING BOTH WAYS

1 *Swatantra Party and Indian Conservatism*, Cambridge University Press, Cambridge, 1967, p. 93.
2 Op. cit., p. 78.
3 Interview, in Calcutta, 21 December 1970.
4 *Hindustan Standard*, 15 March 1971.
5 George Rosen, op. cit., p. 57. An analysis of the occupational background of the delegates to the annual sessions from 1892 to 1909 showed that nearly 40 per cent were lawyers; 25 per cent doctors, teachers and journalists; 10 per cent landed gentry; and 5 per cent businessmen. Ibid.
6 In the process, of course, he alienated Muslims. See Chapter 17.
7 See Chapter 9.
8 Cited in *Seminar*, November 1964, p. 18.
9 Publications Division, Government of India, New Delhi, 1955, pp. 22-3.
10 Op. cit., pp. 175-6.
11 This was ironic; because, only a day earlier, in his report to the conference delegates, the party's General Secretary had stated, 'We have not been able to make much headway towards the socialist society'. Cited in M. Pattabhiram (ed.), *General Elections In India 1967*, Allied Publishers, Bombay, 1967, p. 110.

12 Interview, in Calcutta, 12 December 1970.
13 Cited in Kuldip Nayar, op. cit., p. 42.
14 *Hindustan Standard*, 1 March 1971.
15 Kuldip Nayar, op. cit., p. 45.
16 Reddy, the 'official' Congress nominee, received 405,427 votes; and Giri, Indira Gandhi's candidate, 420,077.
17 *Observer*, 31 August 1969.
18 *Statesman*, 6 February 1970.
19 See Chapter 18.
20 *Overseas Hindustan Times*, 3 June 1972.
21 28 April 1973, p. 786.

CHAPTER 7: THE CONGRESS GOVERNMENT: THE UNFULFILLED PLANS

1 *Sunday Times*, 26 January 1975.
2 10 April 1972.
3 24 October 1975, p. 54.
4 *Indian Express*, 10 August 1972.
5 *Searchlight*, 16 August 1947.
6 *Guardian*, 20 February 1973.
7 p. 9.
8 However, there has been no steady increase in the number of operations performed each year. The number was 1·84 million in 1967–8, but only 1·32 million three years later. *Economic and Political Weekly*, 7 October 1972, p. 2069. See Chapter 19, pp. 271–2.
9 *The Times*, 17 April 1973.
10 *Overseas Hindustan Times*, 10 October 1974 and *Statesman*, 24 February 1976.
11 3 June 1972.
12 *Economic and Political Weekly*, 15 January 1972, p. 115.
13 *Times of India*, 30 August 1971.
14 *Economic and Political Weekly*, 9 September 1972, p. 1861. He estimates that during this period the gross annual rise in personal income in the Punjab–Haryana area has probably been 10 per cent, whereas that in the eastern States has been no more than 2 per cent, barely matching the increase in population.
15 Cited in *Frontier*, 18 October 1969, p. 31.
16 *Frontier*, 1 January 1972, p. 11.
17 *New Left Review*, May–June 1970, p. 45.
18 *Statistical Outline of India, 1975*, Tata Services Ltd, Bombay, p. 39 and *Economic and Political Weekly*, 20 September 1975, p. 1494.
19 *Economic and Political Weekly*, 16 October 1971, p. 2191.
20 *Far Eastern Economic Review*, 24 October 1975, p. 57. The percentage of foreign capital in the total private investment rose from 13 in the First Plan to 24 in the Third. Meghnad Desai, 'India', in Robin Blackburn (ed.), *Explosions in a Subcontinent*, Penguin, Harmondsworth, 1975, p. 23. The net inflow of foreign assistance went up from Rs 254 crores in 1973–4 to (estimated) Rs 2,150 crores in 1975–6. *Business Standard*, 2 March 1976.
21 24 June 1972, p. 1210. See Chapter 18, pp. 252–3 and Chapter 19, p. 269.
22 *Statistical Outline of India, 1972–73*, p. 118.
23 *Statistical Outline of India, 1975*, p. 39, and *Daily Telegraph*, 31 January 1975.
24 Francine R. Frankel, op. cit., p. 12.

25 Ibid., p. 192.
26 Ibid., p. 48.
27 Ibid., pp. 192–3.

CHAPTER 8: AGRARIAN RELATIONS: THE HALF-HEARTED
REFORM

1 Cited in *Mainstream*, 27 December 1969, p. 17.
2 *Times of India*, 2 September 1971.
3 Cited in *Frontier*, 20 May 1972, p. 3.
4 In legal terms, a ryot is a registered holder of a plot of land with permanent, heritable, and transferable rights of occupancy.
5 Cited in George Rosen, op. cit., p. 62.
6 *Resolutions of Economic Policy and Programme, 1924–54*, All India Congress Committee, Delhi, 1956, pp. 17–18.
7 *Statistical Handbook of Bihar*, Government of Bihar, Patna, 1954, pp. 128 and 130.
8 Grigory Kotovsky, *Agrarian Reforms in India*, People's Publishing House, Delhi, 1964, p. 6.
9 *Report of Uttar Pradesh Zamindari Abolition Committee, Vol. II*, Government of Uttar Pradesh, Allahabad, 1948, p. 87.
10 Paul Brass, *Factional Politics in an Indian State*, Oxford University Press, Bombay, 1966, p. 12.
11 Ibid.
12 Bhowani Sen, *Evolution of Agrarian Relations in India*, People's Publishing House, Delhi, 1962, p. 192.
13 Op. cit., p. 213.
14 E. M. S. Namboodripad, *Economics and Politics of India's Socialist Pattern*, People's Publishing House, Delhi, 1966, p. 266.
15 Cited in *Mainstream*, 4 November 1972, p. 17.
16 20 December 1970, p. 18.
17 In West Bengal, the number of landless peasants rose from 1·77 million in 1961 to 3·27 million in 1971. *Deccan Herald*, 25 January 1975. During the same period, in Gujarat, the number of landless labourers increased from being 14·77 per cent of the working population to 22·48 per cent. *Economic and Political Weekly*, August 1974, p. 1434.
18 *Causes and Nature of Current Agrarian Tensions*, Ministry of Home Affairs, Government of India, New Delhi, 1969, p. 19.
19 *Mainstream*, 17 January 1970, pp. 18–21.
20 *Overseas Hindustan Times*, 27 June 1974.
21 See Chapter 1, pp. 5–9, and pp. 12–15.
22 Op. cit., p. 177.
23 5 April 1968.
24 *Mainstream*, 11 April 1970, p. 13. 'This was of course done with the connivance of the authorities,' reported a correspondent of *Mainstream*. 'The Co-operative Department in Uttar Pradesh . . . reeks with corruption.' Ibid.
25 *Times of India*, 1 January 1972. See Chapter 1, p. 6.
26 *Mainstream*, 24 October 1970, p. 13.
27 Cited in *Mainstream*, 4 November 1972, p. 17.
28 Op. cit., pp. 16–17.
29 30 August 1969, pp. 1400–1.
30 Op. cit., p. 295, p. 300 and p. 120.
31 See p. 92.

32 *Mainstream*, 7 October 1972, p. 10.
33 *Mainstream*, 27 December 1969, p. 21. As regards the 47 million acres of cultivable waste land, available to the State governments, only 11·1 million acres had been distributed to the landless by 1968. *Frontier*, 8 November 1969, p. 3.
34 *Statistical Outline of India 1972–73*, p. 24.
35 *Times Weekly*, 26 December 1971.
36 *Seminar*, May 1970, p. 33.
37 *Causes and Nature of Current Agrarian Tension*, p. 9. Agitations for distribution of land to the landless, which occurred all over the country, from Punjab to Assam, and Uttar Pradesh to Kerala, rose from 19 in 1967 to 43 in 1968. Ibid.
38 *Economic and Political Weekly*, 3 October 1970, p. 1629.
39 *Economic and Political Weekly*, 20 May 1972, p. 1008.
40 25 July 1972.
41 *Times of India*, 3 September 1975. '*Malafide* transactions on a large scale, deliberate delay in filing returns of ownership by landlords, the lukewarm attitude of most of the State governments, and the intervention of courts were responsible for the dismal performance,' reported the newspaper's correspondent.
42 Op. cit., p. 204.
43 *Mainstream*, 14 December 1968, p. 16.
44 6 December 1969, p. 1872.

CHAPTER 9: INDUSTRIAL POLICIES: 'SOCIALISTIC' CAPITALISM

1 1 July 1972, p. 1263.
2 *Sardar-e-Aam*, an Urdu daily, Patna, 18 October 1971.
3 Interview, in Madras, 4 February 1971.
4 Cited in R. Upadhyay, *Growth of Indian Industries*, National Publishers, Calcutta, 1970, p. 172.
5 *Statistical Outline of India, 1975*, p. 2.
6 Myron Weiner, *The Politics of Scarcity*, University of Chicago Press, Chicago, 1962, p. 106.
7 Cited in ibid., pp. 112–13.
8 See Chapter 6, p. 72.
9 *The Politics of Scarcity*, p. 114.
10 *Economic and Political Weekly*, 1 July 1972, p. 1263.
11 Cited in *Socialist Digest*, January 1969, p. 35.
12 Cited in Ronald Segal, *The Crisis of India*, Penguin Books, Harmondsworth, 1965, p. 201.
13 *Socialist Digest*, January 1969, p. 34.
14 Cited in *Socialist Digest*, January 1969, p. 41.
15 Cited in Neville Maxwell, *India's China War*, Penguin Books, Harmondsworth, 1972, p. 292.
16 *Foreign Investments in India*, Oxford University Press, London, 1965, p. 143.
17 Paul Brass, op. cit., p. 182.
18 *Party Building in a New Nation*, p. 414.
19 Op. cit., p. 415.
20 See Chapter 5, pp. 68–60.
21 *Statesman*, 16 August 1969.
22 *Mainstream*, 30 September 1972, pp. 10–11.
23 *New Left Review*, May–June 1970, p. 46.
24 *Mainstream*, 11 July 1970, p. 11.

25 Ibid., 30 September 1972, p. 10.
26 *Times of India*, 23 November 1971.
27 *Patriot*, 23 July 1972.
28 *Industrial Planning and Licensing Policy*, Publications Division, Government of India, New Delhi, 1967, pp. 6-8.
29 *Mainstream*, 21 February 1970, p. 17.
30 Cited in *Socialist Digest*, January 1969, p. 41.
31 *Hindustan Times*, 5 May 1972.
32 *Economic and Political Weekly*, 22 April 1972, p. 819.
33 *Hindustan Times*, 5 May 1972.
34 *Economic and Political Weekly*, February 1975, p. 135. The trend continued. 'The accent in public policy from now on is going to be increasingly on the private sector being relied upon to deliver and the government will confine itself to . . . the catering of the economic infrastructure,' wrote the *Economic and Political Weekly* on 17 May 1975. 'The public sector [will be] only the hewer-of-wood and drawer-of-water . . . [while] the private sector enriches itself. . . . . Private foreign capital, the multinational corporations in particular, are being wooed vigorously. . . . The Planning Commission and the Ministries . . . are no longer receptive to ideas that are not vetted in advance either by the FICCI or the Associated Chambers of Commerce and Industry' (pp. 775-6). Following the imposition of emergency in June – a step that was heartily welcomed by the business community – this policy was pursued with further vigour. See Chapter 19, p. 269.

CHAPTER 10: THE TRADE UNIONS: DIVIDE AND RULE

1 Interview, in Bombay, 28 July 1971.
2 *Unions, Employers and Government*, Manakatalas, Bombay, 1966, p. 92.
3 Cited in V. B. Karnik, *Indian Trade Unions*, Manaktalas, Bombay, 1966, p. 37.
4 Cited in N. Pattabhi Raman, *Political Involvement of Indian Trade Unions*, Allied Publishers, Bombay, 1967, p. 102.
5 Interview, in Bhopal, 12 February 1972.
6 Cited in N. Pattabhi Raman, op. cit., p. 148.
7 Op. cit., pp. 193 and 195.
8 Over three-quarters of the 56,800 registered factories in 1969 employed less than fifty workers each. *Statistical Outline of India, 1975*, p. 75.
9 Interview, 4 February 1971.
10 'The Supreme Court today held that the High Courts should give top priority to cases relating to labour disputes,' reported a correspondent of the *Hindustan Times*. 'A four judge bench of the Supreme Court expressed this opinion while disposing of a twenty-year-old dispute between labour and management of a private jute mill of Gorakhpur, Uttar Pradesh.' 31 July 1975.
11 Interview, 3 August 1971.
12 Interview, in Madras, 30 January 1971.
13 Op. cit., pp. 82-3.
14 22 August 1970, p. 1400.
15 *The Politics of Scarcity*, p. 78.
16 *Patriot*, 19 November 1971.
17 *Overseas Hindustan Times*, 18 July 1974. See Chapter 19, p. 268-9.
18 Publications Division, Government of India, New Delhi, 1969, p. 225.
19 *The Illustrated Weekly of India*, 17 May 1970, p. 8.
20 See Chapter 12, pp. 136-7.
21 *Patriot*, 12 February 1972.

NOTES TO PAGES 122-42   305

CHAPTER 11: THE COMMUNIST MOVEMENT: BEFORE 1964

1 *Frontier*, 5 July 1969, p. 5.
2 Cited in *Seminar*, March 1970, p. 41.
3 Cited in Mohan Ram, *Indian Communism*, Vikas, Delhi, 1969, p. 12.
4 *Economic and Political Weekly*, 9 June 1973, pp. 1027 and 1031.
5 Cited in N. Pattabhi Raman, op. cit., p. 98.
6 Ibid., p. 99.
7 Cited in Charles Bettleheim, *India Independent*, MacGibbon & Kee, London, 1968, p. 135.
8 *Constitution of the Communist Party of India, 1958*, Communist Party of India, New Delhi, 1958, p. 4.
9 In 1975, the same Indira Gandhi was to declare a national emergency and imprison tens of thousands of her political opponents on the grounds that they had resorted to 'extra-constitutional' means of agitation. See Chapter 19, p. 262–3.
10 See p. 125.
11 Cited in Mohan Ram, op. cit., p. 202.
12 Op. cit., p. 209.
13 In a national broadcast, on 1 January 1965, the Union Home Minister made unsubstantiated charges that the CPI(M) was preparing for 'armed revolution and guerrilla warfare' to 'synchronize with a fresh Chinese attack, destroying the democratic government of India through a pincer movement which was hoped for but could not materialize in 1962'. Cited in Mohan Ram, op. cit., p. 213. Equally vague charges were to be made against the opposition by the Prime Minister Indira Gandhi on 26 June 1975, in a national broadcast, to justify imposition of a national emergency and the arrest of thousands of political opponents. See Chapter 19, pp. 262–3.

CHAPTER 12: THE COMMUNIST MOVEMENT: AFTER 1964

1 Interview, in Trivandrum, 8 September 1971.
2 *Hindustan Standard*, 1 March 1971.
3 *Seminar*, December 1969, p. 25.
4 Cited in *Economic and Political Weekly*, 25 December 1971, p. 2554.
5 Ibid., 1 November 1969, p. 1738.
6 *Hindustan Standard*, 1 March 1971.
7 *Amrita Bazar Patrika*, 21 April 1972.
8 *Economic and Political Weekly*, 16 September 1972, p. 1911.
9 Interview, in Bhopal, 13 February 1972.
10 Interview with Gopal Banerjee, secretary of the West Bengal CPI, in Calcutta, 19 December 1970.
11 N. Pattabhi Raman, op. cit., p. 48.
12 Op. cit., p. 50.
13 In 1970–1, trade between India and the Soviet Union and Eastern European countries amounted to Rs 902.1 crores (£451 million). *Statistical Outline of India, 1972–73*, p. 62.
14 *Frontier*, 19 July 1969, pp. 7–8.
15 *Statesman*, 4 December 1970.
16 2 September 1972, p. 1763.
17 *Economic and Political Weekly*, 8 December 1973, p. 2161.
18 This will be discussed further in Chapter 13.
19 Cited in Mohan Ram, op. cit., p. 231.
20 *Times of India*, 24 August 1971.

21 M. R. in *Economic and Political Weekly*, 8 July 1972, p. 1301.
22 Of these, sixty were party members, and the rest were 'independents' supported by the party.
23 See Chapter 11.
24 Kerala, with the highest literacy rate in India (60·2 per cent in 1971), has one primary school per square mile, and spends one-third of its revenue on education, either directly or as grants to private institutions.
25 Interview, in Trivandrum, 11 September 1971.
26 *What Happened in Kerala*, People's Publishing House, Delhi, 1969, p. 2.
27 Cited in *Indian Express*, 22 June 1969.
28 *Asian Survey*, November 1970, p. 998.
29 See Chapter 3, p. 37.
30 A CPI(M) leader, who was the head of the United Front government from March 1967 to October 1969.
31 *Frontier*, 22 November 1969, p. 9.
32 16 January 1971.
33 *Frontier*, 24 April 1971, p. 10.
34 Ibid.
35 Cited in *Link*, 14 November 1971, p. 11.
36 Interview, in Kottayam, 12 September 1971.
37 Interview, 30 August 1971.
38 *Citizen*, 8 November 1969, p. 24.

CHAPTER 13: EXTRA-PARLIAMENTARY COMMUNISTS

1 *Liberation*, December 1969, p. 89.
2 Interview, in Calcutta, 9 December 1970.
3 30 October 1971, p. 1.
4 See Chapter 12, p. 147.
5 No strategic or ideological importance need be attached to the choice of Naxalbari as the area of militant action. 'A sick man (of fifty-one) and incapable of participating in any agitation, Charu Mazmudar could guide his followers [only] if their area of activity was somewhere in the vicinity of Siliguri [in Darjeeling district, where he lived],' notes Sankar Ghosh. 'Naxalbari fulfilled this condition; throughout the months of agitation Mazmudar wasable to maintain close touch with its organizers.' Op. cit., p. 99.
6 Cited in Sankar Ghosh, op. cit., pp. 107–9.
7 Ibid., pp. 110 and 113–14. It is worth noting that the strategy of armed overthrow of authority in India was part of the Lin Piao line, which then (in the summer of 1967) called for armed revolutions in Burma and Indonesia as well. This was also the time when the proletarian cultural revolution reached its climax in China and the Chinese Communist Party attacked the Communist parties of North Korea and Japan, and Prince Norodom Sihanouk of Cambodia.
8 Cited in Mohan Ram, op. cit., p. 238.
9 The militant leaders decided that thére had to be at least 250 people in a procession to the house of a 'class enemy' before the attack could be launched: that is, 'revolutionary action' had to have popular support and participation.
10 *New Left Review*, May–June 1970, p. 40.
11 *Liberation*, December 1969, cited in the *Economic and Political Weekly*, February 1973, p. 174.
12 *Liberation*, February 1970, cited in the *Economic and Political Weekly*, February 1973, p. 174.

13 16 August 1969, p. 5.
14 *Liberation*, February 1970, cited in the *Economic and Political Weekly*, February 1973, p. 175.
15 *Frontier*, 6 December 1969, pp. 6-7.
16 Ibid.
17 *Indian Express*, 28 January 1971.
18 Cited in the *Times of India*, 19 August 1970.
19 *Economic and Political Weekly*, 28 November 1970, p. 1913.
20 Cited in *Blitz*, 26 December 1970, p. 5.
21 According to the government sources, during the period of March–November 1970, the Naxalites killed 57 CPI(M) workers while the CPI(M) members murdered 68 Naxalites.
22 Interview with B. G., an active Naxalite in Calcutta during 1970-1, in Delhi, 10 January 1972.
23 13 February 1971, pp. 449-50. Of the 528 schools and colleges in greater Calcutta, 331 were affected by the Naxalite 'actions' of one kind or another during the period of March 1970 and April 1971, with more than 50 institutions being closed down during the peak of Naxalite activity in the winter of 1970. However by the following April all but 15 schools were functioning normally. *Economic and Political Weekly*, 10 July 1971, p. 1374.
24 Cited in *Frontier*, 4 November 1972, p. 15.
25 15,714 'Naxalites and extremists' were arrested during the period of March–November 1971.
26 26 November 1971.
27 Cited in *Amrita Bazar Patrika*, 8 December 1970. As it happened, Charu Mazmudar had, by then, received a set of 'fraternal suggestions' from the Chinese Communist Party, which contained a critical reference to 'Annihilations', and which was meant to be circulated among the Central Committee members, but was not. See p. 161.
28 Cited in *Programme of the Communist Party of India (Marxist–Leninist)*, Leamington Spa, England, 1970, p. 21. Author's italics.
29 *Mainstream*, 2 May 1970, p. 34.
30 Cited in *Programme of the Communist Party of India (Marxist–Leninist)*, p. 24.
31 *Statesman Weekly*, 2 May 1970.
32 Interview, in Delhi, 10 January 1972.
33 Interview with V. Srinivasan, in Delhi, 16 December 1971.
34 *Economic and Political Weekly*, 1 April 1972, p. 692.

CHAPTER 14: WEST BENGAL: REVOLUTION AND COUNTER-REVOLUTION

1 *Frontier*, 13 May 1972, p. 5.
2 Interview, in Bombay, 4 August 1971.
3 *Times of India*, 31 July 1971.
4 *Economic and Political Weekly*, 15 June 1974, p. 938.
5 See Chapter 6, p. 72.
6 The population density of West Bengal – at 1,032 per square mile – is three times the national average.
7 *The Politics of Scarcity*, p. 103. The practice continues. 'I've often passed on money from the industrialists myself,' said Rani Bir Chundur, son of a prominent Congress leader. 'In the 1969 mid-term elections [in West Bengal] the Congress got Rs 60 lakhs [£300,000] from the industrialists.' Interview, in Calcutta, 12 December 1970.

8 *New Statesman*, 8 May 1970, p. 648.
9 Cited in C. R. Irani, *Bengal: The Communist Challenge*, Lalvani, Bombay, 1968, p. 7.
10 C. R. Irani, op. cit., pp. 9 and 11.
11 *Mainstream*, 15 March 1969, p. 12.
12 Interview with G. D., a police intelligence officer, in Calcutta, 11 December 1970.
13 Between July and October 1969, in the district of 24-Parganas alone, 50,000 acres of land were occupied by the landless and sharecroppers; and most of these occupations were legalized by the United Front government. *Times of India*, 4 March 1970.
14 Interview, in Calcutta, 9 December 1970.
15 20 September 1969, p. 1505.
16 *Economic and Political Weekly*, January 1970, p. 207.
17 Ibid.
18 But the Act was denied the Union President's signature, and could not be enforced, since industrial relation is a 'concurrent' subject. See Chapter 4, p. 48.
19 Interview, in Calcutta, 13 December 1970.
20 'One top West Bengal leader of the ruling Congress told me that they were taking the help of Naxalites to fight the Marxists [i.e., CPI(M) members],' stated Kuldip Nayar, op. cit., p. 321.
21 20 February 1971, p. 1.
22 See note 24.
23 *Economic and Political Weekly*, 16 June 1973, p. 1053.
24 'There is a deep political conspiracy about Hemanta Basu's murder,' said Ashok Ghosh, a Forward Block leader, at a public rally in Calcutta in March 1972. 'We asked each and every one, the President, the Prime Minister, the State governor, and the former chief minister [Ajoy Mukherjee] to investigate the murder. Though one year has passed, none has conducted any investigation. So, one concludes, there is a powerful circle behind the murder, that neither the Centre nor the State government dares to touch it.' Cited in the *Economic and Political Weekly*, 11 March 1972, p. 575.
25 19 June 1971, p. 1218.
26 See Chapter 1, pp. 14–17.
27 Interview, 11 January 1972.
28 Interview, 11 January 1972.
29 Interview, 11 January 1972.
30 *Economic and Political Weekly*, 15 April 1972, p. 808.
31 One of the bizarre instances of big business's support to the Congress was brought to light later by Jyotimroy Basu, a CPI(M) MP, in Parliament. He produced a photostat of a document which showed that R. P. Goenka, the managing director of Duncan Brothers of Calcutta, had placed an order, worth RS 500,000 (£25,000), with – and paid the amount to – a printing press for the publication of thousands of election posters carrying Indira Gandhi's populist slogan '*Garibi Hatao*' – 'Remove Poverty'! A demand for and inquiry into the matter by a Parliamentary commission, made by the entire opposition, *including* all the right-wing groups, was rejected by the Congress government. *Overseas Hindustan Times*, 27 May 1972.
32 Although the CPI(M) had all along supported the Bangladesh movement, it was the Congress, as the ruling party, which took most of the credit for its success.
33 25 March 1972, p. 663.
34 *Economic and Political Weekly*, 1 April 1972, p. 691.

35 Cited in the *Times of India*, 2 May 1972. Author's italics.
36 See Chapter 16, pp. 201-2.
37 p. 1465.
38 *Frontier*, 2 September 1972, p. 6.

CHAPTER 15: RIGHTIST FORCES: POLITICAL

1 *Asian Survey*, November 1970, p. 977.
2 Cited in Anthony Elenjimittam, *Philosophy and Action of the RSS for Hind Swaraj*, Laxmi Publishers, Bombay, 1951, p. 149.
3 Cited in Muhammed Ali Kishore, *Jan Sangh and India's Foreign Policy*, Associated Publishing House, Delhi, 1969, p. 74.
4 Cited in Howard L. Erdman, op. cit., p. 256.
5 Cited in *Mainstream*, 28 March 1970, p. 19.
6 When asked whether his organization received money from the Bajajs, a business house linked with the Birlas, Thackeray replied, 'The Bajajs used to maintain the Nehru family. It's okay for the Congress to receive money from big industrialists, so why not us?' Interview, in Bombay, 30 July 1971.
7 Interview, in Bombay, 30 July 1971.
8 Interview, in Bombay, 30 July 1971.
9 *Asian Survey*, November 1970, p. 971.
10 Interview, in Bombay, 30 July 1971.
11 Cited in the *Economic and Political Weekly*, 1 July 1972, p. 1251.
12 Interview, in Bombay, 9 August 1971.
13 *Tribune*, 3 June 1970.
14 4 December 1971.
15 See Chapter 12, pp. 138-9.
16 *Indian Express*, 26 November 1971.
17 *Overseas Hindustan Times*, 14 March 1970.
18 See Chapter 17, pp. 232-5.
19 Motilal A. Jhangiani, *Jan Sangh and Swatantra*, Manaktalas, Bombay, 1967, p. 14.
20 M. Pattabhiram (ed.), *General Elections In India 1967*, Allied Publishers, Bombay, 1967, pp. 77 and 79.
21 *Indian Express*, 27 November 1971.
22 Op. cit., p. 35.
23 *Swatantra Newsletter*, March 1960.
24 *Economic and Political Weekly*, January 1971, p. 284.
25 The strength of the Bhartiya Lok Dal in Parliament was 23-14 in the Lok Sabha, and 9 in the Rajya Sabha. *Overseas Hindustan Times*, 12 September 1974.
26 Op. cit., p. 258.
27 *Sunday Times*, 7 July 1974.

CHAPTER 16: RIGHTIST FORCES: INSTITUTIONAL

1 Interview, 25 February 1972.
2 *United Services Institute Journal*, January–March 1970, p. 141.
3 *Times of India*, 6 February 1972.
4 *Statesman*, 23 May 1973.
5 The religious composition of the Indian section of the army, during the First World War, for example, was: Muslims, 41 per cent; Hindus, including Gurkhas from Nepal, 39 per cent; Sikhs, 16 per cent; and the rest, 4 per cent. Stephen P. Cohen, *The Indian Army*, Oxford University Press, Bombay, 1971, p. 69.

6 Ibid., pp. 50-1.
7 Interview, 24 November 1971. Although the exact breakdown of the army personnel in terms of the State, ethnic or religious affiliation is carried out by the government, the figures are not made available to the public.
8 *India Weekly*, 25 April 1974, p. 5. These figures were revealed by the Central government only to still the fears expressed by Sikh leaders that the traditional policy of recruitment was being changed.
9 13 December 1971.
10 Interview, in Delhi, 9 December 1971.
11 Interview with a Rajasthani cadet, in Jaipur, 21 December 1971.
12 Stephen P. Cohen, op. cit., p. 119.
13 Interview, in Dehra Dun, 25 February 1972.
14 Op. cit., p. 119.
15 Interviews, in Dehra Dun, 25 February 1972.
16 'Elites, status groups and caste in modern India', in Philip Mason (ed.), *India and Ceylon: Unity and Diversity*, Oxford University Press, London, 1967, pp. 231-2.
17 *United Services Institute Journal*, January–March 1965, p. 39.
18 Interview, in Dehra Dun, 25 February 1972.
19 Interviews, in Dehra Dun, 25 February 1972.
20 *India Weekly*, 17 May 1973, p. 3.
21 *United Services Institute Journal*, January–March 1967, p. 36.
22 Ibid., January–March 1963, p. 13.
23 Ibid., October–December 1965, p. 254.
24 Ibid., July–September 1966, p. 126.
25 *Frontier*, 19 October 1974, p. 38.
26 Ibid.
27 *Economic and Political Weekly*, 1 June 1974, p. 846. In January 1976, a Special Correspondent (living in India) put the strength of the Border Security Force at 250,000. *The Times*, 26 January 1976.
28 *Searchlight*, 22 March 1971.
29 *New Statesman*, 7 June 1974, p. 796.
30 *Economic and Political Weekly*, 1 June 1974, p. 846.
31 By 1976 the RAW had become a huge organization with a budget of Rs 14 crores, a seven-fold increase since 1971. *India Today*, 1–15 September 1977, p. 39. Its activities included overseeing revenue and commercial intelligence.
32 *Frontier*, 22 July 1972, p. 2.
33 Ibid. A few months earlier Jyotimroy Basu, chairman of the Public Accounts Committee of Parliament had stated publicly that many of the RAW officials had been trained in America and were known for their anti-Communist leanings. *Amrita Bazar Patrika*, 21 April 1972.
34 *Frontier*, 17 April 1971, p. 13.
35 Cited in *Mainstream*, 9 August 1969, p. 6.
36 Princeton University Press, Princeton, 1969.
37 *Economic and Political Weekly*, 6 November 1971, p. 2287.
38 Publications Division, Government of India, New Delhi, 1970, p. 12.
39 *The Police and Political Development in India*, p. 203.
40 *Statesman*, 25 August 1971.
41 In addition, there are such volunteer organizations as the Home Guards, whose strength in the nine major States, in 1960, was estimated to be over 1 million.
42 *Frontier*, 25 August 1973, p. 12. The actual figures for 1965 and 1970 were Rs 5·76 crores (£2·88 million) and Rs 27·15 crores (£13·58 million).
43 *Frontier*, 19 October 1974, p. 40.

44 *Economic and Political Weekly*, 14 April 1973, p. 691. An analysis of the information released by the government showed that, in 1973, over 70 per cent of deployments of the CRP had been in the non-Hindi-speaking States. *Frontier*, 19 October 1974, p. 40.

CHAPTER 17: THE INTERNAL STRAINS

1 20 October 1973, p. 1982.
2 *Hindustan Times*, 27 February 1972.
3 For the 1971 general election.
4 *Overseas Hindustan Times*, 31 August 1972.
5 *Economic and Political Weekly*, July 1969, p. 1141.
6 Before the communal riots, in 1947–8, when militant Dogra–Hindus caused an exodus of a large number of Muslims in Jammu to Pakistan and Pakistan-held parts of the State, the Hindus were a minority in Jammu. Balraj Puri, a Hindu journalist and author from Jammu, in the *Economic and Political Weekly*, 16 October 1971, p. 2197.
7 K. R. Sundar Rajan in *The Illustrated Weekly of India*, 11 August 1974, p. 17.
8 'Jammu and Kashmir', in Myron Weiner (ed.), *State Politics in India*, p. 17.
9 Op. cit., p. 233.
10 Op. cit., pp. 225–6.
11 Interview, in Delhi, 12 December 1971.
12 Bakshi Ghulam Mohammad was found guilty of substantial charges of corruption and misuse of power, including 'undue financial advantage of the value of Rs 54 lakhs [£270,000] to his family' by a quasi-judicial commission of inquiry, appointed by the succeeding administration in 1965, which published its report in 1967. Balraj Puri in Myron Weiner (ed.), *State Politics in India*, p. 239.
13 See Chapter 18.
14 Balraj Puri in Myron Weiner (ed.), *State Politics in India*, p. 239.
15 Cited in the *Weekend Review*, 7 January 1967, p. 14.
16 *Hindustan Times*, 31 January 1967.
17 S. P. Verma and Iqbal Narain (eds), *Fourth General Election in India*, Vol. I, Orient Longman, Delhi, 1968, p. 244.
18 *Amrita Bazar Patrika*, 7 February 1972.
19 Interview with Balraj Puri, in Jammu, 19 February 1972.
20 *The Times*, 9 March 1972.
21 *Economic and Political Weekly*, 7 October 1972, p. 2056.
22 *Overseas Hindustan Times*, 11 April 1974.
23 *Hindi Against India*, Rachna Prakashan, New Delhi, 1968, p. 121.
24 *Mainstream*, 14 April 1971, p. 12.
25 Cited in P. Spratt, *DMK in Power*, Nachiketa Publications, Bombay, 1970, pp. 34–5.
26 Op. cit., p. 9.
27 Cited in Neville Maxwell, *India and The Nagas*, Minority Rights Group, London, 1973, pp. 23–4.
28 Op. cit., pp. 10–11.
29 Myron Weiner, *The Politics of Scarcity*, p. 44.
30 Op. cit., p. 11.
31 *Statistical Handbook Of Nagaland, 1968*, Government of Nagaland, Kohima, p. 166.
32 *Citizens' Voice* (Kohima), 24 January 1972.

33 *Observer*, 3 September 1972.
34 Cited in Neville Maxwell, op. cit., pp. 28 and 31–2.
35 *Overseas Hindustan Times*, 13 September 1973. But, interestingly enough, this did not lead to the lifting of the ban on foreign journalists, first imposed in 1956.
36 *The Times*, 20 April 1974.
37 28 September 1974, p. 1651.
38 *The Times*, 22 September 1967. The news dispatch was a summary of reports of the official accounts published in the Indian press, since foreign journalists were banned from the Mizo area after the armed uprising in March 1966.
39 Op. cit., p. 19.
40 Interview, 19 April 1971.
41 *The Times*, 13 October 1969.
42 *Seminar*, August 1970, p. 27.
43 M. N. Srinivasan, an Indian social scientist, illustrates Gandhi's religio-political technique thus: 'India was thought of as "Mother India", *Bharat Mata*, and patriotism was love of one's mother, freeing her from the thraldom of an alien ruler. . . . The millennium he [Gandhi] enacted was conceived of as *Ram Rajya* [i.e. Rule of Rama, a legendary Hindu hero-god], and he shared the Hindu veneration for the cow. Two of his central ideas, *satyagraha* or civil resistance, and *ahimsa* or non-violence, had their roots in Hindu and Jain customs and thought.' 'The Cohesive Role of Sanskritization', in Philip Mason (ed.), *India and Ceylon: Unity and Diversity*, p. 26.
44 *Economic and Political Weekly*, July 1969, p. 1150.
45 Cited in Donald E. Smith, *India as a Secular State*, Princeton University Press, Princeton, 1963, p. 389.
46 *The Times*, 13 October 1969.
47 *Times of India*, 29 July 1971.
48 *Indian Express*, 31 December 1968.
49 *Economic and Political Weekly*, January 1970, pp. 187–8.
50 Ibid., January 1970, p. 187.
51 The Indian Union Muslim League, which has only a few members in Parliament, lacks popular following in the country except in Kerala.
52 *Economic and Political Weekly*, January 1970, p. 199.

CHAPTER 18: INTERNAL STRENGTH AND EXTERNAL SUPPORT

1 *Overseas Hindustan Times*, 16 May 1974.
2 *Economic and Political Weekly*, 3 June 1972, p. 1113.
3 *Frontier*, 11 May 1974, p. 11.
4 13 December 1973.
5 *New York Times*, 19 February 1972.
6 *Mainstream*, 30 September 1972, p. 38.
7 *Overseas Hindustan Times*, 16 May 1974.
8 *The Indian Journal of Public Administration*, January–March 1971, pp. 50–1.
9 Cited in A. H. Hanson and Janet Douglas, op. cit., p. 147.
10 *Ministry of Home Affairs Report, 1969–70*, Government of India, New Delhi, 1970, p. 5.
11 See Chapter 14, pp. 172–3.
12 Cited in the *Frontier*, 29 June 1974, p. 6.
13 *Mainstream*, 3 February 1973, p. 16.

14 This figure, obtaining on 31 December 1971, has been rising recently by about a million a year.
15 *Economic and Political Weekly*, 22 April 1972, p. 834. The press censorship, which lasted from June 1975 to January 1977, had the effect of depressing the circulation of small and medium-sized newspapers.
16 *Seminar*, November 1971, p. 12.
17 *Economic and Political Weekly*, 1 March 1975, p. 393. B. G. Verghese contested the employer's action and took the matter to court. At the end of a complicated legal battle, he finally lost his job in September 1975.
18 Ibid., 25 September 1971, p. 2055.
19 *Communism in India*, University of California Press, Berkeley, 1959, pp. 536-7.
20 *Economic and Political Weekly*, 1 November 1969, p. 1739.
21 *The Chinese Betrayal*, Allied Publishers, Bombay, 1971, p. 183.
22 Cited in Neville Maxwell, *India's China War*, p. 282. Coming from the head of a government, which had then, probably, employed as many as 100,000 armed personnel to crush the independence movement launched by a small-sized Naga population, this statement seemed a bit ironic.
23 Neville Maxwell points out that B. N. Mullik was a 'frequent visitor' to the United States, and 'the obvious contact point for the CIA influence'. *The Times*, 24 August 1972.
24 Neville Maxwell in *The Times*, 24 August 1972.
25 *India's China War*, pp. 448-9.
26 *New York Times*, 22 December 1963.
27 *To Move A Nation: The Politics of Foreign Policy in the Administration of John F. Kennedy*, Doubleday, New York, 1967, p. 331.
28 *Statistical Outline of India, 1972-73*, pp. 61-2. This continues. For the nine-month period of April-December 1974, Soviet Russia occupied the top position in imports from India, with America a shade behind. The respective figures were Rs 313·1 crores (£156·5 million) and Rs 308·3 crores (£154·2 million). *India Weekly*, 31 July 1975, p. 6.
29 Cited in the *Times of India*, 21 February 1972.
30 *The Times*, 4 July 1972.
31 *Overseas Hindustan Times*, 14 December 1972.
32 *Statistical Outline of India, 1972-73*, pp. 102-3.
33 Cited in *Frontier*, 7 July 1973, p. 2.
34 14 August 1971, p. 1733.
35 *The Times*, 1 December 1973.
36 *Overseas Hindustan Times*, 27 December 1973.
37 Ibid., 7 November 1974.
38 *Observer*, 16 March 1974.
39 *The Times*, 24 May 1974.
40 *New York Times*, 19 November 1973.
41 *Overseas Hindustan Times*, 17 January 1974.
42 22 December 1973, p. 2239.
43 *Guardian*, 19 May 1975.
44 *Economic and Political Weekly*, 26 April 1975, p. 677.
45 *Daily Telegraph*, 1 August 1975.
46 *Guardian*, 26 September 1974.
47 Cited in *Frontier*, 23 November 1974, p. 12.
48 9 January 1975.
49 These were budgeted figures. *Statistical Outline of India, 1975*, p. 119. The revised estimate for military expenditure at Rs 1,915 crores (£957·5 million) was 14 per cent higher than the budgeted figure. Cited in *Frontier*, 27 July 1974, p. 5.

50 *Statistical Outline of India, 1975*, p. 39.
51 *Economic and Political Weekly*, 21 December 1974, p. 2077.
52 *Statistical Outline of India, 1975*, p. 138.
53 *Economic and Political Weekly*, 22 November 1975, p. 1793. The following year (1974–5) per capita income fell further by 1·7 per cent. *Financial Express*, 1 March 1976.
54 During the first half of 1973, the army was called out seventeen times to restore law and order – a record in post-independence India. *Race Today*, August 1975, p. 179.

CHAPTER 19: THE 'INTERNAL' EMERGENCY:
PRELUDE TO CONGRESS DEFEAT

1 27 June 1975.
2 Cited by Madhu Limaye, a member of Parliament, in *Statesman*, 21 February 1977. The statement was censored at the time.
3 *Times of India*, 10 January 1976.
4 *Indian Express*, 16 March 1977.
5 26 March 1977, p. 519.
6 *Economic and Political Weekly*, August 1974, p. 1431.
7 Op. cit., p. 1429.
8 In contrast, the number of people killed by police firing in the 'Quit India' movement (in 1942) in Gujarat was 12. *Overseas Hindustan Times*, 24 March 1974. During January and February of 1974, the police in Gujarat opened fire on people 347 times, three times the *annual* average for the country as a whole. *Race Today*, August 1975, p. 179.
9 *The Times*, 21 March 1974.
10 'At the best of times India's 1,700,000 railwaymen are underpaid and overworked,' reported Walter Schwarz, a British journalist. 'Even with overtime, only a small minority earn more than Rs 300 [£15] a month.' *Observer*, 19 May 1974.
11 22 June 1974, p. 967.
12 Later, a few of the Congress State chief ministers were to find it expedient to make use of the provisions of the Maintenance of Internal Security Act and the Defence of India Rules to deal with their political opponents.
13 Cited in *India Weekly*, 11 September 1975, p. 3.
14 6 January 1975.
15 It is a measure of administrative sloth in India that it took four years for the election petition to be considered by the High Court. By then, Parliament had finished four-fifths of its normal life.
16 See Chapter 5, p. 66.
17 24 May 1975, p. 809.
18 This was apparently in reference to the crowd that had gathered outside Indira Gandhi's official residence on the day of the High Court verdict, shouting slogans in her favour. 'The busloads and truck-loads of factory workers and municipal employees were cajoled into congregating outside Indira Gandhi's residence . . . to demonstrate "popular" support for her "dynamic leadership",' reported a Delhi correspondent of the *Economic and Political Weekly*. 'The trucks belonged to the New Delhi Municipal Committee and the buses to the Delhi Transport Corporation. Many of the hustlers who organized the demonstrations were local government officials. As added inducement, some of the demonstrators were offered five-rupee notes, and others were given bread and milk.' 14 June 1975, p. 208.
19 26 June 1975.

20 *Overseas Hindustan Times*, 26 June 1975.

21 After the defeat of her party in the March 1977 election, Indira Gandhi openly admitted that she acted alone in advising the President to declare the emergency of June 1975. *The Times*, 7 April 1977. However, she had the cabinet endorse her decision a day after it was taken and executed.

22 Article 352, clause 1, of the Constitution reads: 'If the President is satisfied that a grave emergency exists whereby the security of India or of any part of the territory thereof is threatened whether by war or external aggression or internal disturbance, he may, by Proclamation, make a declaration to that effect.'

23 27 June 1975. It was not the first time that the Congress government had levelled unsubstantiated charges against its political adversaries as a cover for its repressive drive against them. It had done so against the CPI(M) in January 1965. See Chapter 11, p. 134. The only specific charge against the opposition forces this time, that could have been raised, concerned J. P. Narayan's public utterances regarding the army and police. As it happened, this point had been dealt with earlier. 'Last week, J. P. Narayan made it clear in a published interview that he had never asked the army or police to rebel,' reported the *Overseas Hindustan Times* on 1 May 1975. 'All he wanted them to do was to do their duty, and not to obey orders that were illegal.' In an interview with the correspondent of the *Swaraj*, a monthly published in Britain, on 12 February 1976, J. P. Narayan said 'The Police Manual and the Army Acts state that any illegal orders, even if they come from the authorities, should not be obeyed . . . this is written in the Acts. I have personally seen this in the Police Manual. A similar statement is there in the Army Acts.' No. 15, p. 2.

24 Only a brief three years earlier, the same Indira Gandhi had silenced the radical critics within her party with the question: 'Where is the organizational structure and the administrative set-up to implement a more radical policy (of land reform)?' See Chapter 8, p. 103.

25 This was part of the ten-point programme adopted by the Congress in May 1967. See Chapter 6, p. 76.

26 A drive against smugglers, begun in response to the popular protest movement in October 1974, had petered out within a few weeks.

27 This idea was first aired in 1955! The Industrial Policy Resolution of 1956 made a specific mention of it; and the Second Five Year Plan (1956–61) document stated that 'for the successful implementation of the Plan, increased association of labour with management is necessary'. Cited in *Economic and Political Weekly*, 22 November 1975, p. 1757.

28 A few weeks later, participating in a debate in the Lok Sabha, Indira Gandhi herself said, 'Maybe the programme is not all that new'. Cited in *India Weekly*, 31 July 1975, p. 1.

29 *The Times*, 5 July 1975.

30 See Chapter 8, pp. 100–2 and Chapter 17, pp. 212–13 and 221–6.

31 *Economic and Political Weekly*, 29 March 1975, p. 545.

32 'Mrs Gandhi's talk of subversion is quite false,' said Jyoti Basu, a CPI(M) leader, to Gavin Young, a British journalist. 'The CIA is playing around, of course; so is the KGB. It is always there. But not enough to excuse arrests [of people] with no names given and no indication where people have been taken.' *Observer*, 13 July 1975.

33 *Guardian*, 26 July 1975. Significantly enough, more than 90 per cent of the Congress and CPI members of the house attended the session whereas only half of the opposition members, still free, did so. By then, 21 members of

the Lok Sabha and 10 members of the Rajya Sabha were under arrest. *Daily Telegraph*, 8 August 1975. According to a list of Parliamentarians in jail in 14 countries published by Amnesty International on 6 April 1976, India had the highest number (59) behind bars.

34 Indeed, in a unanimous verdict, the Supreme Court judges struck down Clause 4 of the Constitution (39th Amendment) Act on the ground, *inter alia*, that it violated 'free and fair elections', which form an essential postulate of democracy.

35 This was no idle speculation. Referring to the judicial review of V. V. Giri's election to President, in 1969, an Indian journalist, writing anonymously in *The Times*, stated, 'When the President's election was challenged a full bench of the Supreme Court upheld it, though, as one of the judges later confessed, they were far from convinced that the incumbent head of State had told the truth from the witness box. The Court felt, he added, that setting aside the President's election would have an unsettling effect on a national scale.' 7 August 1975. It is worth noting that the High Court judge in Allahabad had remarked that Indira Gandhi had tendered 'false evidence' from the witness box.

36 *New Statesman*, 28 November 1975, p. 670. This number probably included an estimated 35,000 political prisoners that existed *before* the current emergency, nearly half of them in West Bengal. See Chapter 20, p. 283.

37 *Indian Express*, 28 February 1977.

38 *Economic and Political Weekly*, 23 April 1977, p. 684.

39 *Guardian*, 2 September 1977. 'The RAW kept dossiers on every minister at the Centre and in the States, and kept surveillance on brigadiers and above [in the army], and equivalent ranks in the air force and the navy,' states Kuldip Nayar. *India After Nehru*, Vikas, Delhi, 1975, p. 94.

40 Cited in *Daily Telegraph*, 9 June 1976. The existence of this judgment came to light only because a copy was passed on to David Loshak, the *Daily Telegraph* correspondent in Dacca, Bangladesh, and its important points published in the (British) newspaper.

41 *Overseas Hindustan Times*, 10 June 1976.

42 By the time emergency was lifted in March 1977, some 200,000 people had been arrested (or ordered to be arrested) for political reasons: 100,000 under the Maintenance of Internal Security Act, and the remainder under the Defence of India Rules. *Guardian*, 25 November 1977. This figure was four and a half times the number arrested by imperial Britain during the Second World War when the Congress launched its 'Quit India' movement in 1942.

43 *Times of India*, 8 May 1976.

44 'We must not forget that the improved economic performance in 1975–6 was to a large extent due to the return of favourable weather conditions,' said the Finance Ministry's *Economic Survey, 1975–76*. Cited in *Guardian*, 2 June 1976.

45 22 May 1976, p. 761. B. M. Birla, a leading industrialist, pointed out that only about 65 per cent of industrial capacity was being used. *Overseas Hindustan Times*, 13 May 1976.

46 *Economic and Political Weekly*, 26 March 1976, p. 480.

47 *Financial Express*, 17 March 1976.

48 *Times of India*, 5 May 1976.

49 *India Weekly*, 3 June 1976, p. 1.

50 In contrast, the Congress government in Delhi, had used the existence of emergency to extend the life of the State assembly in Kerala by six months,

because it had feared defeat of the Congress–CPI alliance at the hands of the CPI(M) and its allies at the polls due in October 1975.

51 See Chapter 17, pp. 210–14.
52 *Guardian*, 20 December 1975.
53 *Economist*, 4 December 1976, p. 68.
54 *Dawn Overseas*, 25 April 1976.
55 *Indian Express*, 21 March 1976, and *Hindu*, 21 March 1976. Cited in David Selbourne, *An Eye to India*, Penguin, Harmondsworth, 1977, pp. 305–6.
56 *Time*, 4 April 1977.
57 *Statesman*, 11 March 1977.
58 *Economic and Political Weekly*, 12 March 1977, p. 446. The weekly markets began losing popularity, and this had an adverse effect on the rural economy.
59 *Guardian*, 10 November 1976.
60 *Indian Express*, 17 December 1975.
61 Ibid., 18 March 1977.
62 Ibid.
63 *Time*, 4 April 1977, and Friends of India Society, London, *Newsletter*, 16 October 1976. At its peak, reported Lawrence Malkin of *Time*, 'in the city of Muzaffarnagar (population 100,000), vasectomy camps handled between 1,200 and 1,800 cases a day. Each operation took five to ten minutes, and there was often no follow-up when the patient suffered post-operative bleeding, infection or even tetanus.'
64 See p. 266.
65 *Economic Times*, 14 December 1976.
66 See p. 267: the censorship directive dated 5 October 1976.
67 See p. 267.
68 *Economist*, 4 December 1976, p. 68.
69 *Statesman*, 3 February 1977.
70 Despite the fact that the Congress had fought and won the previous election on the slogan 'Abolish poverty', the percentage of those below the poverty line had increased from 39 to 46 during the period 1970–6. *Indian Express*, 11 March 1977.
71 'The Congress is distributing battery cells for transistor radios free of charge in many villages,' reported K. Sundar Rajan of the *New Statesman*, 25 February 1977, p. 240. With an average of five listeners to the radio news-bulletins, the 17·5 million transistor radios in the country provided the Congress with an audience of nearly ninety million, or about a third of *all* voters.
72 *Overseas Hindustan Times*, 5 May 1977, and *Observer*, 14 September 1977. Most of this money was 'laundered' by the methods used at the time of the 1971 election, described on pp. 58–60.
73 *Economic and Political Weekly*, 5 March 1977, p. 409.
74 Since the poor suffered most in these cases, and since the traditionally pro-Congress Muslim and Outcaste voters are largely poor, the Congress lost the support of these substantial minorities to the Janata Party and other opposition groups, with a disastrous impact on its electoral performance. See p. 67.
75 These were the States and Union Territories which had added up impressive figures of sterilizations during the period April 1976–January 1977: Madhya Pradesh, 850,000 (*vs* 112,000 during the previous year); Uttar Pradesh, 700,000 (*vs* 129,000); Bihar, 525,000 (*vs* 166,000); Delhi, 136,000 (*vs* 23,000).
76 See p. 68.

77 Eight years earlier Morarji Desai had been forced to resign as the Finance Minister by Indira Gandhi. See p. 77.

78 At least forty-one political detainees died in jail during emergency, due to torture or lesser physical violence, or deliberate denial of medical facilities. *The Times*, 7 April 1977.

CHAPTER 20: THE FUTURE: PROSPECTS AND POSSIBILITIES

1 *Observer*, 6 November 1977.

2 *Statesman*, 11 August 1977.

3 Op. cit., p. 207.

4 *Economic and Political Weekly*, August 1974, p. 1432.

5 Interview, in Delhi, 16 December 1971.

6 This has been a well-established electoral malpractice by the Congress. See p. 59.

7 *Spectator*, 21 October 1977, p. 8, and *India Weekly*, 13 October 1977, p. 3. Earlier it had been alleged that of the Rs 90 crores (£60 million) collected for the Congress election fund, some Rs 35 crores (£23·3 million) had been misappropriated. *Observer*, 14 September 1977.

8 *India Weekly*, 13 October 1977, p. 8.

9 *Statesman*, 4 October 1977.

10 *Statesman Weekly*, 5 November 1977.

11 *Statesman*, 28 October 1977.

12 Ibid., 2 November 1977.

13 *Hindustan Times*, 10 April 1977.

14 *Observer*, 27 May 1977. A figure of Rs 6,000,000 (£400,000) was mentioned by the *Current*, an Indian weekly. 16 July 1977.

15 Interview, in Sahajapur, 20 July 1977. See pp. 14–5 and pp. 175–6.

16 Interviews with Seva Ram Tyagi and Triveni Prasad Tyagi, landlords of Raghunathpur, a village in Uttar Pradesh, 27 July 1977.

17 *Statesman*, 8 April 1977. Interestingly enough, the estimate of surplus land to become available for redistribution, as result of land reform, fell sharply from 55 million acres in 1961 to 21·6 million acres in 1971, to less than 4 million acres in 1977. See p. 103, and *Observer*, 6 November 1977.

18 Cited in *Observer*, 6 November 1977.

19 *Sunday Times*, 27 March 1977.

20 *India Today*, 1–15 September 1977, p. 17.

21 14 May 1977.

22 *Guardian*, 15 November 1977.

23 Cited in *Economic and Political Weekly*, August 1977, p. 1280.

24 See pp. 288–9, note 54.

25 See pp. 159–62, pp. 171–80, and pp. 202–3.

26 See pp. 14–16, and pp. 168–70. This was borne out by interviews with the voters of Sahajapur, a village in West Bengal, in July 1977.

27 *Indian Express*, 11 March 1977.

28 See p. 156.

29 See pp. 151–2.

30 *Frontier*, 14 May 1977, p. 2.

31 See p. 155.

32 *Frontier*, 14 June 1975, p. 8.

33 Ibid., 9 July 1977, p. 8.

34 *Guardian*, 7 July 1975.

35 *Observer*, 20 February 1977.

36 See pp. 171–80.

37 Addressing senior officials of the Central government in Delhi, Indira Gandhi criticized J. P. Narayan for giving respectability to, among others, 'Marxist-Communists and Naxalites'. *Overseas Hindustan Times*, 10 July 1975.

38 *The Times*, 22 May 1975. 'According to them [the military leaders of the Shan, Kachin, and Karen rebels], the Peking-backed Burmese Communist Party (BCP) . . . is operating for the first time to the west of the Salween river, away from its traditional strongholds along the 2,000 kilometre southern border of China's Yunnan Province,' reported Brian Eads of the *Observer*. 'The Communists, who are thought to have between 15,000 and 20,000 well-equipped troops backed by Chinese "advisers" . . . are now eating into rebel areas and are said to control one-third of Shan States.' 16 May 1976.

39 'A secret document (dated 2 May 1973) recently captured by the Naga Underground, forecast the end of the Naga conflict "within a matter of months" as a result of a counter-insurgency operation headed by Major-General A. R. Dutt, commanding officer of the Eighth Mountain Division of India,' reported the *Observer*, 7 September 1975.

40 See Chapter 17, pp. 227–8.

41 *The Times*, 25 November 1975.

42 4 December 1975. A few months later the Indian Government extended the President's rule in Nagaland, first imposed in March 1975, by another six months. This went on until November 1977 when elections to the State Assembly were held.

43 Cited in *India Today*, 1–15 September 1977, p. 19.

44 *Observer*, 19 June 1977.

45 *Hindustan Times*, 28 July 1977.

46 *Statesman*, 18 July 1977. Jagjivan Ram, the Defence Minister of India, alleged that 'Bangladesh . . . in collusion with China, has been training Naga and Mizo rebels for insurgent activities in India.' *The Times*, 30 August 1977.

47 *Statesman*, 22 June 1977.

48 Ibid., 18 July 1977.

49 *Frontier*, 3 May 1975, p. 6.

50 Interview, 18 January 1972.

51 *Frontier*, 8 March 1975, p. 8.

52 *Indian Express*, 11 March 1977.

53 Significantly enough, within four months of assuming office, the Janata government of Madhya Pradesh had promulgated the Madhya Pradesh Prevention of Public Disorder Ordinance, and arrested three trade union leaders under its provisions. 'It was clear that the Ordinance was directed against the working class and the political opponents of the Janata Party,' noted N. K. Singh of the *Economic and Political Weekly*, 15 October 1977, p. 1764.

54 *Overseas Hindustan Times*, 13 February 1977.

55 *Far Eastern Economic Review*, 24 October 1975, pp. 57–8.

56 Already the post-emergency period has seen a marked decline in the influence of the INTUC and AITUC, and a corresponding rise in the strength of the CITU. *Economic and Political Weekly*, 15 October 1977, p. 1763.

57 *A Report on Causes and Nature of Current Agrarian Tensions*, p. 11. It is worth noting that the voters of the Punjab, the richest State in the Union, returned the largest number of the CPI and CPI(M) members (fifteen in all) to the assembly yet, in the election of June 1977, even though the two Communist parties contested the election on the opposite sides of the political divide.

58 Cited in *Frontier*, 25 December 1971, p. 15.

59 *Times of India*, 29 June 1970.

POSTSCRIPT

1. See p. 279.
2. Of the 294 seats in the Andhra Pradesh assembly, Indira Gandhi's Congress won 175, the official Congress 30, and the Janata 60. In Karnataka, the Indira Congress secured 149 seats out of 224; the Congress 2, and the Janata 59; whereas in Maharashtra, the Indira Congress scored 62, the Congress 70, and the Janata 99.
3. See p. 68.
4. See note 22 of Chapter 19.
5. Cited in *Economic and Political Weekly*, 20 May 1978, p. 825.
6. Cited in *Economic and Political Weekly*, 24 June 1978, p. 1019.
7. Cited in *The Times*, 8 November 1978.
8. Cited in *Economic and Political Weekly*, 10 June 1978, p. 942.
9. *Guardian*, 14 March 1979.
10. *India Weekly*, 29 March 1979.
11. *Hindustan Times*, 31 December 1977.
12. *Economic and Political Weekly*, 14 October 1978, p. 1719.
13. Cited in *Times of India*, 31 December 1977.
14. An indication of the increased strength of the RSS came in mid-April when a Hindu procession, led by a local RSS leader, attacked Muslims in the steel town of Jamshedpur in Bihar on the day of a Hindu festival. The subsequent inter-religious violence left more than one hundred people, mostly Muslims, dead. *Guardian*, 16 April 1979. 'The accounts of correspondents and investigating teams, including a Janata Party panel, have made it clear that the massive orgy of murder, arson, loot, and worse, let loose simultaneously (against Muslims) in several parts of Jamshedpur, was the handiwork of the RSS,' stated *Mainstream*. 21 April 1979.

SELECT BIBLIOGRAPHY

BOOKS

Bayley, David H., *The Police and Political Development in India*, Princeton University Press, Princeton, 1969.

Bettleheim, Charles, *India Independent*, MacGibbon & Kee, London, 1968.

Bhambhri, C. P., and Verma, S. P., *Elections and Political Consciousness in India*, Meenakshi, Meerut, 1967.

Blackburn, Robin (ed.), *Explosions in a Subcontinent*, Penguin, Harmondsworth, 1975.

Brass, Paul, *Factional Politics in an Indian State*, Oxford University Press, Bombay, 1966.

Cohen, Stephen P., *The India Army*, Oxford University Press, Bombay, 1971.

Erdman, Howard L., *Swatantra Party and Indian Conservatism*, Cambridge University Press, Cambridge, 1967.

Etienne, Gilbert, *Studies in Indian Agriculture*, University of California Press, Berkeley, 1968.

Frankel, Francine R., *India's Green Revolution*, Princeton University Press, Princeton, 1972.

Ghosh, Sankar, *The Disinherited State*, Orient Longman, Calcutta, 1971.

Hanson, A. H., and Douglas, Janet, *India's Democracy*, Weidenfeld & Nicolson, London, 1972.

Hardgrave, Robert L. Jr., *India: Government and Politics in a Developing Nation*, Harcourt, Brace & World, New York, 1970.

Irani, C. R., *Bengal: The Communist Challenge*, Lalvani, Bombay, 1968.

Jhangiani, Motilal A., *Jan Sangh and Swatantra*, Manaktalas, Bombay, 1967.

Karnik, V. B., *Indian Trade Unions*, Manaktalas, Bombay, 1966.

Kennedy, Van Dusen, *Unions, Employers and Government*, Manaktalas, Bombay, 1966.

Kidron, Michael, *Foreign Investments in India*, Oxford University Press, London, 1965.

Kothari, Rajni, *Politics in India*, Orient Longman, Delhi, 1970.

Kothari, Rajni (ed.), *Party System and Election Studies*, Allied Publishers, Bombay, 1967.

Kotovsky, Grigory, *Agrarian Reforms in India*, People's Publishing House, Delhi, 1964.

Mason, Philip (ed.), *India and Ceylon: Unity and Diversity*, Oxford University Press, London, 1967.

Maxwell, Neville, *India's China War*, Penguin, Harmondsworth, 1972.

Maxwell, Neville, *India and The Nagas*, Minority Rights Group, London, 1973.

Moorhouse, Geoffrey, *Calcutta*, Penguin, Harmondsworth, 1974.

Mullik, B. N., *The Chinese Betrayal*, Allied Publishers, Bombay, 1971.

Myrdal, Gunnar, *Asian Drama: An Inquiry into the Poverty of Nations*, vol. 2, Penguin, Harmondsworth, 1968.

Namboodripad, E. M. S., *Economics and Politics of India's Socialist Pattern*, People's Publishing House, Delhi, 1966.

Nayar, Kuldip, *India: the critical years*, Vikas, Delhi, 1971.

Nayar, Kuldip, *India after Nehru*, Vikas, Delhi, 1975.

Palmer, Norman D., *The Indian Political System*, Houghton Mifflin, Boston, 1961.

Pattabhiram, M. (ed.), *General Elections in India 1967*, Allied Publishers, Bombay, 1967.

Ram, Mohan, *Hindi Against India*, Rachna Prakashan, New Delhi, 1968.

Ram, Mohan, *Indian Communism*, Vikas, Delhi, 1969.

Raman, N. Pattabhi, *Political Involvement of Indian Trade Unions*, Allied Publishers, Bombay, 1976.

Rosen, George, *Democracy and Economic Change in India*, University of California Press, Berkeley, 1966.

Segal, Ronald, *The Crisis of India*, Penguin, Harmondsworth, 1965.

Selbourne, David, *An Eye to India*, Penguin, Harmondsworth, 1977.

Sen, Bhowani, *Evolution of Agrarian Relations in India*, People's Publishing House, Delhi, 1962.

Sen, S. N., *The City of Calcutta*, Bookland, Calcutta, 1960.

Smith, Donald E., *India as a Secular State*, Princeton University Press, Princeton, 1963.

Spratt, P., *DMK in Power*, Nachiketa Publications, Bombay, 1970.

Tata Services Limited, *Statistical Outline of India, 1972-73*, Bombay, 1973.

Tata Services Limited, *Statistical Outline of India, 1975*, Bombay, 1975.

Taub, Richard P., *Bureaucrats Under Stress*, University of California Press, Berkeley, 1969.

Tinker, Hugh, *India and Pakistan: A Political Analysis*, Frederick Praeger, New York, 1963.

Upadhyay, R., *Growth of Indian Industries*, National Publishers, Calcutta, 1970.

Weiner, Myron, *The Politics of Scarcity*, University of Chicago Press, Chicago, 1962.

Weiner, Myron, *Party Building in a New Nation*, University of Chicago Press, Chicago, 1967.

Weiner, Myron (ed.), *State Politics in India*, Princeton University Press, Princeton, 1968.

Windmiller, Marshall, and Overstreet, Gene D., *Communism in India*, University of California Press, Berkeley, 1959.

INDEX

Abdullah, Sheikh Mohammed, 210–18, 239, 269–70

Aborigines, 35, 223; *see also* Adivasis *and* Scheduled Tribes

Additional Emoluments (Compulsory Deposit) Act (1974), 269

Adivasis, 230–2, 283; *see also* Aborigines *and* Scheduled Tribes

Administration, government, 37–8, 268

Adulteration, food, 32

Advisory Committee on Aboriginal Tribes, 223

Afghans, 4, 166

Agartala, 287

Agricultural workers, 10, 14, 84, 95, 101

Agriculture, 4, 289–90; co-operative, 74; *see also* Land

Ahirs, 195

Ahmad, Imtiaz, 209, 235

Ahmadabad, 236–7, 258

Ahmed, F. A., 262

Ahom kingdom, 222

Aid-India Consortium, 252–3, 269

Air Force, Indian (IAF), xi, 199–200, 250, 253–4

Aizawl, 229–30, 286

Akali Party, 218, 274–5, 282

Akbar, 91

Akhand Bharat, 191

Al-Aqsa mosque, 237

Alcohol, prohibition of, *see* Prohibition

Algiers, 214

Allahabad, 261

Alleppey, 145

Allies, 115, 224

All India Agriculturists' Federation, 190

All India Anna Dravida Munnetra Kazhagam (AIADMK), 274

All India Congress Committee (AICC), 54, 77–8, 80, 107, 110, 279–80; *see also* Congress, Indian National

All India Co-ordination Committee of the Revolutionaries of the CPI(M), 151

All India Co-ordination Committee of Communist Revolutionaries (AICCCR), 151–2

All India Industrial Conference, 106

All India Kisan Congress, 99, 127

All India Kisan Sabha (AIKS), 99–100, 127

All India Muslim League, *see* Muslim League

All India Radio, misuse of, 65–6, 78–9, 172–3, 177, 240, 242–3, 274, 278; *see also* Broadcasting services

All India Railwaymen's Federation, 129

All India Trade Union Congress (AITUC), 113–16, 120–1, 126, 269

All India Workers and Peasants Parties' Conference, 126

AM, 23, 86, 165, 173

America, xi, 76, 130, 138, 248–52, 267, 273

Amnesty International, 284

Amrita Bazar Patrika, 83

Amritsar, 92, 195

Anand Marg, 263

Anand, Major P. S., 199

Ananda Bazar Patrika, 203

Bose, S. C., 72, 166
Bowring, Philip, 83
Brahmaputra, river 222, 250
Brahmins, 5, 12, 219–20
Brahmo Samaj, 166
Brezhnev, Leonid, 140–1, 252–4
Britain/British: and Adivasis, 230;
  Communists, 125–7; Hindus, 166;
  martial races, 194–5; military
  aid, 250; Mizos, 229; Muslims,
  232–3; Nagas, 222–3; rule in
  India, 197
British Commonwealth, 45
British East India Company, 91
Broadcasting services, xi, 65–6, 242,
  274, 276, 278; see also All India
  Radio
Buddhism, 166
Bulganin, N., 131
Bureaucracy, see Administration,
  government
Burma, 222–3, 229, 284, 286
Business community: in Calcutta,
  22–3; Congress and, 58–9, 105–13,
  167; CPI(M) and, 22, 170; election funds and, 58–9, 279; on
  emergency, 269; Janata Party and,
  279–80; Mahatma Gandhi and,
  72, 107; import and industrial
  licences and, 111–12; press ownership and, 243–4; Swatantra Party
  and, 191; trade unions and, 22,
  117–18
Bustees, 20–1

Cabinet, Central/Union, 47
Cacharis, 284
Calcutta, 15–17, 18–23, 106, 157–60,
  167, 172–3, 284
Calcutta Metropolitan District, 19
Caliph, Holy, 233
Cambodia, 284
Camp David, 249
Capital, concentration of, 110–11
Carter, Jimmy, 273
Castes, 4, 53, 55–6, 241–2
Catholics, see Roman Catholics
*Causes and Nature of Current
  Agrarian Tension*, 101–2
Cement, production of, 105
Censorship, press, x, xi, 240, 256,
  262, 264–8, 272–3
Central Bureau of Investigation
  (CBI), 40, 200, 260, 278, 286

Central Industrial Security Force
  (CISF), 200
Central Intelligence Agency,
  American (CIA), 264, 267
Central Intelligence Bureau (CIB),
  172, 177, 200–1, 249
Central Land Reforms Committee,
  90, 102
Central Legislative Assembly, 52–3,
  234
Central Police Department, 200
Central Provinces, 92
Central Reserve Police (CRP), 155,
  161, 171, 176, 200, 205, 249,
  283
Central Treaty Organization
  (CENTO), 131
Central Vigilance Commission, 41
Centre of Indian Trade Unions
  (CITU), 117, 121
Chakravarati, Anand, 66
Chandigarh, 9
Chandola, Harish, 228
Charter of Demands, 260
Chaterjee, Ashim, 156–7, 162
Chaterjee, Dhiren, 21–2
Chattopadhyay, Paresh, 87
Chaudhry, Kishan Chand, 6
Chaudhuri, General J. N., 198–9
Chaudhuri, Kalyan, 156–7
Chavan, Y. B., 279
Chera dynasty, 22
Chhatra Parishad, 174
Chhotanagpur, 231
Chhotanagpur Adivasi Mahasabha,
  231
Chhotanagpur Unnati Samaj, 231
Chhunga, Chal, 229
Chief Censor, 267, 278
Chief Election Commissioner, 57,
  63, 133
Chief Minister, 47
Chin Hills, 286
China, People's Republic of, 73,
  129, 132, 162, 248, 255, 283, 285
Chinaogriala, 50
Chinese revolution, 129
Chins, 284
Chittagong Hill Tracts, 286
Chola dynasty, 221
Chomu, 66
Chopra, Pran, 167, 244
Chou En-lai, 214, 251
Christian missions, 230